The Mythical World of
Nazi War Propaganda, 1939–1945

*The University of Minnesota Press
gratefully acknowledges
the support for its program
of the Andrew W. Mellon Foundation.
This book is one of those
in whose financing
the Foundation's grant
played a part.*

The
Mythical World of
Nazi War Propaganda,
1939–1945

by Jay W. Baird

UNIVERSITY OF MINNESOTA PRESS □ MINNEAPOLIS

504918

Library of Congress Catalog Card Number: 74–83132

ISBN 0–8166–0741–9

For SALLY ESHELMAN BAIRD
with Love and Affection

Acknowledgments

Over the years I have incurred debts to many individuals and organizations in the preparation of this book. The National Endowment for the Humanities and the Alexander von Humboldt Foundation generously supported my stay at the Institute for Contemporary History, Munich, during the academic year 1969–1970 when much of the work was written. The Hoover Institution of Stanford University also underwrote the project with Thyssen Foundation funds, which were supplemented with grants from the American Philosophical Society and the Miami University Research Fund.

My parents encouraged my interest in history from the outset, and I am appreciative of the generous financial and moral support they have rendered over the years. My teacher and friend, Professor Guy Stern, fired my interest in Goebbels and Nazi propaganda when he taught at Denison University in the 1950s, long before he became a scholarly luminary. The enthusiasm he demonstrated as a young instructor freshly landed in the midwest from New York was contagious. The late John Wuorinen and the present Seth Low Professor of History, Fritz Stern, directed my 1966 Columbia University dissertation on Nazi propaganda, and the chapters dealing with the Russian front have been incorporated in the present work. Any strengths which the book may have are in great part attributable to them both, because they set a model for integrity, rigorous scholarship, and style.

Robert Wolfe of the National Archives and Agnes Peterson of the Hoover Institution were extraordinarily helpful in leading me to the sources, and I would also like to thank Heinz Boberach of the German Federal Archives in this regard. The staff of the Institute of Contemporary History—most notably Hellmuth Auerbach and Anton Hoch—made my Munich sojourn both memorable and profitable. Heinrich Pfeiffer, director of the Alexander von Humboldt Foundation in Bad Godesberg and a true Renaissance man, has been most hospitable and accommodating during my research trips to Germany. Walter Laqueur and Henri Michel kindly allowed me to quote from material published in my earlier articles in the *Journal of Contemporary History* and the *Revue d'Histoire de la Deuxième Guerre Mondiale.*

Several other individuals should be recognized here, most notably the members of the Stanford University faculty seminar on the intellectual origins of National Socialism chaired by George Mosse in the fall of 1963. Gordon Craig encouraged my work at that time and thereafter consistently offered me his valuable assistance. Hans Herzfeld and Karl Dietrich Bracher both analyzed earlier versions of this book. James J. Sheehan read the Stalingrad chapter, and my colleague Jeffrey Kimball read the text for errors in military reporting.

My chairmen at Miami University, Harris Warren and Richard Jellison, supported my work at every stage, and I gratefully acknowledge their help. Lee Dutton and Peter Flinterman of the Miami University Library were enormously helpful with bibliographical problems. My greatest debt, however, is to my wife to whom this book is dedicated. She has loyally followed this itinerant scholar from Berlin to New York, from Washington to Palo Alto, from Munich to Claremont, and finally home to the Ohio heartland. It could not have been written without her support.

J. W. B.

Oxford, Ohio
July 1974

Contents

List of Abbreviations

BA	German Federal Archives, Koblenz
BOKW	Berichte des Oberkommandos der Wehrmacht (Daily Communiqués of the Supreme Command of the Armed Forces)
CGD	Captured German Documents Filmed at Berlin Document Center
DAZ	*Deutsche Allgemeine Zeitung*
DW	*Deutscher Wochendienst*
FBIS-FCC-DR	Foreign Broadcast Intelligence Service, Federal Communications Commission, Daily Report
FZ	*Frankfurter Zeitung*
HL	Hoover Library
IMT	International Military Tribunal, Nuremberg
IfZ	Institute for Contemporary History, Munich
MGRC	Miscellaneous German Records Collection
MNN	*Münchner Neueste Nachrichten*
NSDAP	National Socialist German Workers Party
NA	National Archives, Washington, D.C.
OKH	Oberkommando des Heeres (Army High Command)
OKW	Oberkommando der Wehrmacht (Supreme Command of the Armed Forces)
OKW/WPr	Oberkommando der Wehrmacht/Abteilung für Wehrmachtpropaganda (Supreme Command of the Armed Forces/Section for Wehrmacht Propaganda)

RKK	Reichskulturkammer (Reich Culture Chamber)
RMfdbO	Reichsministerium für den besetzten Ostgebiete (Reich Ministry for the Occupied Eastern Territories)
RMfVP	Reichsministerium für Volksaufklärung und Propaganda (Reich Ministry for Public Enlightenment and Propaganda)
RPA	Reichspropagandaamt (Reich Propaganda Office)
RPL	Reichspropagandaleitung (Reich Propaganda Command)
RSHA	Reichssicherheitshauptamt (Chief Reich Security Office)
SB	Sammlung Brammer (Brammer Collection)
SO	Sammlung Oberheitmann (Oberheitmann Collection)
SS	Schutzstaffel (Himmler's Elite Guard)
SD	Sicherheitsdienst (Security Service)
UTW	Ufa Tonwoche (Weekly Newsreel of the Ufa Corporation)
VB-B	*Völkischer Beobachter,* Berlin edition
VB-MA	*Völkischer Beobachter,* Munich edition
VB-ND	*Völkischer Beobachter,* North German edition
VI	Vertrauliche Informationen (Confidential Releases of the Propaganda Ministry)
YIVO	Yiddish Scientific Institute, New York
ZD	*Zeitschriftendienst*

The Mythical World of
Nazi War Propaganda, 1939–1945

I The Mythical World of Nazi Propaganda

The term "propaganda" is more often used than understood. The reason for the confusion is evident: there has never been a definition of propaganda to which all scholars will adhere, as Professor Barghoorn has pointed out in his work *Soviet Foreign Propaganda*.[1] Holt and van de Velde define it as the "attempt to influence behavior . . . by affecting through the use of mass media of communications, the manner in which a mass audience perceives and ascribes meaning to the material world."[2] Harold Lasswell speaks of "the management of mass communications for power purposes."[3] But none of these definitions nor any other is satisfactory in itself to come adequately to grips with National Socialist propaganda.

Nazi propaganda was unique in the way it merged the practical and political with the mythical. Hitler, more than any other twentieth-century leader, focused on the irrational through myths and symbols in his propaganda; all the day-by-day themes he employed were subsumed in the mythical whole, the Hitlerian ethos based on race. The Jewish enemy was clearly defined as the group on which the collective fears of the nation might be directed, and thereby purged. Further, the Hitler cult offered a safe harbor against the storms of dissonant modernity symbolized by mass man. For those who would not respond to the offbeat racial ideas of the National Socialist Party, Hitler offered renewed pride in the German nation, so shamed by Versailles and the subsequent humiliations perpetrated by the Allies.

The peculiar genius of Hitler and Goebbels was to merge the themes of traditional German patriotism with Nazi ideological motifs, a course pursued from the days of the earliest Munich rallies in 1919 until 1945. At many points German biases became indistinguishable from National Socialist thought, a situation the Party exploited by claiming sole authority to define genuine Germanness. By uniting patriotism and Nazi ideology Hitler forged a compelling weapon against what he termed the "immorality of Weimar rationalism," the symbol of cultural decadence, racial impurity, and Jewish putrefaction.

Nazi propaganda has only recently come to receive the attention commensurate with its importance. Both Helmut Heiber's biography of Goebbels and Z. A. B. Zeman's *Nazi Propaganda* are adequate introductory works.[4] Ernest K. Bramsted's *Goebbels and National Socialist Propaganda 1925–1945* is a creditable survey but is flawed by the author's limited use of the captured German records and the inaccessibility of the propaganda elite for interview purposes during the 1950s when the work was being researched.[5] Marlis Steinert offers a cogent analysis of *Stimmung* and *Haltung* in wartime Germany in her *Hitlers Krieg und die Deutschen*.[6]

Myth was at the core of National Socialism, but heretofore this theme has been underplayed in studies on the propaganda of the movement. When Goebbels told his lieutenants in the Ministry for Public Enlightenment and Propaganda during the war that "propaganda does not have anything to do with the truth! We serve truth by serving a German victory," he was voicing his conviction that the authoritarian power network and the mass communication and propaganda machinery all served a higher ideal, the National Socialist world view based on myth and the irrational.[7] It is the purpose of this book to analyze the development of Nazi propaganda during World War II as a function of Party ideology.

Nazi ideology and in turn Goebbels's propaganda embraced a veritable mythical solar system. At the center was the primary myth of Aryan man's racial struggle against the "international Jewish conspiracy," and a descending mythical hierarchy ranged from the Führer cult to the nobility of the warrior's death, from "Jewish-Bolshevik subhumans" to the English "plutocrats." The prime importance which Goebbels assigned the myth of the "international Jewish conspiracy" reflected Hitler's obsession with this theme. As Karl Dietrich Bracher has argued, "National Socialist . . . control and victory over Jews and 'inferior peoples', the völkisch-racial revolution, remained the single genuine core in Hitler's *Weltanschauung* . . ."[8] What made the theory even more effective in the hands of the Nazis was that it was never challenged within the Party in any meaningful way, and as a result nazism did not suffer the dislocations resulting from major theoretical disputes which characterized the Soviet experience.

Hitler's exploitation of anti-Semitism conforms to the dictum that he offered little ideology that was new; instead he utilized themes which already enjoyed considerable popularity.[9] The Jew had been stereotyped long before the Nazis began to make unashamed use of the prejudice. Age-old Christian anti-Semitism was as pervasive as ever, and the Party inherited an especially virulent case of modern man's resentment of an urban, industrial, money-centered civilization. The Jews epitomized this civilization as well as did any other cohesive group.

The widespread contempt for the Jews had been given the appearance of scientific respectability by Gobineau, Vacher de Lapouge, and Houston Stewart Chamberlain. Their racism, Nolte observed, was "first and foremost an instrument of defense of a leading class which was threatened or had already lost its power, but yet which still remained influential, and self-conscious."[10] Franz Neumann has contended that racism was a substitute for the class struggle.[11] Whatever its nature, racism spoke to the needs of modern man and became a natural component of cultural pessimism, whose spokesmen de Lagarde, Langbehn, and Moeller van den Bruck reflected the basic insecurity of the era and contributed through their writings to the hatred of the Jews.[12]

This hatred was exacerbated by the currency given to one of the more clever hoaxes of the modern period, the "Protocols of the Elders of Zion." According to the "protocols," an international clique of Jewish conspirators was preparing to assume total power over all the nations of the world.[13] Despite the absurdity of the "protocols" they were widely disseminated. The predilection of many Germans for the mystical was exploited by the Franconian gauleiter Julius Streicher, whose newspaper, *Der Stürmer,* spread the age-old tales of Jewish ritual murders and magic to a reading public who responded to his unrelenting warnings of the threat to "Aryan womanhood" posed by the stealthy Jew.

According to Hitler, the war was less a struggle among nations than a fight to the finish pitting Aryan against Jew. As Göring declared in a Sports Palace address in October 1942, "This is not the Second World War, this is the Great Racial War. The meaning of this war, and the reason we are fighting out there, is to decide whether the German and Aryan will prevail or if the Jew will rule the world."[14] Hitler began the war, led it, and ended his life with a curse against the Jews on his lips.

In order that the German people would be cognizant of the dangers posed by Jewry, the Nazis produced a documentary film entitled *The Eternal Jew.*[15] Filmed in the ghettos of Warsaw and Lodz and released in 1940, it contrasted Jewish individualism and "self-seeking" with the National Socialist ideal of *Volksgemeinschaft.* Secondly, it revealed that the Jew was motivated solely by "lust for money," the antithesis of the cherished values and ideals of the German cultural tradition. The Jew was a parasite. Not only did he differ from the Aryan in body, but more significantly in soul, for the Jew had no soul!

Pitiable ghetto scenes were shown to incite contempt and hatred for the race which allegedly had urged the Allies to attempt to destroy the Nazi state founded on social justice. After seemingly endless footage of Jewish slaughter practices, which depicted the agony of animals being bled to death, the narrator made it clear that National Socialist Germany would eradicate the perpetrators of such cruelty and barbarity from the face of the earth. The message of *The Eternal Jew* was obvious—a parasitical race dedicated to gold and stealth, and devoid of soul, was fit only for liquidation.

By all accounts, *The Eternal Jew* enjoyed little of the success of the 1940 release *Jud Süss* which featured several of Germany's most outstanding stars in a pseudohistorical dramatization of the Jewish question.[16] Goebbels took a consuming interest in the production of this film which was directed by Veit Harlan and served as a medium to contrast Aryan-Jewish stereotypes. *Jud Süss* was based in part on the career of Joseph Süss-Oppenheimer, who in fact had gained notoreity as a financial adviser to Duke Karl Alexander of Württemberg from 1732 to 1737, but Goebbels's directives to Harlan made a mockery of poetic license. The Nazis' Süss not only cheated the state, but what was much worse he used his position to commit an unspeakable crime against the blood of the German *Volk—Rassenschande*—by defiling a blonde, Aryan maiden played by Kristina Söderbaum. Ferdinand Marian gave a stellar performance as Süss, whose character as the archetype swindler, cheater, and "race defiler" symbolized world Jewry. Only after his lust had run its course—the beautiful seduced victim had found redemption in a drowning suicide and the state was bankrupt—did the Swabian *Volk* awake and demand justice. The last scene depicting Jud Süss dangling from the hangman's noose conveyed Goebbels's brutal message to the German people. Himmler was so impressed with the production that he ordered every SS man to see it.[17] The actors who played Jewish roles were so convincing that they asked Goebbels to announce publicly that they were not Jews but good Aryans merely playing parts as actors in the service of the state.[18] Without question, *Jud Süss* contributed to the radical anti-Semitism already prevalent in Germany and eased the way for the evacuation of the Jews.

Hitler was explicit about the fate of the Jews and several months before the war he warned what lay in store for them: "I want to act as a prophet once more today: if international Jewry should succeed in driving the powers into a world war once more, then the result will not be the Bolshevization of the world and thereby the victory of Jewry, but instead the annihilation of the Jewish race in Europe."[19] This prophecy was clearly echoed early in the war when Helmut Sündermann, second in command to Reich Press Chief Otto Dietrich, published an article entitled "Twilight of the European Jews," which asserted that the end of the "bastardized, poisonous Jewish race" was drawing near. Soon the Jews would be but an "ugly memory."[20] Although public mention of the "final solution" was avoided, every means short of an announcement of the mass liquidations were taken to prepare the nation psychologically for the fait accompli.

The Nazis offered the Germanic myth of racial purity as the antithesis of "Jewish racial decadence and decomposition." God lived in the _Volk._ As an obscure song of the period entitled "You Are the Chain without End" rhapsodized, "That is the meaning of life, that God is astir in one's blood, but God is present only in pure blood."[21] The striving for a pure race demanded in turn the sacrifice of many members of the _Volk_ community so that the nation might live. And Providence, immanent in the _Volk,_ inspired struggle and individual sacrifice which would deliver heroes to the racial community.

War was an important facet of Nazi mythical ideology, for the movement had a dialectic and teleology of its own which was expressed in the symbols of combat. Just as history progressed organically through struggle, so those who made history fulfilled their mission through warfare. According to this world view, war was life spirit fed from the spring of German blood and sanctified by the fallen. The sacrifice of one's blood would ensure eternal life and inspire Germans in the future centuries of the Thousand Year Reich.

German soil was fertile for a new heroization of life. As a U-boat captain observed of his compatriots in _Morgenrot,_ a film of 1933 vintage, during a climactic scene when death lay near in the Atlantic, "We Germans don't know much about living, but in death, yes in death, we're fantastic."[22] Hitler Youth Leader Baldur von Schirach raised a generation on romantic poetry extolling the sweet death of the noble:

> Even if the last stars
> die, and all hope fades away
> still no power can corrupt us,
> still no one will betray the flag.
>
> And even if heaven, hell, and the world
> were to be allied against us,
> we would hold our heads high
> and fight until our last man fell wounded.[23]

The apotheosis of the Nazis' glorification of sacrificial death came with the wartime feature films. In _Stukas,_ ecstatic pilots sing, "We are the black hussars of the air!" on their way to deliver England its "just punishment."[24] In _Wunschkonzert,_ a film which took advantage of the popularity of a regular Sunday request concert feature on the radio, Schwarzkopf signals his comrades by playing a Bach fugue in a church, even though he realizes that this will result in his own destruction. In a macabre marriage of art and force, Schwarzkopf dies a heroic death for Germany, and we last see him bent over a baroque organ going up in flames.[25] *Kolberg*, drawing on a historical parallel with the Napoleonic wars, was released in 1945 to encourage a bold defense against the invaders to the last cartridge.[26] *Kolberg* reflected the declining fortunes of the Wehrmacht and the progressive retreat into myth which characterized Nazi propaganda during the last years of the Third Reich.

The anti-Bolshevik motif was also central to the Nazi mythical structure. Jewry was equated with Marxism in Nazi ideology, a political equation traceable to Hitler's Vienna period: "I discovered the relations existing between this destructive teaching and the specific character of a people who up to that time had been almost unknown to me. Knowledge of the Jews is the only key whereby one may understand the inner nature and the real aims of Social Democracy."[27] According to Hitler, blame for the Marxist "pest" could be laid at the door of that "ferment of decomposition of race and society," international Jewry, which he was certain found its twentieth-century expression in Russian bolshevism's drive to control the world.[28] This, he said, explained the Bolshevik intention to destroy all non-Jewish national states. Thus Hitler concluded that his mission was to annihilate both Jewry and bolshevism and to conquer the source of both—Soviet Russia. Hitler never wavered in his anticommunism; even when all was lost in 1945, he tenaciously held to his fading dream that "it is eastwards, for all time eastwards, that the veins of our race must expand."[29]

The myth of "British plutocracy" also assumed an important place in Nazi ideology. It became the leading horse in the Nazi stable from the outbreak of the war against Poland until Hitler turned eastward in 1941, after which it was relegated gradually to the status of a subordinate myth. But at its height the motif of "British plutocracy" came to symbolize Germany's love-hate for the English, a curious amalgam of respect and jealousy. As Goebbels once admitted privately, "English rule has something really phenomenal about it. I have always felt myself drawn to the English world."[30] For his

part Hitler had long shared this sentiment, and his feelings were
racially inspired: he was convinced that the English were of Germanic
stock and thus fellow Aryans.

Because of their ambivalent attitude toward the English, the Nazis
berated them all the more when the final break came. They rewrote
the history of Great Britain to conform to the charge that the English
character expressed itself in violence, murder, and the exploitation
of enslaved peoples. Goebbels made a timely discovery of the "clique
of plutocrats" who ruled England and were intent on restricting
Germany to its overcrowded territory in central Europe, thereby
suppressing a nation that was in dire need of living space.[31] England,
a country with colonies around the globe, was attempting to deny
the Reich its right to life and would try to starve Germany into
subjection once more just as it did in the bleak days after World
War I. Again it was the Jews, firmly rooted in the cities of England,
who were responsible; as for the English, they were the "Jews among
the Aryan peoples."[32]

The Führer cult was a vital link in the National Socialist mythical
structure and there are remarkable parallels between Christian and
Nazi myths. The Führer was at once Father, Son, and Holy Ghost.
He was the Father because his essence was cosmic and he was sent
to earth on a mission which was both of this world and beyond
it. He rode the wave of the historical dialectic, which would culminate
in the victory of Aryan man, and as the reawakened Barbarossa
he fulfilled the prophecies of the German right wing who longed
for a "great one come from above." He was also the Son, the Son
of Providence, who in his infinite wisdom had created the Aryan
Volk. As such it was Hitler's role to lead his people along the paths
to greatness, a way fraught with danger and one which might demand
that they perish in their own flame in the service of the higher
ideal. The Nazi parallel to the Christian concept of the Holy Ghost
was the spirit of Providence, reflected in the mystical source and
life spirit of the *Volk*. Hitler was at once of this world and beyond.
His flesh was the flesh of the *Volk*, and his spirit was their own
life spirit.[33]

As the sands of time began to run out for Hitler, the more he
and his followers returned to their roots in the irrational and the
more they ignored the world of verifiable reality. General Eduard

Dietl registered the fanaticism of the last ditch at a time when it was obvious that the end was in sight: "I believe in the Führer. The more trying the situation, the more I trust him."[34] When the end came, reality was completely eclipsed by Nazi myth. Instead of announcing the banal truth that Hitler had committed suicide in his bunker, the Nazis claimed that the Führer had died leading a band of loyal followers in a final effort to turn back the "Jewish-Bolshevik" influx into the sacred European heartland.[35] Myth, after all, need not be reconcilable with the truth; but it must be vindicated on the field of battle to survive in the material world.

Before allegedly sacrificing himself for the German people, Hitler cursed them for not measuring up to his greatness; he expected them to perish in the flames of the Reich. He was convinced that blood had betrayed blood, that the *Volk* had betrayed their Führer in the same way that Judas had betrayed Jesus. But such a contention was inconsistent with Nazi ideology, and the caretaker regime under Admiral Karl Dönitz chose to ignore the distinction. In that way the pantheon of National Socialist myth remained inviolable and without inner contradiction until the entire structure collapsed.

The present work will detail the gradual retreat of nazism into myth from 1939 to 1945. National Socialist ideology, at its core an irrational, mystical body of doctrine, failed to survive in a world of objective reality, and there was a remarkable transition in the nature of the propaganda as the war progressed. War reporting could be based on fairly accurate factual accounts during the blitz victories of 1939 and 1940, but the same approach could not be used in dealing with Stalingrad, the loss of Africa, the Allied invasion in 1944, and the final battles of 1945. When they were at the end of their rope, Hitler and Goebbels made one final, frantic effort to survive—they blurred the distinction between Party and nation in an attempt to convince the people that the demise of the one guaranteed the destruction of the other. The red flag flying over the Brandenburg Gate signaled that a more powerful set of myths had prevailed—the symbolic garment for the superior power of the Allied military coalition.

II The Nazi Propaganda Machine and World War II

Javier

Although Germany had never been a country endowed with outstanding speakers, in the twentieth century it had in Adolf Hitler
and Joseph Goebbels two of the most gifted demagogues in the
history of the West, masters of the techniques of mass rhetoric,
men who lent currency to Le Bon's dictum that "the improbable
does not exist for a crowd." The result was the destruction of the
German Empire and the "final solution of the Jewish question."

Nazi propaganda is indelibly linked with the name of Joseph Paul
Goebbels. Born in 1897 in Rheydt, which lies in the western Rhineland
where his ancestors had tilled the Westphalian soil for centuries,
Goebbels was schooled in the Gymnasium and the university and
was profoundly influenced as a young man by World War I, the
Versailles Treaty, and the subsequent instability of the Weimar
Republic. Three factors came to play a major role in forming his
personality: his origins straddling working class and lower middle
class, his clubfoot, and his sharp and penetrating mind. During
Goebbels's early career he evidenced a hatred of his social betters,
an attitude which disappeared once he himself could enjoy the delights
of power. All the more did he bask in the luxurious surroundings
of the Leopold Castle which housed the Propaganda Ministry after
1933, and his two estates—Schwanenwerder on the Wannsee and
Lanke in the Brandenburg countryside—were always a source of

12

pleasure to him. But Goebbels's origins lent him confidence to assume the role of spokesman for German blood and soil. He was never more at ease than when he returned to his simple home on Dahlener Street in Rheydt where he would spend carefree hours of conversation with the "most loyal and characteristic voice of the *Volk*," his mother. During the war he found periodic visits at her home a welcome respite from the frenetic pace of Berlin.

Goebbels's clubfoot was a source of agony to him especially during his youth when he was unable to join in the rough play of his classmates. He was rejected for service in the Kaiser's Army because of his physical disability, at a time when German youth dreamed of heroism in the fields of France. Experience at the front was *de rigueur*, and the seventeen-year-old Goebbels was unqualified for it. He thus came to the realization that henceforth he would have to depend on his wit and intelligence to make his way through life. As he observed, "My foot is a hindrance, I am small and not strong, but nature is just, she gave me instead a brain such as few others possess."[2] Goebbels overcompensated for his clubfoot by making his intellect a showpiece. He became an outstanding student at his Rheydt Gymnasium and in the Germanistic seminars at the universities of Bonn, Freiburg, and Heidelberg. During his career as a National Socialist there were few individuals who did not serve as a target for his cynical remarks or jokes. His public image has remained that of the cunning Mephistopheles, the quintessence of all that is malignant and sinister. Goethe's Mephistopheles met his downfall when he made improper advances to the angels who had come to rescue Faust's soul; Goebbels's end was much less poetic, although equally self-consciously theatrical.

In the field of propaganda Goebbels brought a wealth of experience to bear on the problems of wartime Germany. The experience he gained as the gauleiter of *Kampfzeit* Berlin served him well indeed, for it honed him as a speaker and a fighter. Goebbels's Berlin became synonymous with boldness, daring, and terror. There he addressed countless mass rallies, published inflammatory articles in *Der Angriff*, and learned to appreciate the importance of radio as a propaganda vehicle.

Goebbels was probably the most effective funeral orator since Pericles, and he could turn emotion on and off with but a gesture or two. Some of his most effective propaganda during this period was heard at gravesides, where he eulogized the Party's martyrs and where he would from time to time conjure up a myth to lend new meaning to what otherwise would have been a banal and thoroughly routine death of often rather degenerate human material. The death of Horst Wessel stands as but one example of many. Werner Naumann, subsequently Goebbels's most trusted colleague, has told of the emotional intensity of the afternoon in the Nicolai Cemetery when Goebbels spread sacred German soil over the remains of the Stormer Horst Wessel.[3] The epic of Horst Wessel became widely known throughout Germany on the day of the funeral. Young Naumann, a National Socialist student working in Goebbels's Berlin office at the time, has demonstrated just how adept Goebbels was at creating myths: "Horst Wessel was buried in the afternoon, and I took the train to Görlitz in the evening. In Görlitz I attended a Party rally quite by chance. The name Horst Wessel was on everyone's lips, and when I said that 'I have just come from his burial,' it wasn't long until they had me on the stage where I was to tell them everything I knew about [it]."[4] Had Goebbels decided that Wessel was not worth a myth, he would have gone unsung like the hundreds, even thousands, of other storm troopers who lost their lives in the struggle for "Führer, Volk, und Vaterland." As it was, Horst Wessel became the inspiration for Hitler's most famous Party song.

Goebbels's hatred of the Jews was deeply embedded in his soul. During the war, in May 1942, he demonstrated this aversion by relating an anecdote from his pre-1933 repertoire on the occasion of a birthday celebration for his Communist expert Eberhard Taubert at the minister's Lanke estate. According to Goebbels, late one evening during the Kampfzeit as he was returning home after a rally, he had his driver stop by the Friedrich Strasse kiosks to pick up the latest editions of the Berlin newspapers, whereupon a group of Communists attacked his car and shot the chauffeur. Goebbels pressed his handkerchief against the back of his driver's neck, lay low to dodge the bullets, and together the two of them made it safely to a hospital. Several hours later Goebbels called the hospital to inquire about the condition of his driver, but to his amazement a "Jewish doctor" got on the telephone and informed him that a group of

Communists had appeared at the hospital and had finished there what they were unable to accomplish on the Friedrich Strasse. Goebbels said that the doctor told him, "Our patients get the visitors they deserve."[5] Such was Goebbels's reverie long after any Jews could possibly have been a danger to him.

Goebbels's success in Berlin and throughout Germany was all the more remarkable considering his appearance, which hardly fit the Nazi heroic model. When he first entered crowded rally halls he was repeatedly subjected to derision because of his slight stature, his shallow frame, and his clubfoot which caused a noticeable limp. Wolfgang Diewerge, later to serve as chief of the Radio Section of the Propaganda Ministry, has revealed that his initial reaction upon seeing Goebbels for the first time was cynical: "If he [Goebbels] is an Aryan, then he was damned lucky."[6] But doubts of this nature usually were mitigated once "the Doktor" took the podium.

Women were drawn to Goebbels for the wit and charm he displayed in their company, a characteristic which attracted the wealthy divorcée Magda Quandt to him. Magda's social contacts were of use to Goebbels, and her apartment on the *Reichskanzlerplatz*, which housed the couple after their marriage in 1931, became a center of Nazi intrigue. Hitler was often seen there, and he looked on Magda's home as a place where he could periodically escape from the world of the heroic.[7]

The first phase in Goebbels's Party career ended when Hitler was named chancellor in January 1933, and he spent some anxious weeks until called upon to establish the Reich Ministry for Public Enlightenment and Propaganda on March 13, 1933. Within a matter of several months after assuming his new position, the entire apparatus of public communications had come under his control. Radio, journalism, and the film art fell root and branch into the hands of the Nazis, as did all opportunities for convincing the crowd through demonstrations and mass meetings.[8]

Goebbels's fighting nature was well suited to the period of struggle which was geared to attracting new Party members, gaining contributions to the NSDAP (National Socialist German Workers Party) war chest, and winning elections. But during the period of consolidation of power after 1933 all this would change. Whereas earlier he spoke on the average of five times a week, after the founding of the Ministry the opportunity to display his rhetorical talents came less frequently. Before the assumption of power frivolous hours were scarce, but after 1933 Goebbels simply had too much time on his hands.

Once in power, Goebbels was faced with a radically altered set of variables. His central function was to exalt Hitler to such a degree that people would no longer criticize and analyze his work as they did that of other men, but would look on him as a demigod. This entailed convincing Reich Germans that the policies followed by Adolf Hitler were correct and just, which was no mean assignment. Besides his daily directives to the media, Goebbels sought to fulfill this goal by implementing elaborate Party rituals which promised bread and circuses at recurring times of each year and which the public came to expect like the changing of the seasons.

The celebration of significant dates in Nazi history—anniversaries such as January 30 (assumption of power) and November 9 (anniversary of the 1923 putsch)—was supplemented with blitz propaganda on special events during the 1930s. These included the Nuremberg Party Rallies, Strength through Joy, the opening of the Autobahn, the celebration of the hundred year anniversary of the first German railway line from Nuremberg to Fürth, and the annual Munich Oktoberfest, which now featured in its parade a historic review of Germandom from the earliest times to Adolf Hitler, the opening of the Haus der Kunst in Munich by Hitler, the "resurrection" pageant of the original 1923 putsch martyrs, now placed to rest in Munich's Königsplatz, the opening of the new Reich chancellery in Berlin conceived by Hitler's young architect Albert Speer, the return of the Saarland to the German Reich, the Berlin Olympic Games in 1936, the "Heimkehr of the Ostmark" when Austria became part of the Greater German Reich in 1938, and such massive musical reviews with casts of hundreds as *Siebzig Millionen, ein Schlag,* which delighted Berlin audiences for month after month and which climaxed nightly with the appearance of the famed test pilot Hanna Reitsch descending from the sky in an autogiro, a radical and exciting invention at the time.[9] Linked with the Nazi holiday calendar, such propaganda successes periodically excited the public imagination and tended to undergird the regime. Presented in connection with Hitler's major foreign policy victories they made the Führer irresistible to the great majority of Germans.

Goebbels was very clever at propaganda innovation when special situations arose. One remarkable example occurred on Christmas eve, 1933, in Communist Berlin-Wedding. There, along a street bedecked for a traditional Christmas celebration, the Ministry gathered together the families of most of the Communists who had been incarcerated in Dachau. Party functionaries passed out candy, toys, and clothing to the wives and children, while an SA band provided appropriately sentimental Christmas carols as background music. At the correct psychological moment, as the band struck up "Old Comrades," SS vans rolled up and unloaded a large group of prisoners, who were delivered to their families as free men as a "Christmas gift from the Führer."[10]

Goebbels looked on his propaganda corps as members of a grand symphony orchestra who were to respond to every nuance from the maestro with style and sophistication. He could suffer the inept and the dullard neither in his company nor as a member of his organization. But few could understand, much less emulate, the special relationship between Goebbels and the crowd. He knew how to excite the masses with provocative symbols and images which often had no relationship whatsoever with the truth. Furthermore, both he and Hitler were convinced that the crowd could be disciplined to think, live, and fight heroically in the manner of the National Socialist. Goebbels took Le Bon's most telling dictum for his own: "It is crowds rather than isolated individuals that may be induced to run the risk of death to secure the triumph of a creed or an idea, that may be fired for enthusiasm for glory and honor, that are led on . . . as in the age of the Crusades . . . to deliver the tomb of Christ from the infidel, or as in 1793, to defend the Fatherland."[11]

Goebbels shared with Hitler an appreciation for the fundamentals of mass oratory, and they both realized that if they could convince the crowd, they could govern it as well. In *Mein Kampf,* Hitler devoted a good deal of attention to the problems involved in the formulation of effective propaganda. Germany's attempts to wage psychological warfare during World War I had taught him many bitter lessons. First, propaganda should always be directed to the uneducated masses, not to questioning intellectuals; the larger the crowd, the lower the intellectual level of the speech. Secondly, propaganda should always appeal to the emotions and not to reason; simple themes should be repeated time and again. Material based on objective truth was worthless since the nation "is not composed of diplomats and professors of international law, nor even of people capable of reasonable judgment, but of grown-up children with a predilection for irresolution, doubt, and insecurity."[12] Hitler and Goebbels both followed this simple procedure which had served them well on the road to power and during the period of consolidation after 1933.

Whereas Goebbels's ability to convince an audience was based on his method of logical argumentation with clever irrational additives, Hitler's highly successful appeal was almost entirely clothed in irrational garb, and audiences were often transposed to an ethereal state on a wave of ecstatic emotion. Goebbels was in his element when he addressed a crowd, and his sense of timing, combined with a laboriously prepared, rhetorically splendid, argument of his case, was compelling. But if the situation seemed appropriate Goebbels too could surrender to the irrational. As his lieutenant Eugene Hadamovsky wrote about him in 1933, "It would not really matter what he was speaking about, the masses would want to hear him talk time and time again, to be carried away . . . by his fire and passion."[13]

Goebbels's sinister genius lay in his understanding of the German psyche—he had an acute sense for the problems that individuals and families face. This was a characteristic which would serve him well during some of the most difficult days of World War II. It was his practice to state a theme and then to repeat the motif in polyphonic variations. Goebbels had to be on his guard not to reveal that he held in contempt the human material he was molding, and he had this to say to Germany's intellectuals: "If today an educated person says: 'That is too primitive for me,' then I counter: 'You name me a world view [Weltanschauung] which does not do this to set the masses in motion . . . I can only advise him to listen to the parson in Hintertupfing. He speaks that way too, so that his provincials understand him, and his words are not at all on the level of a sermon which the Pope might deliver in Saint Peters.' "[14]

In order to orchestrate his propaganda properly, Goebbels staffed his Ministry with many capable and efficient men, most of whom were in their late twenties or thirties. It was the minister's practice to conceive broad propaganda policy himself and to leave the tactical details to his staff. The men he chose for the most important positions generally welcomed this kind of freedom; indeed, most of them were intellectuals like Goebbels and they would not have continued to serve him had the chief not allowed them a good deal of room for maneuver. Furthermore, contrary to popular belief, Party membership was not foremost in Goebbels's mind when he sought out able lieutenants; instead, imagination and efficiency were the primary requisites of those who would succeed in his Ministry.[15] Of course he needed loyal "Old Fighter" types to serve as his personal bodyguard and chauffeur, but as a rule intelligence was the sine qua non for service on his staff. Hans Fritzsche is perhaps the most outstanding example of a leading propagandist who did not join the Party until long after he went to work for Goebbels. A man with a caustic style and an articulate radio voice, Fritzsche was the commentator with the largest following in Germany during the war.

During the 1930s several men who would see wartime service with Goebbels rose to prominence within the Ministry, although those who were to succeed in the long run understood that Goebbels's ego could not suffer a competitor to become too popular in the public's eye. Walter Funk served as the number two man in the Ministry until 1937, when he replaced Hjalmar Schacht as minister of economics. Alfred Ingemar Berndt, who functioned in positions ranging from the active propaganda section to radio and press affairs, was rather too headstrong to avoid his ultimate falling out with Goebbels.[16]

Karl Hanke who replaced Funk as state secretary was a bold, efficient propagandist who eventually left the Ministry to become gauleiter of Lower Silesia, but not before fomenting a cause célèbre in the Ministry. Hanke, who had been in Goebbels's shadow for years, finally turned against him in the late 1930s. According to informed sources who served in the Ministry, Hanke was offended by Goebbels's treatment of his wife, Magda, who suffered bitterly as a result of her husband's torrid affair with the Czech actress Lida Baarova, a situation Hanke exploited to enjoy the company of Magda during her period of strain. Naumann speaks of Hanke's repeated childlike, emotional outbursts against Goebbels in the presence of other members of the Ministry staff.[17] This situation opened the way for the naming of Leopold Gutterer as state secretary in 1939. History has not been kind to Gutterer, a man much maligned by his colleagues within the Ministry for his executive incompetence. His rise occurred because Goebbels was looking for a man who would not repeat the "Hanke theater" and cause him embarrassing difficulties. Further, Gutterer had good SS connections—he was promoted to the rank of brigadier general in 1940. An excellent propaganda technician, Gutterer was the victim of the "Peter Principle" and the pressures of intraministerial politics. He was replaced as state secretary in April 1944.[18]

Another example of an intellectual in Party uniform who would spend part of his wartime career as a propagandist was Günter d'Alquen, who had made a name for himself as an enfant terrible while editor in chief of the SS newspaper *Das Schwarze Korps*. D'Alquen was Goebbels's link to Himmler, whom he served as personal staff chief and confidant; thus he was one of the few men who enjoyed the trust of both leaders. D'Alquen had impressed Goebbels when Himmler lent him to the Propaganda Ministry in 1940. At that time Goebbels gave him the key to the safe containing all his secret files, an extraordinary act of trust which d'Alquen never betrayed. Later in the war he commanded the Waffen-SS propaganda troops.[19]

Hans Schwarz van Berk, considered by many of his colleagues to be somewhat of a prima donna, served Goebbels as one of the most influential writers on the staff of *Das Reich*. Witty, versatile, and a master of the understatement, Schwarz van Berk could deliver a news story like few other journalists in the Third Reich. As he has acknowledged, he also was responsible for many news plants in the enemy press during his tenure in the Ministry's Foreign Press Section. Informed by a V-man in the central telegraph offices in Berlin, he often received requests from foreign newspaper and periodical home offices to their Berlin correspondents long before the staff members of those papers did themselves. In this way he was rapidly able to order one of the men on his staff to prepare the news story desired by the *Guardian*, the *Times*, or *Life* and deliver it to the party who had requested it through neutral channels.[20]

Goebbels's relationship with Schwarz van Berk was a stormy one. On several occasions the two engaged in heated arguments about editorial policy, which would culminate in the young writer's expulsion from the irate minister's office. More than once Schwarz van Berk submitted his resignation, but invariably Goebbels would extend his apologies. He would endure this kind of insubordination provided that a man produced for him, and Schwarz van Berk refused to become a government official precisely in order to maintain his independence.[21] After writing in Berlin during most of the war, he returned to the front with the *Leibstandarte SS "Adolf Hitler"* to avoid the worst excesses of what he termed Goebbels's "theater of annihilation" in 1945.

Wolfgang Diewerge, a lawyer who served as director of the Ministry's Radio Section and later as chief of the Reich Propaganda Office Danzig–West Prussia, was an articulate, efficient, convinced Nazi on whom Goebbels could depend.[22] A colonel in the SS, Diewerge drew on a long history as a Party propagandist. As a Reich speaker, he had addressed audiences from Finland to South Africa, and Goebbels used him with success to carry out some of his ad hoc anti-Semitic campaigns before the war. He was especially effective in conceiving and disseminating whisper propaganda, a technique to be discussed in detail below.

Dr. Eberhard Taubert was another notable figure in Ministry circles. Taubert had attracted Goebbels's notice when he was a student at Berlin, where he had commenced his life's work as a professional anti-Bolshevik. Goebbels employed him in the Propaganda Ministry, where he began with a modest title and ultimately rose to direct the important office "Ost und Anti-Bolschewismus," as well as its subordinate agencies "Anti-Komintern" and "Vineta."[23] Taubert was concerned with every question that involved the Soviets, and he waged an unceasing campaign against the "Red East" until 1939, when as a result of the Hitler-Stalin Pact he was forced to take a two-year respite. At that time Goebbels busied him with farm-city population problems and anti-Semitic propaganda. In June 1941 he was unleashed against the Soviets once more.

Werner Naumann, the éminence grise of the Propaganda Ministry, enjoyed a meteoric career as Goebbels's protégé.[24] He possessed the virtues Goebbels sought in his staff: intelligence, loyalty, devotion to duty, ruthlessness, ambition, and a conscience at ease with criminality. As the years passed Naumann moved up in the Ministry to become head of the *Ministeramt.* As such, Goebbels had no closer personal friend or adviser, no man he trusted more than Naumann.

whom he molded in his own image; the latter responded, because he was made of the same material as was his chief. In order not to appear to compete with Goebbels—Naumann was himself an accomplished speaker—he went to great lengths to stay behind the scenes. Naumann, like so many other officials in the Propaganda Ministry, held a rank in the SS, a situation Goebbels found reassuring (Naumann rose to the rank of brigadier general).

Both Hitler and Himmler trusted Naumann, although Bormann judged him to be a dangerous rival.[25] It had somehow come to Hitler's attention that Naumann had performed heroically in the *Leibstandarte SS "Adolf Hitler"*; as a result, the Führer never wavered in the favor he showed him.[26] Hitler's trust was deepened as a result of Naumann's loyalty during the 20th July crisis.

In 1944, Naumann pushed Gutterer aside and took over his post as state secretary in the Propaganda Ministry. Gutterer admits that his position within the Ministry had visibly weakened by early 1943, when he began to notice that he was often being sidestepped in the chain of command between Naumann's *Ministeramt* and the various sections.[27] His resignation in 1944 merely confirmed a situation which had long existed.

When the end came in 1945, Naumann was at Goebbels's side fanatically demanding resistance to the last bullet. In a sense, he was to Goebbels what Bormann was to Hitler. Hitler reaffirmed the trust he had in Naumann—who at that point was only thirty-six years old—by naming him propaganda minister in the cabinet he appointed in his last will and testament.

Hitler and Goebbels worked from the basic principle that all propaganda media must operate according to strictly defined ideological guidelines; yet they expected Nazi maxims to appear in multicolored garb. The Führer once elaborated on what he demanded from his journalists, an admonition which pertained to all propagandists: "We want men who, when they develop a theme, do not first of all think of the success the article will bring them or of the material benefits it will give them; as molders of public opinion, we want men who are conscious of the fact that they have a mission and who bear themselves as good servants of the state. . . . Today the journalist knows that he is no mere scribbler, but a man with the sacred mission of defending the highest interests of the state."[28]

By 1938 it was apparent that nazism's greatest struggle lay over the horizon. As Hitler surveyed the chances of realizing his dreams, he knew that the burdens which a war would place on the propaganda corps would be extremely challenging. He had been dismayed by the lack of martial enthusiasm on the part of the Germans during the Sudeten crisis of August and September 1938.[29] To alert the press to its role in a future war, Hitler invited four hundred of the Reich's leading journalists to a private address in Munich on November 10, 1938. The crowd was an imposing one and included Hess, Goebbels, Amann, and Rosenberg.

The thrust of Hitler's message was obvious. In his words, "It was necessary gradually to prepare the German people psychologically and to make clear to them that there are some things which only force, not peaceful means, must decide." In the hour of decision the German people, a nation as strong as Krupp steel, must stand body and soul behind their Führer. The propagandists' common goal must be to rally to their leader's side a people who were "true believers, united, confident, and absolutely reliable," a people who would fanatically believe in the final victory. The press thus shared with Hitler and the Party the responsibility to lead the *Volk* to their grand, epochal destiny.[30]

Once hostilities commenced in 1939, Goebbels experienced little difficulty in shifting his operation to a wartime footing. The "Minister Conference" which he held each morning at the Wilhelmsplatz provided him with an effective medium to direct German war propaganda; as such it was a valuable weapon in psychological warfare.[31] The conferences were attended by anywhere from forty to sixty people including the senior Ministry officials and representatives of the various public media. There Goebbels issued the directives of the day on the most important war news, albeit within the parameters established in the OKW communiqué regarding the progress of hostilities on any given day and in the "daily directives" of Reich Press Chief Dietrich to all German journalists, both of which were issued by the Führer headquarters. The conferences reflected Goebbels's personality, style, and determination to outwit the enemy. According to the participants, more than one was a propaganda tour de force. Whether Goebbels was treating the Battle of France or the flight of Hess, startling U-boat victories or the serious reverses in Russia, he was seldom at a loss for words. Those present learned that he was capable of embellishing a victory in Ciceronian style one day and offering an obvious lie as the truth on the next. Goebbels's personal direction of the conferences was all-important. One of his adjutants, Wilfred von Oven, has quipped that when the minister was away from Berlin the tone at the conferences was like a rabbit breeding club.[32]

The exigencies of the war demanded of Goebbels a much more intense concern with propaganda tactics than had been the case after the Nazis' assumption of power. His directive "Guidelines for the Execution of NSDAP Propaganda," issued at the outbreak of the war, outlined the means he expected his staff to employ in disseminating propaganda.[33] Goebbels's concern was how best to direct the Party to summon its reserves of energy and ingenuity in order to influence public opinion, with the goal of mobilizing every citizen to contribute uncompromisingly to the cause of victory. The means included the radio and newspapers, mass meetings, illustrated lectures, films, posters, brochures, pins, and "whisper" or person-to-person propaganda.

Besides issuing propaganda guidelines, Goebbels often introduced innovative techniques for the technical delivery of war propaganda. One example of this was the "Special Announcement," conceived to dramatize German blitz victories during the first years of the war.

Prince von Schaumburg-Lippe wrote of an encounter at Goebbels's palace on the Wilhelmsplatz shortly after the attack on Russia which illustrated the minister's ability to maximize the effectiveness of music as an accompaniment to the spoken word. For some time he had been looking for an impressive fanfare to accompany news releases of German military triumphs. Goebbels blithely told the prince to follow him, and without a word they went through the corridors until he sat down at the piano and began playing. Goebbels roamed through motifs of Wagner and Liszt, and still with no word about what he was up to he kept seeking the proper score. He played for over an hour, and "suddenly he played Les Preludes. He began to concentrate on but a part of it. He had what he wanted. He repeated it once, twice, and added variations. He seized on the score which the German people heard repeatedly in the following years when a great victory against the Russians was announced. The signal of the German radio for announcements on the East—Special Announcements! 'Now I've got it,' he said. He repeated this passage several times, stood up then and drawing a deep breath he added: 'Thank God—I have found the best. This is it and this it will remain! What do you think of it?' "[34]

Another personal sounding board for Goebbels was his weekly lead article in *Das Reich*. From the first carefully timed appearance of this newspaper during the victorious campaign against France in 1940 until the last issue in April 1945, Goebbels went through the sometimes agonizing routine of meeting a weekly copy deadline. If his task was easy enough during the days of blitz victory, it became an onerous burden later in the war when he had to treat serious German reversals. Without question *Das Reich* was the leading German newspaper of the period, and it was read both in Germany and abroad with great interest as an indicator of Nazi policy. To ensure the widest possible dissemination, Goebbels's article was read over the radio every Friday evening.

Goebbels, like the English, made use of "black" or "gray" propaganda, as distinguished from the pronouncements of the officially recognized government media. One of his favored techniques was "whisper" or person-to-person propaganda, a subtle form of propaganda never before used in any country on such a massive scale. *Mundpropaganda* was predicated on the conviction that there were many themes in wartime better approached through channels which concealed the governmental origin of the information. It was employed only when public mention of the sensitive issues in question had to be avoided.[35]

Now and then person-to-person propaganda was utilized to conceal preparations for impending campaigns. An example of this occurred a short time before Hitler's attack on Russia, when Goebbels's staff launched a rumor that troops with special qualifications in amphibious warfare were being collected along the Channel coast "for the imminent landing against England." On other occasions, Goebbels released news about the future deployment of new weapons by German armies, topics which could not be treated in the public media for reasons of security. Several weeks before the first German snorkel submarines were launched, *Mundpropaganda* channels had floated a rumor that Hitler was "about to deploy a new type of submarine which did not have to surface for six weeks."[36]

Black propaganda was very useful during the air war over Germany, and Goebbels's staff was able to counter exaggerated English and American claims about the damage Allied air fleets had inflicted. Should Sefton Delmer or Lindley Fraser of the BBC claim one evening that an important weapons factory in Krefeld had been destroyed, the next morning at his press conference Goebbels would turn to Wolfgang Diewerge and request that he disseminate the news through *Mundpropaganda* personnel that the Krefeld factory had suffered only minor damage. For obvious reasons Nazi public media would harm the German cause if they were to announce publicly that the factory was producing at a higher level after the raid than before it—and that with the roof blown off the plant. Such a claim would serve as an open invitation to the English to pay a return visit to Krefeld to finish what they had begun.

Some whisper propaganda was prepared for selected provincial audiences. For example, *Mundpropaganda* channels quieted the fretting wives of the workers in the famous Schweinfurt ball-bearing plants, favorite targets of Allied bombers, by sending their personnel to the Bavarian villages housing the evacuees and having them drop the news at Frau Meier's Konditorei in Mittenwald that the wives' men were safe in the factories because of new camouflaging methods. In another case, Düsseldorf families evacuated to the bucolic Black Forest were assured that BBC assertions to the effect that Düsseldorf had been pulverized were false, and exact block by block reports were released enumerating the names of streets and sectors of the city which had not been touched or were only partly damaged.

Yet another effective means of spreading *Mundpropaganda* was through church groups and club meetings. For example, when Goebbels wanted it to become known that Hitler was planning a counterattack against the invasion front in France in 1944 or that cadres for sixty new divisions were being formed, he turned to church and club channels. If a simple peasant heard from the old president of the Saint Elizabeth League that the Führer was about to do these things, he tended to believe it. And more often than not, the old president had read about the news in his monthly paper, which was fed items from the Propaganda Ministry.[37]

the war the two men fought a battle for control of the German press, a relentless struggle which neither man completely won or lost. On several occasions Hitler had to intervene personally to settle disputes between them.[42]

For his part, Goebbels attempted to sidestep Dietrich's influence over the journalists by inviting selected editors to his daily press conferences. The minister's prestige within the press corps was much greater than Dietrich's, and as a result the line Goebbels dictated more often than not prevailed. Dietrich fought back by issuing the daily "Tagesparolen des Reichspressechefs" from the Führer headquarters, which incorporated Hitler's detailed directives to the newspaper editors. The *Tagesparolen* were initially issued in 1940 at the suggestion of Dietrich's zealous staff man Helmut Sündermann, who conceived of them not only as an efficient method of transacting daily business, but as a way to checkmate Goebbels's efforts to undercut Dietrich's authority.[43] The nominal chain of command for the daily directives was Hitler to Dietrich to Goebbels. But Dietrich's power stopped outside the gates of the Führer headquarters, because it was Goebbels who transmitted the directives to the newspapers in his own press conferences.

Hostility between Goebbels and Dietrich reached a new high as a result of a rather amusing incident in 1940. Purely by coincidence, both men delivered addresses on the same day, Goebbels at a rally in Münster, Dietrich at a meeting of the press in Wiesbaden. Each expected headline billing, and both issued directives accordingly. Ernst Braekow, Fritzsche's assistant in the Ministry's domestic press section, acting as a barometer of the actual power of the men involved, gave the Goebbels speech the primary billing. When Dietrich realized what had happened, he was enraged and fired Braekow, but ultimately he could do nothing but register another defeat at the hands of Goebbels.[44]

Goebbels, who was prepared to sacrifice a friend of many years standing for a bon mot, did not hesitate when an opportunity offered itself to humiliate an enemy like Dietrich, and on several occasions the minister's devilish humor was turned on the Reich press chief. Perhaps the best instance of this occurred one day when the Führer's intimate circle was gathered for luncheon at the Reich chancellery. Dietrich, who had not yet spoken, suddenly leaned forward and said, "My Führer, this morning, while I was taking a bath, I thought of a good idea." At that, Goebbels, who was never at a loss for a biting remark, turned to Dietrich and without changing his expression interrupted him, "Herr Dietrich, you should take more baths."[45] Goebbels, to be sure, enjoyed the game of cat and mouse, especially when his adversary was on Dietrich's intellectual level. But Dietrich continued to cause him a great deal of embarrassment, and he was unable to shed this particular thorn. Goebbels often told Naumann that "he was waiting for the day when the stupidity of Herr Dietrich would get on the Führer's nerves to such a degree that he would never want to see him again."[46]

A dramatic event involving Dietrich early in the war against Russia exacerbated tensions in the extreme. In October 1941, Hitler dispatched Dietrich to Berlin to announce to a gala conference of the world press that the last hour of bolshevism had struck. Goebbels's advisers have remarked that on that day the minister nearly cried. He had long fought the overly optimistic news policy emanating from the Führer headquarters; now he was presented with an unbelievably absurd situation. Ironically Dietrich served as a convenient target for Goebbels's differences with Hitler on the question of basic propaganda strategy; Hitler, after all, was responsible for Dietrich's announcement.

In the summer of 1942 Dietrich won a new, if tenuous, lease on life as a result of the "Order of the Führer for Securing Co-operation between the Reich Propaganda Minister and the Reich Press Chief of August 23, 1942."[47] Both men agreed to its stipulations which reaffirmed the status quo except for the clause obligating Goebbels to issue directives to the press only through Dietrich. Actually, it settled nothing, and Goebbels continued to hold the upper hand over the press.

Relations continued to deteriorate between the two and were brought to a head when a few weeks later Dietrich endeavored to strengthen his position in Berlin by naming Helmut Sündermann to the post of vice Reich press chief. This pleased neither Goebbels nor the members of the press corps who found Sündermann's high-handed methods intolerable. Goebbels was irate because his effort to place a press liaison officer of his own next door to Dietrich at the Führer headquarters had been checkmated by his adversary.

Goebbels's complaint to Bormann about the Sündermann appointment infuriated Dietrich who threatened to resign for the third time
if Goebbels did not stop meddling with the Reich press chief's
directives and prerogatives. Hitler refused to release him, remarking
that "you can't come and go as you please with me."[48]

Sündermann turned out to be something of a problem for Goebbels,
because he was a man who held his ground. Hans Fritzsche, who
in March 1942 reported to the Sixth Army in the field after resigning
his position as chief of the domestic press over bitter policy differences
with Dietrich, probably would not have lasted a few weeks in his
Ministry post subject to the tender mercies of Sündermann. The
latter has made it clear that he did not regard Goebbels as his superior,
nor did he afford him any more respect than all the other Nazi
ministers.[49] Although Sündermann did establish his quarters in the
Propaganda Ministry, he was loyal to Dietrich and never consulted
with Goebbels on any questions of common interest. Without Sündermann in Berlin, Dietrich's influence would have paled to the minimum, but Sündermann's fighting nature guaranteed Dietrich continued influence over some members of the press corps.[50]

As the war drew to a close, Goebbels finally witnessed Dietrich's
demise. In June 1944 he gained a veto power over the daily directives,
which removed one source of irritation. At last, on March 30, 1945,
Hitler fired his Reich press chief who he was convinced had been
sabotaging not only his "scorched earth" and "Werewolf" propapanda
directives, but also those protesting alleged British and American
atrocities on the western front.[51] Goebbels now had every public
medium under his control, a fact entirely without significance so
late in the war.

Goebbels had serious differences with Hitler about the tone of
military reporting emanating from the Führer headquarters. He was
especially disgusted with the daily military communiqués. Hitler
regarded the communiqué primarily as a propaganda weapon in
the psychological warfare he waged against the Reich's enemies; he
never considered using them solely as factual reports on the course
of military operations.

The communiqué largely dictated the line on military news to
which the entire propaganda apparatus conformed. There were
several steps between its first formulation and the final draft released

to the world press. Initially, the reports of the day's fighting were sifted by the three Wehrmacht branches and then sent to the OKW/WPr, where the first draft was written. It was next sent to General Alfred Jodl who took an active interest in the communiqués and who had the responsibility of preparing the final copy before presenting it to Hitler. Thus, from one step to the next in the preparation of the communiqués, political considerations became increasingly important.

Although Hitler expected absolutely reliable reports to reach his headquarters from the various sectors of the front, he felt free to make use of them just as he pleased, a discretionary power often approaching the cavalier.[52] Any item which did not meet the Führer's approval was dropped, and he added sections at his pleasure. Not only did he read and approve the communiqués, but often enough he dictated portions of them; none was ever released without his signature.[53] Because of Hitler's misuse of this traditionally respected medium of information, the communiqué gradually lost its credibility,[54] until by 1945 it had become little more than a sounding board for Hitler's last-ditch fanaticism. One German reeling after an Allied raid gave vent to his disgust by panning the communiqué with the following wall inscription: "HAVE PULLED BACK FROM ENEMY'S POSITIONS ACCORDING TO PLAN AND LIVE FROM NOW ON AT LUDENDORFF STREET 18. RETREAT CARRIED OUT UNHARASSED BY THE ENEMY."[55] These words summed up the feelings of countless people, who no longer read the communiqués because they were so misleading.

Two directives by General Jodl reflect the changing nature of the communiqués. In the first of these, dated June 18, 1941, Jodl wrote that the "basis for the entire German military news reporting (Wehrmacht Communiqué, Special Announcements, Commentaries, Propaganda Company Reports, etc.) is the truth. . . . The German Wehrmacht Communiqué is the honest account of the actual events on the battlefield. . . ."[56] In contrast to this position, Jodl noted in his directive of October 25, 1944, that the communiqué "must . . . represent a compromise between the purely factual account of the military situation and the psychological and propagandistic conditions, which cannot be ignored. The greatest effect of the Wehrmacht Communiqué lies in its trustworthiness. It can and, to be sure, must frequently conceal the truth, but it may never replace

people in his gau, thus hoping to influence policy in the *Ministeramt*.
Or, as was more often the case, they were written by men who
were more interested in protecting their own positions than in offering
an objective assessment of public opinion on sensitive issues.[81]
Considering Goebbels's reaction when he read that morale was poor
in any particular area, it is hardly surprising that his subordinates
did not level with him.

The weekly SD reports, written in Office III of the *Reichssicherheitshauptamt,* were a much more reliable indicator of public opinion.
The genesis of the wartime SD reports ("Meldungen aus dem Reich")
was remarkable; they were the result of one of Hitler's memorable
outbursts on the day he attacked Poland. Although the Führer often
depended on his loyal paladin Himmler for information on the home
front, he ordered the Propaganda Ministry to prepare an analysis
of the popular reaction to the war with Poland on that fateful day.
State Secretary Gutterer obediently took the report to the Reich
chancellery, which was bustling with military and Party brass. Hitler
asked Gutterer for his report, and upon reading it he took note
of the fact that there were several spontaneous demonstrations in
Vienna protesting the war. Taking Gutterer and Himmler into the
Wintergarten of the Reich chancellery, Hitler flew into a rage. After
attacking Gutterer, he trained his fire on the Reichsführer SS, asking
him, "Why in God's name didn't your office report that to me?"
It was the first that Himmler had heard about antiwar demonstrations,
and he withdrew to check the report with the Vienna SS. Once
Himmler had confirmed the information, Hitler forbade Gutterer
ever again to indulge in gathering intelligence material.[82] Gutterer
later met with Reinhard Heydrich of the SD and together they worked
out an arrangement for the wartime SD reports.

Gruppenführer Otto Ohlendorf who edited the SD reports saw
to it that they were characterized by an honesty which was uncommon
in the Nazi state. Ohlendorf's goal was to influence opinion at the
highest level with absolutely objective assessments which knew no
favorites. Ultimately, this brought him into disfavor with Bormann
and led to the discontinuation of the reports in the wake of the
belt tightening that followed the attempt on Hitler's life in July 1944.[83]

As long as the SD showered praise on the Party elite, no protests
resulted; but as the war dragged on, the widespread pessimism was

accurately reported. As a result, Goebbels took steps to limit their circulation to a few key individuals in the Ministry, and he made an unsuccessful effort to allow only Göring, Himmler, and Bormann to receive them besides himself. Hitler, for his part, ignored them. After Stalingrad, Goebbels felt that they served the interests of a handful of "defeatists" in the governing circles of Berlin who confused the opinions of a "few highly-placed bureaucrats" with the general mood of the German people.[84]

Stalingrad marks the watershed in delineating Goebbels's shift from a combination of factual-mythical propaganda—which characterized his approach during the early years of the war—to an increasing dependence on irrational themes at the expense of factual war reporting. The myths of Stalingrad, of the "Jewish-Bolshevik world conspiracy," and of the Führer's infallibility became the leading motifs in his ideological orchestration which culminated in 1945 with the Nazi elite's return to its mystical roots, as Goebbels drummed out the demise of the Third Reich. Long before he had struck the *Untergangsmotif* that emphasized the war as an ideological struggle, a "fight for life or death"; in 1945 he demonstrated that he was absolutely in earnest about it.[85]

III The Battle of Poland

As a result of some eighteen months of planning commencing early in 1938 both in the Propaganda Ministry and in the OKW/Section for Wehrmacht Propaganda, it was relatively easy for Goebbels to shift German propaganda machinery to a war footing in 1939. The campaign of vilification against Poland in August 1939, signaling the imminence of war, posed no technical difficulties. Hitler and Goebbels agreed on the strategic and tactical direction for propaganda on the Polish question, which embraced planning for all contingencies. But the Poles, Hitler's first victims in his eastern-oriented Weltanschauung, were tertiary enemies and were treated as such even during the military campaign which was to last less than five weeks. The Jews, the English, and the Poles—these were the Reich's enemies, in descending order, during the German-Polish war.

The Hitler-Stalin Pact posed major problems for Goebbels which he was unable to solve. Photographs of hardened Communists exchanging toasts with Nazi diplomats and of Stalin in a friendly *tête-à-tête* with von Ribbentrop shocked people conditioned by some twenty years of anti-Communist propaganda to distrust, even to hate, the Soviets. Hitler realized that only his total control over the media would enable him to carry out what seemingly everyone knew to be a tactical diplomatic maneuver.[1] On the other hand the Non-aggression Pact reassured many Germans who were convinced that

Hitler had avoided a two-front war, thereby delivering the Reich from its proverbial "encirclement."[2] Yet the Führer's reference to the Russian treaty of friendship in his Reichstag address of September 1 raised more puzzling questions than it answered:

I am particularly happy to be able to tell you of one event. Russia and Germany are governed by two different doctrines. There was only one question that had to be cleared up. Germany has no intention of exporting its doctrine. Given the fact that Soviet Russia has no intention of exporting its doctrine to Germany, I no longer see any reason why we should still oppose one another.

This political decision means a tremendous departure for the future, and it is a final one. Russia and Germany fought against one another in the World War. That shall and will not happen a second time. This pact was greeted in Moscow too.[3]

If people remained confused about the Hitler-Stalin Pact, all the more clearly did they read the danger signs during the escalation of the Polish crisis. To be sure, there was little that was new in the Nazis' treatment of the Polish Corridor question, the German minority problems, and the "Polish provocations." But the manner in which the propaganda was worded reflected the rapidly deteriorating state of affairs; the situation became more emotionally charged with each passing day after the announcement of the German-Russian understanding on August 23. Although the diplomatic front was fluid during the week before the outbreak of hostilities while Hitler frantically attempted to win a guarantee of neutrality from the English, this was not discernible in Nazi propaganda which pursued a seemingly unalterable course toward war. Frothy headlines heralded this belligerent spirit: "Renewed Horrible Polish Acts of Terror," "Panic and Chaos in Poland,"[4] "Polish Flak Fires at Reich Minister Stuckart,"[5] "Poland Orders Full Mobilization."[6]

Nazi propaganda at the outbreak of the Polish campaign established a pattern that was to be followed with each subsequent declaration of war. The Wehrmacht's drive into Poland from Silesia, Pomerania, and East Prussia was touted as a counterattack, a preemptive strike against a strong enemy poised to join hands with England in driving a dagger into the back of the Reich. Within a matter of hours, Hitler went before the Reichstag to announce that Versailles was a dead letter: "Danzig was and is a German city! The Corridor was and is German!" The Poles, he said, had misunderstood his peaceful intentions and at the instigation of England had refused to send a representative to him to talk peace. Polish general mobilization and the accompanying atrocities and border provocations allegedly had compelled him to answer force with force: "Since 5:45 this morning, we are shooting back!"

Hitler promised that his only goal in the war was to right the intolerable wrong done in the Corridor and at Danzig and to terminate the state of civil war on the Reich's Polish border. He stretched the "hand of friendship" to England and France in an effort to keep both powers neutral in the conflict. The borders with France were final, he declared; the West Wall would forever remain the frontier between their two countries. Hitler promised England friendship and close cooperation as its reward for guaranteeing him a free hand in Europe.

Hitler ended the Reichstag meeting with a remarkable symbolic gesture to draw attention to the fact that he was the first soldier of the state, a man cognizant of the needs of the *Volk* and of the mission that Providence had decreed for him as Führer of the Reich. He pledged that he would not remove his field gray uniform until victory had crowned his efforts, or he would not live to see its end. This strangely prophetic remark signaled that the war to come would be waged according to the radical precepts of Nazi ideology which knew only total victory or death. "I have never learned the meaning of one word," he admonished the nation, "and that is surrender."[7] Ultimately he expected the entire nation to soar with him on his eagle's flight to the Walhallian heights where glory was enshrined or to die a proud death in the attempt.

Hitler reaffirmed his conception of himself as the inheritor of the Germanic tribal chieftain's role as the first soldier of the clan in his message to the "Eastern Army": "I myself, as an old soldier of the World War and as the commander-in-chief, am moving my headquarters to the front to be at your side."[8] His arrogance was echoed in Göring's Order of the Day to the Luftwaffe which was composed in ecstatic, Hitler Youth style: "The Führer has ordered you into action. Your greatest hour has arrived . . . Flyers! You will annihilate the enemy in lightning attacks wherever he fights or retreats in desperate flight. You will destroy and pulverize the enemy with your zealous, self-sacrificial deployment (mit letztem opferfreudigem Einsatz) . . . Our beloved Führer is leading us, and the whole nation, unified in National Socialism, is marshalled behind you. There is only one possible outcome: victory."[9]

No sooner had the Wehrmacht launched its offensive into Poland than Hitler fulfilled his promise of twenty years standing to bring Danzig and the Corridor "home to the Reich." Gauleiter Albert Forster, a Bavarian transplant in the Hanseatic city, exchanged telegrams with Hitler that stressed not only the political significance of the event but the National Socialist ideological interpretation as well. In Nazi jargon, the blood of the Germanic east now flowed and merged with its source in the heartland.[10]

Throughout the first two days of September Hitler was haunted by the prospect of a war against England which, he affirmed, might mean "finish Germaniae."[11] He clung to the chimera that a local war against Poland was still a possibility, and Goebbels dealt gingerly with Anglo-French sensibilities for the time being. For example, he forbade the media to refer to the "outbreak of war"; the designation "hostilities" better suited his purposes. Nor were the English people to be maligned; only their leaders, "eternal warmongers, who are directed by the Jews, the international capitalists, and the demo-plutocrats," were to be defamed.[12] Propaganda directed to France appealed to anti-English prejudice and established a thematic sequence which became the hallmark of Nazi propaganda until France lay prostrate in June 1940; by opposing Germany, Frenchmen allegedly would shed their blood for English interests alone. A typical rhetorical question took this form: "Why should the flower of French youth die while engaged in a hopeless sacrificial offensive against the impregnable West Wall at the bidding of Jewish Parisian lawyers who take their cues from London?"[13]

Following the English and French declarations of war, the Führer, disappointed and fearful for the future, launched an acrimonious propaganda onslaught against England. His "Message to the German People" gave notice that their struggle for peace and justice had been misinterpreted by "the English and the Jews" who dared to challenge fate and declare war on the Reich. His earnest endeavor to remain at peace with England had been spurned, he claimed, "but the British government has deceived itself on one thing: Germany in the year 1939 is no longer the Germany of 1914! And the Chancellor of today's Reich is not Bethmann-Hollweg!"[14]

Hitler's message to his Party comrades on September 3 embraced the threefold purpose of reawakening the idealism of the *Kampfzeit*, preparing them for radical solutions of internal problems, and bringing the war into line with Nazi ideology. He resuscitated the myth of 1918 whereby "Jewish-Bolshevik" elements at home "stabbed the Reich in the back" and caused its defeat, and asserted that such a situation under his regime was inconceivable. The burden of history fell on the shoulders of the Party members, whom he admonished to lead lives of exemplary frugality. Death awaited those who engaged in war profiteering, and merciless liquidation would be the lot of internal enemies who dared to oppose the war: "The brave soldier at the front must feel that his life is more important to us than those of traitors at home."[15]

It was but a matter of hours after the English had declared war on Germany that Captain Lemp, skipper of U-boat 30, mistook the steamer *Athenia* for a destroyer and sank her without warning some two hundred miles off the coast of the Hebrides.[16] Although some 140 persons were drowned, this consideration was not paramount in Hitler's assessment of the situation; what disturbed him was that twenty-eight Americans had lost their lives in the attack. At a time when he wanted to avoid a provocation against the United States, he could ill afford to admit that a German submarine had sunk the *Athenia*. To have done so would have offered Roosevelt a cause parallel to the sinking of the *Lusitania* which played an important role in ultimately bringing the United States into World War I. Hitler's initial reaction was to forbid the U-boat fleet to attack passenger vessels, even when sailing in convoys.[17] Next he issued a public denial that Germany was involved in the incident.

In a propaganda directive dated September 6, Hitler answered the English charge that a German torpedo had sent the *Athenia* to the bottom with the disclaimer that all German submarines were under strict orders to obey the Hague Convention stipulating that passenger vessels of belligerent nations must be warned and civilians brought to safety before sinking. Further, he argued that no German naval vessel was even remotely near the area in which the *Athenia* was sunk, thus absolving the Germans of guilt in the affair.[18] For his part Goebbels accused Churchill of ordering the sinking, and he took this fabrication to the nation over all radio networks on the evening of Sunday, October 22.[19] He cited as evidence the alleged testimony under oath of one "Gustav Anderson of Illinois," a travel agent who had been aboard the *Athenia*, before United States congressional investigators Francis Case of South Dakota, Overton Brookes of Louisiana, and Walther Pierce of Oregon.[20] According to Anderson, the British had loaded munitions aboard the ship, a fact which Goebbels chose to interpret as Churchill's preparation to sink her. Anderson also told the investigators that British destroyers shelled the sinking hulk, which Goebbels took as ample proof that "the liar Churchill" had planned its destruction in order to force the United States into war immediately as England's ally. Goebbels offered as further "proof" Anderson's testimony that he saw no U-boat periscope or any other evidence of a German attack.

The fact of the matter was that the Germans themselves were not certain who sank the *Athenia* until Captain Lemp of U-boat 30 docked in Wilhelmshaven on September 27, some three weeks after the sinking.[21] Admiral Dönitz was there to meet the ship and was the first to learn that U-30 had indeed sunk the *Athenia*.[22] Hitler was so concerned that he went to Wilhelmshaven himself the day after U-30 had docked to interview the crew.[23] In an effort to conceal the truth, the crew was sworn to secrecy, and a general directive forbade all public references to the matter. Quite inadvertently a slip occurred in the provinces when the *Westphälische Neueste Nachrichten* included the *Athenia* in a list of U-boat victories which it published in mid-October 1939.[24]

The anti-English air war propaganda began during the first week of hostilities in answer to the RAF's symbolic raid against Cuxhaven and Wilhelmshaven on September 4, an attack which surprised and irritated Hitler and Göring. The Wehrmacht communiqué reporting it claimed that over one-half of the attacking English aircraft had been shot down and that neither raid caused any damage whatsoever because of the effectiveness of the combined German air and flak defenses. Thereafter the English commenced a concerted propaganda campaign from the air. Royal Air Force bombers flew over widespread populated areas of Germany and dropped a wide assortment of leaflets. In a speech to Berlin defense plant workers Göring made a threat which he later would have cause to regret: "If they continue to fly about in the clouds at night at ridiculous heights in order to drop their stupid little propaganda sheets, then I really don't give a damn. But woe to them should they ever try to exchange a bomb for a propaganda pamphlet . . . revenge will come immediately."[25]

The same pomposity characterized German reporting on the Battle of Poland. Hitler's year of glory had begun, and the media described the Wehrmacht operations as the quintessence of the war of movement. "The Führer at the front" was a recurring theme during the Battle of Poland. Enjoying a luxury he could ill afford during the Russian campaign to follow, Hitler delighted in posing for the photographers and film artists in situations which recaptured the camaraderie of the Great War and which conjured up images of Siegfried as well. Hitler was "with his soldiers" when they returned the Corridor to the German homeland and when they moved into Warsaw. A headline of September 12 which read "Decisive Battle Watched by the Führer" left no doubt that it was Hitler's "strategic genius" which was leading the Army in the dash across Poland and which in a matter of eleven days had "annihilated the Polish Army west of the Vistula."[26]

Hitler seemed to be everywhere the action was, and he assumed roles ranging from that of the greatest military commander of all time to the healer of the wounded. On one occasion he was depicted inspecting the officers and crew of the battleship *Schleswig-Holstein* which had figured so prominently in the German capture of the fortress Westerplatte near Danzig. At several points Hitler was shown surrounded by beaming troops; at other times he was grouped with officers as he peered through field glasses to watch the progress of the battle. He was also seen in the guise of the Messiah with thankful women and children who had safely returned "home to the Reich" clustered about him to offer their humble expressions of gratitude. A photograph of Hitler visiting the *Leibstandarte SS "Adolf Hitler"* in the field conveyed a twentieth-century version of the *Führer-Gefolgschaft-Treue* motif. And at Danzig on September 19 he donned the cape of liberator, remarking that

I once decided never to come to Danzig before this city was returned to the German Reich. I wanted to come here as your liberator. And it is my good fortune that this hope has been realized today.

I am now being rewarded for countless anxious hours, days, weeks, and months. Look on me . . . as the delegate of the German Reich and of the entire German people, which now receives you in our eternal racial community, never to let you be taken from us again.[27]

To exalt the Führer's role in the Battle of Poland took little imagination, but it was quite another thing to deal with the problems that the Soviet occupation of its sphere of influence presented. On September 17 Stalin ordered his army to occupy the Russian sector of the corpse of Poland, placing the Red Army as far west as the Narew-Vistula-San rivers. Accordingly, a joint German-Soviet communiqué, released on September 17, attested that the Soviets acted for reasons of self-defense. Since Poland no longer existed as a state, the Red Army allegedly was forced to intervene to protect the Russian national minorities in eastern Poland, who otherwise would have to face the consequences imposed by chaotic conditions beyond their control.[28]

Goebbels moved decisively to confront the sensitive question of Soviet intervention in the war. To avoid any embarrassing Russian claims about sharing credit for the victory, the call went out that the campaign was essentially completed except for mopping-up operations. Goebbels also took steps to allay suspicion of Russian aims in Poland by assuring his countrymen that the Soviet occupation was being made in cooperation with the Wehrmacht. And the communiqué of September 18 maintained that German troops had pulled back to the demarcation line separating the German and Soviet occupation zones according to the agreement between the two powers.[29] Further, von Ribbentrop announced that the "German-Soviet Boundary and Friendship Treaty," signed in the early morning hours of September 29, guaranteed lasting friendship between the German Reich and the Soviet Union.[30]

The public terms of the treaty published in the German press disclosed very little of what was actually agreed upon. But when the German minorities in Estonia, Latvia, Lithuania, and the Soviet zone of Poland began to stream into Reich German territories, many people were alerted to the fact that they had been deceived about what was going on behind the scenes. In fact some 1,000,000 Germans in Volhynia and Galicia were scheduled for resettlement in Poznan and Pomerania, and the 16,000 Germans in Estonia, 70,000 in Latvia, and 45,000 in Lithuania all were slated for expulsion and relocation within the boundaries of Greater Germany.[31] The fate of these people who were pawns of Hitler's machinations upset many Germans who would not, on the contrary, show the least concern for the lot of the Jews or the Poles, and Goebbels found the question very awkward indeed. The outbreak of the Finnish war in November 1939 added to the rumors about the actual state of affairs between Hitler and Stalin.[32]

The regime also faced a credibility gap in its handling of the tragic death of General Werner von Fritsch. Although Hitler's scandalous allegations that von Fritsch was guilty of homosexual acts when he was commander in chief of the Army were little known outside limited Army and Party circles in Berlin, his death while attached to Artillery Regiment 12 on the front lines in Poland gave rise to myth and legend. Traditionally, historians have argued that von Fritsch sought death at the front in a desperate attempt to clear his name and regain his honor.[33] More recently this view has been refuted with the contention that von Fritsch's religion and character precluded his seeking death by suicide, a position upheld by evidence from the general's adjutant Lieutenant Rosenhagen and other witnesses.[34]

By ordering a state funeral for General von Fritsch, Hitler established a cynical pattern that was repeated in the burial of Field Marshal Erwin Rommel with full military honors in 1944. His Order of the Day to the Wehrmacht of September 23 set the tone for the propaganda dealing with von Fritsch: "On 9.22.1939 the former Commander-in-Chief of the Army Baron von Fritsch fell in battle before Warsaw. Colonel-General von Fritsch was in command of Artillery Regiment 12 which he led in the Polish campaign . . . On the morning of 9.22 he was in the front lines before Warsaw. Here he was killed by machine gun fire as he led his troops forward. The German Wehrmacht lowers its flags to honor the gallantry of this exemplary soldierly conduct. To demonstrate its high esteem the war flags of Artillery Regiment 12 will fly at half mast until his burial."[35] Hitler also dispatched a telegram to Baroness von Fritsch, conveying his "deeply felt sympathy" at the loss of her son.[36]

Goebbels sensed the seriousness of the assignment before him when news of von Fritsch's death first came over the wire services from the front to Berlin, and he put out a call to his staff for extreme caution and circumspection.[37] As a result the initial coverage was brief, factual, and unemotional. But the Nazis staged an elaborate state funeral which featured an address by von Fritsch's successor as commander in chief of the Army, Walter von Brauchitsch. In his tribute General von Brauchitsch referred to von Fritsch as "one of the best men that the Prussian-German Army had ever known," a man whom the Führer called upon to mold the weapon which he "would put to the service of the National Socialist Reich." "Werner Freiherr von Fritsch," von Brauchitsch concluded his homily, "your soldiers, your comrades, have come to offer you final honors. Our hearts, our gratitude, and our loyalty will be with you today and forever."[38] Göring offered the wreath of the Führer, who had absented himself from the ceremonies, and he was followed by Mackensen, Raeder, Keitel, Hess, Milch, and Goebbels.

There were certain news stories which conjured up such negative associations that Goebbels attempted to have them forgotten altogether. The von Fritsch affair was one such example, and he pursued this goal with unwavering zeal throughout the following months. Yet a curious series of events took place on the first anniversary of von Fritsch's death when the *Kieler Neuesten Nachrichten* requested permission to publish a memorial article about him. Normally an article on a former commander in chief would be welcomed, but when the Kiel editors submitted this one to the censors of the Schleswig-Holstein Reich Propaganda Office, permission to publish it was denied "on the orders of the Propaganda Ministry."[39] Goebbels himself was behind the directive, and at his press conference of September 23, 1940, he forbade all future memorial articles dealing with the general. Fritsch had become an unperson.

Fritsch's death gave rise to many rumors, some inaccurate, but some very revealing. According to one of them, Himmler and other anti-Fritsch conspirators within the Party were responsible for his demise. Others conjectured that von Fritsch had sought death at the front to free his soul of some terrifying burden caused by his

enemies.[40] Whatever was behind his mysterious death, it did not
sit well with many people, least of all with the officers and men
of the Army who had divined that a Party-Army power struggle
had destroyed von Fritsch. A group of noncommissioned officers
and men of the Third Infantry Regiment stationed in Poland vented
their wrath in a most extraordinary way—they fired off a heated
protest to their commander in chief von Brauchitsch.[41] If this letter
is any indication, the news of von Fritsch's death must have caused
a sensation at the front. After complaining that "the organizer of
our Army is not good enough for the front pages" and further
that Hitler had not bothered to attend the funeral of von Fritsch,
they demanded revenge: "Since we took an oath to Hitler, we expect
in turn that he show loyalty to the man who created the Wehrmacht.
Is that asking too much? We are of the opinion that the little leader
of the black pigs [Himmler] . . . has taken his revenge on Fritsch.
We will find a way . . . to take care of the black pig. We ask your
excellency respectfully to send the ass with ears on an inspection
trip to the front lines. We'll take care of the rest." There is no
evidence to suggest that von Brauchitsch answered this passionate
appeal.

Following the conclusion of the Battle of Poland, the Nazis stepped
up the tempo of their anti-English propaganda and began a moderate
campaign against the French who until then had been all but ignored.
"England and France Responsible for the Continuation of the War"
was the headline summarizing a propaganda campaign which culminated in Hitler's victory address before the Reichstag on October
6. The respected *Frankfurter Zeitung* echoed the refrain that "the
decision for war or peace falls squarely on the shoulders of London
and Paris."[42]

The peace offer Hitler made to England on October 6 was an
earnest effort to turn back the clock and to secure his own position.
The Führer desperately wanted peace with England, and in the
fall of 1939 he might well have guaranteed the integrity of the
British Empire had London in turn recognized the new order in
Poland and given him a free hand on the continent. But Hitler
went about his "peacemaking" in a peculiar manner. His references
to the British Empire could not be construed as friendly by any
stretch of the imagination; instead, his tone was coarse and threaten-

ing. Some nations like England, he said, had so much, while others like Germany had so little. Our 80,000,000 have to live somehow, he declared: "If 46,000,000 Englishmen on their home island have the right to control 40,000,000 square kilometers of land, then it is no injustice if 82,000,000 Germans demand to live on 800,000 square kilometers and to plow their fields and cultivate their crafts."[43]

He appealed to the English to see reason, to understand that he meant them well. Now that the injustices of Versailles had been reversed, the Reich and England could join hands in peace and friendship and lead the world to a greater future. Hitler, not for the last time, warned the English that this was his final offer of peace. Should they spurn it, they alone would be responsible for the continuation of the war: "Mr. Churchill might be convinced that Great Britain will win this war. I don't doubt for a moment that Germany will win it. Fate will decide who was right."[44]

Following Hitler's address it was widely rumored that armistice negotiations were taking place, a fact which demonstrates just how pervasive the desire for peace was in Germany. It was no secret that German enthusiasm for the Polish war was something less than overwhelming at its outset, and there was little sentiment favoring even a limited war over the Danzig and Corridor questions.[45] The peace rumors climaxed on October 10, when word began to spread that King George VI had abdicated and the English had signed an armistice.[46] Work stopped in the plants, and clerks quickly closed their shops to celebrate the victory. In Berlin large groups formed to rejoice at the news. At the University of Berlin the announcement that an armistice had been signed was made in one of the larger lecture halls, and it set off a massive gathering of students who cheered the news. At a small railroad station near the capital people rushed to greet a passing troop transport: "You can go home, the war is over!" Even the Berlin stock exchange was fired by the news which induced a flurry of buy orders for Reich securities. And the official telegraph service transmitted word of the "armistice" throughout the Reich.

The armistice rumors peaked on the day Hitler had scheduled to open the 1939 Winter Help Campaign, a coincidence which only heightened the tension as people awaited word from the Führer that the war was over. A special announcement of the *Reichsrundfunk* at noon on the 10th offered an official denial that an armistice had been signed. But popular imagination refused to repudiate the chimera. Neither the radio address by Daladier on the same day, in which he turned down Hitler's peace offer, nor that of Chamberlain on October 12, demanding "deeds not words," dampened optimism that there was still a chance the war might be concluded. The SD reports of October 13 to 25 continued to reflect this hope which only gradually faded away.

Goebbels, who sensed the English will to fight more accurately than Hitler, also understood that the German people were not yet psychologically ready for an extended period of suffering and deprivation.[47] Thus he took steps to prepare for a war of longer duration than either the Party or the country at large really wanted. The Polish campaign had hardly been completed when he ordered whisper propaganda channels to quash illusory peace rumors and to take up the theme that although Germany had sought to avoid war the nation would fight to the bitter end.[48]

One method which he followed in pursuing this goal was to glorify the Wehrmacht in newsreels and feature films, and the first documentary production of the war, *The Campaign in Poland,* continued Leni Riefenstal's practice of linking the film art with myth. *The Campaign in Poland,* which reviewed the highlights of the offensive, made Germany's victory seem inevitable. Hitler's infantry, Panzer, and air units were depicted in an inexorable, cascading leap to greatness which, it appeared, no power on earth could possibly stop. The campaign was interpreted as an important step toward the realization of Hitler's goals, an organic development placing the Reich in step with world and universal history. The message was clear; no earthly power, least of all the Polish Army, could resist the forward march of the German Wehrmacht, the bearer of a world historic mission.

No photographs of German dead were included, because this might tend to distort the visual mystique of grandeur which the film was meant to convey. But the horror of the German onslaught was accurately portrayed in footage showing Stuka wings diving into action in support of Panzer and infantry columns advancing below and in scenes of the battleship *Schleswig-Holstein* delivering its devastating point-blank fire against the Westerplatte. There was also extensive coverage devoted to Hitler's activities—"inspiring the troops," greeting *Volksdeutsche,* lunching in the field with common soldiers, "re-opening churches closed by the Polish reign of terror," and delighting in his Warsaw victory parade. Response to *The Campaign in Poland,* as well as to the weekly newsreel coverage, was enthusiastic.

Once the campaign had been completed, Goebbels began to treat the racial question extensively. On October 7, 1939, Hitler had named Himmler "Reich Commissar for the Strengthening of the German Race" and had ordered his death squads to begin their barbarous acts of mass murder and to commence the "resettlement" of the 1,500,000 Poles slated for expulsion from the territories annexed to the Reich.[49] Although Goebbels did not treat the subject of extermination publicly, except indirectly late in the war, his immediate assignment was to lay the groundwork for the day when the truth would be revealed. In 1939 this meant interpreting Hitler's radical racial solutions for the German people in the east.

Goebbels began his campaign of "racial education" at his press conference on October 20, 1939, by calling on his staff to guarantee that the image of the "Jewish-Polish-Subhuman" became "firmly rooted in the German's subconscious." The press, responding to Goebbels's directive, began a series of articles dealing with Polish Jewry. The description of Lublin, the "ghetto of all ghettos" in Nazi parlance, was representative of this genre: "Filth is a way of life here. The old and the young, the men and the women, all lie about in nothing but filth. An indescribable stench is in the air."[50] Typhus was running through the ghetto, and the disease could not be controlled under such unhygienic conditions. The thrust of such propaganda was to leave people with the impression that the Jews, "filthy and diseased," were fit only for extermination—in the same way that one kills roaches and bacilli. But this policy could not yet be admitted, and the Nazis denied it for the time being. "Unlike other colonizers, we are not carrying out any liquidations here. Instead, we're putting the Jews to work for the Reich."[51] Goebbels took several precautions to conceal what ultimately would become the "final solution of the Jewish question." For example, he forbade public announcement that Hans Frank had been appointed governor of the *Generalgouvernement,* the Polish rump state, because people reading between the lines might divine that the area was to become the collecting ground for "asocial elements" fated for extermination.[52]

Propaganda directed to the SS, on the other hand, dealt openly with the murders. Young SS trainees, who would be expected to participate in future exterminations, were informed of the activities of their comrades in the *Einsatzgruppen* in Poland. As an SS indoctrination pamphlet entitled *Grenzkampf Ost* worded it, "Criminal and guerilla units flourished in Poland before the Germans moved in there. Merciless deployment of the SS and of the German police played a significant role in normalizing this situation."[53]

Goebbels's second goal after the conclusion of hostilities—to obliterate the designation "Poland"—was motivated by both diplomatic and racial considerations. "The theme of Poland," Goebbels told his press conference, "must become uninteresting." The English might quietly forget that they had gone to war to protect "Versailles Poland," which had disappeared, and they might sue for peace. Secondly, Poland was to be forgotten because this "unnatural state" was a product of the dictated peace of Versailles. The sooner the designation "Poland" was forgotten, the sooner would Reich Germans come to see this eastern territory as part of Germany proper.

Ribbentrop took 482 documents and 350 pages to describe English and Polish guilt in a "white book" which the Foreign Ministry published in mid-December. Bearing the title *Dokumente zur Vorgeschichte des Krieges,* it included selected documents that "proved" that Poland had waged a campaign to annihilate the Germans and that Warsaw cooperated completely in England's concerted drive to "destroy Germany root and branch." In his preface to the "white book" von Ribbentrop clearly outlined what purpose it served. The German people, he said, would not lay down their weapons until they had realized their goal, which is "the military annihilation of the enemy and then to secure for the German people against every future threat the living space to which it is due."[54]

There was to be no peace with England. The Polish war was over, and the "phony war" had begun. According to Goebbels, no matter what the future might bring the nation could look back with pride to the blitz victory in Poland. The end of the first phase of the war found the Nazis linking their propaganda to traditional Hohenzollern national symbols in an effort to unite the country behind the Führer. In 1939 they called on the spirit of Frederick the Great, as they would so often during the war:

The "King Frederick March" was never so touching as it was here deep in the heart of Warsaw. The Führer has called our Reich the Frederician Germany, and he expects today the same trust and determination, the same strength and confidence which once gave the great King of Prussia the strength to defeat a host of enemies. This confidence and trust, this fanatical will and stubborn determination which inspired Frederick the Great and his troops has inspired us as well in these hours which have been crowned by the victorious Battle of Poland.[55]

IV The Phony War

The "phony war"—the period between the defeat of Poland and the German attack on Denmark and Norway in April 1940—presented the German, British, and French propagandists with an inordinately important assignment. An ominous quiet puzzled and distressed the public in both the Axis and the Allied camps. On the continent the battles were being fought for the time being primarily by the experts in psychological warfare, while a series of dramatic naval engagements was eagerly followed by the public.

Many factors further confused the international scene. Although the English were in the war to stay, French determination was open to question. One of the world's great armies had not attacked the weak German western front during the Polish campaign. Once the Poles had been destroyed, the French seemed all the less eager to "die for Danzig," and the face which they showed the world was one of weakness and division. It became increasingly clear that France would fight only if it were attacked by German land and air forces, and some doubted its determination given even those circumstances.

The mood of the "phony war" was bizarre and unreal, as William Shirer's radio spots from Berlin illustrated. On September 28, 1939, for example, he interviewed U-boat Captain Schultze for the folks at home. Schultze turned out to be an engaging personality as he related the details of the sinking of the British ships the *Royal Scepter* and the *Firby*. Shirer spent Christmas with the men of the German fleet docked in the harbor of Hamburg. Yet another incident involved Louis Lochner when he joined selected foreign correspondents on an inspection tour of the West Wall as guests of the Propaganda Ministry. A German general later sacked for his indiscretion provided one of the war's lighter moments as he guided the journalists along his sector of the fortifications. Acting as if his historical moment had arrived, he ordered a batteryman to describe his weapon, which turned out to be a Russian field piece from the Crimean War. Next, for some musical diversion, he ordered the radio turned on, but it happened to be tuned to Radio Strasbourg, an offense punishable by imprisonment or death according to Goebbels's decree on enemy broadcasts. Pierre Huss of the International News Service, amazed at the candor displayed by a general of the victorious Wehrmacht, could only tell his German hosts: "This general is a darling; we love him."[1]

The "phony war" was a war of nerves which challenged Goebbels's resourcefulness, and on occasion he made remarkable tactical blunders. The *Ark Royal* affair was one such case. Overly eager to claim German naval victories, Goebbels boasted in mid-September 1939 that the English aircraft carrier *Ark Royal* had been sunk in a combined air–U-boat attack and he later made the modest claim that the English loss of this vessel was equivalent to the Germans' losing ten infantry divisions in the field. A month later Goebbels urged his staff repeatedly to pose the question, "Where is the *Ark Royal?*"[2] In that way he hoped to be able to force the English to admit that the Germans had indeed sunk her. A cartoon later in the month depicted Churchill in a diver's outfit holding a press conference aboard the sunken hulk of the *Ark Royal*.[3]

British silence on the location of the *Ark Royal* was based on the conviction that nothing was to be gained for the time being by denying the Nazi report. Her reemergence on the high seas fit for action following a layup for repairs would be most dramatic. Late in December German intelligence reported that the *Ark Royal* was ready for battle. When Goebbels learned that the carrier was operating in South African waters and heading for Capetown, he asked the Navy's liaison man to the Propaganda Ministry how he was going to handle the embarrassing situation. He received the abrasive rejoiner: "I don't care to express an opinion on that, Herr Reichsminister, the *Ark Royal* was sunk by the Propaganda Ministry not by us."[4] Goebbels covered his tracks as best he could by ordering that all further discussion of the case was to cease.[5]

The German Navy scored enough triumphs in the first year of the war to make cheap propaganda campaigns on the *Ark Royal* model unnecessary. The U-boat fleet was operating with marked success against English merchant ships, and some individual vessels were credited with extraordinary kills. The most dramatic of these was the mission of Lieutenant Prien of U-47 who sank one of Great Britain's notable battleships, the *Royal Oak,* in the harbor of Scapa Flow. The plans for the mission were prepared by the German U-boat chief Admiral Dönitz, who had never forgotten the abortive raids into Scapa Flow during World War I.[6] Leaving Kiel on October 8, 1939, Prien steered a course toward Scotland. He successfully negotiated U-47 into the harbor on October 13, braving both the dangerous currents and the barrier formed by sunken ships which was supposed to have rendered such attacks impossible. Once he had passed Kirk Sound the entire treasure of the harbor lay before him. Having spotted the dream of every U-boat commander, the masts of two battleships, he attacked. The *Royal Oak* exploded and went down in a matter of minutes, taking 786 officers and men to the bottom with her, while the *Repulse* was damaged. Then Prien edged away as stealthily as he had come.[7]

Prien became a hero overnight in response to orders that he "must now be celebrated as one of Germany's heroic figures. Just as once Weddigen was the rallying cry for heroism at sea, now Prien has renewed the old glory of the U-Boat fleet with his even more impressive deed."[8] The weekly newsreel set the tone with footage of the *Royal Oak* on maneuvers with the fleet, followed by shots of Prien flying with his entire crew from Wilhelmshaven to Berlin "in the Führer's own aircraft."[9] Finally Prien, now a *Volk* hero, enters Berlin amid the pomp and display prepared for him by the Party and the Navy. He and the crew report to the Führer who greets them in the Reich chancellery.

Prien's bold deed epitomized the heroism which nourished the myths of National Socialism, and Hitler basked in the glory of his men. Addressing the crew members, he drew a contrast between their courage and the "cowardice" of the German government in 1918 which had surrendered the fleet to the enemy in the very same harbor of Scapa Flow. Hitler praised them lavishly, claiming that their example would forever inspire the German Navy.[10]

Prien's autobiography, which the Deutscher Verlag rushed to the press under the title *Mein Weg nach Scapa Flow,* also spread the legend. It appeared that Prien's entire career was but a preparation for his Scapa Flow mission, and he, like Hitler, was touted as a simple man from the *Volk* whose only goal in life was to serve his people. The crowning chapter of *Mein Weg nach Scapa Flow* was not so much the description of the mission itself, but the recognition which Hitler gave to it. Lieutenant Prien related the scene in the Reich chancellery in a classic propaganda vignette:

The cheering of the throng outside could only be faintly heard, here inside it is quiet. The adjutant comes and announces: "Der Führer!" He walks in. I have seen him several times before. But I have never felt the greatness of this life so strongly as at this moment. . . . the dream of my youth had been realized, and perhaps it is the greatest thing in life to experience the dreams of our youth. But what a life his was next to mine. A man who felt the shame and misery of his country to be his own shame and misery wanted a free and prosperous Fatherland. He had faith and he acted . . . an unknown man among eighty million people. His dream came true, his hopes were realized.[11]

Prien's account integrated his deed with National Socialist ideology by bringing the warrior myth full circle with the words, "The only important thing for men is to have the heart of a fighter, to forget oneself in the service of a greater cause."[12] Prien's days of glory were numbered; U-47 was lost with its entire crew in March 1941 somewhere in the Atlantic south of Iceland.[13] The name of Lieutenant Prien thus joined the list of Nazi martyrs who had "fought the good fight and died for a greater ideal."

While it is simple enough to engage in a propaganda campaign when one has successes like the *Royal Oak* to describe, on the other hand defeats can challenge the best propagandist. Such was the case when the British sank the *Graf Spee* in December 1939, a reversal which Goebbels mishandled as badly as he had the *Ark Royal* affair.

The *Graf Spee,* displacing 12,000 tons and mounting twenty-eight guns, one of three German pocket battleships which operated with the battleships *Scharnhorst, Gneisenau, Tirpitz,* and the *Bismarck,* offered some nervous moments for Churchill and the Royal Navy.[14] To meet the threat of the German surface fleet, Churchill formed nine hunting groups which joined the convoy escorts and amassed a force of seven battleships, five aircraft carriers, and fourteen cruisers.

The hit-and-run tactics of the *Graf Spee* had proved very successful. In a single mission to the Indian Ocean in the fall of 1939, it accounted for nine ships, totaling 50,000 tons.[15] Captain Langsdorff, having completed his mission in the Indian Ocean in November, sailed the *Graf Spee* westward past the Cape of Good Hope toward Montevideo, Buenos Aires, and the mouth of the La Plata River. It was his misfortune to cross paths with Churchill's hunting pack "G" which was patrolling the waters off the east coast of South America and stood ready to engage the enemy at the mouth of the La Plata on December 13.[16]

The *Graf Spee* joined battle with the British cruisers *Exeter, Ajax,* and *Achilles* in a seesaw fight which tested the ingenuity of the commanders on both sides to the limit. Although she severely punished all three of the British cruisers, the *Graf Spee* herself suffered very serious blows, and Langsdorff put into the neutral port of Montevideo where he hoped to find a safe haven while undergoing repairs. The Uruguayan government, however, ordered Langsdorff to leave Montevideo within seventy-two hours, which did not provide the time necessary to prepare for battle. The British then began an exceedingly sophisticated news campaign claiming that they had reinforced hunting group "G" with an even stronger force which lay in wait for the kill in international waters outside Montevideo. Captain Langsdorff was deceived about the size of the opposing force which grew more menacing with each subsequent English newscast. He was convinced that besides several cruisers the English had rushed the aircraft carrier *Ark Royal* and the battle cruiser *Renown* to the area, when in fact both ships were several thousand miles away.[17] Langsdorff sent a telegram to Hitler on the 16th describing the hopeless situation and offering three alternatives: to fight his way through to Buenos Aires, to scuttle the vessel, or to intern her.[18] Raeder wired Hitler's order for the *Graf Spee* to fight her way out of the trap, and, if this were impossible, for Langsdorff to scuttle her. Internment was out of the question.[19]

On the morning of December 18, Langsdorff headed down the harbor channel at Montevideo and, with a great crowd of curious Uruguayans in a holiday mood watching, scuttled the *Graf Spee* in the shallow waters off the coast. Langsdorff, who was interned with his crew in Buenos Aires, opted for suicide. On December 19, he wrote a letter to the German ambassador in Buenos Aires which was forwarded to Hitler. In it he defended his actions and declared, "For a Captain with a sense of honor, it goes without saying that his personal fate cannot be separated from that of his ship . . . I can now only prove by my death that the fighting services of the Third Reich are ready to die for the honor of the flag. I alone bear the responsibility for scuttling the pocket battleship Admiral Graf Spee. I am happy to pay with my life for any possible reflection on the honor of the flag. I shall face my fate with firm faith in the cause and the future of the nation and of my Führer."[20] On the next day, Captain Langsdorff was dead, and he followed von Fritsch to the halls of the forgotten heroes, never to be mentioned again.

Goebbels's handling of the *Graf Spee* news violated his own principle of propaganda uniformity and led to serious misgivings about the reliability of German war reporting. Part of the problem resulted from his being misled by the initial OKW communiqué which was in essence a victory announcement, claiming that after sinking two English steamers at the mouth of the La Plata River while suffering only a "few hits" herself, the *Graf Spee* was able to damage severely both the *Ajax* and the *Achilles*. The *Exeter* was allegedly so battered that she had to withdraw from the battle. Offering no explanations for the reason, the OKW blandly reported that the *Graf Spee* had put into the harbor of Montevideo.

Evidence on Goebbels's treatment of the *Graf Spee* affair is confusing and fragmented. On the one hand, the minister seemed to pursue a cautious news policy and at his press conference on December 14 he warned Fritzsche that the seventy-two-hour time limit offered by the Uruguayan government would not be sufficient to return the *Graf Spee* to seaworthy condition.[21] Two days later he hedged against the possibility of losing the ship by charging that the English had resorted to the use of mustard gas, a violation of international law which doomed the *Graf Spee* to destruction.[22]

If Goebbels did indeed believe that the *Graf Spee* was about to be scuttled, he would have made certain that the news media conformed to his initial cautious directives. But this was not the case. The *Völkischer Beobachter* claimed a magnificent German victory on December 15 in a lead story which held that the *Graf Spee* showed "no sign of damage whatsoever."[23] The heroic German victory allegedly had caused a sensation throughout the Americas, and tens of thousands of people crowded the hills above Montevideo to watch a spectacle which pitted one brave German vessel against three English cruisers.

The Propaganda Ministry compounded the confusion when the *Reichsrundfunk* broadcast a story on the *Graf Spee*'s "victorious naval battle near the La Plata," the "eyewitness account of a neutral observer."[24] Yet another report featured an interview with Captain Langsdorff aboard the *Graf Spee* which left the impression that the captain and crew were hearty and healthy and their ship in excellent condition. Spirits were high and the crew had even begun to decorate for Christmas.[25]

At long last the Germans began to learn the facts. As the *Völkischer Beobachter* worded it, "Once the *Graf Spee* had steamed into the La Plata, the enemy began to concentrate all their available forces in that area: aircraft carriers, battleships, heavy and light cruisers, destroyers, and U-boats are lurking out there waiting for the moment when they can pounce upon this single German ship which they could not overcome in a naval battle."[26] Before confirming that the *Graf Spee* had been lost, Goebbels sought to lessen the impact of the bad news by commencing an intensive ad hoc campaign stressing recent German naval and air victories. Finally, the truth was admitted in a radio broadcast on December 18: "The time necessary to return the 'Admiral Graf Spee' to seaworthy condition was denied by the government of Uruguay. As a result the Führer and Commander-in-Chief has ordered Captain Langsdorff to destroy the ship. This took place in international waters."[27] A few days later he issued instructions that the subject be dropped.[28]

The *Graf Spee* propaganda was a fiasco, and Goebbels suffered a personal reversal as a result; the public, expecting that the ship would fight her way to safety, was confused and disappointed. The naval authorities also were at odds with Goebbels. Raeder, Dönitz, and most of the naval elite had the impression that he made their work a good deal more difficult than it already was because the *Ark Royal* and *Graf Spee* propaganda was delivered with a flamboyance which did not square with the facts. When the German News Bureau announced that Churchill had conceded the battle of the South Atlantic on the day after Langsdorff scuttled the *Graf Spee,* the Navy's anger reached a new high. They had come to the end of the line with Goebbels. A Naval High Command communiqué to the OKW/WPr decried the situation: "As far as the Naval High Command sees it, such propaganda is a failure which not only leads the public to question the credibility of German military reporting, but beyond that it offers the enemy material for effective counterpropaganda which works to our disadvantage."[29] This analysis was justified; according to one SD report some people were of the opinion that "the English fleet would be destroyed by the end of the year [1939]."[30]

Anti-English propaganda reached a fever pitch late in 1939 as the Nazis campaigned against the "only country which holds out for war now." Although the German public entered the war reluctantly, there is evidence that a considerable number of people began to count on a cheaply won victory against England which would preclude their suffering the effects of bombing raids or shortages of food and coal. The SD attested that "confidence in the success of a war of annihilation against England has risen" and that "there is a growing feeling among the German people that our Wehrmacht is invincible."[31] The victory in Poland, Hitler's repeated emphasis on German military might, and news of victories at sea all fed the war fever, and the anti-English song "Denn wir fahren gegen Engelland," played at the conclusion of the OKW communiqués and after propaganda broadcasts, was going over well.[32]

But all these factors were but a prelude to the dramatic days of November when the Nazis charged that the English were responsible for the attempt to assassinate the Führer at the Bürgerbräukeller in Munich. Yet the bomb plot was not attributable to either the British Secret Service or the SS, as some have argued. It was staged by a single conspirator, Georg Elser, a cabinetmaker who spent several nights before Hitler's appearance in the Bürgerbräukeller preparing the device.[33]

Had Hitler followed his usual practice of remaining for a time with the "Old Fighters" after delivering his speech on the evening of November 8, he might well have been killed. But by a quirk of fate, which Hitler interpreted as a reaffirmation of his messianic role, he was already aboard a special train en route to Berlin at the time the bomb exploded. Instead of killing Hitler, the bomb took the lives of seven Nazis and wounded some sixty others.[34]

News of the bomb plot set off a spate of rumors throughout the country: Hitler and many other high Party officials were wounded, Rosenberg had fled, Streicher had been shot, and Crown Prince Wilhelm had been beheaded.[35] There were in fact spontaneous demonstrations against the Jews, who were suspected of being in league with the English in planning the nefarious crime, and some people expressed the hope that Göring would dispatch the Luftwaffe to punish London. Loyal teachers led their children in singing the hymn "Nun danket alle Gott," and there was a general sense of relief that the nation had been spared the loss of its Führer while the country was at war.[36]

The Nazis lost no time in giving maximum play to the assassination plot. The *Völkischer Beobachter* set the tone of the propaganda dealing with the affair by stressing the "miraculous rescue," a theme which reinforced the myth of Hitler as savior of the Reich.[37] The shedding of the blood of the "Old Fighters" who were killed on November 8 offered added material to buttress this motif, which was a Nazi counterpart to the myth of the Christian martyrs who had died that others might live and that truth might be revealed. An elaborate ceremony was prepared to honor them which featured the martyrs lying in state before the *Feldherrnhalle*, funeral music played by the Munich Philharmonic, and a death march down Ludwig and Leopold streets to a common burial in the North Cemetery.[38] The *Volk*, it was held, showed its devotion once more to the "Old Fighters" by offering homage to the fallen. Hitler appeared unexpectedly at the ceremonies, and his final salute to the fallen comrades symbolized the union of *völkisch* blood with the blood of the dead.[39] His greetings to the bereaved relatives were less an act of mourning than an admonition for all Germans to summon the strength to see the Reich through to the final victory.

Rudolf Hess, who Naumann characterized as a "priest for mothers and old women," made a brief address at the funeral which extolled the blood myth: "The stream of blood which flows for Germany is eternal—the sacrifice of German men for their Volk is eternal—therefore Germany will also be eternal, the Germany for which you sacrificed your lives. Dead comrades, sleep in the peaceful love of your Volk . . ." Now, according to Hess, the good work had to be continued with the Führer at the helm:

The spirit which is moving our people was given witness once more in the words of the wives of two of our fallen comrades who said today: "It is more important that the Führer lives than our husbands." The Führer lives! In boundless gratitude we all feel today as if he had been given to us anew. How many tears of joy have been shed for him! How many fervent prayers have been said on high for him. The miracle of his rescue has enhanced our belief in him. Providence has spared our Führer in the past, and Providence will spare our Führer in the future, because he has been sent on a great mission . . . To our enemies we call out: You wanted to take the Führer from us and you have only drawn us closer to him. You wanted to weaken us and you have only made us stronger . . . The German victory will express our gratitude to these, our dead.[40]

Once the assassination attempt had been grounded in Nazi myth, the propaganda network set to work to trace the attempted murder to the British Secret Service. Goebbels knew that the regime's foes would endeavor to link the bomb plot with Hitler's domestic enemies. Consequently he directed attention abroad in an attempt to unite the Reich in one common, steadfast bond faithful to the Führer. The press directive of November 9 was worded to leave no doubt that the explosion resulted from the complot of the English and the Jews.[41] In an attempt to put the damper on rumors about the resistance in Germany, he ordered Crown Prince Wilhelm and Prince August Wilhelm to make public appearances.[42]

German propaganda dealing with the *Attentat* reflected the Nazis' confusion over who was really behind the plot. To cite but one example among many, although Goebbels instructed his staff to underplay the role of individual personalities and to concentrate their fire on groups, cliques, and the English, the stories of November 22–23 focused on Otto Strasser. This drew attention to the opposition in Germany and to émigré activities abroad, two subjects the minister wanted to avoid.[43] The tumult within the Party over the Bürgerbräu affair was reflected in public opinion. Rumors continued to spread and according to one of them Himmler, whom Hitler called "der getreue Ekkehard," had the bomb placed in the Bürgerbräu.[44]

Hitler was convinced that the English were behind the plot and refused to believe the report of Himmler's commission directed by SS Oberführer Nebe which maintained that Georg Elser had worked independently of any third party.[45] The sooner the affair was forgotten, the better it was for Himmler, but the foreign press corps kept the matter alive for weeks with their recurrent query, "When will Elser be tried?" Himmler and the other Nazis found this disconcerting.[46] The case was slowly forgotten; the pace of the war was such that even the attempt on the life of the Führer could not command the stage for more than a matter of a few weeks. Only a pseudo-documentary book entitled *Murder! Espionage! Assassination!* written by a team of professors under Walther Koerber of Munich University muddied the waters once more by attempting to lay full blame for the assassination plot on the English Secret Service.[47]

The excitement had hardly died down when Goebbels faced a severe crisis resulting from Russia's attack on Finland late in November 1939. Using border provocations as his excuse, Stalin launched four armies under Marshal Timoschenko against Finland, a nation of only three and a half million people which was capable of fielding ten divisions at the most. At the same time that their armies struck westward, the Russians bombed Helsinki and shelled the southern coast of Finland.

World opinion sided immediately with the Finnish cause, as did Nazi Germany. Under the circumstances Hitler and Goebbels faced a serious problem because they were forced to take a propaganda line diametrically opposed to German public opinion as well as to their own convictions.[48] It was impossible for them to side publicly with the Finns during their period of "friendship" with the Soviet Union.

Hitler drafted the official government position on the Russo-Finnish war in an unsigned article entitled "Germany and the Finnish Question," which was published in the December 8 issue of the *Völkischer Beobachter*.[49] The article was a thinly veiled apology for his inability to come to the aid of Helsinki in its hour of distress. For his part Goebbels found it difficult to suppress his true feelings, a situation made even more trying because of the heroic resistance of the Finns.[50] But for the time being, the eastern alliance took first priority. As Goebbels's spokesman von Strumm told the press on December 3, "You should . . . avoid revealing . . . what we all feel in our hearts. A headline like 'Finnish Resistance' is to be avoided. Our oil deliveries won't come any faster as a result. We help neither ourselves nor the Finns with such headlines."[51]

Hitler and Goebbels took solace in the thought that, although the Finns would have to suffer in the short run, ultimately hell would break loose on the Russians. Throughout the period of the three-month war they maintained a facade of neutrality. When the Russians finally were able to subdue Finland in mid-March 1940, Party functionaries dutifully argued that the Russians had fought against great odds in Finland, a prevarication which everyone knew to be ridiculous. "Finland," it was argued, "could have found better ways . . . to end its conflicts with Russia, if only it had chosen the path of reason."[52]

Nazi propaganda on the Finnish war contributed to the spread of the most bizarre rumors. Some people, expecting that the Russian quid pro quo to Germany for Finland would take the form of immediate military support in an imminent western campaign, began to speculate that Soviet troops were already moving into the staging areas along the Siegfried Line. Furthermore, the Soviets allegedly had joined their submarine fleet to the wolf packs of Admiral Dönitz in order to score a knockout blow against England, a rumor attributable to the success of the passenger liner *Bremen* in steaming out of New York in the fall of 1939 and making it safely through the English blockade to the Russian port of Murmansk.[53]

Nazi propaganda reflected the nearly surrealistic atmosphere of the phony war; at no time was this more pronounced than during the Christmas season. Propaganda focused on the German soldier at the front, united in spirit with his loving *Volk* at home. Scenes in the West Wall filmed for the weekly newsreel showed cozy, *gemütlich* groups of soldiers finishing their holiday banquet, drinking wine, and singing appropriate carols. The lighted candles of a Christmas tree reflected warmth and contentment, and the mood was one of reverence, comfort, determination, and good will.[54]

But to believe Nazi propaganda, what made Christmas for the men of the Wehrmacht was to have the first soldier of the Reich, Adolf Hitler, pay them a visit "at the front." As the *Völkischer Beobachter* described it, the scene was one of complete surprise and jubilation as the Führer appeared unannounced at the various bunkers and installations bearing gifts of chocolate, sweets, and *schnaps*. A photograph of the Führer was featured depicting him surrounded by the men of the *Leibstandarte SS "Adolf Hitler"* at a Christmas dinner. In an outpouring of romantic ecstasy, Hitler's presence at the front was likened to the light of the candles in a fir tree, which symbolized the "victory of light and justice over darkness and death."[55] A new dimension was thus added to the synthesis of National Socialism, the Germanic sagas, and the myths of Christianity.

The theme of unity between homeland and front which Goebbels employed in his Christmas propaganda was continued long after that season had faded into memory. A vehicle for this was the extremely popular song request show *Wunschkonzert* which became an immediate hit after its inception in 1939. Following the first week of programing, the Propaganda Ministry received a stream of requests from the front which soon numbered more than 30,000 a week. The show became a playground for the stars, and an important calling card for rising artists.[56] Goebbels placed a premium on the quality of the musical selections presented, and he expected the artists who served without remuneration to look upon their work as a sacrifice for the front. Gustav Gründgens, Lola Anderson, Zarah Leander, Marika Rökk, Willy Birgel, Grethe Weiser, and Karl Schmitt-Walter headed the list of stars who week after week answered requests from the front for musical selections which were transmitted to millions of civilians and servicemen huddled around casino and bunker radios. Any Sunday might bring performances ranging from the height of pathos, when sentimental poetry conveyed the melancholy words of separated lovers or extolled the virtues of a fallen hero, to lively folk music from the Alps.

The general impression of comfort, security, and strength conveyed by Goebbels's West Wall propaganda and the *Wunschkonzert* did not sit at all well with the Army, which worried about its image. Many complaints were directed on high about this matter, and one lieutenant from a propaganda company wrote a sarcastic letter to the OKW/WPr reporting that there were jokes going around about the men guarding Germany's lifelines in the west. According to one of them, life in the bunkers was so soft that men were taken to the hospital for injuring their fingers playing chess. The lieutenant wanted it made clear that life in the bunkers did not consist of lying about on bearskins.[57]

A Wehrmacht spokesman fired off a letter to the OKW/WPr complaining that the home front was getting the idea that life at the front was fun and games, coffee, radio, *Wunschkonzert* and "Strength through Joy" entertainment. The soldier, he said, does not understand this and finds it irritating. Life amid land mines and reconnaissance missions was no dream assignment, he argued; some 3000 men had lost their lives along the French border.[58] The complaints resulted in a general press directive in mid-December which ordered an end to such reporting.[59] But it had little perceptible effect, and stories from the West Wall continued to emphasize the good life there.

Prominent gererals who had time on their hands during the phony war employed their talents by writing articles praising the virtues of the Wehrmacht. This had the threefold effect of countering the bear rug–bunker image, honoring the German Army, and working hand in hand with the Nazis in their propaganda effort. General von Brauchitsch wrote one such article for the *Völkischer Beobachter* entitled "The Frederician Soldier and the Present."[60] In a gesture which would become commonplace by 1945, von Brauchitsch detailed the virtues of the Prussian soldier under Frederick the Great. The Frederician soldier respected authority, he was disciplined, schooled in the tradition of heroic self-sacrifice, and steadfast in his loyalty. He served a system which was based on cooperation between the army, the bureaucracy, the bourgeoisie, and the farmer. When the soldier under Frederick the Great went to battle he did so with a song on his lips, asking God to give him the will to carry out his duty with valor and strength. It was now the soldier's duty to act in the best Frederician traditions and follow the Führer until the mission begun by the Great Frederick was fulfilled.

General von Rundstedt authored an article in this genre which appeared in the *Völkischer Beobachter* in March 1940. Published under the title "Sacrifice for Germany," it admonished the soldiers of World War II to emulate the example of their brothers in the Great War. Although written by a man who allegedly sympathized with the resistance against Hitler, von Rundstedt's article could just as easily have been written by Hitler or Goebbels: "The heroic death of a German soldier is not something to be forgotten. Instead, it should inspire everyone who remembers it to die in the same way, to be as strong, unswerving, and obedient, to go happily and as a matter of course to his death (selbstverständlich und freudig zu sterben)."[61] The present war had been forced on Germany, von Rundstedt claimed, and he characterized it as a struggle for justice and freedom which was being fought under the Führer's leadership.

Throughout the winter Goebbels engaged in a bitter propaganda duel with Churchill whom he characterized as an "unteachable hood, a strange mixture of dilettante, windbag, and arch-deceiver" who "like a terrified little boy lost in the forest cries out 'I'm not afraid.' "[62] Hitler echoed the theme of Churchillian blood wrath in his addresses of January 30, February 24, and March 10, 1940, which were notable more for the light they shed on Hitler's conception of the war as a cataclysmic struggle to the death than for any revelations about the future course of the war against England.[63] Hitler found it impossible to think in any other terms than the heroic "either-or" of the Germanic tribal past translated into National Socialist myth, yet the public thought in more traditional terms in delineating war aims.

As a tactical device to conceal the scope of Hitler's aspirations, Goebbels kept Hitler's plans vague. All the Führer seemingly expected from the war was a "just and lasting peace" with the guarantee of adequate living space.[64] It offended both of them that Churchill enjoyed a great measure of credibility abroad with his claim that England was fighting for the freedom of all peoples and the sanctity of treaties.

Mutual recriminations about the relative merits of the RAF and the Luftwaffe consumed much of the energies of London and Berlin propagandists throughout the winter. The English interrupted their pamphlet campaign with only an occasional bombing raid and as a result, when the RAF dispatched a fleet of bombers against a German target, the Nazis invariably claimed dramatic defensive victories. After the raid against Sylt in January, Goebbels charged that terrifying German flak drove the raiders from German soil before they could set two twigs afire.[65] While the English missions were described as pathetic, the Nazis made much of their own forays over the Channel.

Time alone would teach the Nazis respect for the English air arm, as Goebbels's use of the RAF propaganda film *The Lion Has Wings* graphically illustrates. During the phony war he arranged for the film to be shown throughout the Reich so that "it might have a first class burial amid a storm of laughter," and he even invited representatives of the foreign press corps to the screenings.[66] But in February 1941 after the Battle of Britain the minister made use of the film for a radically different purpose; he ordered the entire Berlin and provincial propaganda staffs to view private showings of *The Lion Has Wings* which he now realized was a commendable example of effective war propaganda.[67]

The English proved themselves to be no less adept in their leaflet campaign over Germany. Seldom did a day pass when several towns and villages were not showered with leaflets dropped by English war planes. Goebbels became disturbed about the dangerous potential of this propaganda, and he asked to be informed about the content of the leaflets.[68] There was no little humor in the pamphlet war. When a Nazi national holiday was about to be celebrated, the RAF would drop a flyer with an appropriate message, such as "We congratulate you on the 30th of January" or "We'll be giving a warm reception to the Führer on the 9th of November."[69] They mocked Deputy Führer Rudolf Hess's ponderous Christmas message of 1939, an "Open Letter to an Unmarried Mother": "Cannon fodder wanted, legitimate or illegitimate. Send offers to Rudolf Hess. Password: 'The Führer needs soldiers.' "[70]

Goebbels operated from the conviction that "when the weapons resound, the Muses need not be silent," and as the Reich's cultural czar he was in a position to direct both the artists and the public to look on cultural activity as the most precious expression of Western civilization for which German soldiers were making the supreme sacrifice.[71] He repeatedly stressed that the component groups in the *völkisch,* organic state—from intellectuals to workers, from peasants to soldiers—were all part of the war effort and should drink at the fountain of the Germanic spirit. The most outstanding example of this was the Bayreuth War Festival productions of the works of Richard Wagner.

The war transformed Bayreuth, heretofore known as the shrine of the rarefied Wagnerian elite, into a democratized playground of the "fighting National Socialist Volk." This development resulted from a boyhood dream of Hitler's, whose spirit was one with the mythical heroes of the Nibelungen-Wagnerian sagas. Wartime Bayreuth hosted a more representative cross section of the German people than at any time before or after the war. Soldiers from the front and workers in war industries filled the Festival Theater to hear performances of *Parzifal, Tristan,* and the *Ring* cycle. Some of them might see the Führer himself in attendance, because early in the war he had the time available for such diversion. Before performances he could be seen on the veranda outside the theater on the hill which overlooks the town of Bayreuth and the Franconian countryside, beckoning to the crowd below who were awaiting the trumpet fanfares which would call them to join him in worship at the shrine of the Reich's Holy Grail. In this way Hitler contributed to the myth of Germanic cultural superiority which was being threatened by the forces of the racial underworld.[72]

But during the winter of 1939–1940 Goebbels had to deal with matters considerably more pressing than German culture, for he faced a serious morale problem resulting from the shortages of food and coal. The SD reported protests throughout many areas of the Reich from people who were suffering without fuel; they took their most remarkable form in Erfurt where the situation deteriorated so badly between Christmas and New Year's that the police had to be called in to protect coal trucks because angry crowds were attacking them and stealing the coal.[73] The coal shortage also had its effect in war industries, and many plants were forced to shut down.

Food shortages produced equally disturbing results. By the end of January 1940, the potato ration was down to two pounds per person a week, and often enough even this meager supply could not be provided.[74] Long lines of persons waiting to buy potatoes were reported even in Berlin and Vienna. To be sure the public was in no mood to accept the fare served up to them that the Freemasons were responsible for the situation. The shortages encouraged a flourishing black market, and irregularities in supplying customers became the order of the day. Payoffs, bribes, and under-the-table trading became commonplace.[75]

Rumors of an imminent peace continued to circulate early in 1940, despite Goebbels's efforts to prepare the nation for a long war.[76] But there were others who expressed the hope that the struggle with England would soon "cut loose in a big way" so that hostilities might be successfully ended early in 1940. Those anticipating an extension of the war—an exciting affair for some deceived by the false heroism of The Campaign in Poland, which played to cheering audiences during the winter—did not have long to wait. The campaign in Scandinavia, the prelude to the Battle of France, was about to begin.

V Blitzkrieg 1940: "The Reich Rescues Scandinavia"

Hostilities in the year 1940, which climaxed Hitler's success in his drive for total control of the continent, began with a bold offensive against Norway and Denmark. Both Germany and Great Britain were concerned with Norway for strategic and economic reasons, and both powers stood ready to violate its rights as a neutral to realize their goals. For Germany the country represented an industrial lifeline of fundamental importance, because the Norwegian ice-free port of Narvik disgorged the Swedish iron ore which Hitler so desperately needed to wage aggressive war. Norway would also guarantee safe U-boat havens, and it would put the Germans in a much more favorable position to guard the North and Baltic Sea ports. And from Norway Admiral Raeder could operate more successfully against the English mine-laying tactics which played such an important part in their attempt to blockade Germany. An occupied Norway would provide the Luftwaffe with several airfields from which to launch air strikes against England and would enable Hitler to put more effective pressure on Sweden which was maintaining an uneasy neutrality.

Winston Churchill, first lord of the Admiralty, understood the strategic importance of Norway for Great Britain's defense, and he sought to checkmate German ambitions there. Throughout the winter of 1939–1940 the English fleet kept a close watch over Norwegian waters in an effort to counter German initiatives there, and in February it scored a success in the *Altmark* affair which, although of minor military consequence, nevertheless was a propaganda coup. The *Altmark,* a German auxiliary ship, had been operating with the *Graf Spee* until the latter's demise in December. There were some three hundred English seamen aboard the *Altmark* who had been rescued by the *Graf Spee* during the course of her search and destroy missions. Suppressing a natural inclination to steam for home port straightaway, the skipper of the *Altmark* bided his time and steered a course toward Germany several weeks later. On the evening of February 16, 1940, the *Altmark* was in Norwegian waters in Joessing Fjord south of Egersund when the *Cossack,* an English vessel, heaved alongside her and freed the prisoners, killing several Germans in the course of the scuffle. The *Cossack* steamed homeward as stealthily as she had appeared.[1]

The *Altmark* affair was significant for a number of reasons. Even though the case of a maritime vessel sailing in neutral waters with prisoners aboard was not defined in international law, England nevertheless challenged Norway's rights as a neutral by its action.[2] Oslo protested, but received the answer that only a technical violation of international law had occurred.[3] The affair indicated to Hitler that his enemies could be just as cavalier about the rights of neutrals as he and that Churchill might be planning to mine the Norwegian coast or even to join the Norwegians in a cooperative military venture. The *Altmark* case was galling to Hitler personally, not the least for the historic associations it conjured up in his imagination about German weakness after 1918; subsequently, he issued orders for the German occupation of Norway and Denmark.[4]

The Germans wove variations on the David and Goliath theme in their *Altmark* propaganda with headlines such as "Cowardly Surprise Attack on the 'Altmark': British Government Congratulates the Murderers."[5] Pictures of the two vessels were placed side by side with the accompanying caption, "unarmed German merchant ship," "murder ship—the destroyer *Cossack,*" and quotations like "All of Italy is enraged" registered the "indignation of world opinion." The combined radio, press, and eyewitness reporting on the *Altmark* brought tensions to such a fever pitch that many people expected the spring offensive to be launched momentarily. When Hitler did not deliver a blow in revenge immediately, there was widespread dissatisfaction and Goebbels ordered an end to all discussion of the incident.[6]

The English cabinet decided to take action in Norway within a day of Hitler's launching of "Weserübung." Although Churchill had been pressing the cabinet for months to approve his plan to cooperate with the French in mining Norwegian waters and occupying Narvik, Stavanger, Bergen, and Trondheim, it was only on April 3 that he received the go-ahead for "Operation Wilfred."[7] On April 8 the British began to mine the coast of Norway, and a day later the Wehrmacht struck in the north.

Hitler, in his original order for Weserübung on March 1, structured the general propaganda line to follow the attack: "The fundamental goal of this campaign is to give the undertaking the character of a peaceful occupation, which has as its goal the protection of the neutrality of the Nordic states with force of arms."[8] As a result "Germany Saves Scandinavia from English Aggression" was the theme which accompanied the occupation of Norway and Denmark.[9] This remarkable "rescue" employed the services of over 100,000 men and almost the entire German Navy. General Nikolaus von Falkenhorst's battle plan called for an extraordinarily sophisticated cooperative effort of the three services in landing operations slated for Oslo, Kristiansand, Stavanger, Bergen, Trondheim, and Narvik.[10] The blitz had thus been unleashed once more, and anxiety grew as the nation awaited the first substantial news from the north.

The war in Scandinavia placed many obstacles in Goebbels's path which he did not have to face in dealing with any other campaign. Because Norway and Denmark were of "Aryan" stock, the basic assumption was that they were friendly nations. Yet the propaganda line that the German occupation was a protective maneuver meant to shield two friendly nations from a life of slavery under the "plutocracies" was obviously contrived. Goebbels counted on a rapid victory in the north to counter criticism of his weak propaganda position on the question, and the failure which he suffered was the result of a campaign of a much longer duration than either he or Hitler foresaw.

At the outset of the hostilities Goebbels took appropriate steps to lend credence to the shield motif, and a general order of April

10 forbade any discussion of a victory of German arms in that theater
or of Quisling's collaboration with the Nazis.[11] All references to the
strategic advantage offered by Norwegian bases for use against
England were prohibited as well. Newsreel coverage was devoted
to the rescue theme, and one sequence pictured German officers
saluting the king of Denmark "as he took his daily ride through
Copenhagen." The general impression conveyed was that the Danes
had accepted the protection of the Germans with open arms and
that they would continue as before, happily producing milk and
cheese for a hungry continent secure in the thought that Hitler's
Wehrmacht stood as a bulwark to guarantee their neutrality.[12]

Ribbentrop remarked to a press conference staged for foreign
journalists that "England has raped Scandinavia and the Führer has
today answered this crass breach of international law: the German
Wehrmacht will see to it that for the duration of the war no Englishman
or Frenchman will dare show his face in Norway or Denmark.
Germany has rescued the people of Scandinavia from annihilation
and will guarantee bona fide neutrality in the north until the
conclusion of the war."[13] Simultaneously von Ribbentrop made public
the official note which Berlin presented to Oslo and Copenhagen
on the day of the attack. Singularly low-keyed in tone, it was not
a declaration of war at all; instead it catalogued the alleged misdeeds
of England and France in Scandinavia while issuing the warning
that resistance would be met with force. He promised that the
independence of Norway and Denmark would be respected in the
future as it had in the past.[14]

On the morning of the attack the Danish government decided
not to resist the invaders, and King Christian X accepted the German
memorandum under protest. But matters took a different course
in Norway where King Haakon VII and the government evacuated
Oslo and established headquarters in a safer inland haven where
they directed the military resistance, thereby reflecting the bankruptcy
of Nazi propaganda. It would take Hitler two months to subdue
the combined English-Norwegian defense, and although land casualties were light, the Navy suffered a series of savage blows.

Hitler won the tactical advantage of surprise by occupying all of
Norway's major ports within twenty-four hours of the initial attack,

but the fleet was in an exceedingly precarious position tucked into the confines of the fjords where the occupying troops disembarked. All ten destroyers deployed at Narvik were lost, and at Bergen English dive bombers sent the cruiser *Königsberg* to the bottom. At Kristiansand an English submarine so badly damaged the cruiser *Karlsruhe* that she had to be sunk by the crew; and at Oslo the 18,000-ton heavy cruiser *Blücher* was sunk and the pocket battleship *Lützow* was put out of commission.[15]

Goebbels, who had claimed on April 10 that the Scandinavian operation was "the boldest, most audacious military undertaking in modern history," was faced with a problem which he never solved satisfactorily.[16] Hitler, overwrought about the naval operations in the north, pursued a calculated policy of concealing German losses during the first week of the campaign. Initially the OKW admitted only the sinking of the *Blücher* and the *Karlsruhe*; the public had no inkling of the loss of the *Königsberg* and the serious damage done the *Lützow*. Furthermore, the OKW did not concede the reversals at Narvik but instead reported that an English naval attack had been thrown back at the cost of three enemy destroyers.[17] The general impression was that the campaign was moving along according to plan.

Although more and more people tuned in the BBC to try to ascertain the facts, Hitler refused to abandon his propaganda of deception even after the English sank the last of the ten destroyers which Raeder had engaged at Narvik in a devastating attack on April 13. The result was confusion, and an irate public demanded the truth. While the OKW communiqués maintained an official silence on Narvik, Goebbels sensed a propaganda reversal and ordered coverage of Captain Bonte's "heroic destroyer fleet" which would stress his numerical inferiority to the enemy.[18]

The German people saw through this smoke screen, and when they picked up their morning papers on April 15 and read the headline "Heroic Fight of Heavily Outnumbered German Destroyers," the handwriting was on the wall. Their suspicions were confirmed when the OKW released the following communiqué two days later written in unmistakable Hitlerian style: "The Commander of the German destroyer fleet, Captain Bonte, died in the defense of Narvik in a heroic struggle against overwhelming odds. Some two-thirds of the crewmen of the destroyers which are now out of action . . . have been added to the Army units defending Narvik."[19]

The echo in the provinces was a complete repudiation of the official news policy on the Norwegian campaign.[20] An OKW account on English losses in Norway without corresponding statistics on the Wehrmacht served as another source of irritation. Hitler's policy tended to encourage rumors of outlandish proportions. According to one of these, the entire German fleet had been wiped out in Norway.

The SD issued a brutally frank analysis of the current news policy, designating three general areas of concern.[21] First, the public demanded to know the truth; it had come to regard the OKW communiqué as just one more vehicle to convey Nazi propaganda rather than as a reliable indicator of the progress of the war. A managed news policy such as that pursued during the campaign in Scandinavia was felt to be an indication that the leaders did not trust the people. Secondly, the Party could depend on the effects of seven years of intensive National Socialist propaganda to meet any crisis. And finally, the nation expected casualties commensurate with the risks involved in any particular campaign. Many people were not concerned about high losses in Norway because it was their fervent hope that the struggle with England would be intensified and would bring a showdown early in 1940.

Goebbels was unable to recoup the ground lost at the onset of the Norwegian campaign. and the English made the most of their advantage. Seldom was their combined radio and leaflet barrage more effective, and they took the occasion to point out the inconsistencies in Hitler's naval propaganda and to charge that Norway proved that "Party hacks and informers, the vanguard of Siegfried's rule, do not carry the banner of a free humanity but instead a thinly concealed Asiatic despotism."[22] Nor was Goebbels able to deal firmly with the deleterious effects of the news which reached Germany from Switzerland. According to the Baden SD, reports from Switzerland found their way into the border areas and caused serious morale problems for the authorities. Businessmen passed on information and the Swiss newspapers they smuggled across the frontier were eagerly read. This was not the first time, nor would it be the last, that the Swiss incurred Goebbels's wrath, and he was of the firm conviction that one day the independent state of Switzerland would have to disappear.[23]

During the first week of May as Goebbels was occupied preparing the propaganda camouflage for the imminent strike against France, he let the Norwegian campaign gradually recede from view, despite the fact that heavy fighting was taking place for possession of Narvik. At his press conference on May 7, Goebbels ordered that "Narvik must disappear as a theme in the war news and under no conditions should our prestige be laid on the line there."[24] The German attack on France launched two days later became a veritable symphony for propagandists in need of good copy, and it completely swallowed up coverage of the Norwegian campaign until the Allied forces had withdrawn in June.

On May 28 an Allied force of 25,000 men made up of British, French, and Norwegian units reinforced by a Polish brigade succeeded in driving General Dietl from Narvik.[25] Although the town had fallen at 2 o'clock on the morning of the 28th, Goebbels made no mention of it in his next press conference which was devoted to the surrender of Belgium. The OKW never admitted the loss of Narvik, but Goebbels felt so pressed by the effects of BBC counterpropaganda that he made an exception to his own rule against directly answering London by remarking that "this pile of ruins has become meaningless for us."[26]

Following the English evacuation of Narvik on June 8, just a few days after Dunkirk, Goebbels was in a position to chirp the gleeful refrain that the Wehrmacht had driven the English "invaders" into the sea on two fronts. Narvik became a *Deutsches Heldenlied*: "Today the heroic resistance which Major General Dietl has rendered against overwhelming odds in Narvik was rewarded with total victory. *Ostmark* mountain troops, Luftwaffe units, as well as our destroyer crews have achieved eternal military glory in this struggle of two months. Their heroism has compelled the allied land-sea-and air forces to evacuate the Narvik and Harstad areas. The German flag now waves over Narvik . . . Surrender negotiations are in progress."[27]

It was not by chance that Hitler showered glory on General Dietl; he was a kindred soul from the Alps, a Nazi general true to the Führer's heart. Dietl came to symbolize the heroic Nazi "new man" whom the Party exalted as an audacious fighter who knew no fear, a man who lived only to fight Aryan man's life-or-death struggle. No other general except Rommel would enjoy this kind of acclaim. The place of "Generalleutnant Dietl, der Sieger von Narvik," was assured in the Nazi mythical pantheon, and the "Shield of Narvik" medal was struck and issued to all participants in the battle.

The Nazis attributed the German victory to the racial stock of the Narvik troops, men from the soil of Carinthia and Steiermark: the "blood flowing through their veins also flows through the veins of the Führer." "Words have no meaning in the face of such deeds," Fritz Zierke wrote in the *Völkischer Beobachter.* "No one can give more to Germany than did these sons of the Alps . . . Today the German people, tremendously proud, greet their sons who have won eternal glory far in the north."[28]

On June 14, the OKW published a final report on Norway which Hitler himself had edited.[29] The aircraft carrier *Glorious* headed a long list of British ships sunk off the coast of Norway, which included a cruiser, ten destroyers, and nineteen submarines. Although the OKW reported German naval losses, the public was in no position to realize how seriously the fleet had been weakened. Thirty-three percent of the entire German cruiser fleet and 50 percent of its destroyers had been sunk. There was no mention that the *Lützow, Scharnhorst,* and *Gneisenau* had all been put out of action. The listing of six U-boat losses did not tell the real tale; the submarine fleet of Admiral Dönitz came out of the Norwegian campaign seriously demoralized because of the technical faults in torpedo construction which were revealed during their unsuccessful combat operations.[30]

It was clear, however, that the German Army, Navy, and Air Force had carried out a very difficult operation under trying conditions. Surprise, boldness, and imagination had all played a role in this stunning military victory. Swedish ore routes had been secured once and for all, and submarine havens were now at Germany's disposal for the naval war against the Allies. Bases were secured which would become important once the German-Soviet war broke out a year later; from Norway the Germans could raid the Allied convoys following the northern route to Russia via Murmansk.[31]

To attach any more significance to the strategic advantages gained as a result of the Norwegian campaign would be illusory. The significance of the Norwegian air bases for the coming Battle of Britain was minimal, and General Jodl complained during the course of his testimony at Nuremberg that "the Norwegian coast gave us no strategic advantage for the air attacks against England."[32] The 300,000 men whom Hitler assigned to occupy Norway acted as a drain on German manpower until 1945.

Any analysis of Nazi propaganda on Norway must assess it as a series of blunders. No one comprehended this more clearly than Goebbels who later remarked at a Ministry staff meeting that Nazi news policy during the battle for Scandinavia was a failure.[33] In an effort to close the book on Norway, he did not include a single speech or radio broadcast dealing with the northern theater in his carefully selected compendium of major addresses and writings for this period which was published in 1941 under the title *Die Zeit ohne Beispiel.*[34] For these months, quite understandably, he chose selections concerning the Battle of France.

The campaign in Scandinavia ended on the same note on which it had begun: Germany's enemy was the English plutocratic clique, not the people of Norway and Denmark.[35] But many Germans knew what was taking place all along, Goebbels's rescue propaganda notwithstanding. The Nazis made no attempt to reconcile their earlier propaganda line regarding the "Aryan Nordics" with the appointment of Josef Terboven, an Essen Party boss, as Reich commissar of Norway, and it was generally expected that Hitler would maintain control of the country once the war was over.[36] The negative impression which the military reporting on the Norwegian front made on the public was eclipsed by the euphoric *Heldenlied* on the Battle of France, and it was all but forgotten when Hitler realized his dreams in the small clearing in the forest of Compiègne when all France lay at his feet.

VI Victory in the West: The Battle of France

The Battle of France offered Goebbels a model propaganda situation which he exploited almost flawlessly, and his propaganda motifs were orchestrated in such a way that a message was offered at once to the Party, the nation, the remainder of intimidated Europe as yet untouched by the hostilities, and the world at large. The components he stressed were the following: an external "threat" to the Reich's security, countered by Hitler's timely deployment of the Wehrmacht; a six-week campaign of unparalleled success that seemed to prove the superiority of National Socialists élan and determination which, in a matter of a few weeks, delivered a victory that Imperial Germany could not attain during the course of four years fighting at an enormous cost of life; a campaign which was to demonstrate that the Nazi state based on Aryan cohesiveness represented a system superior in both spiritual and material strength to France's "Jewish-Negro racial mélange" and to England's "plutocratic and democratic decadence"; the destruction of the armed forces of France and the humiliation of the British who were routed and sent scurrying home from the beaches of Dunkirk, defeated and demoralized; and finally, Hitler's dramatic gesture of appearing with his paladins to present the armistice terms to the French at Compiègne, a symbolic act registering Hitler's consummation of victory in 1940, his profound debt to his comrades in arms in the Great War whose honor was

84

thus avenged, and a warning to the English that they best come to terms with the Greater German Reich. The Battle of France was to classic Nazi victory propaganda what Stalingrad was for the situation of penultimate defeat. Each propaganda campaign served as a model of its genre.

During the course of the Scandinavian offensive, Goebbels was already preparing the way for his subsequent *Westfront* propaganda by alleging that the English and French were planning to carve up central Europe for themselves and that the United States would guarantee the arrangements.[1] As "documentation" he featured a doctored photograph of Sumner Welles of the United States posing with the French premier Paul Reynaud, which was superimposed on a map of Europe delineating their respective spheres of influence. France was to gain its long-sought Rhine frontier while England would guarantee Poland's advance all the way westward to the Oder River. Germany was to be divided into two states, Prussia and Bavaria. The Hapsburgs were to be returned to the Austrian throne and were to rob Hitler of sections of southern Germany, while Mussolini would be forced to cede Venice and Trieste to Vienna. Even Czechoslovakia was to have its share of rump Germany; Prague would control Saxony under the English-French new order. The Netherlands and Belgium were to be united and would fall easily into the English sphere of interest.

Nazi propaganda before the Battle of France followed the pattern for delayed attack situations established in August 1939. Once again Hitler accused his enemies of preparing a surprise attack on the Reich, and once more the level of tension grew to unbearable proportions as the German onslaught was delayed. In the case of Poland, the repeated halts in the German marching orders were attributable to Hitler's frenetic diplomatic offensive aimed at keeping Great Britain out of the war. On the other hand in May 1940 heavy fog determined that he cancel on several occasions the initiation of "Case Yellow" in order to launch the offensive at the most propitious moment.[2]

Hitler himself directed what the propaganda line should be. On May 3 Goebbels, and in turn the propaganda corps, was ordered to commence a campaign charging that the English were about to strike in the Mediterranean and the Balkans.[3] For days the combined radio and press network decried the "imminent English attack" against Italy's positions in the Mediterranean area. Even the respected *Frankfurter Zeitung* raised the query regarding what would happen to *mare nostrum* and to the reborn Roman Empire should the British designs be successful, and concluded that Mussolini's new Italy would deal with any English resort to force in kind.[4]

In their attempt to draw attention away from France and western Europe, Hitler and Goebbels did not stop with the Mediterranean; they also charged that the English, unable to win a foothold in Norway and searching for new areas in which to expand the conflict, now had designs on the Balkans as well. Yugoslavia, Greece, Rumania, Bulgaria, and Egypt were all in danger of immediate occupation by "Perfidious Albion," an allegation which Goebbels set about to prove. Accordingly, on May 7, only three days before the German strike in the west, the *Völkischer Beobachter* "revealed" that Chamberlain and Reynaud had agreed on a joint strike into the Balkans, an action which would commence on May 20.[5] According to the Nazis, German intelligence had been able to intercept a telephone call between the Allied leaders on April 30 and had transmitted this shocking news to the Führer. To judge by Nazi propaganda, there was no limit to what the English might do to challenge the freedom of other peoples.

At the time when the Mediterranean-Balkan deception was being carried out, and only one day before Hitler unleashed his divisions westward, Goebbels returned to the theme of the imminent English-French aggression in the Low Countries. In a directive released some forty hours before the May 10 dawn attack, Goebbels ordered his subordinates to counter the English-inspired charge that Germany was about to begin an offensive in Holland and Belgium. According to this directive, "It must become clear that this is nothing more than a typical British diversionary maneuver which resulted because it has become general knowledge that the British were about to launch another aggressive attack in their attempt to spread the war."[6] Goebbels had reverted to his "Stop the thief!" motif by accusing London of pursuing the exact course taken by Hitler. This propaganda in preparation for war was followed without compromising Goebbels's own diversionary maneuver to the south and southeast. Furthermore, by pointing the finger at London just before Hitler's own strike,

Goebbels could all the more easily characterize the German assault either as a preemptive blow to head off the English or as a counterattack. As it developed he used both techniques, and the themes he employed before May 10 merged smoothly with those he ordered for the Battle of France.

The propaganda deception in early May demonstrates just what effect such an operation can have when carried out by a totalitarian propaganda apparatus utilizing tight censorship controls. According to the SD, the German strike into France and the Low Countries came as a shock to most Germans who had believed that the English were about to move into the Mediterranean and the Balkans.[7] In this case Nazi propaganda was successful because Goebbels made use of his principle that if lie one must, then lie in a big way to increase one's chances of credibility.

Goebbels's propaganda during the week preceding May 10 also stands to support two further observations about his tactics. The first is that Goebbels gave great weight to the proper timing of his propaganda. He understood that to bring any particular propaganda compaign to a climax at the wrong time was tantamount to negating its effects entirely. On Monday, May 6, 1940, he urged his radio and press directors to be certain that there was stilll room for elasticity and maneuver in Germany's propaganda posture as of Wednesday May 8. This directive was well conceived, because as it turned out foggy weather forced Hitler to postpone the campaign until dawn on the tenth. There was still time for Goebbels to raise the fever pitch to a new high (what he called *Steigerungsmöglichkeit*), and on May 8 he ordered Hans Fritzche to direct the press "to intensify the panic which is beginning to spread, and to do everything possible to incite more unrest and to bring tensions to a peak."[8]

The second general principle which he followed during this period was to utilize alleged foreign sources to increase the credibility of his own propaganda. The German people, Goebbels was forced to admit, were intelligent enough to know when they were being led down the garden path. If Berlin alone were to raise the battle cry that the English were about to strike again, this would have made German propaganda less than believable. But by quoting sources, or alleged sources, such as Rome, Helsinki, Stockholm, and Bern to the effect that the London aggressors were about to cut loose once more, Goebbels was able to deliver his point more adeptly, as the SD reports of the week in question attested.[9]

The Goebbels apparatus adjusted smoothly to the onset of the campaign in the west. Convinced that his timing had been perfect and looking with a real sense of anticipation toward a campaign which would dim memories of the difficulties associated with the battle for Norway, he launched his Battle of France propaganda with vigor. Addressing the German people on a nationwide hookup on the morning of May 10, he asserted that Hitler had proved dramatically that his contentions of the last weeks and months were correct.[10] It was clear now, he said, where England and France were about to strike; they had already begun moving their troops into Belgium and Holland when the Wehrmacht was deployed to meet that threat. The forces of England and France, along with their Belgian and Dutch accomplices, would have to pay the price for their ill-considered attack.[11] Goebbels, elaborating on the theme of the German "counter-strike" in his press conference of May 11, emphasized that England and France "were the ones who declared war on us and now they were going to have to pay for it. This war which they began is now coming home to roost (Ihr eigener Krieg breche nun über sie herein). Under no circumstances can we allow ourselves to be maneuvered into the role of aggressor again."[12]

Finally, to give his propaganda added momentum, Goebbels conjured up once more the motif which the Nazis had hammered on in one form or another for years and which would become common-place once the Soviet war broke out—the horror theme option, that is, the threatened annihilation of the German people. Since the enemy planned to starve and slaughter "millions of the Reich's women and children," it was imperative that Hitler launch a defensive blow to protect them.

Hitler's "Proclamation to the Soldiers of the West Front," which broached the theme of life or death for the German people, was intended to send the Wehrmacht into battle reassured that theirs was a just struggle. Hitler, who himself had conceived the Mediter-ranean-Balkan deception, now accused the English and French of doing exactly what he had done—focus attention away from the imminent attack through Holland, Belgium, and Luxemburg in order to conceal their dastardly aggression:

The hour of the most decisive struggle for the future of the German nation has arrived.

For three hundred years English and French power brokers have tried to check every effective consolidation of Europe, but above all to keep Germany weak and divided. France alone declared war on Germany thirty-one times to realize this goal.

But it has also been the aim of the British imperialists to keep Germany divided under all circumstances and to deny the Reich the food and resources necessary to support a people 80,000,000 strong . . . The German people neither hates nor feels enmity toward the English or French people. But the question today is whether we will live or whether we will perish.

In a matter of weeks the brave troops of our armies vanquished the Polish enemy driven on by England and France, thereby ending the danger in the east. Whereupon England and France decided to attack Germany from the north. Since April 9 the German Wehrmacht put an end to this danger too.

Now something has happened which we have felt to be a threat and a danger for several months. England and France are now attempting to push across Holland and Belgium into the Ruhr by employing a gigantic deceptive maneuver in southeast Europe.

Soldiers of the western front! Now your hour has arrived. The campaign which begins today will decide the fate of the German nation for the next thousand years. Now carry out your duty. The German people is with you in spirit.[13]

Ribbentrop in his conference with the German and foreign press on the morning of May 10 summarized several documents with propaganda value emanating from the Foreign Ministry, the Wehrmacht High Command, and the Reich Ministry of the Interior. Taken together they amounted to a reiteration of Hitler's charge that the English were caught in the act of landing troops in Holland and Belgium, troops which were destined to destroy the Ruhr industrial complex, the heart of the Reich's security system. Belgium and Holland, whose military staffs allegedly had surrendered all their independence to the military clique in London, had shared in planning the destruction of the Third Reich. Ribbentrop claimed that he had documentary evidence to prove this contention, but for obvious reasons he did not produce it for the press. In a pallid replay of the identical claim made persuant to the occupation of Norway, von Ribbentrop declared that Germany had taken the necessary steps to protect the neutrality of Holland and Belgium against the English-

French aggressors. Ribbentrop, as impudent as ever in his dashing blue uniform, reflected Nazi arrogance at the height of its power when he concluded the press conference with the boast that now Germany "would settle accounts with these despots once and for all."[14]

The official notes from the Foreign Ministry to the governments of Belgium and Holland embraced an eight-point attack outlining the transgressions of Brussels and the Hague; these papers included the primitive charge that, in addition to repeated violations of their neutral status, both powers had allowed the "English Secret Intelligence Service" to operate from their countries in an attempt to "incite a revolution in Germany." Not only had the English been permitted to use the territories of these "neutrals" for a base, but both military and civilian officials of Holland and Belgium were said to have worked hand in hand with the "criminals." Furthermore, they had encouraged the English military buildup which was to culminate in a surprise attack on the Reich. As a result of these provocations and other unfriendly acts, Holland and Belgium had forced Hitler to take steps to guarantee their bona fide neutrality. Ribbentrop's statement closed with a reiteration of Germany's position that it was entering Holland and Belgium as a friend and protector, an assertion qualified by the warning that a misinterpretation of Germany's magnanimous gesture in the form of resistance would be answered in kind.[15] A brief note to the government of Luxemburg appended to these memorandums was much milder in tone, although the meaning was the same.

Keitel's statement, representing the OKW's assessment of Belgian and Dutch complicity in the alleged English buildup at strategic points throughout their countries, had been completed by May 3 in anticipation of Hitler's aggression. Also released on May 10, it was a tedious report which few people read but which added to Hitler's case against the English.[16] A joint communication issued by Himmler and Minister of the Interior Frick used the Venlo incident, which had culminated in the arrest of the British agents Best and Stevens, to spin off other evidence to buttress the charge that the Belgians and Dutch were guilty of working with the English Secret service in an attempt to join with German opposition circles to assassinate the Führer.[17] Taken as a whole, these documents published at the outset of the Battle of France represented an extensive yet belabored justification for blatant aggression.

The first reactions to the strike in the west were ecstatic and were qualified only by Hitler's warning that the campaign would demand heavy sacrifices. Few doubts were expressed about Germany's final victory, because the conviction was widespread that the Führer was entirely in command of the situation. The great majority of Germans believed, or wanted to believe, that the English and French were in fact preparing an attack on the Reich through Belgium and Holland when Hitler acted decisively to stop them.[18]

Success is slow to feel the pangs of conscience, as German attitudes during the Battle of France clearly demonstrate. Unlike the cautious mood of September 1939, there were few doubters in 1940; the lightning campaign in the west pitched the country into a war fever particularly receptive to Goebbels's propaganda of heroism. Few cared about the rights of the independent states of Belgium and Holland; the SD summed up the situation by saying that "the people have since the beginning of the war not only been awaiting an occupation, especially of Holland, but they have deemed it necessary."[19]

Goebbels's initial directives were in part based on complaints raised by the Army and Luftwaffe high commands, which issued a directive for press coverage of the operations in the west on May 10. Piqued by the reactions to the campaign in Norway which they were convinced Goebbels had mishandled, the military wanted precautions taken to avoid a propaganda campaign of arrogant overconfidence. The military commands expected the radio and press to approach the campaign conservatively and not to raise unwarranted hopes for a blitz victory on the model of the Battle of Poland. After all, the Maginot Line, perhaps the world's most intricate defensive system, faced the Wehrmacht. Reporting on the course of the campaign was to be kept in low key until the decisive confrontation with England and France had been brought to a successful conclusion.[20] Reacting to the wishes of the military command, which in effect expressed his own predilections considering the deleterious results of the Norway experience, Goebbels ordered Fritzsche to direct the press to indulge neither in "exaggerated optimism nor in a wild panic" to the successes or failures of the campaign to come. They should understand that temporary reversals do not decide a campaign; therefore, the editors should be ready for all eventualities and should be able to integrate reversals smoothly into their overall propaganda strategy.[21] As the campaign developed, these forewarnings proved to be unnecessary.

As the Wehrmacht rushed headlong from victory to victory in a campaign lasting only six weeks, it was all Goebbels could do to keep up with the rapid pace of the German advance. Special Announcements of the OKW, heralded by dramatic trumpet fanfares, were heard with remarkable frequency during the Battle of France. The campaign gradually took on the aura of a crusade as the stanzas of the *Frankreichlied* signaled the Reich's mission in the west:

> Comrade, we are marching in the west united
> with the bombing squadrons, and though many of
> our best will die, we will smash the enemy.
> Forward, onward, onward. Over the Meuse,
> over the Scheldt and Rhine, we'll march
> victoriously through France . . .

> They tried to destroy our Reich, but the
> mighty West Wall held them back. We're
> coming to dash the old rotten world to
> bits. Forward, onward.

> Comrade! We're marching and fighting for
> Germany, ready to die, 'til the bells peal
> the new era from tower to tower!
> Forward, onward.[22]

Alfred Rosenberg, assessing Germany's mission, integrated the Battle of France with Nazi ideology in an article he published in the *Völkischer Beobachter* on May 12. Rosenberg asserted that the war had entered a new phase; it was now a revolutionary war, a war which pitted Europe—led by the National Socialist Reich based on strength, work, and virtue—against the forces of "decadent Jewish-Plutocratic-Democratic Piracy." The struggle would be decided on the field of battle where Germany's revolutionary ideal would prove victorious.[23] Rosenberg's proclamation of Europe's revolutionary war was a forerunner of the "Europe united" motif which would become a bulwark of National Socialist propaganda during the Battle of Russia. According to the myth, all Europe looked to Hitler to lead the revolutionary war against injustice and exploitation of the continent by the English plutocrats whose nefarious money-grubbing would now be brought to an end once and for all. Rosenberg, by conjuring up the symbols of light versus darkness, and of "Germanic National Socialist purity" as opposed to "Jewish-English-French moral decadence," provided the ideological foundations for the Battle of France which Goebbels was to embellish in his propaganda.

The propaganda storm attendant on the opening of hostilities served to lessen the impact of the news that Chamberlain had been forced out of office and replaced by Winston Churchill. Under normal circumstances the naming of Churchill would have become the subject of propaganda accounts lasting a week or more. But at the time it seemed of secondary importance, although it tended to reinforce not only Rosenberg's "revolution of Europe" theme but the entire anti-English propaganda strategy up to that point. Churchill emerged as a German-hating beast of World War I vintage, a war monger without parallel, the "quintessence of the decadent English plutocrat," a man destined to fail in his attempt to repress the tidal wave of history represented by the National Socialist Reich. According to the *Völkischer Beobachter,* "A system which allows such men as Churchill and Reynaud to take power is destined for destruction."[24]

As the first reports of the German successes began to come in, Goebbels analyzed them and proposed contingency propaganda strategy for both the short and long terms. Early on in the campaign he intended to be very vague about the Wehrmacht's progress westward in order to maximize the effectiveness of the major victories once they could be announced.[25] Next, he proposed to spread terror among Germany's enemies with propaganda dramatizing the new weapons and tactical units being employed. The surrender of Eben Emael—one of the world's most powerful fortresses—within thirty hours after the beginning of the offensive occasioned propaganda of this type.[26] Goebbels spread tension by capitalizing on the mysterious wording of the OKW report announcing the fall of the fortress, a cryptic communiqué stating that it had been taken by troops using "offensive weapons of an entirely new type." This in turn led to rumors that the weapons in question included a nerve gas which was effective for several hours.

Thirdly, Goebbels ordered that all necessary steps be taken to avoid any sympathy for Belgium and the Netherlands. To further that end, and to reinforce the nascent "Europe united" theme, he commanded the German radio to begin playing old Dutch and Flemish war songs in order to stress their origins as part of a greater Germanic cultural unity.[27] Next, to further Hitler's stratagem of making it appear that the Schlieffen Plan was in operation once more, Goebbels directed the progaganda corps to focus as much attention as possible on the Netherlands-Belgian fronts in order to conceal the aim of the major strike through the Ardennes Forest to the Channel.[28] This last goal was carried through flawlessly, and the general impression from May 10 to the capitulation of the Netherlands five days later was that the main force of the German strike was concentrated in the north.

At the same time that Goebbels was carrying out these objectives he began a buildup of the central idea of his entire campaign—that it was the English who were responsible for the spread of the war. Anti-French propaganda was very much in the background at this juncture. To believe this propaganda, the Englishman was the quintessential war criminal, responsible for all manner of atrocities in 1940, including the Luftwaffe's attack on Rotterdam.[29] The Netherlands had been duped by the English who had involved the Hague in their concerted policy to gain total control of Europe. Guilt lay not with the Dutch people but with their government whose treachery opened the floodgates of western Europe to the forces of English aggression. The German line seemed confirmed when Queen Wilhelmina sailed for London to establish a government-in-exile after the surrender of the Netherlands on May 15.

Goebbels took measures to avoid speculation about future German annexations in western Europe.[30] Woe to the editor who would relate all the frustrations of World War I trench warfare to the new situation and who might be misguided enough to contemplate the possible German annexation of Eupen-et-Malmédy, Alsace-Lorraine, Luxemburg, Antwerp, or the Channel ports. The battle in the west was being fought not for German aggrandizement, but so that the Reich and each individual nation in Europe could enjoy the delights of a free and independent development in an ordered environment. Hitler, it goes without saying, would provide the order. At times he also caused the confusion, and embarrassed Goebbels in the bargain.

One such case involved the annexation of former "Reich territories" in the west. Hitler announced on May 18 that he was reversing yet another injustice of the Versailles Treaty by bringing Eupen, Malmédy, and Moresnet home to the Reich, lands which would never again be returned to alien Belgian control.[31] Hitler thereby violated Goebbels's standing order that the topic of possible German annexations in the west was not to be broached. What would have cost a mere propagandist his job, or even worse, became a much heralded fait accompli once the Führer had uttered the magic words. Such were the shifting winds with which Goebbels had to cope.

The Goebbels machine, concentrating on the Belgian and Dutch fronts, offered the public an integrated saturation campaign to cover the progress of the battle. Radio broadcasts of the propaganda companies reporting from the front provided dramatic coverage of significant engagements which were particularly well received because of their timeliness. The following Propaganda Company broadcast from the fortress of Eben Emael on May 11 serves to demonstrate the mood of heightened realism which characterized these reports:

In the midst of the front along the Belgian border we meet the captain who . . . led the daring attack on the bridges of the Albert Canal. Captain Koch, an austere, tall, athletic, muscular person, tells of the order which won the Knights Cross for him. At dawn on May 10, he was on German soil. The paratroopers jumped over the area which they must protect against attempted demolition . . . The men stormed in like lions and within a short time they had secured the bridgeheads . . . Around noon the infantry had arrived . . . But the unit's greatest achievement was to enclose 1000 Belgians in a fortress. Lt. Witzig had guided his planes directly over the fortress . . . His was to be the bold strike. With complete surprise and despite heavy resistance the commander and 1000 Belgians were taken prisoner, after an infantry unit attacking from the north succeeded in linking up with Witzig's unit.

These two distinguished actions on this the first day of the great German offensive in the west serves as a model for all the fighting troops . . .[32]

This report celebrated the Nazi "German fighter" stereotype—that the National Socialist warrior was a brave, audacious, Aryan specimen ready to give his life for Führer and Fatherland. He knew no fear. He was soldierly and honorable in his conduct with the enemy and fair in his treatment of noncombatants. He knew who he was, from whence he came, and the system he was defending. That he could be ruthless when the necessities of war demanded it became clear in the OKW Special Announcement on the bombing of Rotterdam. Stuka attacks combined with the threat of a concerted Panzer blow had forced the city to capitulate, "thereby avoiding its destruction."

The impression left by the first newsreels of the spring offensive was one which would be cultivated throughout the campaign: Hitler had launched a relentless drive which could be slowed only occasionally by enemy resistance; German success was assured because of its technical, moral, and material superiority over the enemy.[33] Shots of diving Stukas, of tanks rushing over hill and valley from one village to the next with amazing rapidity, and of blond, Nordic soldiers in battle all conveyed the feeling that the National Socialist Wehrmacht was an incomparable striking force.

The news that the Netherlands had capitulated in five days evoked an ecstatic reception in the press and radio. An editorial by Wilhelm Weiss of the *Völkischer Beobachter* assessed the significance of the victory by contrasting it to the standstill of 1914 when the weakened German right flank became bogged down at Mons and Maubeuge and turned south instead of occupying important points all the way to the sea. What a difference 1940 had made in the Schlieffen Plan, Weiss continued; not only was the German right flank secure now that the coast had been reached in the Netherlands, but the Atlantic was in German hands all the way to Norway.[34]

Weiss also stressed the danger to which England was exposed now that the Wehrmacht controlled the strategic North Sea and Atlantic positions, an advantage which Major Erich Murawski echoed in his radio analysis of May 15. It appeared that England had never been in such mortal danger, because now Hermann Göring's Luftwaffe, which "ruled the skies," held bases much closer to England. Targets lay on the average only 250 kilometers from the Netherlands, and German war planes could now reach them in forty minutes flying time. And they would come even closer since the Wehrmacht, now freed in the Netherlands, could strike southward to force its way into the ports and airfields of Belgium.

With the campaign in the west in full swing, the Nazis intensified their glorification of Hitler, "the greatest military commander of all times," whose genius, dedication, and inspiration had made all these wonderful things possible. Reich Press Chief Dietrich published a hymn of praise to Hitler which extolled his military virtues.[35] According to Dietrich, the bond between the Führer and the Wehrmacht was unbreakable; it was a tie based on faith, trust, and loyalty which only soldiers could really comprehend. Hitler's men recognized his military genius, his depth of strategic understanding, and they knew that he personally was up front with them at his headquarters, constantly reviewing plans with his generals. His entire being was devoted to his men, and he knew no danger. As the first soldier of the state, he made frequent trips to be with his fighting men and to recognize the bravest by personally awarding them medals of the highest distinction. He was the genius of total war and only he understood its intricacies. The Führer, Dietrich continued, would deliver the final victory.

Goebbels elaborated on the theme "Front and Heimat" in propaganda intended to reinforce the bond between the home and fighting fronts. His directives to Heinz Goedecke, the voice of the Sunday *Wunschkonzert*, reveal how he proceeded to accomplish this goal.[36] The concert on Sunday, May 19, was to be a tour de force featuring the mayors from the home towns of Knight's Cross winners in the west conveying greetings to the front. When the soldiers heard "Bells of the Homeland," "It's Great to Be a Soldier," or "Antje, My Blond Baby" radioed to their casinos, they would know how much the home front appreciated their heroic fighting spirit.

As the Wehrmacht advanced westward at a remarkable pace, Goebbels again took precautions to suppress what might turn out to be unwarranted optimism. On several occasions he directed the propaganda elite to water the coals of victory ecstasy in order to avoid a propaganda reversal.[37] This entailed avoiding speculation about the future course of the campaign and adhering strictly to factual military reporting. The OKW, fearing that the propaganda machine was running ahead of events and disquieted by Nazi flamboyance and exaggeration, once more brought pressure to bear on Goebbels to be more conservative in his approach to the war in the west.[38]

But hedging of this nature proved unnecessary, because no sooner had orders been dispatched to the radio correspondents and editorial writers to trim their sails than another dashing victory was scored. Furthermore the officers of the Wehrmacht High Command/Section for Wehrmacht Propaganda, who repeatedly called for a conservative posture, themselves were powerless in the face of the OKW communiqués which Hitler edited and which became more enthusiastic as the German forces surged toward the Channel. There was little which could be done when the OKW reported on May 21 that German units had reached the Channel at Amiens in "the greatest offensive operation in history," a boast traceable to the Führer. This news of the greatest importance was preceded by the fanfare of the French campaign and appropriate march selections and was followed by the playing of the *Englandlied.*[39]

As a result the Propaganda Ministry, taking its cue from Hitler and the OKW, began to speak of the French campaign in terms of a "rout." The reports from the front bore out this contention as Lieutenant Kurt Hesse's account from the area of Cambrai attests:

As I write these lines, the battle rolls on. You simply cannot employ another expression for it. Modern tank warfare presents an entirely new mode of combat. Hundreds of armored vehicles roll forward across country at a speed of 30, 40, or 50 kilometers an hour after information from land or air reconnaissance units has been sifted to prepare the way for the attack. One finds the divisional general of this new, unique cavalry out front or riding the first wave, a new type of Seydlitz but not unlike him, who must have the eyes of a hawk to make decisions and to act instantly if an opportunity to strike presents itself. Today you really have to speak in terms of a great Panzer weapon. To a great degree it dominates this war . . . You must acknowledge the tank corps as the standard bearer of the best German military tradition.[40]

With accounts such as this, few would doubt the supremacy of the Wehrmacht.

Goebbels timed a massive anti-French propaganda campaign for the climax of the Battle of France; as the fluid situation at the front developed, this coincided with the Dunkirk withdrawal during the first week of June. But until that time, he had to be satisfied with anti-French propaganda dealing with three issues: the barbarism of the enemy, a favorite subject of his; atrocities and war crimes, originally conceived as a counteratrocity campaign but continued after the success of the original action to become a theme on its own merits; and finally, the inhumanity of the combined English-French air raids.

Goebbels was very sensitive about the Allied claim that France and Britain were the standard-bearers of civilization who were fighting to protect it from being destroyed by the Nazi barbarians. In his capacity as president of the Reich Culture Chamber, this irritated him because, according to the book, it was National Socialist Germany which nourished and protected the culture of Western civilization. Allied propaganda had become so effective that Goebbels ordered counterpropaganda both at home and abroad on this issue. Heretofore, it had been deemed sufficient to treat it solely by way of short-wave radio. Goebbels, in a shallow gesture, directed his staff to stress the general flowering of culture under both National Socialism and Italian fascism.[41]

Goebbels next launched an attack on the French for their alleged violations of the Geneva Convention in connection with their treatment of parachute troops and airmen parachuting from destroyed planes. On May 12, Reynaud charged that the Germans had deployed parachute troops wearing Dutch and Belgian uniforms and civilian clothes in violation of the Geneva Convention; such men were to be shot on sight.[42] Goebbels's first reaction was to announce in a press conference that the Germans would not "hesitate a moment" to take reprisals for such illegal enemy action. At the same time, in an effort to stir the waters, he ordered that the question should be raised whether every German parachutist really was to be shot. This ruse was consistent with Goebbels's general dictum for propaganda: to always have something to say, no matter what the circumstances, to keep the enemy on his guard, and to appear bold. As it developed in this case, he had not first checked with the OKW/WPr on a common line.

The OKW answered Reynaud's charge with such force and with such blatant threats of its own that even Goebbels was embarrassed. On May 13 the OKW called the allegation a lie, maintaining that if Reynaud were a soldier he would know that the Wehrmacht had added parachute troops to its regular forces long before the war broke out and had trained them for their special functions. Their uniform could under no circumstances be confused with those of the enemy, much less with civilians. Should Reynaud really intend to murder brave parachute troops, he could expect a corresponding German counteraction. For every single German soldier killed in this manner, ten French prisoners of war would be executed in retaliation.[43] Ribbentrop entered the fray and sent notes to London, Paris, Brussels, and the Hague warning them of the consequences of their violation of international law.[44]

Goebbels, always jealous of his prerogatives as propaganda minister, saw his prejudices reconfirmed by the behavior of the Wehrmacht High Command in this case. As he told his men at the Ministry, the OKW had committed some rather astounding tactical blunders by its announcements of the 10:1 kill ratio. First, by making public the Wehrmacht's peacetime training of the parachute units for their special tasks in the war, it was implying that the armed forces had planned for the war all along and stood ready for take-off orders long before September 1939. As Goebbels realized, this made a mockery of his propaganda that the Battle of France, the Netherlands, and Belgium was really a preemptive strike to counter the imminent Allied blow through the Low Countries into the Ruhr. Goebbels was offended by the OKW's statement for a second important reason. By warning the enemy that they could expect ten prisoners of war to be murdered for every German, the OKW did nothing but harm the German cause, because now the French would fight all the harder as a result of the threat.[45] Although Goebbels directed his own men to set the picture straight immediately, Hermann Göring was not told about the order. During the course of one of his many bombastic press conferences, the Reichsmarschall not only reiterated the OKW statement, but fanned the flames of fear by warning that the Führer would not leave his brave parachute warriors in the lurch.[46]

The third phase of Goebbels's stage one anti-French campaign consisted of claims of atrocities allegedly committed by the French Air Force. The most outstanding example of this was the false charge that the French had bombed Freiburg in Breisgau on May 10, killing thirteen children and causing substantial damage to the city. What Goebbels could not admit was that Luftwaffe formations, mistaking Freiburg for a French town over the border, had themselves carried out the raid.[47] By claiming that it was the French who were responsible, he thereby accomplished the dual purpose of furthering his atrocity propaganda and concealing the blunder of Göring's overzealous flyers. The weekly newsreel made much of this "outrageous example of French inhumanity." The footage which dealt with the Freiburg attack began with scenes depicting the Wehrmacht's excellent treatment of enemy civilians in the Battle of France, asserting that the Luftwaffe was under orders to protect the homes and belongings of French civilians. In a classic Nazi transition, the *Wochenschau* then transferred the scene to Freiburg where "innocent children had become the victims of French treachery inspired by the English." A view of the school destroyed "by French terror bombers" supported the point that Hitler was indeed the protector of Western civilization.[48]

The few raids which the Allies in fact flew over Germany during the Battle of France evoked Goebbels's righteous indignation, while they were a great source of embarrassment to Göring's overweening pride. The public soon learned that it was nonsense to expect immediate revenge for any particular attack, Party rhetoric notwithstanding. The propaganda advantages which the Allies gained with their raids early in the war were far out of proportion to the damage they actually caused; a handful of very light air raids in May tended to undermine morale in western Germany.[49]

The SD reported that throughout May the most incredible rumors were circulated which spread fear on the one hand and lack of trust in German news reporting on the other. This situation was the direct result of Goebbels's policy to provide only limited information on air raids. It was his feeling that the less said about them the better; for this reason he ordered that news of the bombings was to be covered only in the provincial press of the areas involved. But few were fooled by this propaganda tactic which caused serious repercussions; the result was that most Germans believed the damage to be much greater than it actually was. And when deliberate falsification of the number of people killed in a raid became common knowledge, as happened in the Hanover area, Goebbels was roundly cursed.[50] Indiscriminate talebearing by train personnel who rode through the western territories tended to exaggerate the effects of the Allied raids as did the letters written by people in the threatened areas to their friends and relatives to the south and east. According to the SD, "These rumors are very widespread and one can hear them everywhere in the trams, trains, in the shops, and on the street; they have led to substantial unrest among the people."[51] This was just the beginning of a morale problem which was exacerbated as the air war increased in intensity. But for the time being the public's attention could be focused on the Battle of France.

The campaign in France was at its height when Goebbels went to work on his first editorial for *Das Reich,* a new weekly newspaper which he hoped would increase both his own prestige and that of the National Socialist cause.[52] The timing for the initial issue was auspicious. When his editorial entitled "An Epoch without Parallel" appeared on May 26, the Wehrmacht was in the process of concluding its victorious campaign for northern France and Belgium, and the Allied withdrawal from Dunkirk was about to begin.

Divisiveness within Belgian ruling circles played into Goebbels's hands as well. On May 28, Belgium surrendered unconditionally on the orders of King Leopold III, who went into German captivity; the Belgian premier Pierot, on the other hand, established a government-in-exile in London. This was grist for Goebbels's mill, and he relished the opportunity to exploit inter-Allied hostility. His hopes were fulfilled when both Reynaud and Churchill denounced King Leopold's act as a betrayal of the Allied cause. At this point Goebbels launched a caustic attack on the Allies under the heading "The Missed Opportunities":

One often asks the question: what are they really thinking about, this Churchill and Chamberlain, and Reynaud and Daladier? My answer is: absolutely nothing. They are so arrogant and presumptuous that they think they can afford not to think at all. If I were an Englishman or a Frenchman I would ask in desperation today just what my government had done during the five hard winter months. And the answer must be: nothing except to contrive blustering, cheap paper victories and to fabricate slander and evil . . . Oh blessed naïveté!

But now the western offensive is breaking in over these plutocrats. Now they must deploy their armies in tough, bloody fighting, the same armies which were taught to believe that they only needed to wait in the Maginot Line and that they would hang their washing on the Siegfried Line . . . But now they're suddenly raising the hue and cry that we're attacking them. This wasn't what they wanted. of course. They had fully expected a bloodless war in which German soldiers didn't fight, but instead German women and children starved. Now they have suddenly been awakened to reality. They lounge about in their churches and pray. In a provocative act of hypocrisy they claim God as their ally and whine to the whole world to pull their chestnuts out of the fire . . .

They continue to be fresh, arrogant, stupid, and cowardly, pedestrian politicians who had the audacity to join battle with a world-historic genius who once quite correctly observed that he felt cheated by fate for allowing him only mediocrities as opponents. . . . But they will go down in history as the gravediggers of a world grown rotten and indolent which one only has to jolt to topple it.[53]

As the Battle of France climaxed, Goebbels moved into phase two of his anti-French propaganda campaign, which involved switching to highly emotional saturation propaganda on the race issue. No one knew better than he the difficulty involved in teaching the Germans to despise the French. Respect for French civilization and culture was deeply embedded in the German soul; even Frederick the Great, the Nazis' hero without equal, had preferred French to German culture. As a result he turned to the myth of "French racial degeneration" to explain what reason could not fathom.

Goebbels had but a very short time to prepare the nation for Hitler's radical solution of the French problem. Every conceivable anti-French prejudice was to be played upon, including Versailles, the occupation of the Ruhr in 1923, and the alleged plans of Reynaud to partition Germany. A nation which had not hesitated to use black occupation troops in the Rhineland after World War I was now attempting to destroy civilization itself with a sinister plan to turn the "racial underworld" loose on what remained of cultured Europe. France, Goebbels charged, had become a nation of "verniggerte Sadisten" and the German people should know the dangers which this specter posed: "Through our tireless work we must see to it that the German people are consumed with rage and hate against corrupt, Freemason, diseased France within two weeks."[54] With his emphasis on the "Jewish-Negro-French" subculture, Goebbels was clearly preparing the way to interpret the Battle of France in terms of the blood myth.

The propaganda apparatus proceeded to launch an attack on the Jews in the French government who were responsible for the decline of France. A cartoon in the SS newspaper, Das Schwarze Korps, juxtaposed an oversized, military figure representing Clemenceau against a Lilliputian figure of Mandel, the Jewish French minister

of the interior. The caption read "1918—a man; 1940—a Mandel."[55]
French Jews were said to be leading the nation to destruction in
league with their henchmen in the international Jewish conspiracy.
Not only were the Jews responsible for destroying the once great
French nation, but Mandel, "the symbol of the black and Jewish
racial mélange," was taking steps to liquidate the good elements
still remaining in France.[56]

Rosenberg struck up the identical theme in an editorial he wrote
for the *Völkischer Beobachter* which linked France's decline to the
loss of its racial purity:

> The French armies have been destroyed by the blows of the German
> Wehrmacht. One found in their ranks the best of the French elite
> troops but also the dregs of humanity in the Foreign Legion and
> among the several African races. Taken together they embody today's
> France; as they have said, they all want to "save the culture of Europe."
> Only after Europe, which has finally awakened, catches a glimpse
> of the physiognomy of this whole racial mélange which is fighting
> here on the sacred soil of cultured Europe will they be able to really
> grasp what a decisive struggle has been waged in Flanders.

Clearly, Aryan man was pitted against racial impurity, and the victory
of the Wehrmacht stood as evidence that the pure would triumph
over the impure. Here in the west two worlds were in mortal combat:
"Chosen spokesmen pronounced the mulattisation of Europe to be
the new French national idea. After that white and black were no
longer races, but only white and black Frenchmen, or if you like
black and white niggers." Thus the racially pure Frenchman no longer
existed, and it was the Third Reich's moral duty to history to fill
this vacuum and rescue European civilization from destruction: "One
only has to imagine for an instant what would result if these millions
of armed blacks were set loose on European soil in league with
the French and English and were victorious over the German Army.
There would would be a racial degradation which could never be
made good again and which would destroy everything which all
the people of Europe have created over the centuries."[57] Rosenberg
concluded with the admonition that the only alternative was Adolf
Hitler, a messianic figure who would return Europe to its greatness.

After ten days of this type of saturation propaganda, the SD
reported that a "complete shift" in German attitudes toward France

took place during the first week of June. Even though many people recognized that Goebbels or some Party source had contrived the propaganda, this caused no difficulty except for a few scattered queries regarding why the Party had just now discovered the "Jewish-African" threat in France.[58]

In general Goebbels's campaign accomplished its objectives. For example, the article "We've Had Enough," published in *Das Schwarze Korps* on June 6 calling for the Wehrmacht to liquidate the French threat, was well received. Munich, among other areas, advocated the ouster not only of the French Jews, but of the "ruling clique" tied to England as well. The highly sensitive propaganda charging that black troops had committed atrocities evoked an intense reaction. "Blood isn't enough to pay for that!" was one woman's response to a film report of the alleged French atrocities, and she added for good measure that France must be dealt a lasting reminder for its crimes.[59] But it was Innsbruck which recorded the most radical reaction to Goebbels's campaign. Feelings ran so deeply there about the alleged atrocities committed by the French colonials that to set matters right "they should gas the whole gang of them." Only in that way could the sufferings of the German soldiers be avenged.[60]

Propaganda concerning the alleged illegal treatment of German parachute troops resulted in demands from the public that the Nazis punish the Allied prisoners of war. "The French don't have the right to be handled decently any more" was one voice speaking for many. People on the home front could not understand why prisoners were being dealt with according to the precepts of international law. Newspaper and film reports which demonstrated that enemy prisoners of war were being well cared for caused an outraged reaction. Such was also the case when Göring's *Reichsluftfahrtministerium* published photographs in its illustrated magazine *Der Adler* showing the favorable treatment being accorded to the English prisoners captured in Norway.[61] This did not sit well with people who had been fed a propaganda line so primitive that they understood only immediate revenge and radical solutions.

Nazi propaganda reached a crescendo when the British and Allied forces made their way out of Dunkirk, having "fought down to the last Frenchman." The English had tried a cowardly escape but had been "forced to fight against their will" as a result of the onrush of the German advance. In the light of such "craven behavior," was more proof needed that the English system was unjust, that their plutocracy was sick, and that the Wehrmacht should eject them from the soil of Europe?

At Dunkirk the facts would have spoken for themselves. But Goebbels took the occasion to launch a bitter attack on Churchill whose speech after the Belgian surrender he called an "unparalleled perfidy." All Churchill wanted was for the Belgians to bleed themselves dry to cover the English retreat. Just as in the case of Poland and Norway, he had betrayed another ally. He had turned on the Belgians, giving his soldiers free reign to plunder and rob, all the time claiming that he was there to protect them. What a protector, shipping out his army at Dunkirk, loaded down with Belgian loot in a callous display of "allied unity." These "English criminals" know neither justice nor military virtue. Churchill, according to Goebbels, now added insult to injury by deriding King Leopold for his justifiable decision to save his troops from needless death and suffering, instead of delivering them up to become English slaves.[62]

The OKW report of May 30 told the frightening tale of Dunkirk: "The great battle of Flanders and Artois is approaching its end with the annihilation of the English and French armies deployed there. Since yesterday the expeditionary army is in complete disarray. It is fleeing into the sea leaving its vast war matériel behind. The enemy, either swimming or in small boats, is attempting to reach the English ships lying at anchor which our Luftwaffe is pounding with devastating effect."[63]

The Nazis embellished their reports with appropriate commentary: the German pincers were closing in and were about to win the greatest military victory since Cannae.[64] The success of the German operations was the result of a brilliant strategic plan which called for speed, encirclement, and complete destruction of the enemy. According to Major Carl Cranz, the English flight was the "death dance of Dunkirk," the end of the empire, a battle of annihilation which ushered in a new era in world history.[65] The lesson was clear: if ever a total victory had been won in battle, Dunkirk was its symbol.[66]

On June 4, the day the Germans captured Dunkirk, the OKW published its first extensive communiqué on the war in the west. It clearly had Hitler's stamp upon it, claiming that the battle in

Artois and Flanders would go down in military history "as the greatest battle of annihilation in world history"; it was won by the heroism and glory of troops inspired by the moving force of National Socialism, whose heroic spirit ensured an esprit de corps precluding the chance for a second "miracle of the Marne." According to the report this explained why the Allied forces of England, France, Belgium, and the Netherlands gave up 330,000 prisoners of war and why the military hardware of seventy-five to eighty divisions was completely lost to the enemy. The Luftwaffe had taken its toll on the English as well, and the OKW claimed to have sunk twenty-four warships and sixty-six merchant vessels. On the other hand, not a single German ship had gone down. The OKW reported 10,000 German dead and 43,000 wounded. The reward for this heroism had been great; not only had the Netherlands and Belgium surrendered, but the forces of both England and France had been routed. And of great importance for the future, Greater Germany now controlled the entire eastern and southern coasts of the North Sea and the Channel.[67]

Hitler released an order of the day to the "Soldiers of the Western Front" extolling their military virtues: "My trust in you was boundless. You have not disappointed me . . . The boldest plan in military history has been successful because of your unparalleled bravery, endurance of hardship, devotion to duty, and your fighting spirit . . ." The battle for the freedom of the German people would continue until the enemy was annihilated. "All Germany is with you in spirit," he concluded.[68]

When the Dunkirk withdrawal ended and the Wehrmacht was preparing for the drive against the French forces in the south, Günter d'Alquen, the young, articulate editor of *Das Schwarze Korps*, excited the romantic imagination of the World War I front generation as he scanned the gently undulating hills of Flanders, the battleground for so many at a time which now seemed so distant. His lines convey the rhapsodic ecstasy of those days:

We would have nothing today were it not for the sacrifice of those lying here in countless graves who are celebrating a proud resurrection and to whom we offer fervent gratitude, deeply humble yet proud.
Langemarck is not far from here. Perhaps many of us without knowing it are passing over fields once soaked with the blood of our fathers.

The sun is hot over Flanders's green meadows. Spring is everywhere in all its glory, so fresh and bracing, and the columns move forward along the broad highways toward their last victories for the great Reich.[69]

Now that the campaign had been won for all practical purposes Hitler permitted Mussolini to enter the war against France. On May 30 the Italian ambassador Dino Alfieri visited Hitler at the *Felsennest* and delivered Mussolini's offer to enter the war a week later. Hitler, who wanted to commence his southern offensive from the Somme-Aisne front at that time, politely turned down this proposal and wrote a warm letter thanking Mussolini for his support and asking him to delay his declaration of war. The Duce agreed and postponed the undertaking until June 10.[70] Hitler was thereby assured that he would not have to share the role of conquering Caesar with his comrade to the south.

The Führer needed the Duce for symbolic and propaganda purposes; he harbored no illusions about the potential of the Italian armed forces. But the theme of a united Fascist front was purchased at considerable cost to Goebbels's efforts; Italy was to become one of his most unrelenting problems until the end in 1945. Even before the Duce opened his much heralded "Alpine front" against France, the Germans were suspicious of him and mocked him unmercifully. As early as the first week of the war in the west, the Germans had been complaining about the Italians. "Why hasn't Italy entered the war?" was the question so often asked. Reacting negatively to Mussolini's pompous anti-English speeches, the German people were of the opinion that the time for speechmaking was over, whereas the time for action was at hand. "Italy apparently wants to enter the war after it already has been won" was the general reaction to the flamboyant Duce.[71]

The Associated Press caused Goebbels some headaches over Alfieri's visit with Hitler on May 30. Goebbels also conferred with Hitler on the same day, leading the foreign correspondents to speculate that they were meeting to formulate a propaganda release in connection with Italy's declaration of war, which appeared imminent. When Goebbels learned that the Berlin office of the Associated Press had teletyped this interpretation by way of Switzerland, he was outraged.[72] In order to quiet the rumors he wanted little or nothing to be said about Italy, and he demanded extreme caution in handling the Italian question until further notice.

The stage was set for Italy's declaration of war when the Wehrmacht met with success in its southern pincers operation. Although Mussolini declared war against France and England on June 10, his forces remained immobile for over a week. They did not attack until June 19, and the modest success they enjoyed was solely the result of their being supported by the Germans who moved against the French positions from the rear.

Nevertheless, the Nazis attempted to cloak the Italian entrance into the war with the glory of the Caesars. Goebbels's directive called for special editions to report what he termed the exceptionally intense, emotional, even ecstatic German response to their great Fascist ally's action, a falsification which in no way reflected the average German's true feelings on the matter. There was no shortage of material to cover this "act of world-historic importance" which included the Duce's speech in Rome, the German government's declaration of gratitude, the Führer's telegrams, Alfieri's speech from the balcony of the Italian embassy in Berlin, and "the enthusiastic rallies of the Berliners at the embassy and throughout the Reich." Goebbels went the limit to cultivate pro-Italian sentiment and endeavored to create the impression that Italy's struggle "shoulder to shoulder" with the German Reich was of the greatest importance. But the more Goebbels tried to quell criticism of Italy, the more widespread it became.[73]

Hitler's telegram to the Duce was featured to buttress the pro-Italian propaganda:

The world-historic decision which you announced today has moved me deeply. The German Wehrmacht is proud to be able to fight at the side of its Italian comrades. Growing disregard of Italian national interests by the power brokers in London and Paris . . . has brought us together in the great struggle for the freedom and future of our peoples . . .
Duce of Fascist Italy! Be assured of the eternal fighting spirit of the German and Italian Axis.[74]

Photographs showing Hitler and Mussolini in conference were prominently displayed under the caption "Two Peoples—Two Leaders," and Admiral von Prentzel published an article claiming that the Italians were the dominant naval power in the Mediterranean.[75]

A picture of the Duce in a characteristic arrogant pose, helmet tightened for action, was featured along with an article in *Das Reich* touting the considerable military strength of the Italian armed forces.[76] Photographs taken at Hitler's meeting with Mussolini at the Brenner Pass in March 1940 appeared as well, to emphasize the close cooperation the two leaders had demonstrated throughout the war.[77] But the entire campaign had all the force of an ant swimming upstream; the German people remained unconvinced.

The SD reports substantiate the claim that the Italian declaration of war caused little excitement in the country. Instead, the overriding sentiment was that the Wehrmacht should have administered the coup de grace alone; Italians tagging along in the field would only mean trouble. Some with genuine foresight warned that ultimately Germany would have to step in to defend the Italian interests throughout the Mediterranean area. Those with the best memories even recalled the "Italian treachery of 1915."[78]

When it took the "mighty Italian war machine" over a week to budge, German criticism became more outspoken, a situation very disconcerting to Goebbels. He spread the rumor through whisper propaganda channels that an immediate Italian advance was undesirable for reasons which must remain secret and that Mussolini would attack at the most propitious moment.[79] A week later matters had become even worse. Although the Italians managed to launch an offensive, it ground to an immediate halt, and the discrepancy between their performance and Rome's exaggerated news releases became ever more glaring. The most notable example of this occurred when the Italian press announced a "Major Attack on the Alpine Front" at the very time that the Germans were engaged in peace negotiations.[80]

Goebbels, in a desperate but futile effort to quiet the complaints which were filtering down to Italy and were threatening a crisis in German-Italian relations, once more ordered the media to take steps to improve the situation. "The press," he urged, "was to tactfully counter the rising tide of contempt and hatred of the Italians."[81] As an alternative to reporting on the performance of the Italian troops in the field, it would be better if the press were to ignore news from the Alpine front and concentrate on how helpful the Italians had been during the past winter. Matters reached a new low when a radio station carried a feature on salad preparation at the very time that Hitler was meeting with the Duce in Munich on June 18.[82] The drama at Compiègne temporarily overshadowed this particular problem, but tempers ran high as the Italians gained the spoils of victory paid for by German blood.

The stirring events in France at once terrified and captured the world's imagination. Paris, so long the goal of troops shackled in a hopeless war of attrition from 1914 to 1918, fell to Hitler's Wehrmacht on June 14. The way was thus opened for one of the wildest spontaneous celebrations of the entire war, as people became delirious upon hearing news which seemed to assure the capitulation of France and a rapid end to the war.[83]

For the first time since 1871, German soldiers marched into Paris:

We bow our heads awed and moved by the greatness of this hour. All our feelings, all our thoughts are turned to those who sacrificed their lives to gain this victory. The clipped march of the German battalions which passed in review on this hot summer day before the magnificent palaces of the French capital stirs in our hearts anew. And the oak leaf crown which adorns their foreheads we also place in this unforgettable hour on the helmets which crown the simple wooden crosses between the Somme and Aisne and Seine and Marne. Living and dead, the fighting and home fronts, everything which is German in the whole world is immersed in the strains of a ceremonial hymn of jubilation, pride, and mourning.[84]

Paris had an indescribable hold on every soldier who marched past the commanders assembled to review them on the Place de l'Etoile. Officers and enlisted men alike, whether they were educated or uneducated, understood the significance of Paris and the grip it held on the civilized world. But in Nazi jargon Paris was the "playground of the Jews" and a "parasitical ruling clique," the breeding ground of filth and evil which Hitler would restore to its former greatness. The Nazis made much of the disciplined entrance of the troops into Paris, which was declared an open city. Neither robbery nor pillaging was said to have marked their coming, only the pounding of the jackboots on the boulevards as the field-gray columns advanced to embrace elusive Marianne, the capital of the French Empire.[85]

Paris had a peculiar fascination for Hitler for two reasons, which he revealed during the course of his dawn visit to the city on June

28.[86] First and of greatest importance it had been the capital of Napoleon's empire, and Hitler paid a visit to his tomb at the Invalides, where the quiet of the Paris dawn mingled with his own thoughts of past and future grandeur. Moreover, Hitler was attracted to the architectural beauty of the city, which served to inspire his own monumental building plans to make Berlin a suitable habitation for a war god. Hitler's "official" architect Albert Speer accompanied him on his tour of Paris with this end in view.[87] Paris was for Hitler both a symbol of bygone greatness and an admonition of what he must accomplish in the future.

The fall of Paris spelled the imminent capitulation of France. On June 17, Pétain called for armistice negotiations with the Germans, a step which was announced with fanfare in the Reich. For the record, Hitler was to meet with Mussolini to agree on the positions to be taken during the subsequent armistice negotiations.[88] Accordingly, the two leaders rode in triumph through Munich on June 18 and carried out their discussions at the *Führerbau*. A communiqué announcing Hitler's "complete agreement" with Mussolini on the future course of the armistice negotiations was undescriptive in the extreme.[89] Anyone doubting the nature of the Führer-Duce relationship had only to await the armistice negotiations at Compiègne where Hitler, feeling no compulsion to share the glory, excluded Mussolini. The Italian-French armistice was completely separated from the German negotiations and was signed in Rome.

Goebbels served a dual purpose by intensifying his last minute anti-French propaganda campaign. First, he wanted to avoid the possibility of any falsely sentimental pro-French opinion in the country; the French would receive the stern but just punishment they deserved. German control must become so complete that the French could not threaten the Reich's security "for three or four hundred years," he submitted. Goebbels's second motivation was precautionary in nature. He ordered the continued coverage of the progress of the campaign, understanding that a long lapse might ensue between the announcement of armistice negotiations and the actual signing of a peace treaty. This would tend to avoid unnecessary disappointment should the consummation of the victory be delayed.[90]

Goebbels was beside himself when the June 18 issue of the *Völkischer Beobachter* made a mockery of his directives. Not only did the Berlin edition carry the headline "France Capitulates," but page one featured a nostalgic article stressing the pathos of Pétain's address to the French people. What made the matter worse was that the story focused on Pétain's role in World War I when he was acclaimed as the savior of Verdun. The *Völkischer Beobachter,* the organ of the NSDAP, was thus used to exemplify poor reporting.[91]

As mop-up operations progressed, Goebbels's caution proved unnecessary. The presentation of the German demands before the French representatives was scheduled for the afternoon of June 21 in the forest of Compiègne. Goebbels set to work to prepare coverage on this event, never divining that this would be the last such victory he would have to celebrate. Compiègne represented the height of Hitler's power and prestige, and he personally planned the drama to take place there, employing every possible historic and symbolic nuance to be savored as all France lay at his feet. At Compiègne Hitler was his own propagandist.

Compiègne, as Hitler staged it, had a fourfold message. Above all, it symbolized victory for the corporal who, like all soldiers of the German Army, experienced a profound shock when Germany announced its surrender on November 11, 1918. As Hitler strutted from one French victory monument to another on that warm June afternoon, he suddenly paused and read the following inscription: "Here on the eleventh of November 1918 the criminal pride of the German Empire . . . was vanquished by the free people which it tried to enslave."[92] As the Führer raised himself to his full height and spread his feet in a gesture of defiance, he was acting for his World War I comrades-in-arms. Compiègne represented the consummate revenge for this German soldier who after 1918 unfurled the banners anew with the slogan, "Comrades, you were victorious after all!" (Ihr habt doch gesiegt!) The battles of the Marne, Verdun, and the Somme were all relived at Compiègne.

Not only was Compiègne a personal triumph for Hitler, but it also was an act of revenge on behalf of the Wilhelmine Reich against the scandalous Versailles Treaty. For that reason Hitler ordered that the identical railway car in which the German delegates had signed the armistice on the morning of November 11, 1918, be returned to the sacred ground where it had stood just twenty-two years previously. It would now be a silent witness to the turning of the tables as General Keitel presented the terms of Germany's demands to the French delegates, General Huntziger, Ambassador Noël, Vice Admiral Leluc, and General Bergeret.[93] Hitler was surrounded by several leading Nazis as he entered the wagon-lit to present the German demands to the French delegation. He personally inserted the following message in the preamble, which Keitel read aloud:

when the historic Forest of Compiègne was chosen for presentation of these conditions, it was to wipe out once and for all in an act of just retribution, a memory which was no heroic chapter in the history of France, but which the German people felt was the worst humiliation in world history.

France has been defeated and broken in a single campaign of bloody battles. Germany does not intend to demand from such a brave opponent humiliating armistice conditions nor will it engage in abusive armistice negotiations.

The aim of the German demands is 1. To end the fighting 2. To gain security in the continued struggle against England which was forced on Germany 3. To provide the basis of a new peace, which will deliver retribution for the injustice done the German Reich at bayonet point.[94]

Hitler put his triumphal afternoon to a third purpose—to warn England that they would also do well to sign peace with the Reich. As Hitler marched out of the railway car past the honor guard and listened to the band strike up the national anthem and the *Horst Wessel Lied,* the ceremony took on as much meaning for the English as for the French. Although his "final peace offer" to London would be announced a few weeks later, his intent was already clear: either a peace treaty or annihilation.

Hitler lent to Compiègne yet another meaning, one which offered cohesiveness and unity to all the others, for in his mind it had ensured the success of all Germany's aims. The victory over France, hegemony on the continent, revenge for Versailles, and fulfillment of the mission begun in the Great War would never have been possible, Hitler believed, had it not been for the birth of National Socialism. If Marx and Lenin could point to the dialectic in history guaranteeing victory, Hitler spoke instead of the mythical oneness of blood and soil, of strength and virtue, of valor and struggle to greatness;

Compiègne symbolized this forward surge, this movement in history. The point was not lost by Wilhelm Weiss whose report on Compiègne pointed out the strange coincidence that June 21, the day the ceremony was held, also had a celestial importance. For June 21, 1940, was the day of the summer solstice. The meaning was clear. As the heavens moved, so moved the Greater German Reich! The new Germany must prevail.[95]

Goebbels's extreme caution in reporting the events at Compiègne led to one of the great news leaks of the war. Fearful that direct radio coverage from the railway car would invite unsolicited and undesirable remarks from the French delegates which would embarrass the conquerors, Goebbels ordered that a transcription of the proceedings should first be brought to Berlin to be evaluated there by a team headed by Fritzsche; only then was the minister to make the final decision on the direction the news would take. The delay which this involved opened the way for William Shirer to release the news to the United States that the French had accepted the German conditions and had signed the armistice at 6:50 on the evening of June 22. This meant that the American public was informed of the signing some two to three hours before the Germans themselves.[96]

Goebbels did not release word of the German-French armistice until June 25, while the clauses of the Italian-French agreement were held back yet another day.[97] The announcement of the conclusion of the French armistice negotiations was elaborately orchestrated. After the fanfare and the communiqué, the national anthem and a verse from the hymn "Nun danket alle Gott" were played. Finally, following a pause, the strains of the *Englandlied* were played, to remind everyone where the next piece of business lay.[98]

Hitler addressed the following proclamation to the nation: "German people! In only six weeks of heroic combat your soldiers have concluded the war in the west against a brave opponent. Their deeds will go down in history as the most glorious victory of all times. We fervently thank Providence for his blessing. I order that the Reich flag be flown for ten days, and the bells be rung for seven."[99] Hitler, always longing for the strength of the lion, the agility and grandeur of the eagle, could think only in extremes; the victory, his victory, was the greatest ever to be experienced in world history.

Goebbels, whose loose interpretation of truth was notorious, switched propaganda gears on June 25, 1940, to correspond to the new situation. Quite without warning he ordered that "the hate propaganda against France must cease immediately."[100] The *Frankreichlied*, the song of the campaign, was not to be played again. Bygones were bygones, and an anti-French propaganda posture would only be detrimental to relations between Pétain and Hitler. The French campaign ended as it had begun—with all propaganda weapons trained on England.[101]

The propaganda apparatus responded to this directive, but only too well. No better example of this could be found than in Goebbels's own *Das Reich*. The same issue which carried news on Compiègne showed photographs of German soldiers taking in the sights of Paris, wondering at the architectural beauty, and buying silks, perfumes, and other luxury goods for their wives, lovers, and the folks at home. It must have occurred to some people that this was rather difficult to reconcile with Goebbels's and Rosenberg's warnings of just a week before about "Negroid, Jewish Paris."[102]

The general impression to be culled from German propaganda after the armistice was that it was regrettable that France had to become involved in the war at all. After all, the real fault lay with the English who had influenced the leaders in France to wage war against a Germany which only wanted the best for the French people. Pétain came off looking not unlike a grayed Siegfried figure, summoned from the past to save France and to join the Führer's surge to greatness. Hitler himself had a weakness for field marshals of World War I vintage. The anti-Semitic and generally Fascist tone of the Vichy regime was given favorable comment in reports on France.

By July, pro-French sentiment had become so widespread that Goebbels had to call a halt to it. In the years past, he said, Germans had indulged themselves in a "kitschigweiblich" sentimentality which played a significant role in Germany's missing some of its best historic opportunities. Now the same thing was happening once more in the form of misguided propaganda on France and its leaders. He admonished the press and radio corps "to make France unpopular once more."[103] Despite these directives, the pro-French trends remained essentially unchanged. The more Goebbels attempted to make the French less popular and the more he tried to reverse German attitudes toward its Italian ally, the less success he enjoyed in both endeavors. Anti-English propaganda worked at cross purposes with the anti-French motifs. It was impossible to evoke a poisonous anti-English feeling and expect this hatred and distrust automatically to spill over the Channel to France. The basic "hate England" propaganda strategy, which was overriding, tended to cast any resentments against France into the shadows.

If Pétain's actions were too pro-German and sympathetic to Hitler in the early days of Vichy, it was a problem Goebbels would have welcomed later in the war. But in 1940 it served as a source of embarrassment to him, because it tended to ascribe more prestige and power to France than the Nazis desired or than even an objective assessment would permit. What especially disturbed Hitler and Goebbels was that hardened Nazis fell into the "trashpile of sentimentality" even after the German Wehrmacht had taken only six weeks to rout the forces of France and all its allies. At the end of July 1940 he called a halt once more to "the flood of articles on Vichy, Paris, and France in general." "France as a great power is destroyed and will never rise again," he declared, and added for good measure, "As far as Europe is concerned, France is a second rate nation."[104] Ultimately Goebbels suggested a course which he might well have ordered weeks before—he warned his subordinates simply to keep quiet on the whole subject.[105]

Luxemburg, Alsace, and Lorraine were annexed and brought "home to the Reich," although Hitler did not include this among the armistice provisions. The Battle of France had thus reunited "blood with blood," and Versailles, which has subjected these purportedly "German provinces" to foreign rule, was avenged. As the Wehrmacht advanced across the Rhine into Strasbourg and took one fortress after another along the Maginot Line, the feuilleton featured romantic poems and "homeland" articles, hymns of devotion to "Germanic" Alsace and Lorraine. They were reminiscent of the propaganda of an identical genre which accompanied the return of Danzig and the Corridor to the Reich. Professor Kurt von Raumer, in the article "Between the Rhine and the Vosges" published in *Das Reich,* heralded the "liberation" of Alsace and Lorraine which had been German since the Allemani tribe first sank their spears in the soil of the area. Photographs of farmers in the fields, of valleys, hills, and castles all were used to transmit the message that Alsace and Lorraine were German. "These territories," von Raumer concluded, "bespoke through blood and history their perpetual marriage with Pan-Germandom."[106]

Goebbels attributed the "greatest military victory of all times" to the entire German racial community. To win the battle, individuals had delivered themselves to the greater good of the whole: "The German Reich idea and the national ethos of the German racial community have received the most noble consecration and the ultimate glorification through the fighting, dying, and victory of the German soldier."[107]

The meaning of Compiègne was given visual manifestation in the documentary film *Sieg im Westen,* a rapturous glorification of armed might in the service of a criminal cause. Released in 1941, the film was divided into three thematic areas. To set the stage, it first demonstrated just what it was that the German Wehrmacht was protecting, featuring scenes of the Germanic countryside, children playing, peasants working in the fields, sheep grazing, and other examples of the *Heimat* genre against a peaceful, bucolic panorama. The Peace of Westphalia, the encirclement motif, the "hunger" blockade after 1918, and the dictated peace of Versailles all led up to the theme of the most recent threat to the Reich—English and Allied armies poised to plunge a dagger into the Ruhr in 1940. Should they have been successful, the future of Christian civilization would have been in doubt, a point made more graphic by scenes of German soldiers entering a French Gothic church which had been "bombed by the enemy." A common soldier moved by the greatness of his mission struck the chords of a Bach fugue to lend new dimension to the profound fact that the Battle of France was a struggle for civilization itself. Elaboration of the racial underworld theme was provided by footage of gyrating French colonial troops participating in a tribal dance. To dramatize English arrogance, strains of the popular song "We'll Hang Our Washing on the Siegfried Line" served as musical accompaniment to the evacuation at Dunkirk.

Traditional German military elitism was blended skillfully with repeated affirmations of determined National Socialist leadership. The result was the stereotype of the "German fighter" which cast

Aryan man in heroic poses on the classic Greek model. He was less an individual than he was a type; strength, pride, and courage were his hallmarks.

Scenes depicting Hitler's strike westward conveyed the impression of relentless forward movement, professionalism, and invincibility which was enhanced by scenes of men moving bravely into action armed with the ultimate in weaponry and military hardware. Songs and marches eased their fatigue. One never saw a dead German soldier in the entire film—only troops grimly determined on victory shown in battle or moving ahead on their forward march. The impression was one of comradeship, unity, and élan in the service of Führer and Fatherland. After all, as the commentator noted, they were deciding the course of history for the next thousand years.

The climax of the film depicted Hitler's moment of triumph at Compiègne. With the clear intent of linking God's will with Hitler's mission, *Sieg im Westen* drew on the strains of the Old Netherlands Hymn of Prayer, now put to use to serve a cause far different from that of its Calvinist composer:

> We gather together to ask the Lord's blessing;
> He chastens and hastens his will to make known
> The wicked oppressing now cease from distressing:
> Sing praises to his Name; he forgets not his own.
>
> Beside us to guide us, our God with us joining,
> Ordaining, maintaining his kingdom divine;
> So from the beginning the fight we were winning;
> Thou, Lord, wast at our side: all glory be thine!
>
> We all do extol thee, thou leader triumphant,
> And pray that thou still our defender wilt be.
> Let thy congregation escape tribulation:
> Thy Name be ever praised! O Lord, make us free![108]

With Providence supporting the Wehrmacht's victory, surely England would be punished as well. The Battle of France was over. The Battle of Britain could begin.

VII The Battle of Britain

Before the Battle of Britain, Nazi propaganda on the English question had reflected a measure of constraint attributable to the fact that Hitler still clung to the chimera that England might sue for peace. Once the Führer had realized the hopelessness of this illusion, Goebbels in turn could begin a campaign in which his invective knew no restraint. Driven by a burning hatred, he waged the propaganda war against England with piercing blows embellished and styled with cynical finesse. He seemed to delight in the assignment.

German propaganda before the Battle of Britain had featured the theme of the "Plutocratic-Jewish" domination of the "pirate state England." Anti-English tracts, some crude and others based on pseudo-scholarship, flooded the bookstalls after September 1939. Martin Dibelius's *British Christianity and British World Power* and Giselher Wirsing's *100 Familien regieren England* competed for the public's attention with *My Lady* and *My Lord* and countless pamphlets on English "air piracy."[1] Goebbels's speeches and columns in *Das Reich* became the focal point for what he claimed was an increasing worldwide recognition of English perfidy. Directive after directive issued at his daily press conferences ordered the intensification of the anti-English propaganda campaign.

The alleged English conspiracy to rule the world was an integral part of the assault. Their far-flung empire not satiating an inordinate lust for power, the "plutocrats" were taking steps to control the four corners of the globe. Jewish financial interests and English lords who had sold their birthright to the Jews were combined in a plot to achieve this horrendous objective.[2] England's goal was to annihilate Germany, to destroy the accomplishments of the Third Reich, and to enslave a brave people.[3] The "plutocrats" had commenced their work of destruction in Poland, Scandinavia, France, and the Low Countries. Although soundly defeated there, they continued to violate all the rules of warfare by initiating a campaign of "air piracy" over Germany. What made it worse, according to Goebbels, was that the English criminals held the Bible to their hearts and spewed forth hypocritical prayers to conceal their atrocities. His *Reich* editorial of June 16, 1940, expressed the quintessential racist statement of the war against England: "The English are firmly convinced that God is an Englishman. In their character mélange of brutality, mendacity, sham piety, and sanctimonious Godliness, they are the Jews among the Aryan race."[4]

Churchill became the symbol of "Perfidious Albion." He was "Plutocrat Number One," a whisky-guzzling, cigar-chomping, bovine, decadent liar, who hardly could be classified as a member of the human race. He was leading his people to destruction and most assuredly would go down with them. England now stood alone, its dupes having been betrayed one by one; now its hour of destruction was at hand. According to *Das Reich,* "Churchill doesn't know how to get his head out of the noose."[5]

Goebbels, realizing the added dimension that music gave to his propaganda, fostered the *Englandlied* which became the symbol of the struggle against England.[6] Based on the World War I poem by Hermann Löns which the bandleader Herms Niel—the darling of the *Wunschkonzert*—put to music in 1940, the song of the English campaign became very well known indeed. "Denn wir fahren, denn wir fahren, denn wir fahren, gegen Engelland!" was the famous line which caught on so readily. As the Battle of Britain neared, it was played following the Special Announcements and on other ceremonial occasions as well. Not only Goebbels, but von Brauchitsch, Raeder, and Göring realized that it enhanced the Wehrmacht's prestige and they called for its frequent use.[7] The strains of the *Englandlied* conjured up memories of World War I:

Today we'll sing a little song,
We'll drink our cool wine,
and our glasses will ring out
Because we must, we must depart.

Give me your hand, your sweet hand
Goodbye, my darling, goodbye, goodbye
For we sail, for we sail, for we
Sail against Engelland, against Engelland, Ahoi!

Our flag, it waves on the mast,
Announcing our Reich's power,
Because we'll no longer let
The English insult it.

If the news comes that I have fallen
That I'm sleeping in the waves, don't cry
For me my darling and remember
My blood flowed for the Fatherland.[8]

Anti-English sentiment was brought to a fever pitch, and there was widespread anxiety to get the "final campaign" of the war started. The RAF bombing offensive was taking its toll, although it had not yet begun in earnest. After a few raids over German cities, there were demands that London should be annihilated as revenge. According to the SD, the country was "waiting with increasing anticipation for the great attack against England . . . since the feeling of hatred . . . could not reach a higher pitch than it is now."[9]

As the nation awaited a mortal blow similar to that inflicted on Poland or France, rumors assumed an increasingly sinister form. Talk of "miracle weapons"—such as "liquid air with electronic dust" which would instantaneously kill anything in its path or new bombs which were so heavy that no single warplane could carry more than one of them—became commonplace. Some rumors curiously reflected current innovations in weapons technology. An example of this was speculation about future German use of a revolutionary new aircraft which could fly over 1000 kilometers per hour. This was an accurate prediction of the jet project which was begun later in the war and then sidetracked.[10]

The British attack on the French fleet harbored at Mers-el-Kebir, which resulted in the sinking of several capital ships on July 3, offered Goebbels a striking propaganda issue. Sensing the embarrassment which Mers-el-Kebir caused Churchill and the English, he immediately launched a vituperative propaganda campaign around the general theme that England's "betrayal" of France was more obvious than ever, now that the "English pirates" had engaged in a savage surprise attack on their own ally. The English had now outdone their Dunkirk caper with a brutal act which would go down in history as the model of villainy between one ally and another at war, the antithesis of Germanic *Bündnistreue.* If there were any decency left in England, he argued, the responsible elements would demand Churchill's immediate resignation.[11]

Hitler returned to Berlin with appropriate pomp on July 6. Goebbels had prepared the capital for a magnificent victory celebration, complete with flower-strewn streets, courtesy of the maidens of the *Bund deutscher Mädel* organized for the occasion. Although Hitler would have infinitely preferred a feeler from London indicating that England was ready at last to talk peace, no such peace offer was received. Still clinging to this forlorn hope, Hitler took the occasion of his Reichstag speech on the evening of July 19 to offer Churchill a settlement once more. According to impartial observers, the Führer was in his best oratorical form that evening, and his style reflected more the mood of a man confident of victory offering a just peace to the weak than that of one consumed with hatred and fear. Hitler, posing as one who meant only the best for the English people, made his "final peace offer":

My conscience now dictates that I make one more appeal to reason in England. I am in a position to do this not as the vanquished asking for something, but as the victor calling for reason. I see no reason why this war must go on. I deplore the carnage which will result. And I would like to spare my own people . . . Mister Churchill might brush off my pronouncement with the cry that this is only proof of my fear and doubt in our final victory. At least my conscience will be free after what follows.[12]

On the same evening that Hitler offered peace to the English, he awarded the spoils of victory to his generals in the form of rank and decorations. Göring, beaming like a schoolboy, headed the list with his new designation as Reichsmarschall. And in a move which he would later have cause to regret, Hitler named no less than twelve field marshals and promoted nearly thirty other high-ranking officers.

These were the victors of Poland, Norway, and France, and Hitler, the "greatest field marshal of all times" at the height of his own military glory, would suffer no loss in prestige by honoring his military men. This celebration, comparable only to the pageantry of Rome and the Caesars, would be the last of its kind. The day of blitzkrieg victories was over for good with the exception of the peripheral Balkan interlude in the spring of 1941. Never again would Hitler shower his generals with such recognition. On the contrary, more and more they were to become the objects of his distrust and symbols of a Prussian elite out of step with the National Socialist revolution.

The English were not long in answering Hitler's new tender of peace. Within an hour after the conclusion of his Reichstag address, the BBC had categorically refused the German offer. Should there have been any lingering hope in Hitler's mind, it was dashed by Foreign Minister Lord Halifax's radio broadcast three days later. The English, he said, would go on fighting, no matter what the cost.[13] The die was cast.

Goebbels spoke of Hitler's peace initiative as if it were one of the missed opportunities of world history: the plutocrats did not want peace, they wanted war. Although they might speak of fighting on "no matter what the cost," Goebbels answered that it wouldn't cost the rich lords a shilling, for they had transferred their wealth to safe foreign havens for the duration. The good hard working, respectable people of England would have to suffer instead. Goebbels dismissed Lord Halifax's use of the term "determination" with a singularly cynical retort. It was this same determination, he said, which left Warsaw a rubble heap, which led "cowardly" Queen Wilhelmina to demand that the Dutch continue the battle after her escape, and which inspired Reynaud, "once he himself was off quite safe," to demand that the *poilu* continue his senseless resistance.[14] Goebbels ordered that from now on the English were to receive the full propaganda treatment and that the anti-English propaganda, which had been tempered considerably before Hitler's peace offer, was to be set on a war course.

Strict instructions followed forbidding speculation about the nature of the coming attack against England. The public, on the other hand, had begun a spate of rumors about an invasion even before Hitler dictated orders for "Sea Lion" three days prior to his Reichstag address of July 16.[15] Hitler took the next decisive step in preparing "Sea Lion" on August 1, when he issued Directive Nr. 17 which called for stepped-up air and naval activity against England.[16] The success of any invasion attempt would depend upon German air superiority and to achieve it he commanded Göring to commence an all-out offensive against the RAF.

The Battle of Britain falls into three distinguishable yet overlapping phases. The first ran from August 13, which Göring named "Adler," until September 17. This was the period of the classic dog fights and Channel battles which witnessed Göring's unsuccessful attempt to wipe out the RAF in the skies. Stage two consisted of the blitz against London and lasted until late November 1940, merging with stage three which saw the Luftwaffe turn against England's industrial centers in raids beginning in November. It peaked with the famous bombing attacks carried out against Coventry and Birmingham, but continued roughly until May 1941 when Hitler set about to launch the Soviet war.[17]

Goebbels's propaganda campaign during phase one of the Battle of Britain led to an extremely overoptimistic appraisal of German chances for victory among the public. During the period of relative quiet between Hitler's Reichstag address of July 19 and *Adlertag* on August 13 when Göring could finally launch his air armada following repeated cancellations owing to poor flying weather, Goebbels had a problem on his hands. A Reich accustomed to blitz victories could not understand the reason for the delay.[18] As Goebbels observed, the public during the first week of August expressed anxious complaints about the delay in launching the Battle of Britain. But when it did commence, the reporting on German exploits would not leave them disappointed.

The thrust of Nazi propaganda during August and September was that England was approaching its doom. This in turn led to the popular conviction that the war would soon be ended with a total German victory. And although Goebbels time and again tried to condition the people to expect another war winter, his own enthusiastic accounts of the "air victories" over England were counterproductive. Ultimately he would have cause to regret the direction of his propaganda campaign.

On the eve of *Adlertag,* Rudolf Hess, addressing the faithful in

Vienna in connection with von Schirach's recent appointment as gauleiter, predicted that the Battle of Britain would destroy the British Empire: "England will be amazed at the power that the German nation can muster, when all its strength is brought to bear in this war." [19] Churchill, he said, had refused to make peace after an honest offer on the part of the Führer and would now have to suffer for his mistake. The irony was that it would be Churchill himself who would have the last say in the Battle of Britain. And English endurance would inspire the loyal paladin Hess to undertake his hazardous flight to England nine months later in his hopeless attempt to arrange peace.

The air battle had no sooner begun than the Nazis, characteristically, touted the campaign as unique in world history. The clear inference to be drawn was that a Luftwaffe blitz would work as smoothly as the campaigns in Poland and France. Nothing would deter the victory of Göring's air force; the strategic initiative, technical superiority, and skilled, inspired pilots guaranteed it.

Reports from the skies over England sang the praises of the young German pilots. Typical of this genre was that of war reporter Fritz Mittler whose eyewitness description of the "Horst Wessel Squadron's Greatest Day" captured the drama and tension of the Battle of Britain:

The great call to battle arrived. Shortly after lunch we are huddled around the staff captain who announced that we were off. The engines of our two-motored fighters are already roaring, singing the song of battle. Clouds of sand and dust whirl about the field as we fly off to meet the enemy . . .

We come closer and closer to our goal. The flight directly below us is to attack an airfield in the vicinity of the large passenger airport of Croydon. Now it is slowly coming into view . . . But we do not remain mere observers of this gigantic bombardment. *The first enemy fighters appear, Spitfires and Hurricanes.* And now the dance breaks loose. We have been waiting for it. They didn't name our planes "Destroyers" for nothing. We not only destroy these enemy attacks, we destroy every enemy fighter that comes in sight. The plane dives and plunges, swerves and lunges, fires its machine-guns and shells, and the motor howls—all this seems to take place at once . . .

Now we too enjoy the luck of the fighter corps. A Hurricane has just veered off before us and escaped the guns of the Messerschmitt

110 . . . but we've got a bead on her. I hear the crack of gunfire
lacing the air, and move into a climb. I see the Hurricane falling
like a wounded bird with flames pouring out of her, until she plunged
into the water not far from the mouth of the Thames. And then
our guns are ablaze once more . . . and this Hurricane has enough
too and it shares the fate of its predecessor . . . I was thrilled to
have taken part in this battle . . . But what was even greater was
the news we got when we landed that our wing chalked up six
kills and that the whole squadron, our *"Horst Wessel" Squadron*,
knocked out five English aircraft on that day.

The name of Horst Wessel means the ultimate in devotion to duty.
With hard-earned pride German fighter pilots bear this name in
battle—until the final victory is ours.[20]

Such rhapsodizing became commonplace during this phase of the
war and added to the prevalent mood of overconfidence. There
seemed to be truth in the claim that the final destruction of England
had begun when Goebbels announced the "total blockade of England."
A nation which had grown fat while German children starved in
the dark days of 1918–1919 was now to pay a long overdue bill,
and with interest.[21]

When the German air armadas were grounded for several days
because of inclement weather, English counterpropaganda claimed
that the RAF had written an end to the German blitzkrieg. This
led to a violent reaction from Goebbels who offered the cynical
retort that "a couple of rainy days will not save the Empire."[22] He
ordered a full propaganda return blast against London, stressing
themes which he hoped would be effective for domestic consumption
as well.[23]

He had other problems to handle, the most disturbing of which
was the effect the RAF bombing raids were having on German morale.
At the time when Germany was supposed to be dealing a death
blow to its mortal enemy across the Channel, the English were flying
bombing missions of their own across the length and breadth of
the Reich. The English raids were not on any large scale whatsoever,
and their effect was mainly symbolic. But the propaganda value
of the August attacks on Berlin and Hamburg was immense. Germans
could not reconcile Göring's boasts about the strength of German
air defense and his periodic threats of revenge with the fact that

night after night and day after day they had to run for cover in the air raid shelters.

Goebbels used two techniques to counter the propaganda effects of the English raids. The first of these involved the repeated assertion that most of the raids caused little or no damage. The second was a good deal more subtle, with Goebbels turning to his favored ruse of dispatching foreign correspondents as guests of the Propaganda Ministry to targets which the BBC claimed had received serious damage. For example, following the English raid on Hamburg in early August the minister sent representatives of the foreign press corps to check at first hand the BBC assertion that the port had been pulverized. As Shirer, a witness on that day, has written, there was indeed very little damage to be seen. "The port," he said, "had not really been affected by the bombings."[24] And it surprised him that the RAF had not done more damage after two months of continuous bombing.

In a lead story in the *Völkischer Beobachter* which had Goebbels's stamp on it, the minister attacked "Churchill's lie" that Hamburg had been demolished as a "fantastic British fantasy" engendered by their "fear psychosis." Citing the evening New York papers which had been "written by Jews" all too eager to swallow the "ridiculous English deceptive maneuver," Goebbels launched a vicious attack on the English:

The conclusion to be drawn from this revolting nonsense is obvious: *conditions in England are abominable . . .*

It demands a considerable lack of judgment and even incompetence to take the fearful outbursts of these helpless bankrupts seriously and to trumpet them as the story of the day. How often the world has been shamelessly lied to by London in this war . . . and how preposterous these lies were which were conceived only to conceal the miserable state of affairs in England.[25]

Goebbels's second technique to counter the bad impression engendered by the bombing was to claim that the English spirit of inhumanity drove them to bomb targets of no military value whatsoever, thus consigning helpless women and children to a flaming death. Not only were these raids in violation of international law, Goebbels charged, but they proved that the English humanitarian propaganda was bankrupt. And the pilots whom Churchill dispatched on these terror missions were no longer men representing a proud imperial military tradition. Instead, they were beasts of the air, pirates on the wing.

According to Goebbels, English pilots who had no appreciation for Western civilization had the temerity to attack some of Germany's most famous and sacred cultural shrines. Who but a beast could bomb Goethe's garden house and the Goethe Park in Weimar?[26] Who but a culture destroyer would have the gall to bomb Bismarck's mausoleum at Friedrichsruh? In this manner Goebbels, who was extremely sensitive to the English charge that the Nazis were determined to destroy all things of cultural value, tried to negate this telling Allied propaganda motif.[27] After the raid on Berlin on the night of September 11, he flew into a rage of pious indignation.[28] Why, he asked, would the English kill women and children in the capital of the Reich? For what purpose did they bomb the Brandenburg Gate, the Reichstag, and the Academy of Arts? For nothing more than a criminal prank, he supposed.

Goebbels cited the British attack on the Bethel hospital complex near Bielefeld on September 19—which killed nine epileptic children and wounded twelve others—as the quintessence of the English contempt for the human race. He offered the explanation that the strength of the German air defenses triggered the English atrocity. The RAF pilots, he claimed, having been beaten back from flying farther into the heart of Germany, looked for easy targets upon which to unload their bombs. Seeking false glory on the cheap, they decided to go for preschool hospital patients.[29] The Bethel raid was widely covered in both radio and press accounts and served as useful material for newsreel editors as well. Goebbels observed that the same people who had enrolled Christ as their new ally—and had distributed a million and a half crucifixes to prove it—had already betrayed Him just as they had Poland and France in their hypocritical self-righteousness.[30]

But counterpropaganda could not conceal the Party's increasing embarrassment about the bombing. Had Goebbels been in a position to seal off the damaged areas and to avoid public mention of the subject, he most assuredly would have followed this course. But this option was not open to him, and even attempts at limited coverage backfired, because no subject offered itself as better material for rumors. Nazi propaganda notwithstanding, the German people began to speak of the RAF with respect.[31]

Hitler addressed the nation on the evening of September 4, as stage one in the Battle of Britain was about to reach its climax. Speaking from the Berlin Sports Palace, he gave full vent to his hatred of England. Seldom had the Führer indulged in more bitter sarcasm than when he directed his comments to the English tuned in across the Channel. Promising the Germans that he prepared every move with great care in an unhurried, self-assured way, he delivered this cynical question to his listeners: "And if they become curious in England and ask 'Well, why hasn't he come?' Just wait, he's coming. Don't be so curious all the time." Motivated by his own desire to have ended the campaign in August, he was forced to substitute bluster for victory. He dealt with the RAF bombing of the Reich in the same manner: "If the British air force drops two, or three, or four thousand kilograms of bombs, then we will drop 150,000, 180,000, 300,000, 400,000, a million kilograms." The threats reached a climax as Hitler blared, "And if they announce that they are going to launch massive attacks against our cities—then we will pulverize their cities. We'll put a stop to these night pirates, so help me God."[32]

Within a matter of days the Germans began full-scale attacks against London. From September 7–17, Göring committed his entire armada.[33] Victory hung in the balance as the RAF dueled with the Luftwaffe in the battle which would prove so decisive in the future course of war.

This was to be Göring's grandest hour, and much to his delight photographs featuring him in various command poses became standard front page copy: the Reichsmarschall peering through binoculars across the Straits of Dover; the Reichsmarschall smiling as he and his staff watched Luftwaffe formations converge over the Channel, target London, from the "Holy Hill" at Cap Blanc Nez along the coast; the Reichsmarschall stooping over an operations map with an appropriately heroic look on his face, an affectation which he shared with Mussolini; the Reichsmarschall receiving the reports of his pilots just back from the travails of the air battle.[34] To demonstrate that there was at least one field marshal who knew no fear, he himself flew a mission over London on the evening of September 17, much to the dismay of Hitler. This caused some consternation among the public as well, who feared for the safety of their "Hermann," and Goebbels was forced to block news of the flight.[35]

Göring was the heir to the tradition of Baron Manfred von Richthofen, the nation's leading air ace of World War I, who was celebrated anew during the Battle of Britain in a poem by Heribert Menzel. Entitled "To the Young Dead Hero," it romanticized the exploits of von Richthofen with Nietzschean ecstasy. The message to the Reich's young fliers was obvious:

Glimmering he climbed towards the opening, and he caused the heavens to thunder, out of the grey cloud bank he came like the flaming lightning, Hunted an eagle among the sparrow hawks and drove it back in a rage, and how many he forced down lifeless.

He flew alone, it seemed he was charmed, his glory was in the stars, Idolized, boys sang songs for him, Far off in the homeland mothers prayed for him, and his bold face inspired his comrades.

Germany, with silver wings he climbed high to the heroes, to the Gods, they loved him and we sang of his immortality, they heard our prayer and nodded assent, they gave him to us forever, his upraised face peered from the ruins.

The God remained silent and legends lingered like clouds over the ruins and we did not muse on the hero. Brave, proud face, you pure youth, you bring good fortune to our dreams, you are our model in all battles.

Who would say that a hero dies? Even in ten thousand years his name will cause enemies to tremble and will make hearts ready to dare the impossible as he did, if that must be. Knowing what he expects, he flew the gleaming cornet's path for many.[36]

At the same time that Goebbels warned his subordinates not to make it appear that the end of England was near, both the radio and the press followed exactly this course.[37] Day after day until the middle of September headlines spoke of London as a "city damned," helpless before the onslaught of the German Luftwaffe which "reigned supreme over London." Churchill was violently attacked for not providing adequate bunker shelter for London's poor, while his clique of lords enjoyed the good life in their luxuriously outfitted bomb shelters.[38] This, the Nazis charged, was the prime example of an unjust state, pursuing an unjust war by unjust methods. Simultaneously the Party tried to show that Germany was attacking only military targets in London, in contrast to the English "terror flights" over Germany. Goebbels's *Das Reich* devoted its September 15 issue to the air war over England under the headline "The Just Answer: Why London Burns." The entire gamut of anti-English propaganda was mustered to demonstrate that from the first day of the war the English had provoked Hitler until he was forced to mete out the punishment which they deserved.[39]

Goebbels continued to foster whisper propaganda about the coming invasion of London, until Hitler postponed "Operation Sea Lion" indefinitely on September 17. Fritzsche visited the coastal areas in France which allegedly were "teeming" with preparations for the coming invasion, and he returned to deliver the appropriate propaganda material to the media. The thrust of his message was that the invasion would come off without a hitch no matter what the time of year or weather conditions, once German air superiority over England had been "stabilized."[40] Even after the 17th, rumors about the coming invasion continued to circulate, a situation which Goebbels encouraged. For the time being, the theme was too useful as propaganda against England.

The propaganda disseminated during the Battle of Britain was counterproductive to a great degree. Nothing illustrated this more clearly than the candid SD reports which disclosed just how poorly the propaganda campaign had fared. According to one of them, people were complaining about the fact that the air battle was "lasting so long." After all, they said, "if Warsaw and Rotterdam fell in a matter of days, certainly London could not hold out for more than three weeks."[41] This alone reflected an astonishing naïveté regarding the differences between the Polish, Dutch, and English campaigns. The nation, not to mention the leadership, was very slow to realize the seriousness of the RAF's challenge to the Luftwaffe. Some were so poorly informed that they believed that if the Luftwaffe really bore down on the English the campaign could be ended rapidly. It seemed inconceivable that any enemy in the world could successfully defy Hitler.

At the end of September the truth about the Battle of Britain was revealed when Goebbels implied in *Das Reich* that there would be no invasion of England in 1940. The final victory had already been guaranteed on the continent, and the only thing left undecided was the exact timing of the British defeat. There was "no time limit on this," Goebbels wrote, "although Germany would like to shorten it." A public experienced in picking up signals could chirp, "Nightingale, I hear you singing."[42] Victory was not in sight, and they could count on another war winter.

Nevertheless some overzealous writers went about their business as if nothing had happened. Their reports might well have been adaptable to the Battle of France, but hardly to the campaign against England. With all the passion of an inspired Hitler Youth, one propagandist submitted a report which included these fateful lines: "Now we await the orders of the Führer. We are ready at a moment's notice to carry the flag of our victorious revolution against England and to raise it over the British Isles."[43] The report was censored for obvious reasons.

Other evidence that the tide had turned against the Reich in the Battle of Britain came with the realization that the *Englandlied* had been phased out toward the end of September.[44] No longer did a trumpet blare followed by the now familiar lines conclude Special Announcements, OKW communiqués, and *Wunschkonzerte.* The campaign song was relegated to the archives, and Goebbels took steps to eliminate other popular songs like "England, We're on Our Way" and "Infantry to England," offering the lame excuse that some of the verses were "rather Bolshevik" in tone.[45] This ridiculous contention could not belie the fact that the Wehrmacht simply was not going to invade England.

Although Goebbels initiated an "anti-illusion campaign" in October 1940 and made every effort to convince people that England was in a hopeless position even if its demise was not imminent, most Germans remained unconvinced.[46] It was generally agreed that even if only half the German claims were true, then the staying power of the British public was commendable.[47] There was also a good deal of skepticism concerning the exceedingly high claims of English aircraft losses. People turned more than ever to the BBC for a closer look at the news.

The continued bombing raids over the Reich were hardly calculated to spread confidence. As the traumatic effect of the first few attacks was experienced, Hitler began to receive heavy deliveries of mail from anxious parents, appealing to him to send their youngsters to the protected villages and countryside.[48] As the months rolled by and it became clear that civilians were indeed in great danger, Hitler decided to expand the administrative apparatus of the "Fresh Air for Children" program—begun by Baldur von Schirach in peacetime—for the new situation. Care was taken to avoid use of the word "evacuation." The first group of children left Berlin on October 7, 1940, and they would be followed by some 250,000 in 1941 and thereafter by millions seeking the safety of the countryside.[49]

Their evacuation led to rumors reflecting irritation and fear over just what this precaution revealed about the German war effort, and the cloak of secrecy which enveloped the evacuation worsened the spreading doubts. Goebbels, who had ordered that there was to be no public mention of the youngsters' transfer, himself was to blame for the fact that the public was unprepared for the measure and thus reacted in an emotional and frightened manner.[50] Their shock took many forms. One soldier's wife wrote her husband at the front that a Party man had just stopped by their house and said that the evacuation of their children was not mandatory but that those who did not cooperate would be placed on the "extra list," a euphemism for uncooperative individuals certain to be punished.[51] Goebbels took steps to correct his tactical error by threatening any persons who spoke of a mandatory evacuation with incarceration in a concentration camp, and he ordered a "person-to-person" propaganda campaign stressing the voluntary nature of the operation.[52]

Subsequent propaganda dealing with the evacuation theme was unconvincing. Richly illustrated booklets bore the message that the Reich's children were safe and sound tucked away in the Alps, at the shore, or in some sleepy Moselle village. Photographs of pretty girls and of ardent, blond youths set off against appropriate scenic backgrounds conveyed the distinct impression that they were experiencing National Socialist tourism rather than an improvisation caused by inadequate air defenses, a kind of "Strength through Joy" for tiny tots. *Youth in the Reich* carried the following Hitler quotation from the 1930s as a dedicatory message which should have caused even the dullest minds to pause and think: "It is your duty to get to know Germany so that you learn to love it with all your heart."[53]

The combined effect of the failure to defeat England, the bombing raids, and the evacuation of the children spread a mild panic throughout the country. A Baden-Baden luxury hotel offered "peace and quiet from the nightly air raids" to those who could afford the time and the price. Evacuees from Berlin spread the rumor in Dresden that English fliers had dropped bacilli of an unknown disease, thus starting the spread of a plague which was raging out of control. Another tale had it that a whooping cough epidemic in the capital had forced the closing of all children's clinics, and that the disease was spreading to Dresden and beyond. According to another story, children refused to enter the bomb shelters because they could not stand the sight of the dead.[54]

British propaganda leaflets capitalized on this insecurity. Germans supporting the Allied cause were enlisted to prepare leaflets which by all appearances seemed to be official Nazi Party communications. One of these, allegedly distributed by the "Kreisleiter," conveyed a message from a Party mother figure, or, in Party jargon, the "Kreisfrauenschaftsleiterin," which spoke to the situation of the German woman. Whereas one of the great fears was that the nation would have to endure another war winter, the "Party representative" warned that a harsh winter lay ahead and that even more serious food and coal shortages would ensue. The women were advised to hoard foodstuffs as a precaution—a violation of government statutes on hoarding. Finally, playing on the fears related to the air war, the "representative" told them to sell their heavy inflammables and to buy gold and jewelry which they could easily carry with them out of the bombed and endangered areas. Leaflets of this nature were effective, and Goebbels made it known that he wanted to be informed about the wording of every last one dropped over the Reich.[55] As it developed, the dreaded food and coal shortages occurred before winter had really set in.[56]

As late fall faded into winter, German hopes for a final victory in 1940 gradually died out. Hitler was forced to substitute bombast and arrogance for an announcement of final victory. His speeches of September 4, November 8, and December 10, 1940, as well as that of January 30, 1941, reflected the altered situation. Although the Führer promised in September that "we're coming," by January he was warning that the British would meet disaster should they try to invade the continent.[57] His claim in Munich's Löwenbräukeller on November 8 that Churchill had decided to attack the Reich with his weakest weapon, the RAF, had an especially hollow ring. He and Molotov carried out some of their discussions a few days later in the Reich chancellery bunker where they had sought refuge from British bomb loads. This led Molotov to raise the reasonable query regarding just whose bombs were pounding Berlin.[58] The propaganda effect of the raids was so adverse that the anniversary speech of January 30, 1941, had to be held at the uncommon hour of 4:30 P.M. which defied Nazi tradition but was necessary because the English had made a habit of paying visits to rally cities on anniversary nights.[59]

Some people began to pin their hopes for final victory on a spring offensive and were encouraged by Hitler's speeches which stressed Axis solidarity, the Wehrmacht's supremacy, and the German direction of the entire economy of Europe.[60] Some even looked for a German landing in England when the weather cleared in the spring. But repeated air attacks against the Reich cast doubt on Hitler's boast that a final victory was assured. Little did the public divine that as a result of Hitler's failure to gain air supremacy over England, which was a prerequisite for "Sea Lion," he had decided to strike east against the Soviet Union; he issued the necessary orders for "Barbarossa" on December 18, 1940.[61]

During the late fall and winter Goebbels went to great lengths to take the edge off the disappointing outcome of the Battle of Britain, stressing that for all intents and purposes the English were defeated but that it took time to wear down an old, decrepit world empire. He repeatedly directed the media to play down sensational announcements (e.g., "Southhampton No Longer Exists"), warning that this would raise unwarranted expectations about the imminent fall of England.[62] With the coming of the new year, he ordered that bombing news be relegated to the second page, except for raids of extraordinary importance. Cynical reporting on Churchill and "English hypocrisy and deception" became standard fare during the period before Germany's Balkan offensive in the spring of 1941. For understandable reasons, the anti-English propaganda campaign of the 1940–1941 winter was received with a grain of salt and not a little resentment.

It was an impossible assignment to bridge the gap between Theodor Seibert's remark in the *Völkischer Beobachter* in October 1940 that "the fact that we are standing here at Cape Gris Nez itself guarantees our victory" and the back page coverage allotted to the air offensive against England in the new year.[63] Goebbels tried to mitigate this psychological disadvantage, but with meager results. Following the November Coventry raid his staff trained its guns on the English denial of damage to Germany's war industries, observing that "judged by this madness, Shakespeare's Falstaff was a blunderer."[64] Churchill's "rape of human reason" defied description, and "he has a lot to learn before he reaches his quiet, secure haven in Canada."[65]

In what was to be his final Christmas message to the German people Rudolf Hess echoed the official optimism that the English cause was lost: "Let England wage an air war just as long as it wants to. But without a doubt the day is coming when she'll be at the end of her rope."[66] And before England reached that point it would have to endure unspeakable suffering for its arrogance. According to *Das Reich,* the English "trudge down night after night into the subway shafts, sit there for fourteen hours in dirt, misery, defecation, and disease, and wait for the miracle which Churchill has promised them."[67]

Exactly when the Germans lost the Battle of Britain is debatable. But symbolically the defeat was registered when Rudolf Hess flew to England on May 10, 1941, to seek an accommodation with Churchill.[68] At the greatest risk to his own personal safety and reputation he attempted to gain two objectives: to fulfill Hitler's dream of cooperation and peace with England and to avert Hitler's need to attack Russia, which Hess correctly judged would destroy his leader, the Party, and the nation. His decision was inspired in part by the credence he gave to dreams and to the mystical world of astrology, which only reinforced his determination to save the Third Reich. Hess dreamed that his former professor at Munich, the famous geopolitician Karl Haushofer, bid him to carry out a mission of world-historic importance to England. Having obtained the use of a Messerschmitt 110, he was successful in getting a copy of the current cross continental air security zones.[69] Hess instructed his adjutant to deliver a letter of explanation to the Führer several hours after his departure.[70] Hitler was astounded by the message and said that he hoped Hess would "crash in the ocean." The news brought about a major crisis in the Party; for one solid week the Hess case dominated the Nazis' attention.

Goebbels admitted that he had spent some sleepless nights in fear that the English might exploit the Hess affair in their propaganda, and his first reaction was to order an official silence in the German press and radio.[71] The conference Hitler held with his Reichsleiters and gauleiters at the Obersalzberg on May 13 determined the direction of German propaganda regarding the affair, which resulted in the bewildering diagnosis that insanity had driven Hess to his deed. According to the official account released to the media on May 14 which established the Party line, the moonstruck Hess had become obsessed by the idea that he could effect an understanding with England by personally communicating with the Duke of Hamilton. In his desperation Hess had been encouraged to act boldly by mesmerizers and astrologers, to the point where he believed he could avert "the total annihilation of the British Empire." The official communication concluded that "the National Socialist Party regrets that this idealist fell victim to his crazed ideas."[72] So much for the official line.

It was a great relief to Goebbels that the English did not wage a concerted propaganda campaign regarding the Hess affair. Nevertheless the Party had to deal with a psychological problem of the first magnitude, which Goebbels compared to the Strasser, Röhm, and von Blomberg affairs. As the minister told his assistant Rudolf Semmler, the flight of Hess was the propaganda equivalent to the desertion of an entire army corps.[73] As always when the objective situation seemed the most depressing, he resorted to the Hitler myth, the Nazi moral equivalent of the Christian belief that all things work together for good to those who believe in him. In his words, "We believe in the divine mission of the Führer. We know that in the end what appears to do us the most harm has worked in our best interest."[74]

Goebbels took steps to transform Hess into an "unperson" on the model so common under the Stalin regime. First, following his May 19 summary of the affair to his staff, during which he asserted that the policy of "dead quiet" had proved successful (after all, he had just come from Aussee in Gau Upper Danube where he had mixed among the people—simple farmers and woodcutters—and their opinion was that the Hess flight was only a "razor knick on the German face"), Goebbels declared that the case was closed. Woe be it to the editor or commentator whose lips should utter the name of Hess! Next, he sent a directive to all Party offices ordering that their copies of Hess's photograph (de rigueur in Nazi offices just like those of the Führer) were to disappear immediately. Then the Army officer corps was warned not to allow troop morale to fall noticeably as a result of the behavior of the Deputy Führer. Finally, knowing full well that Germans who ever listened to the BBC would surely take this opportunity to get at the truth, he reiterated the warning about the severe penalties for listening to the enemy radio and announced some recent sentences from the Special Tribunals for "Radio Criminals" of from four to six years' imprisonment each.[75]

With these steps Goebbels was able to offset the worst effects of Hess's precipitate action. The first popular reaction was one of dismay and depression which led to one of the most remarkable outbursts of rumors during the entire war. According to one of them, the following men had been summarily executed: the Party ideologue Alfred Rosenberg, Agriculture Minister Darré, the Reich Protector of Bohemia and Moravia von Neurath, as well as Gauleiter Wagner of Munich. Further, the gauleiter of Franconia, Julius Streicher, along with Count Helldorf, Berlin police president, had been arrested. One rumor proved to be correct—that the airplane manufacturer Willy Messerschmitt had been arrested along with many other close associates of Hess, including his wife, Ilse, and Professor Haushofer.[76]

A rash of rumors could be overcome easily enough, but the loss in dignity to Hitler and the Party elite was another matter. People were not about to believe that Hess had suddenly lost his mind. If that were so, why was it that the Party allowed an insane man to keep his position as Deputy Führer for so many years? There were many jokes about this particular inconsistency, and when the chief interpreter of the Foreign Office Paul Schmidt returned from Rome, his gardener asked him, "Did you know that we were being ruled by a lunatic?"[77]

As the months and the years rolled by and as Rudolf Hess became but a faded memory, Nazi Party men still thought of him as a dedicated National Socialist who had sacrificed his reputation in the service of Hitler and the war effort.[78] But whereas the mock heroic flight of Göring over London symbolized Germany's drive for total continental power, that of Rudolf Hess radiated the sick smell of defeat.

VIII Balkan Interlude: Spring 1941

Much of the winter of 1940–1941 was devoted to naval propaganda which dominated the news while Hitler laid plans for the offensive in the east. German naval strategy was based on the conviction that England could be defeated by a blockade which would cut off the foodstuffs and raw materials vital to its war effort. Although both Admirals Raeder and Dönitz had been hurried into the war long before they felt the Navy was ready to fulfill its strategic role, they undertook their assignment with vigor and limitless energy. And though their tactics embraced a combined air, surface, and underwater offensive, hope for ultimate success was placed in the submarine fleet.[1]

The Naval High Command based its victory target at 750,000 tons of enemy shipping per month, and it was reckoned that a year of such pressure would bring England to heel. During the second half of 1940, the Germans consistently sank 380,000 to 450,000 tons per month—July 1940–March 1941 resulted in 3,080,060 tons—a figure disturbing to both Churchill and Dönitz but for different reasons.[2] Nevertheless the Germans maintained a facade of complete confidence in victory and Admiral Raeder declared in a speech to Bremen shipyard workers in January 1941 that "today we are faced with the fact that England is moving ever more swiftly toward its unavoidable demise. No power on the earth can deter the force

141

of destiny." In 1941 the German Navy would succeed where it had failed in 1917, he concluded.[3]

Raeder scorned the United States for the Lend-Lease Agreement which provided Great Britain with fifty vintage destroyers, and the complaint was often repeated in 1941 as Nazi hostility toward Washington became increasingly intense. The *Völkischer Beobachter* launched a tirade following one of President Roosevelt's "fireside chats" on lend-lease, asserting that "even if they were able to deliver the goods, they would arrive too late anyhow."[4] Goebbels's caustic *Reich* article entitled "Britannia Rules the Waves" wove variations on this theme, and an official naval spokesman claimed in a radio address in the spring of 1941 that England had not faced such danger "since the days of the Spanish Armada."[5] The general impression conveyed was that the submarine fleet, the "Stukas of the sea," was in complete command of the situation, and, operating with the four battleships *Scharnhorst, Gneisenau, Bismarck,* and *Tirpitz,* represented an unbeatable combination.

Several major reversals dispelled this chimera. Two of the Reich's leading U-boat commanders were killed and a third was taken prisoner in March 1941. Prien, the hero of Scapa Flow, went down on March 8 in U-47 after tangling with Convoy 293, and a week later Kretschmer and Schepke were lost as the destroyers of Convoy HX. 112 made a mockery of the Nazis' naval propaganda.[6] With the loss of Prien and Kretschmer Germany was deprived of two of its most popular heroes, and thereafter Goebbels terminated the naval propaganda based on the deeds of individual submarine commanders.[7]

The shock had hardly abated when news was received that the *Bismarck* had been sunk following a hunt by seemingly half the English fleet. *King George V, Prince of Wales, Repulse, Victorious, Reknown,* and *Ark Royal* were all deployed in an effort to destroy the *Bismarck,* which had been engaged against the battle cruiser *Hood* which was sunk on May 24. Following a bitterly fought engagement, the *Bismarck* was sent to the bottom on May 27 as she steamed toward a haven on the coast of France.

Poor communication between the Navy and the Propaganda Ministry exaggerated the effects of the reversal. Although the authorities had several days to prepare the public for the bad news, they did not avail themselves of the opportunity. Instead they covered the sinking of the *Hood* with considerable fanfare, and the OKW communiqué made matters worse by announcing that the "battle was proceeding without German losses." Then abruptly the last message from Fleet Commander Lütjens to Hitler from the *Bismarck* was released: "Ship unmaneuverable. We are fighting to the last shell. Long live the Führer!"[8] The predictable result was that the public was not only disappointed, but angered as well.

Serious complaints about news management further complicated the picture.[9] Germans who tuned in the BBC learned of the disaster hours before word of it was released from Berlin. Furthermore, it appeared strange to many people that a sudden "illness" forced the cancellation of Fritzsche's caustic and witty commentary on the news and that Goebbels avoided the issue entirely in the subsequent issue of *Das Reich*. Finally, the loss of the *Bismarck* was irreconcilable with the current line from Berlin on the decline and fall of the Royal Navy. Goebbels hastened to alleviate the negative effects of his naval propaganda by giving dramatic coverage to German successes in Crete; further, he became increasingly involved in coverage of the dramatic sequence of events in the Balkans.

In an attempt to secure his right wing for the coming Russian offensive, Hitler prepared to act decisively in the Balkans during the spring of 1941. Hungary and Rumania were already aligned with the Axis bloc, and Bulgaria joined the Three Power Pact on March 1, 1941. Yugoslavia was the last holdout, and after spirited diplomatic bargaining with both Berlin and London, the government of Cvetkovic rather haltingly signed the Three Power Pact on March 25. Thus the ethnic tug of war in Yugoslavia between the Serbians, who would never align with Germany, and the Croats, who would hear of nothing else, apparently had tilted in favor of the latter. But even before the new treaty with the Axis could go into effect, a coup d'état staged by Serbian nationalists led by General Simovic forced Prince Regent Paul into exile, thus transferring power to King Peter II, a youth in his middle teens. Hitler, concerned by anti-German demonstrations in Belgrade and the pledges of support for the regime by the church, Serbian nationalists, and the military, decided to deal with Yugoslavia mercilessly.[10]

Goebbels initiated a propaganda campaign to prepare public opinion for the coming events in the Balkans. This included charges of English aggression in Greece and references to the inorganic Yugoslavian state allegedly composed of a collection of mutually hostile races. "Chauvinistic Serbian power seekers" were said to be charting a dangerously belligerent course vis-à-vis the Reich. German propaganda was so suggestive that it led to rumors about the Führer's plans to handle the situation. Goebbels warned his staff that public opinion had outraced the course of events; they were to tone down the campaign but to "keep the fires stoked" nonetheless.[11] Hitler's offensive in the Balkans, begun on April 6, ended this tactical problem.

Hitler established the propaganda guidelines for the Balkan offensive in an emotional "Proclamation to the German People," in which he asserted that the real enemy in Yugoslavia and Greece was England, not the peace-loving populations of those nations.[12] Some disreputable Greek and Serbian leaders had sold their nations' independence for English Secret Service blood money. As a result, the only possible way to guarantee justice and reason to the area was for the Wehrmacht to make its might known there. Hitler promised that the Reich would continue the fight until the last Englishman had fled from the Balkans.

Meeting with his staff at the outbreak of the campaign, Goebbels launched a tirade against Yugoslavia's "seventeen year old king who was not mature enough to master the intricacies of his toy horn and peashooter, but who now had the audacity to stumble onto the world stage by betraying the world's leading power." He had ample material on hand to appeal to every ethnic group in the Balkans; in Yugoslavia, this meant tossing bones to the Serbs, Croats, Slovenes, and even some Ruthenians, among others.

Goebbels laid stress on the necessity to condition the German people not to expect a blitz victory like that of 1939–1940. The terrain, he said, made a longer campaign mandatory, and bitter guerrilla fighting could be expected. To avoid the mistakes he made during the Norwegian offensive, Goebbels demanded caution in covering what he termed a peripheral campaign. German romantics who might take pity on the Greeks were to be discouraged from confusing Socrates and Plato with the contemporary "clique of mercenaries" operating in Athens. Finally, he proposed the *Prinz Eugen Lied* as the official song of the Balkan campaign.[13]

Goebbels was unrelenting in his claim that "he who marches with the English, marches to his death," and he cited the bitter experience of the Poles, Norwegians, Dutch, Belgians, and French. The fate of misguided politicians in Greece and Yugoslavia would follow this pattern, and one day soon they would quietly retire from their homelands and take up residence in a London luxury hotel where they would join Beck, Pierlot, and Sikorsky in a melancholy game of Europe in a sandbox. As for the English, they could be expected to bid their erstwhile allies "bye-bye" at the opportune moment and ship out for home as they had in France.[14]

The Yugoslavian forces which joined battle with the invaders were woefully unprepared. Thirty to 40 percent of those eligible for armed service were Croats who refused to rally to the banner raised by their Serbian archenemies. The army was poorly outfitted and possessed neither the equipment nor the technical skills to wage modern warfare. Yugoslavia entered World War II without a tank force, and it was at a 4:1 disadvantage in air strength. German troops, attacking from Austria, Hungary, Rumania, and Bulgaria against an enemy virtually surrounded before the first shot was fired, moved ahead at a pace which brought the surrender of Yugoslavia in twelve days. German losses were very light, while the Wehrmacht took 344,000 prisoners. King Peter went into exile in London, the British Expeditionary Force was expelled, and the sovereign state of Yugoslavia, born at Versailles, ceased to exist.[15] Hitler celebrated his victory in a Reichstag address on May 4.

Goebbels was in his element as a result of the victory, and he prevaricated the story that the English—desperate and on the run—had murdered the Greek minister president Koritzis.[16] The fact was that Koritzis could not bear to be witness to a German occupation, and he opted for suicide. Goebbels also warned Roosevelt that he had been promising more than he could deliver to his allies and that he should redirect his course toward a reasonable goal; to deal with England, the quintessence of "Falstaff redivivus," was to court disaster.

He mercilessly parodied FDR's offer to come to the aid of Greece and Yugoslavia in an article reminiscent of Voltaire. It seems that Roosevelt sent his son "Jimmy" as an emissary to faraway lands. His first stop was supposed to have been Belgrade, but the Waffen-SS beat him to it. He then continued his journey to Crete where he met with the king of Greece, to whom he sang a melancholy song about the planes, tanks, and weapons which the United States would have delivered "had events not progressed so rapidly." Then "Jimmy" rushed off to the neighboring kingdom of Yugoslavia. There King Peter asked him exactly how many planes he might expect for the Yugoslav air force. "And Jimmy Roosevelt answered promptly, 'As many as you need, your majesty!' Now the High School Student-King Peter Karageorgewitsch is smart enough to know that it would be better to receive a few dozen planes for his vanished state right away, rather than as many as he wanted after the war from Jimmy Roosevelt. Our chronicler does not inform us if he voiced this opinion."[17] Clearly, the days were past when Berlin avoided the American theme.

During the pause between the German occupation of Crete, May 20–June 1, 1941, and the launching of the war against Russia three weeks later, Emperor Wilhelm II died at his residence in exile at Doorn in the Netherlands.[18] Coverage on his passing was in very low key and went almost unnoticed. The German people were hardly consumed with interest in the kaiser or the Wilhelmine era at this point in their history, and the year 1941 was no time for romantic melancholy and reminiscences of any kind, much less for a man and a period which the Nazis were convinced they had superseded. The result was a bland statement to the effect that the kaiser was dead, that he had always wanted the best for Germany, but that he represented a system which had fallen short at the threshold of destiny.[19]

Hitler did the minimum expected of him under the circumstances. He sent a wreath to the kaiser's funeral where he was represented by Reich Commissar for the Netherlands Seyss-Inquart. A parade in regimental strength paid last respects to the monarch. Professor Karl Richard Ganzer analyzed Wilhelm's career in an article for *Das Reich* which laid bare his weaknesses and which placed the Wilhelmine era in historical perspective. Wilhelm II was not a Führer type, Ganzer wrote; he was more a personality "who wavered ineffectually between performance and fantasy, reason and rhetoric, between instinct and vague mist."[20] Wilhelm II was the symbol of an "unfulfilled" epoch. The message was clear. What the kaiser left unfulfilled, the Führer would fulfill. Within a week the Battle of Russia had begun.

IX The Soviet War: From Minsk to Moscow

Goebbels was faced with a serious challenge in interpreting the Russo-German Nonaggression Treaty, and there is a good deal of evidence demonstrating that he was unable to convince the Germans that the pact was not a tactical maneuver which in time would be reversed. There was barking in the kennels almost from the first, and the situation was exacerbated as a result of the Russo-Finnish war during the winter of 1939–1940. As the SD reports of the period disclose, the public was not so naïve as the Nazi leadership supposed. Goebbels's film release *Bismarck* was timed to lend credence to Hitler's treaty with the Russians by drawing on historical parallels from a period in which German relations with Russia were on a relatively cordial footing. Yet the public could not be persuaded that Hitler and Stalin's "friendship" was genuine when at the very time that *Bismarck* was premiered with appropriate fanfare pretreaty anti-Bolshevik films such as *Henker, Frauen, und Soldaten* and *Flüchtlinge* continued to be screened by reason of a bureaucratic oversight.[1]

Gradually public distrust of Russian aims took the form of rumors about serious differences between Hitler and Stalin during the winter of 1939–1940. Soviet annexation of the Baltic states and the seizure of Bessarabia and North Bukovina in 1940 only spread the conviction.[2] Goebbels tried in vain to reverse the tide of public opinion by ordering his staff to interpret these events in low key to counter the suspicion that the Führer was taken off guard and to minimize the importance of the events in the east in comparison with those in western Europe.[3] The public sensed Hitler's chagrin about the timing and manner of some of the Soviet annexations. As was often the case, some Germans remained one step ahead of Goebbels by divining that Moscow's ultimatum to Rumania had taken Hitler by surprise because the radio and press reports on the seizure began after the Red Army had moved into the disputed territories.[4]

Despite Nazi propaganda, it became increasingly clear to the German people that war with the Soviet Union was inevitable. Yet the façade of friendly relations continued, and in September 1940 the Soviet exhibition at the Leipzig Fair indoctrinated Reich Germans into the delights of life in the Russian proletarian-peasant paradise. SD informers wrote irritated reports about German workers being very impressed by the Soviet exhibition, as witnessed by their cordial remarks in the Russian pavilion's guest book. Some complained that they were not being given a "true" picture of conditions in the Soviet Union by the Nazi establishment.[5]

The German-Italian-Japanese Pact, signed in Berlin on September 27, 1940, a ten-year mutual defense and economic agreement, violated the spirit of the Hitler-Stalin Pact because it conjured up images of a new anti-Comintern alliance. Goebbels took steps to dispel this impression, and *Das Reich* carried an important article by O. P. Häfner denying "the allegations of the allies" that German-Soviet differences in the Baltic and the Balkans coupled with the new agreement with the Italians and Japanese had rendered the Hitler-Stalin Pact a dead letter.[6] To be sure, it was an old trick of Goebbels to link undesired German opinion with "the Allies" in an effort to stamp it out. Here the ruse was broadened to include a discussion on the importance of the German-Soviet trade agreements which provided for Russian delivery of grain, mineral oil, wool, and tobacco in exchange for machinery and capital. *Das Reich* concluded with the observation that the west could not offer the Russians the same advantages and that the ideological differences between nazism and bolshevism were of little consequence compared to the deep cleft separating communism and capitalism.

Molotov's state visit to Berlin in November 1940 presented Goebbels with a problem. Since most Germans knew that there were serious differences between Hitler and Stalin, Goebbels took pains to prepare a reception for Molotov which would not appear overly enthusiastic, but yet would be polite.[7] This resulted in an order that only a moderate number of people were to line the streets to welcome Molotov in Berlin and that Soviet flags would be distributed in limited numbers. Coverage on the visit was extremely low-keyed and concealed the bitter hassle which ensued between Hitler and Molotov over Finland, Rumania, Bulgaria, and the Three Power Pact.[8] Nevertheless there were widespread rumors that war with the Soviet Union was imminent, and there was talk of German troop transfers to the east in preparation for it. Within a month after Molotov had departed from German soil, Hitler issued Directive Nr. 21 for "Operation Barbarossa," authorizing the OKW to commence plans for an attack on Russia.[9] The addition of Bulgaria to the Three Power Pact on March 1, 1941, and Foreign Minister Matsuoka's state visit to Berlin later that month only exacerbated tensions.[10] The overthrow of the Yugoslav regent, Prince Paul, after he followed the Bulgarian example raised German-Soviet tensions to yet a higher threshold. The Russian-Japanese Nonaggression Pact, signed in Moscow in mid-April 1941 further confused the international situation.

During the winter the German High Command began elaborate planning to conceal preparations for the coming attack on the Soviet Union. On February 15, 1941, the chief of the OKW, Keitel, issued a directive outlining a strategy of deception, which he divided into two periods.[11] In the first of these, from February to mid-April 1941, all means were to be taken to maintain complete secrecy regarding "Operation Barbarossa." During the weeks just before the attack, when the German preparations could no longer be concealed, the stratagem was to make it appear that the invasion of Great Britain was about to begin. In an effort to confuse the situation further, appropriately placed sources were discretely to claim that the troop movements in the east were part of "the greatest undertaking in deception in the history of warfare," which was being carried out in order in divert the world's attention from the cross-Channel invasion. German troops were also to be deceived, and Keitel directed that they were to be led to believe that "Sea-Lion" was next on the Führer's agenda, although preparations for it had already been canceled. Even the troops slated to fight on the eastern front were misled by the same story, and the day before the attack they were unsure about their ultimate deployment.[12]

In another directive, dated May 12, 1941, Keitel emphasized the importance of misleading both the Wehrmacht and the civilian population.[13] Deceptive rumors, which Keitel hoped would quickly find their way back to Germany, were to be spread among the troops. One of these rumors, which he himself suggested, was that the divisions in the east were to be transferred to staging areas on the coast of France. Simultaneously with this artifice, the High Command would break the eastern divisions' mail connections with the homeland, thus stimulating the kind of atmosphere in which rumors thrive. To maintain secrecy within Germany, Keitel also assured that the Reich ministries would continue their preparations for the invasion of England. He authorized the naming of English interpreters as well as other persons who were to take part in governing a conquered England.[14] Some of Keitel's directives were ingenious; for example, Minister of Armaments and Munitions Fritz Todt was authorized to transfer a number of his personnel from the western coastal areas to the east so that they might spread rumors to the effect that the preparations for the invasion of England were progressing apace.[15]

Goebbels played a major role in the campaign of deception, and he used the medium of his press conferences to mislead not only the members of the foreign press corps, but his own staff as well. He announced to his advisers and section chiefs on June 5 that a landing would be undertaken against England within three to five weeks, and he set them to work preparing material for use in connection with the invasion. For example Heinrich Glasmeier was assigned the task of preparing an "England fanfare" to precede Special Announcements heralding the coming victories, and whisper propaganda channels were to disseminate material about "the coming visit of Stalin to Berlin." State Secretary Gutterer set a team of seamstresses to work in the Hotel Kaiserhof to carry out a "top secret assignment for the Führer"—to prepare Soviet flags for "Stalin's visit." He knew that the Kaiserhof was the best possible launching pad for rumors in Berlin.[16]

Goebbels's conferences with the foreign press were staged with a huge map of England and its possessions serving as a visual background for his remarks. Next he carried out a stratagem reminiscent only of the comic opera, when he published an article entitled "The Example of Crete" shortly before the attack on Russia, hinting that Germany's action in Crete was merely a prelude to a possible landing in England. According to a prearranged plan, Jodl ordered Fritzsche, the chief of the Press Section of the Propaganda Ministry, to recall the "Crete" issues of *Das Reich* from the newsstands, and Goebbels temporarily withdrew "in disgrace" to round out the hoax.[17] For the next few days the minister visited Hitler only in secret, forgoing his customary luncheons at the Reich chancellery. He went to the chancellery for secret visits with Hitler in an unmarked car, his face hidden behind a newspaper.[18] There is no evidence to support Goebbels's exaggerated hopes that the little plot would confuse the Allies. But taken as a whole the campaign of deception most assuredly confused the Germans. Propaganda Staff Chief Werner Wächter remarked that there were so many rumors abroad in Berlin before the Russian campaign "that in the end there wasn't an ass who knew what was going on." [19]

However, some Germans had a very accurate understanding of the future course of the war, despite the government's attempts at concealment. The great majority expected war to come with the Soviet Union sooner or later, and according to the SD report of March 27, 1941, it would break out "after England had been defeated." One rumor even named May 20, 1941, as the exact date for the attack against the Soviet Union, which was in fact the day proposed by Hitler in his Directive Nr. 21 of December 18, 1940. Yet another rumor circulated in May 1941 which held that up to 180 German divisions had been transferred to the eastern borders in preparation for an attack; this was fairly accurate because by May 20, 1941, 120 of the 153 German divisions which would attack a month later were in the eastern assembling areas. As the date of the offensive neared, there was a remarkable correlation between rumor and truth.[20]

The launching of the offensive was the occasion for a long-planned propaganda barrage which once more lent some measure of ideological cohesion to Nazi propaganda toward the Bolsheviks. At 5:30 on the morning of the attack, Goebbels read Hitler's war message to the German people. The Führer's statement represented the link from the traditional, pre-1939, anti-Bolshevik propaganda—which had been interrupted by the temporary pact with the Soviet Union—to the propaganda of the war, which was to become progressively more virulent in tone. Without question, Hitler was on home ground once more. He began by relating his great relief at finally being in a position to speak frankly after so many months of forced silence, months in which he had been burdened by many cares. He had a good deal to explain. Anticipating a propaganda theme that was to be repeated often during the summer of 1941, he offered excuses for ever having made a pact with the Soviet Union in 1939: "I did it only out of a sense of responsibility to the German people," he declared. Hitler offered several examples of Soviet breaches of treaty commitments and touched on points that were covered more extensively in a statement delivered the same morning by von Ribbentrop in a press conference at the Foreign Ministry.

Hitler stressed the Soviet threat to the nation, charging that the Russians had deployed 160 divisions on Germany's border and were poised to attack the Reich. But he had countered their imminent strike with a preventive blow which had saved the homeland from disaster:

But therefore the hour has come in which it becomes necessary to move against this plot of the Jewish-Anglo-Saxon warmongers and of the Jewish rulers of the Soviet Union.

German people! At this moment a movement of troops is taking place which in its scope and expanse is the greatest that the world has ever seen . . . The German eastern front stretches from East Prussia to the Carpathians. . . .

The task of this front is no longer to protect single countries but to ensure the security of Europe and thereby save them all.

I have therefore decided today to put the fate and future of the German Reich and of our people in the hands of our soldiers once again.[21]

Soon after Goebbels had finished reading Hitler's proclamation which described the war as a great ideological struggle, it was left to von Ribbentrop to employ the language of international law in his press conference for the home and foreign press corps which was held in the council room of the Foreign Ministry. Ribbentrop's charges fell into three general categories: Soviet breaches of its treaty commitments with Berlin, its aggressive designs in the Baltic and the Balkans, and its attempt to destroy Germany. The foreign minister claimed that although Germany had carried out its commitments under the German-Soviet Pact to the letter, including adherence to the clearly delineated spheres of influence and the reciprocal nonaggression agreement, Soviet Russia had not followed suit. It had continued the activities of the Comintern, exploited Germany's military gains in Poland, and bolshevized the entire Baltic area in violation of the German-Soviet Pact. Ribbentrop further decried Moscow's strong-arm tactics in annexing Lithuania, Bessarabia, and parts of Bukovina. He charged that Stalin, not content with controlling the Balkans and much of the Baltic area, was about to crown his nefarious plot by striking a dagger into the back of Germany. Hitler's preemptive blow had checkmated Russia so that a superior civilization and culture might "free the way for true social progress in Europe."[22] By stressing Germany's cultural mission, von Ribbentrop attempted to justify a war of aggression. He thereby put international law to the service of the myths of Nazi ideology.

The German propaganda media trumpeted variations on the themes of Hitler and von Ribbentrop.[23] Many newspapers published special editions announcing in bold headlines "The Decision of Fate in the East: The German Answer to the Russian Betrayal."[24] The Führer was applauded for his insight in warding off the danger to the Reich and for uniting Europe in the struggle against the enemy. For months Nazi propagandists reiterated the charge that the Soviets had planned the war for years and asserted that it was only Hitler's decisive action which had rescued Europe from destruction.[25]

During the first days of fighting on the eastern front, the High Command blocked all war news of significance. Suddenly, the tension was broken on June 29 with twelve dramatic Special Announcements written by Hitler himself, each preceded by a musical fanfare. The OKW claimed dashing breakthroughs along the entire front, and the destruction of two surrounded Russian armies was imminent. Motorized and Panzer divisions were reported to have raced past this pocket and to be pushing toward the area of Minsk.[26]

Despite the announcement of German successes, the SD reports reveal that the High Command's policy of withholding major news items and managing the news for propaganda purposes in this manner was poorly received.[27] In this particular case, the twelve Special Announcements were read over the radio at one-hour intervals, and listeners were required to devote an entire Sunday to waiting for them in order to learn of the major war developments. Many people realized that much of the material had been lying on the desk of the Wehrmacht High Command for days. The SD report on the reception of Hitler's Special Announcements reflected widespread resentment, which detracted from the mood of victory he intended to create.

Reich Press Chief Dietrich was adamant in his charge that Hitler had prepared the Special Announcements personally and that the Führer had ordered Goebbels to follow his directions: "Hitler thought the idea brilliant. Then criticisms from an irritated public began pouring in. These criticisms were reported to Hitler, who ignored them and responded with violent fury to all recommendations that the practice be discontinued."[28] Goebbels took steps to head off any such errors in the future. An undated diary fragment revealed his irritation about the incident: "I had a very heated argument with the Führer Headquarters about the way in which we will release the Special Announcements tomorrow. They were actually serious in suggesting once again that they be released piecemeal throughout the day, separated by intervals of an hour or an hour and a half. I regard this as nothing short of catastrophic. We will have the same miserable results as we had the last time. The public feels itself duped, and rightly so; in my opinion they are fully justified in demanding that the Special Announcements should be promptly released . . . I buttressed my case with a whole series of arguments and proofs and was ultimately successful. The Führer ultimately gave me full powers over the Special Announcements . . ."[29] Thereafter, Goebbels made certain that they were presented effectively.[30]

The Nazis experienced similar problems in forging their anti-Bolshevik propaganda. Although they were quick to revive and adapt their traditional anti-Bolshevik, anti-Jewish propaganda to the war situation, they were never able to convince the nation that the war against the Soviet Union was unavoidable and that Hitler had indeed warded off an imminent attack from the east.[31] Goebbels began his vain attempts to argue these points in his *Das Reich* article of

July 6, 1941, in which he linked Hitler's timely strike against the enemy to the "saving European civilization" motif.[32]

Goebbels had a good deal more success with the "Europe united" theme, which emphasized that the continent had never been so unified as it now was and that the Reich and its allies together would complete the task at hand—the destruction of bolshevism. For the time being, Germany's leading role in the struggle was to be played down in the interest of allied unity. The war thus became part of a pan-European historical tapestry. The *Berliner Illustrierte Zeitung* focused its attention on this theme in an article entitled "Against Europe's Enemy and England's Friend," which carried photographs of Italian, Spanish, and Nordic units preparing for deployment against Russia.[33]

Another subject which Goebbels stressed was the horror of life under bolshevism. He issued statements from veterans of the Russian front to make this traditional Nazi motif more credible. His article of September 28, 1941, quoted a letter written by one Josef Zezetka, a soldier fighting on the eastern front, to a local Nazi official of his home town of Donawitz: "I too was never certain . . . and could never believe in its [the National Socialist] greatness. But now I have seen everything and ask even today whether I might be accepted as a member in the great German Workers Party, should I live through the war. In case I die, I will die gladly for Germany. . . ."[34] This letter, Goebbels declared, was from a man who earlier was a dedicated Communist. The minister claimed that this was typical of the countless letters being received in Germany, and he assigned Wolfgang Diewerge the task of compiling several of them in pamphlet form for distribution at the front as well as in the Reich. Diewerge has attested that there was no shortage of documentary material to work with; he had thousands of letters to choose from which had been addressed to the Propaganda Ministry and were in fact unsolicited testimonials from eyewitnesses at the front. The general theme was that living in a good clean German barnyard would be preferable to the filth of Soviet Russia.[35]

Nazi reporting on the progress of Europe's crusade against bolshevism became progressively more strident during the summer of 1941 and peaked with the announcement of total victory in the east in October. Astounding successes on the field of battle brought ecstatic claims of the Wehrmacht's superiority. The *Münchner Neueste*

Nachrichten intoned on July 12, 1941, that the German successes were without parallel in world history. Bialystok-Minsk left the battles of Sedan, Cannae, and Tannenberg in the shadows as successful campaigns of encirclement.[36] By late July the Nazis were claiming that the "enemy no longer operates under a unified command."[37] The campaign, it appeared, was already as good as won.[38]

It has subsequently come to light that Hitler was purposefully exaggerating the OKW communiqués during this period in order to win an important political objective—to bring the Japanese into the war against the Soviet Union immediately. In July 1941 the explosive political situation in Japan culminated in Foreign Minister Matsuoka's fall from power.[39] Matsuoka was unable to steer a course between his own position, that Japan should enter the war against Soviet Russia without delay, and that of his colleagues in the Konoye government who opted for playing the waiting game and continuing the cat-and-mouse diplomacy with Hitler's Reich and the United States. Matsuoka faced powerful enemies at home, including the army, and he could not prevail. All the urging of von Ribbentrop that the Japanese government strike at once against the Bolsheviks came to naught. Matsuoka's many enemies in the highest echelons of power in Japan were too sophisticated to believe von Ribbentrop's assertion on July 1 that total German victory in Russia was but weeks away.[40] Japanese policy at this point was to await the favorable moment to strike the Soviet Union, and the general feeling was that that moment had not yet come, despite German victory propaganda which went far beyond the objective military situation after only one month of the Russian campaign.[41]

The celebration of the Wehrmacht's victory at Smolensk, which netted some 310,000 prisoners in August 1941, was but a prelude to the highly emotional reporting on Kiev in September which, besides resulting in the capture of 665,000 more prisoners, was heralded in the *Völkischer Beobachter*'s banner headlines as "Kiev: Battle Cry of the German Victory."[42] Little did the Nazis realize that Kiev was the last such legitimate triumph which they would have to celebrate in their old style.

During the war, attitudes of the German elites toward the Soviet Union and its various national subgroups were tangled and inconsistent. Hitler never wavered from his opinion that all of the eastern nationalities were by nature inferior to the German race. Himmler and Bormann concurred in this extreme positon. Goebbels at first took the "Russian-Jew-Subhuman" stance, but he later reversed himself radically when the folly of Hitler's *Ostpolitik* was revealed as a major disaster.

Rosenberg, who was appointed Reich minister for the Occupied Eastern Territories in 1941, had his own ideas on the problem. While agreeing with many of Hitler's plans for occupied Russia, he could not accept the theory that all the Russian peoples were subhuman. As Alexander Dallin points out in his *German Rule in Russia: 1941–1945*, Rosenberg held that the Great Russians were the bogiemen, "the kernel and symbol of Russian-Mongol backwardness," and that one must view the nationality problem with this fact clearly in mind.[43]

Rosenberg's policy for the east was based on the hostility toward the Great Russians displayed by the various national groups within Russia itself, and he envisaged a group of buffer states, "protected" by the Reich, to surround the Great Russians. Among them would be the Baltic nations, Belorussia, the Ukraine, the Caucasus, and central Asia. Rosenberg agreed to the policies that united all the Party factions: the Soviet party administrators were to be liquidated, and the Soviet state had to be destroyed.[44]

Dallin distinguishes three major groupings among the Party leaders on the eastern question. Opposing the Hitler-Bormann-Himmler syndicate, which was unalterably opposed to all the eastern nationalities, there were individuals who favored German exploitation of the widespread anti-Soviet hostility within Russia. This group opted for uniting all anti-Bolshevik Russians under the swastika and envisioned a sovereign Russian state as well as independent nationality groupings. Rosenberg took a position midway between these extremes.[45]

Hitler's position has been documented in countless directives as well as in the records of his conversations. First of all, he planned to gain control of the rich agricultural and mineral resources of Russia and at the same time to secure Germany's eastern frontier. He also set great store by his plan to liquidate the Soviet governing class.[46] According to Hitler, a sovereign Russian state of any kind was out of the question. His aims were to control, colonize, and exploit: "Nobody will ever take the east from us! . . . We shall soon supply the wheat for all Europe, the coal, the steel, the wood." He looked forward to the day when the control of Russia would tip the scales of world power in favor of a Europe dominated by Berlin. In such a situation, there would be no fear of a blockade. Space would no longer be a problem, and he would be free to breed a pure race in the conquered territories. Hitler intended to control all the country west of the Urals with an occupation force of 250,000 men and a corps of ruthless administators. He regarded the Slavic population as fit only for slavery: "As for the ridiculous hundred million Slavs, we will mold the best of them to the shape that suits us, and we will isolate the rest of them in their own pig-sties; and anyone who talks about respecting the local inhabitants and civilizing them goes straight off into a concentration camp!" [47]

Hitler was parroted by Himmler, who made several statements to the SS during the war on the subject of Aryan supremacy. The classic remark came in his Poznan address on October 4, 1943, when he declared that it was inconsequential if ten thousand Russian women died building a Panzer trap; what mattered was the completion of the fortification for Germany. Moreover, if the whole lot of eastern peoples must starve, so be it, just as long as Germany was assured of slaves for its culture.[48]

It is clear that attitudes within the Wehrmacht toward the question of eastern nationalities were as diverse as those among the Nazis, ranging from Field Marshal Keitel's complete subservience to Hitler to the opposition of the officers of the resistance. Most of the generals of the Führer headquarters as well as the commanders in the field were content to hide behind their oath to the commander in chief, whether or not they agreed with Hitler's policies.

Field Marshal Keitel executed the Führer's orders ruthlessly and shares responsibility for the death of several million Russian prisoners of war who perished in the camps under his administration.[49] His directive, "Instructions for Handling Soviet Prisoners of War in All the Prisoner of War Camps," dated September 8, 1941, stated that the "Bolshevik has lost every claim to be treated as an honorable soldier according to the Geneva Convention."[50] He instructed the guards to parade their superiority over the prisoners and to meet resistance with force; escapees were to be shot without warning. He also ordered that Bolshevik agitators were to be dealt with by "special measures, free from bureaucratic and governmental influences." The prisoners in the camps were to be separated into national groups and then subdivided into those who were (a) politically undesirable, (b) politically harmless, and (c) politically very trustworthy. The SS "Deployment Groups" were authorized to treat them as they saw fit, and the camp commanders were warned that they were to work closely with the SS groups in this connection.

An Army General Staff directive of November 1, 1941, which purported to speak for Commander in Chief von Brauchitsch, offers another illustration of Hitler's close control over the Army's eastern policies. The directive concerned the food situation in Russia and pointed out that if the Russian urban population should starve during the coming winter, the Bolsheviks were to be held responsible, since they had confiscated the supplies and in some cases had destroyed them. Therefore, "the city population . . . will have to starve." The soldiers of the Wehrmacht were warned not to offer any of their own food to the civilians, because by doing so they would be harming the German cause. They were counseled to remain hard in the face of starving women and children.[51]

As a general rule, the farther one traveled from Hitler's headquarters, the more humane were the Army directives regarding the treatment of the Russian population. Indeed, many field commanders issued orders that the Russians were to be treated as allies. Some went so far as to declare, "Whoever among the indigenous population participates in the struggle against Bolshevism . . . is not our enemy but our fellow-fighter and fellow-worker in the struggle against the world-foe."[52]

Several officers proposed a radical shift in Germany's eastern policy. One of the most impressive position papers was the report of General Gehlen dated November 25, 1942, which discussed the partisan danger. Gehlen, the chief of the *Fremde Heere Ost,* called for an end to the Nazi "subhuman" policy. He suggested that the only sensible way to confront the partisan movement was to establish a regime that would be benevolent enough to preclude the formation of the partisan bands. In addition, he maintained that Berlin should guarantee the Russians some type of self-rule for the future. Finally, he proposed that units of Russian troops should be formed to join in the Wehrmacht's struggle against bolshevism.[53] As Dallin observes, "It was the increasing likelihood of defeat that spurred more and more men in the Army to embrace politics as the nostrum that might salvage what could not be won by arms: political warfare rose on the bitter yeast of defeat."[54]

The Army almost from the beginning of the campaign put Russian "Hiwis" (Hilfswillige) to work in paramilitary capacities. Furthermore, soon after the invasion German officers began to organize former Red Army men into units under German command, and thousands of them saw action against the Soviets as early as 1941. A desperate military situation would force Hitler to the expediency of the Vlasov experiment late in the war. The captured Russian general Vlasov was proclaimed head of the "Committee for the Liberation of the Peoples of Russia" (KONR) in November 1944, and under his leadership several thousand Russians saw service in the field during the closing months of the war. The wheel had turned full circle; Slavic "subhumans" fought side by side with "Aryans."

On the other hand, German recruitment and utilization of forced labor illustrated that the most powerful Nazi policy makers felt that the Slavs were subhumans and should be treated as such. During the course of the war, nearly 2,800,000 Russians were forced to work for the Third Reich. They lived under very unsanitary conditions and were treated inhumanely.[55] Their designation as "Eastern Workers" suggested their inferior status. Furthermore, all of them were required to attach the mark of opprobrium—"Ost"—to every article of clothing they wore. This approximated the requirement for Jews and concentration camp inmates, and the Russians resented it deeply, calling it their "dog label" or "Jew's star."[56]

The problems which befell the propaganda minister as a result of the mistaken eastern policies were legion. The war in Russia had not progressed many months when Goebbels, like so many others, had come to the conclusion that Hitler's Ostpolitik was ill-advised. He recognized the folly of treating all the Russian peoples as inferiors since it not only demoralized Russians employed in German defense industries and those who served in the military volunteer units, but it alienated the various Russian national groups, such as the Ukrainians and the Caucasians, who would have rallied to Hitler's cause had they been treated correctly.

Goebbels described the faults in the Reich's policies toward Russia in his diary, arguing that the only reasonable course was to put an end to the "subhuman" propaganda and instead to dramatize the Reich's war against bolshevism rather than against the Russian people. He proposed the creation of puppet regimes in Russia, a step which would establish a favorable climate for collaboration by the eastern peoples with the Nazis. He also favored ameliorating conditions in Russia to demonstrate Germany's good intentions.[57] He began to work toward these goals by radically altering the content of his own eastern propaganda, which henceforth was much softer on the Slavic question than the Party radicals would have liked. Goebbels also took steps to challenge Himmler and Bormann by employing Gutterer, Taubert, and Tiessler to front for him in the intra-Party ideological battle which he was about to provoke.[58] The first skirmish was not long in developing and took a dramatic form in 1942 after Goebbels became incensed at the publication and dissemination of *The Subhuman,* a wildly racist SS pamphlet which symbolized the utter stupidity of Hitler's *Ostpolitik.*[59] Goebbels, through his straw men, was to join battle with Himmler over this issue, which became one of the more bizarre causes célèbres involving the Nazi hierarchy during the war.

The Subhuman was the classic expression of Hitler's racial theories, in comic-book format. The cover featured photographs illustrating the contrast between "subhumans" and Aryans, while the text consisted of scattered pseudoscientific, pseudohistorical assertions characterized by falsification and exaggeration. A subhuman was defined as that which biologically appears to be a man but which in reality differs fundamentally, representing a lower order than the animal kingdom; the swamp was his natural element. The Jews, quite predictably, had been the leaders of this underworld from the beginning of time, and one of their first acts was the "Purim Festival," in which Jewish hate was responsible for the annihilation of "75,000 Aryan Persians." The SS contended that the lesson to be learned from such scientific truths was simple: Germany's mission was to come to grips with the twentieth-century manifestation of the "Jewish-Bolshevik will to destruction."

The crudity of *The Subhuman* aroused Goebbels's ire, and furthermore he had received a very negative report about it from Taubert who had taken an inspection trip to Russia with members of Rosenberg's ministry, the OKW, and the *Reichssicherheitshauptamt.* There Taubert had learned firsthand the reaction of the Russian people to the designation "subhuman." As a result Goebbels decided to act, and in the late summer of 1942 the first in a long series of letters written by Taubert and signed by Gutterer was dispatched to the *SS-Ministeramt* and the *Reichssicherheitshauptamt,* suggesting that *The Subhuman* be withdrawn from circulation in the east and be given very limited circulation in western Europe. The response was immediate. The chief of Himmler's *Ministeramt,* Obersturmbahnführer Rudolf Brandt, fired off a letter to Ohlendorf of the SD complaining that the Reichsführer was enraged about the meddling. He wanted to know exactly what persons in the Propaganda Ministry were responsible for it so that he could take appropriate action. Himmler was especially offended because he personally had edited the text of the pamphlet "at least six or more times."[60] Months passed, and the names of the culprits were not forthcoming; nevertheless, *The Subhuman* continued to be distributed through SS channels.

Himmler did suffer some second thoughts over the winter as the result of conversations he had with his trusted confidant Günter d'Alquen. D'Alquen was a man who fearlessly spoke his mind to the Reichsführer throughout the war, and during the course of an inspection flight to Waffen-SS units deployed in Russia in February or March 1943, Himmler handed him a copy of *The Subhuman* and solicited his comments. D'Alquen answered that the brochure was a disaster and gave a candid analysis based on some thirty to forty discussions with officers and men at the front. He repeated this performance on subsequent occasions much to Himmler's chagrin. More than any other factor, the men of the Waffen-SS and Wehrmacht units were unimpressed by starry-eyed ideology which referred to an enemy they had come to respect as "subhuman." For them, "one straight shooting bazooka had more cultural value than the Marienburg" and certainly more than the vain theorizing of *The Subhuman.* Although Himmler generally put great store in d'Alquen's judgment, he took no action to reverse a policy so dear to the Führer's heart. He refused to change course on *The Subhuman* to the bitter end.[61]

Goebbels's team once again plunged headlong into its mini-battle after the trauma of Stalingrad had subsided. Employing SS Major General Gutterer to sign his letter, Taubert once more raised the issue of *The Subhuman* in a remarkably arrogant dispatch to Himmler dated March 5, 1943. After reiterating the points of dispute which he had outlined to the Reichsführer the previous summer, "Gutterer" continued,

Therefore I should like to suggest that you take another look at the brochure with these points in mind. I feel that it should be withdrawn from Germany and from the occupied eastern territories, in an unobtrusive manner. . . .

On the other hand in my opinion the brochure can continue to be sold in the western European countries, just as long as there are no eastern volunteer units or eastern workers deployed there.

I request that you inform me about the result of your rechecking and about your decision just as soon as possible.[62]

Himmler was enraged by this condescension from a subordinate in his own SS, and he told Gutterer on March 12, 1943, that he had been "astounded" by the letter.[63] "I would really be interested in knowing which pictures supposedly would keep the eastern peoples from volunteering for the Army," he said. "I regard this assertion to be typical of those which we get so often from the military; we old National Socialists have to be on our guard not just to simply parrot them uncritically," he added. In a letter from Brandt to Gottlob Berger, chief of the *SS-Hauptamt,* dated April 14, 1943, the Reichsführer is quoted as having said that Gutterer should be thrown into the front lines with the *Leibstandarte SS "Adolf Hitler,"* so that he could discover for himself just what "fine people" these Slavs really were.[64]

Himmler and Brandt conceived a plan to wedge Naumann between Gutterer and their unknown enemies at the Propaganda Ministry, and he was contacted in this connection.[65] However, what began as a clever scheme to use the fanatical and trusted Naumann to carry Himmler's banner came to nothing for the simple reason that Naumann was one of the few people privy to Goebbels's plot, and he never considered entering the lists in a battle which he only stood to lose.

Berger's letter to Brandt of April 17, 1943, continued the fight.[66] Berger was enraged over the manner in which Himmler had been treated by a Goebbels man, and he took the opportunity to condemn the propaganda minister's work, charging that German propaganda had reached a low comparable to 1918. In a humorous aside, Berger assured Brandt that he was not suffering from a "persecution complex"; rather, the SS had many enemies "not because we have really done something wrong, but because we work, not complain, remain true to the Führer and forge ahead." Therefore, not a word of *The Subhuman* would be changed, and "absolutely nothing" would be done about the complaint. Furthermore, "when I have the chance I'm going to have it out with Gutterer," Berger concluded.[67] As late as the fall of 1943 Himmler—through Brandt, Ohlendorf, and Berger—was still searching for the culprits in the Propaganda Ministry who were intriguing against him.[68] It never occurred to him that the plotter was the Reich minister of propaganda himself.

Although Goebbels failed to have *The Subhuman* withdrawn, he succeeded in scoring a tactical victory in his attempt to ameliorate some of the worst features of the Nazis' anti-Slavic racial policies. Two major directives which Goebbels issued in early 1943 called for a radical shift in policy regarding the treatment of the eastern peoples within the Reich. The first of these, issued in February 1943, was addressed to the Party offices, and the second, signed by Bormann, took the form of a *Merkblatt* to all government bureaus, including the appropriate offices of the SS.[69] According to these memorandums, there was to be a radical change in the treatment of the eastern national groups within the Reich, because the country needed all available assistance to win the final victory; help from Slavs in the effort was to be welcomed, and they should be led to feel that a German victory was in their best interest. The Party and government elite was admonished to handle the question of the eastern national groups with exteme care in any future public statements which it made on the subject. Thus the deleterious effects of Hitler's Slavic policies were mitigated to some degree.

On the whole Nazi anti-Bolshevik propaganda was inconsistent, unsophisticated, and unconvincing.[70] And as the months and years passed, it became increasingly sterile because Goebbels was caught in a dilemma. He was unable to reconcile Hitler's basic ideological position that the Bolshevik system was archaic, bankrupt, and decadent with the objective organizational and military performance of the Soviet Union and the Red Army during the war.[71] Although he recognized the problem, Goebbels never successfully came to grips with this basic inconsistency.[72]

X The Battle of Moscow

During the fall of 1941 Nazi propaganda reached a high pitch of optimism as victory over the Soviet Union seemed imminent. Hitler made the bold prediction in his Sports Palace address on October 3 that "the enemy is already broken and will never rise again." Less than a week later, on October 9, he audaciously dispatched Dietrich from his headquarters to Berlin, where he was authorized to announce to a jubilant meeting of the German and world press that the end was nearing in the east: "The annihilation of Army Group Timoschenko has decided the campaign in Russia . . . The Soviet Union is done for militarily (erledigt) as a result of this last powerful blow which we are delivering."[1] Allowing that some desperate resistance remained, he asserted that Timoschenko's armies could not possibly fight their way to freedom, thus shattering the miserable hopes of the fireside strategists in Moscow, London, and Washington. The Führer was so certain of victory that he was already planning to release several divisions and reduce munitions production. The newspapers had their greatest day of the war proclaiming the demise of the Red Army.[2]

Dietrich never lived down this blunder and he had to take the blame for Hitler's miscalculation. Long after the war was over he was still feeling the pangs of embarrassment, and he explained in

166

his memoirs that Hitler had dictated the victory release and ordered his trip to Berlin: "I had no reason to doubt what the Commander-in-Chief told me so spontaneously in his headquarters about the events in Russia, with the specific purpose of making it public."[3] Dietrich argued that he even had General Jodl double-check the Führer's statement. There is no doubt that Hitler believed that Moscow lay undefended before his advancing Panzers and that the decisive blow had been struck. In a radical reversal of his earlier conservative policy in reporting news on major battles in progress, he felt that the time had come to inform the German people and the world of the Wehrmacht's success.

There was a good deal of opposition to the claims of total victory. The soldiers in the field were disgusted with the talk about victory and von Brauchitsch complained directly to Hitler, who replied that he had been motivated primarily by reasons of foreign policy and that he had intended to impress the Japanese.[4] If Hitler was indeed trying to entice the Japanese into declaring war on Russia, he was entirely unrealistic about the intentions of his Tripartite Pact ally. In mid-August, following the fall of Matsuoka, the ruling circles in Tokyo had confirmed their earlier decision not to join in the struggle against the Soviet Union in the immediate future.[5] The Japanese, furthermore, had decided by early September that the "situation favorable to our Empire" which would develop sooner or later in the Soviet Union most probably would come "after the middle of this coming winter (1941–1942)."[6] The Japanese were so seriously involved in the events leading up to the replacement of Konoye with General Tojo as well as with their diplomatic maneuvering with the United States that Germany's assertion that Soviet Russia was defeated did not have the desired effect. By October the Japanese had something entirely different in mind; they were hoping that Hitler would very soon bring about a negotiated settlement of the Soviet war in order to be able to free troops to join them in their coming war against the United States and Great Britain.[7] Hitler had completely misread Japanese intentions.

Goebbels was enraged by Dietrich's press conference which he viewed not only as an indefensible violation of his strategic principle of propaganda orchestration, but as an absurd tactical blunder brought about by reckless overconfidence. Goebbels's young subordinate at the ministry, Rudolf Semmler, noted in his diary: "Goebbels thinks we have seen today the biggest propaganda blunder of the war . . . It made a tremendous sensation; Goebbels says it was done with unbelievable irresponsibility. He is foaming with rage. First because Dietrich has got himself quite undeserved credit; secondly because the impression will be given at the front and among the people that the war is really as good as over." [8]

The propaganda minister had nothing but contempt for such premature talk of victory. As early as October 1, 1941, he had issued a directive scheduling a propaganda campaign of six months' duration which admonished the Germans to rely on discipline, endurance, and perseverance in order to fight their way through to the final victory. "The Führer alone began the struggle for the salvation of the German people . . ." he wrote, and "he will also conclude this final period of great struggle with victory." [9] Long before Moscow, Goebbels, like many Germans, sensed in what direction the military events were tending, and he expected at least one more war winter. He ordered that there was to be no talk of easy victories. [10]

Hitler's Munich address of November 8, 1941, hinted that the war might well last into 1942 and set the stage for Goebbels's "new propaganda line" which entailed shifting propaganda strategy from optimism to realism. [11] In the words of the minister, "The speech of the Führer will mean the high point in this development which . . . for every citizen was a sobering account of the fact that the struggle is still hard and that there is no end in sight." [12]

Goebbels dispatched an important directive to the gauleiters on this theme in mid-December, elaborating on the propaganda strategy for the coming winter. It was released under the title "The Necessity of Preparing the Nation to Cope with All the Eventualities of the War." [13] Goebbels complained that some persons had not yet realized that "there was a war going on," but that they had better learn it immediately. He observed that the Soviets knew how to cope with the war, because they did not hesitate to use ruthless methods to keep their people in line. It was to be no different in the Reich. Therefore the Germans must be told the truth about the war: "The radio, press, speakers, and person-to-person propaganda . . . must hold nothing back in reporting the war. Most people today are very realistic about the war situation. Therefore we must describe the war situation as it really is . . ."[14]

One of the most significant statements of the "new line" was Goebbels's *Reich* article of November 9, 1941, entitled "When or How?" In this piece he admonished the German people not to concern themselves about *when* the German victory would come, but to concentrate instead on *how* it would be achieved. He called for dedication, sacrifice, and a willing spirit on the part of every German. Should they meet the challenge, victory would bring with it abundant new food resources, living space, and raw materials; on the other hand, defeat would mean the end to Germany's national existence.[15]

Goebbels's attempts at reversing the propaganda strategy were modified as a result of Hitler's treatment of the propaganda on the Moscow campaign. At a time when the German drive on Moscow might best have been concealed pending the outcome, he put his prestige on the line, leaving no doubt that the Soviet capital was the goal of the campaign. On November 25, the *Völkischer Beobachter* carried a map on page one in the shape of a bull's-eye, with Moscow at the center.[16] But in the first week of December, the attack ground to a halt before Moscow, and the Red Army launched a major counteroffensive.[17]

A person reading between the lines might well have divined that trouble was brewing, because after the end of November the subject of Moscow all but disappeared from the newspapers and radio programs, while the public was bored with the Nazis' timeworn diversion technique. On a day when the High Command did not mention the battle for Moscow, an account of eighty brave Germans capturing the Soviet troop transport *Stalin* shared top billing with an Ickes address "before a crowd of Jews" at Chicago.[18]

More compelling fare was offered by a timely variation on the "Europe united" motif, occasioned by the late November Berlin meeting of Germany's fellow Anti-Comintern Pact allies. Ribbentrop took the opportunity to stage an elaborate ceremony in the new Reich chancellery building, where the six former signers (Germany, Japan, Italy, Hungary, Manchukuo, and Spain) joined with representatives of Bulgaria, Denmark, Croatia, Rumania, Slovakia, and the "Chinese Nationalist" government (the Japanese puppet regime at Nanking) in signing a five-year renewal of the treaty which pledged each nation's support of the Reich in the common struggle against bolshevism. But the public hungered for more specific news on the progress of the drive toward Moscow.

The Japanese attack on Pearl Harbor set the stage for a violent German propaganda assault on the United States preceding Berlin's declaration of war on December 11. German anti-American propaganda had come full circle. Traditionally the Nazis had attacked the United States as the playground of the Jews, but with the outbreak of the war in 1939 the order went out that the United States was to be treated with great caution to avoid provoking its entrance into the European war at the side of its traditional English and French allies.[19] Throughout 1940 the Nazis maintained a façade of moderation toward Washington, but Hitler took a new course in his address of January 30, 1941, when, despite disclaimers of friendship, he warned that any attempts to aid the English by sea would be met with force.[20]

The following eleven months featured anti-American propaganda which reached a higher threshold of intensity with each ensuing act on the part of Roosevelt and the Congress to demonstrate their loyalty to Great Britain and occupied Europe. The Lend-Lease Bill passed by Congress on March 11, the Atlantic Charter issued jointly by Roosevelt and Churchill in August, and the exchange of fire between the American destroyer *Greer* and a U-boat were three landmarks on the road to war, and Goebbels treated them as such.[21]

Hitler acted on the conviction that Roosevelt was a syphilitic who surrounded himself with Jews like Frankfurter and Morgenthau and thus was unable and unwilling to seek an accord with the New Order.[22] As such Roosevelt was a tool of the universal enemy, international Jewry, and proved it by his membership in a New York chapter of the Freemasons. Thus, the anti-American propaganda was easily merged with Nazi ideology based on anti-Semitism. All the themes used in connection with the United States flowed from this principal motif, which was summarized by Goebbels when he remarked that "there on the other side of the big pond an unscrupulous clique of Jews, capitalists, merchants of death, bankers, and newsmen stealthily pursue their criminal goal of maneuvering the United States into the war despite the fact that the American people does not support them."[23]

Hitler's reaction to the outbreak of war with the United States was characteristically visceral and racially motivated. According to Goebbels, "The Führer naturally deeply regrets the heavy losses which the white race will have to suffer in East Asia. But we're not to blame for that."[24]

The Japanese attack on Pearl Harbor relieved some of the pressure resulting from the setback at Moscow which Hitler sooner or later was forced to admit. The news from the Pacific offered a welcome shield from the adverse effects of the OKW communiqué of December 8 which announced that severe weather conditions had brought a halt to the German offensive in Russia for the year: "The continuation of operations in the east, and the methods pursued in waging war there, will be determined from now on by the beginning (Einbruch) of the Russian winter. Only local combat is taking place along broad stretches of the eastern front."[25] For several days after Pearl Harbor, all news reports were dominated by the coverage of Japan's bold offensive, and the Russian campaign received only passing reference.[26] Excuses for Moscow would have to be conjured up soon enough.

It was but three days later, on December 11, 1941, that Hitler went before the Reichstag to deliver his first major address following the setback at Moscow. Disappointment awaited those who expected a statement of substance in regard to the eastern front. Gone forever were the days when Hitler could declare to the world that the final compaign of the Soviet war was being launched. The best he could promise was that "with the return of summer weather there will be no obstacle to the continuation of this advance."[27] In an attempt to divert attention from the defeat before Moscow, Hitler concentrated his fire on Roosevelt and at the same time pledged lasting solidarity with the Japanese. He made it clear that the Reich would fight side by side with its loyal allies until the final victory.

Before Moscow, Hitler had been celebrated in German propaganda as the "greatest military commander of all times"—an infallible strategist. Because his prestige could not suffer the onus of the recent defeat, he laid the blame on the generals for his own errors of judgment. Commander in Chief of the Army von Brauchitsch headed the long list of generals who were forced into retirement for their "failures" in the campaign. In this manner the Führer "exonerated" himself for the defeat, a tactic hardly surprising in view of his contempt for his officers. Brauchitsch reinforced the myth of Hitler's strategic infallibility by concluding his final Order of the Day to the Army with a tribute to his chief, in which he declared that "the Führer will lead us to victory. Face the future with unflinching determination. Everything for Germany!"[28]

Despite Party propaganda, many people perceived that Hitler was holding von Brauchitsch responsible for the failure to supply the front with the necessary winter outfitting, despite the public announcement that he was retiring because of "heart trouble."[29] As Dietrich observed in his memoirs, "Brauchitsch's dismissal at this moment meant far more than the elimination of a level in the chain of command which was troublesome to Hitler. He sent him to the desert as a scapegoat because of the winter catastrophe in the East, which was accompanied by a lack of winter outfitting for the German soldiers, a situation which had deeply shocked the nation. He himself wanted to pose before the German people as the righteous one, the avenging nemesis of the unquestionable mess in the Army supply system."[30]

Goebbels's initial reaction to the news of the shortage of winter clothing for the troops was acute embarrassment and anger, and he had visions of people saying, "There you can see how Goebbels lies!"[31] His fear was justified, but in this case the lying was not of his own making since he had been misled into believing that the winter needs of the soldiers were well taken care of in advance. In October Goebbels had asked General Jodl about this and had been told not to worry because by the time the Russian winter set in the troops would be warm and comfortable in their winter quarters in Moscow and Leningrad. He had also been taken down the garden path by Army Quartermaster General Wagner who had staged a propaganda show in Smolensk where he exhibited the winter clothing issued to all the men on the eastern front. As a result, in mid-November he had directed that the nation be reassured that all the needs of its men were being met to face the rigors of winter in Russia.[32] But as the German troops began to suffer, the truth could not be concealed; many people obtained firsthand reports from men on leave or by way of letters from the front. The military authorities quickly took action to put a stop to these complaints as well as to halt the rumors of Soviet atrocities.[33]

Goebbels conceived plans for an extraordinary ad hoc propaganda campaign to meet the threatened crisis in morale. He took steps to redirect the home front's fears by calling on every individual in the Reich to participate in a massive clothing collection campaign for the troops—"the Christmas gift of the German people to the eastern front." Launched by a national radio address shortly before Christmas with a generous larding of Goebbels's pathos, the collection scheme had two goals, the practical and the political.[34] Christmas was a season during which the Germans' will to fight might easily give way to a feeling of melancholy. To avoid this, the minister endeavored to instill a spirit of cooperation and dedication to the cause of victory.[35]

Although the collection campaign tended to confirm the worst reports about the east, nothing was to be gained by avoiding the truth. The fact that the clothing did not reach the front until March 1942 was irrelevant to the propaganda success which resulted. The collection became an exercise in mass participation on a national scale, and Goebbels could boast that "carrying out this collection was a work of love for the German homeland, and therefore it was more a deed of the national community than one of propaganda . . . "[36]

In order that the home front should not be deprived of a face-to-face encounter with bolshevism, Goebbels staged an exhibition in 1942 called "Soviet Paradise," which featured "original" mud huts, torture chambers, and corpses. The minister was quite satisfied with the exhibition; he described it in his diary as a "classic example of effective propaganda" that left an overpowering impression on the viewer.[37] It had been so successful that after its première in the Lustgarten in Berlin, it toured the provinces as well. Skeptics circulated a joke to the effect that people from Berlin's run down Acker Street complained to Goebbels about sending the exhibition on tour because "they wanted their furniture back."

The effectiveness of Nazi propaganda had ebbed to one of its lowest points during the winter of 1941–1942. The defeat at Moscow came as a profound shock to the German people, and many of them understood its far-reaching implications. This was true both at the highest levels of command and among much of the public at large. The prospect of a long war in Russia opened up many frightening possibilities. On balance, German war propaganda in the year 1941 had been a failure because victory was the only eventuality for which the public had been prepared. There had been no contingency planning, no propaganda strategy which could be adjusted to temporary setbacks on the field of battle. The blame clearly lay with Hitler, for Goebbels had long fought the excessive optimism of the Führer headquarters. That both had profited from the experience became clear in the development of the myth of Stalingrad a year later.

XI The Myth of Stalingrad

The forging of the propaganda on the Stalingrad debacle formed an important chapter in the development of psychological warfare in World War II. Begun as a tactical innovation to interpret the Wehrmacht's declining fortunes on the Volga, it was to assume the proportions of an important Nazi myth. The outcome of the battle and the conception of the myth were developments which few could have foreseen.

Although Hitler firmly believed that the final victory would be consummated in 1942, Goebbels continued to demand caution; in May he issued to his staff an order entitled "No Propaganda of Illusion."[1] The Führer, having in 1942 deployed against Russia 240 divisions totaling three million men, expected Stalingrad to fall by late summer. Units of the Sixth Army fought their way to the River Don by mid-August, battled for the suburbs later that month, and entered Stalingrad itself early in September. The next months were to witness one of the most bitterly fought engagements of the entire war, and for some time it appeared that Stalingrad was about to fall. By the second week in October, German troops had captured the tractor plant and a large part of the workers' settlement, and had secured several beachheads on the Volga. By the end of the month, four-fifths of Stalingrad was in their hands. It seemed that it would be only a matter of time before the entire city would be theirs.

Having learned a lesson the previous year, Hitler instructed Dietrich to warn the journalists to exercise restraint in reporting on the battle for Stalingrad in order to avoid raising unwarranted hopes among the public. Instead of stressing the capture of localities in and around Stalingrad, they were to accent the bitterness of the fighting and the bravery of the German soldier. Stalingrad was to be referred to as a fortress which had to be stormed; if the campaign slowed down, the strength of the Soviet fortifications would serve as a ready excuse.[2]

At no time did the Nazis claim that Stalingrad had fallen, and for once Hitler's caution paid dividends. Instead of announcing victory, the news media emphasized that a harsh struggle to capture Stalingrad lay ahead. This report from the *Frankfurter Zeitung* of September 13, 1942, was typical: "Every step must be fought for, every position must be stormed by Stukas, as well as by the sappers with their flame throwers, only to be finally taken by infantrymen using hand grenades and bayonets."

But Hitler himself was overconfident. Dietrich has written that as early as mid-August a Special Announcement lay on Hitler's desk announcing the capture of Stalingrad: "That event was expected to occur hourly."[3] A month later, on September 15, when it seemed that victory was his, the Führer ordered the press to prepare special editions for the news of the fall of Stalingrad. Detailed instructions were issued for press coverage on the victory that was never to be.[4]

Hitler showed signs of being on the defensive in his address at the Sports Palace on September 30. He reviewed the goals of the offensive of the previous year and claimed that Germany had gained all of them; everything expected from the 1942 offensive had already been realized, i.e., the capture of the Soviets' last grain, coal, and oil-producing areas and the rupture of the last significant link in their communications network, the Volga. He went on to declare that Stalingrad ensured the success of the last goal: "You can be quite certain that no human being will push us from that spot." But he revealed his uncertainty by answering the "people on the side of the enemy" who questioned his judgment as well as the "crusty old reactionaries" who "might be somewhere among us." He seemed to be making excuses, and he made a point of stressing the difficulties encountered in supplying the army and in repairing and building bridges, roads, and railways:

If there are people on the side of the enemy who say, "Why are they suddenly stopping?"—then I can answer: because we are careful . . . because we stop at any point for as long as is necessary to bring our supplies in order . . . people with any understanding of military problems will admit that the amount of territory which we have captured in a few months is itself something unique in the history of the world . . . If someone now says: "But the Russian does get through after all"—yes, we have to admit that they are a type of swamp human and not European. It is more difficult for us to advance in this muck than it is for those people born in the morass.[5]

There was a good deal more complaining in the next weeks. The SS organ, *Das Schwarze Korps* (October 29, 1942), contended that if Stalingrad were being defended by the English or Americans, its capture would have taken only a few days; there was a world of difference between the war in the west and that in the east "because the Bolshevik is a beast." Even if a man's background was that of a British colonial butcher or a Chicago gangster, at least he recognized the laws of Western civilization; the Bolsheviks on the other hand refused to realize when a struggle was useless and continued to fight to the last man. Thus Stalingrad represented the quintessence of the Soviet comtempt for the human race.

The German High Command for its part attempted to explain the slowdown of the campaign by asserting that the German forces were exercising caution and as a result were avoiding forced prestige victories and unnecessary casualties. But until early in November the OKW communiqués continued to report "mopping-up operations" in Stalingrad; then the Nazis reverted to their diversion technique, and the communiqués from the front paid little attention to Stalingrad. After occupying the front page for months, the campaign was abruptly relegated to a few lines on the back pages and often received no mention at all. Public attention was directed instead to the occupation of southern France and to German successes in naval engagements.

But as late as November 9 Hitler was still claiming victory; in his Munich address to the Old Guard he declared, "I wanted to take it [Stalingrad] and—you know—we are modest, we really have it! There are only a few very small places left there. Now the others say: 'Why don't you make faster progress?'—Because I don't want to create a second Verdun there, but prefer to do the job with small shock-troop units."[6]

This sort of bragging was undoubtedly disconcerting to Goebbels, who was dissatisfied with the propaganda disseminated by the Führer's headquarters during the Stalingrad campaign. Hans Fritzsche has written that in October 1942 Goebbels called him to Berlin to offer him the post of director of the German radio. At that time the minister revealed his plans to make a complete change in German war propaganda. He complained that the official propaganda was too optimistic, whereas many Germans were pessimistic about the outcome of the war. He blamed Dietrich for the fact that the German newspapers had lost all their influence among the public, and he even attacked Hitler for "not seeing the problem correctly," since he was so busy with other matters.[7]

This explains why Goebbels repeatedly stressed the great sacrifices that each German had to make if the Reich's future were to be made secure and the final victory won. He began to emphasize the dangers that faced the nation should the Germans not be equal to the tasks before them. In his Munich address in mid-October, and again in Wuppertal a month later, he broached a theme which became increasingly important in his propaganda following Stalingrad—that the German people were fighting for their very existence and faced possible annihilation. To emphasize the seriousness of this claim, he wrote in *Das Reich* on November 15, "We have thrown our whole national existence into the balance. There is no turning back now."

The fulfillment of his prophetic words came with the massive Soviet counteroffensive launched on November 19, consisting of a pincers movement against Stalingrad and a simultaneous drive toward the west by forces vastly superior to the German in both numbers and striking power. On November 23 the jaws of the Soviet pincers met at Kalach on the Don, surrounding and trapping twenty-two German divisions. Details concerning General Paulus's attempts to secure Hitler's permission to break out of the caldron, Göring's false promises to supply the suffering troops who lacked adequate ammunition, food, and winter clothing, and the failure of the newly formed Army Group Don under Field Marshal von Manstein to break through and relieve the men at Stalingrad are all well known. Hitler's prestige could not suffer the loss of Stalingrad, the city that symbolized his personal struggle with Stalin, and he feared the psychological effect of such a retreat. His decision not to call for withdrawal was to lead to disaster.

Hitler was reluctant to allow the High Command to release news of the Russian counteroffensive, and not until November 24 did the communiqué report that the Soviets had broken through the German positions southwest of Stalingrad and in the Don bend. There is little question that this admission was forced on Hitler by the Soviet Union's own Special Announcement, which was made public on November 23.[8] The High Command did not mention the Soviet breakthrough to the north of Stalingrad or the fact that the Sixth Army was completely surrounded. It attributed the breakthrough in the south to Russia's "irresponsible deployment of men and matériel." In an attempt to diminish the importance of the Soviet counteroffensive, the press was ordered to keep its reports on the German defensive battle in a low key.[9]

For the next two months, as the German armies were being pushed westward and the Sixth Army was being gradually destroyed, Hitler concealed the facts in the official war news. At many a juncture during this period the drafts of the OKW communiqués submitted to him included reports on the unfavorable developments in Russia, but the Führer invariably changed their content.[10] He was intent on making no public mention of the crisis. Nazi propaganda, therefore, completely ignored the Soviet encirclement at Stalingrad.

With no mention of Stalingrad beyond a few lines in the communiqués, uneasiness on the home front mounted. Germans accustomed to following the war were left with a confused picture of the progress of the campaign; maps of the Soviet Union gradually disappeared from the newspapers and the OKW spoke in generalities, avoiding references to towns or place names. According to an SD analysis of German morale late in November, there was a general feeling of "insecurity and anxiety" which German propaganda in no way assuaged.[11] The Germans wanted facts about the eastern front, not contrived reports on U-boat victories or reaffirmations of Axis solidarity. The bankruptcy of the propaganda in this period was illustrated by the fact that reports on a new institute of Italian studies in Berlin made the headlines.[12] What coverage the press did give to Stalingrad was misleading. For example, the OKW camouflaged the failure of the von Manstein offensive in late December to rescue the Sixth Army. The German public was not told that the last genuine attempt to break through to the beleaguered forces at Stalingrad had failed.

Goebbels attempted to reassure the nation. He declared in a Sports Palace address on December 5, "We are absolutely convinced that in Russia the better man, the better race, the better political philosophy, and the better leadership will win the ultimate victory, as they always have throughout the history of the world."[13] In his New Year's message he attempted to soothe taut nerves by comparing the crisis of the Moscow winter with that of 1942–1943, when "we already see the light in the distance: the light of the new morning which awaits us."[14] Through his person-to-person propaganda he spread the rumor that the Wehrmacht was fully outfitted to meet the rigors of the Russian winter.[15]

Hitler's message at the year's end made no mention of the progress of the campaign in the Stalingrad theater, a certain sign that trouble was brewing there. Germans hoping for victory announcements, or even for a sign that something favorable was imminent, remained disappointed. An SD report dated January 4, 1943, noted that "the seriousness of the hour made an especially marked impression, which was intensified by the fact that this time the Führer had made no predictions concerning the future course of the war."[16] In order to assess the situation independently, Goebbels flew the Stalingrad veteran Fritzsche back to the beleaguered Sixth Army to obtain a firsthand report for him. The propaganda minister himself distrusted the official communiqués.[17]

To counter the suspicion and cynicism spreading throughout Germany, ministry channels let it be known that although the communiqués represented the "absolute truth," certain facts had to be concealed until a more propitious time in order to protect the troops at the front. Several SD reports show that many people knew the forces deployed at Stalingrad were surrounded. Some even expected the Sixth Army to be evacuated from the Volga stronghold. Interrupted mail deliveries from Stalingrad added to uncertainties and rumors, as did the doubts voiced by veterans of the Russian front on leave in Germany.

In his diary entry for December 12, 1942, Goebbels attacked the SD reports and their severe criticism of the official war news. He absolved himself of all blame, since he "had always fought for an open news policy" and would continue to do so. "The German people can stand it," he declared. "I'll see that at least our supplement to the OKW communiqué handles things subtly."[18] But dissatisfaction continued to spread and to cause concern. To counteract the growing criticism, Bormann dispatched a directive, "on Hitler's orders, and in cooperation with the Reich Propaganda Chief," commanding the Nazis to strike out against the "incorrigible pessimists and small-minded philistines." He instructed his party colleagues to demonstrate aggressive leadership and to set an example of belief in final victory. When necessary, they were to employ force, as in the early days of the movement. In this way "the Party will make the decisive contribution to victory, as it has always done."[19]

But there was to be no victory at Stalingrad. The first weeks of the new year brought the catastrophe along the Volga to its end. On January 8, 1943, the Soviets offered the helpless Sixth Army terms of surrender, warning General Paulus that annihilation was the only alternative to capitulation. After receiving the German refusal, the Russians began their final offensive at Stalingrad on January 10 and made rapid progress. On January 22, Paulus wired Hitler a description of the situation at Stalingrad: there was no longer a possibility of stopping the Russian advance; the Sixth Army had neither food nor supplies; there were 12,000 unattended wounded. He concluded with the hopeless query, "What orders should I give to troops who have no more ammunition and are being attacked by heavy concentrations of artillery, tanks, and infantry?" and added, "A quick decision is essential, since total breakdown is already beginning at some points."[20] Hitler replied that there was to be no surrender; it was clear that he expected the Sixth Army to hold its position to the last man.

Paulus was obedient to the end. On January 30, the tenth anniversary of Hitler's appointment as Reich chancellor, Paulus wired his congratulations to Berlin: "On the anniversary of your accession to power, the Sixth Army greets its Führer. The Swastika still waves over Stalingrad. May our struggle be an example to present and future generations and encourage them never to capitulate in a hopeless situation. Then Germany will be victorious. Heil, mein Führer."[21]

The German divisions, encircled and broken into two narrow pockets, were severely battered. Paulus surrendered the southern pocket on January 31, but units holding out in the north resisted until February 2. In the course of the battle some 124,000 German soldiers had been killed. Ninety thousand others went into Soviet captivity, of whom only about 5000 ever returned to German soil. Some 40,000 German wounded and specialists had been flown home while the battle still raged.[22]

At last, during the final weeks of the battle, steps were taken to prepare the nation for news of the disaster that ultimately would have to be made public. A decisive shift in German war propaganda followed Goebbels's conference with Hitler on January 13; for more than eight hours the two discussed the radical changes required. Hitler gave the minister permission to remove the veil surrounding Stalingrad and at the same time to explain gradually to the German people the grave situation as it actually existed on the entire eastern front.[23]

On January 16, the OKW admitted for the first time that for weeks the German troops at Stalingrad had been engaged in a defensive battle against an enemy who was "attacking from all sides." This confirmed the rumors that the worst had happened. The communiqué of January 22 reported that, despite heroic resistance, the Soviets had effected a breakthrough in the western sector of the Stalingrad front. The report of January 25 declared that the German armies had won eternal honor for their valiant and sacrificial struggle; two days later the OKW went so far as to speak of those units of the Sixth Army that were "still able to fight . . . clinging to the ruins of Stalingrad."

The press was instructed to dramatize the heroism and self-sacrifice of the men at Stalingrad in order to urge a more dedicated war effort on the German home front. Stories about the Sixth Army's glorious tenacity in its defense of the Fatherland bore headlines such as "Hold Fast—To the Last Man," "The Heroes of Stalingrad," and "The Führer Honors the Heroic Band at Stalingrad." Heroism, sacrifice, and bravery—these were the themes that drummed out the demise of an entire army.

The Stalingrad propaganda campaign was stepped up on January 30, the tenth anniversary of Hitler's assumption of power. Göring spoke to a Wehrmacht rally that afternoon at the Reich Air Ministry: "We recognize a powerful heroic song of an unparalleled battle; it is called 'The Battle of the Nibelungen.' They too stood four square among the raging flames, and quenched their thirst with their own blood, but they fought to the last." Göring then compared the men fighting at Stalingrad to the Spartans at Thermopylae: "Only one sentence stands in this narrow pass: 'Wanderer, when you arrive at Sparta, report that you have seen us dead here, as the law commanded.' And one day the history of our own times will read that 'should you come to Germany, then report that you have seen us fighting in Stalingrad as the law, the law of national security commanded' . . . it is ultimately a matter of indifference to the soldier whether he fights and dies in Stalingrad or Rzhev, in the deserts of Africa or the snows of Norway."[24]

On the same evening Goebbels spoke to a rally at the Sports Palace. He read a "Proclamation of the Führer," in which Hitler made a single reference to Stalingrad: "The heroic battle of our soldiers on the Volga should be an urgent reminder to everyone to contribute his best to the struggle for Germany's freedom and for the future of our people." For his part, Goebbels used the occasion to reaffirm Germany's trust in the Führer as the war against "Jewish-bolshevism" moved toward its climax. "There is no such word as capitulation in our vocabulary," he cried.[25] Goebbels touched also upon the theme of total war, but in terms that were mild in comparison with his "total war" address in the same hall three weeks later. What was strange about the January 30 rally was the lack of attention paid to the important question of Stalingrad. The SD reported that this neglect did not go down well with many people. Hitler and Goebbels realized that the propaganda coverage of the disaster had to be treated in an extraordinary fashion. Neither factual reporting nor traditional misrepresentation would serve their purpose, and they decided that the sacrifice along the Volga could be explained only by way of a myth. Reality was thus to be reinterpreted.

Hitler and Goebbels were agreed on the Stalingrad propaganda strategy, which clearly showed Goebbels's influence on Hitler in the formulation of the main themes. From the first the Nazis refused to admit that the Sixth Army had surrendered. Instead, they did violence to the truth in the matter by claiming that the entire Army had been destroyed and had fought to the last man. The daily directive of February 3 gave full instructions to the press:

The heroic battle for Stalingrad has ended. In several days of mourning the German people will honor their brave sons, men who did their duty to the last breath and to the last bullet, and as a result have broken the back of the Bolshevik assault on our eastern front. The heroic battle for Stalingrad will become the greatest of all the heroic epics in German history. The German press has one of its greatest tasks before it. In the spirit of the special OKW communiqué to be issued later today, the press must report this stirring event, which outshines every feat of heroism known to history, in such a manner that this sublime example of heroism, this ultimate, self-sacrificing dedication to Germany's final victory, will blaze forth like a sacred flame. The German nation, inspired by the eternal heroism of the men of Stalingrad, will demonstrate even more nobly than before those spiritual and material qualities which assure the nation of the victory it is now more fanatically than ever resolved to win.[26]

Goebbels did his utmost to give meaning to the great loss. His campaign reached an emotional intensity that exceeded even the victory celebrations of the summer and fall of 1941. The manner in which he relayed the news that Stalingrad had fallen was very effective. The radio broadcast of the Special Announcement opened with solemn marches, followed by drum rolls and the three stanzas of one of the saddest of all German war songs, "Ich hatt' einen Kameraden." Then came the announcement of the fall of Stalingrad, followed by the playing of the German, Italian, and Croat national anthems. After three minutes of silence Beethoven's Fifth Symphony was played, and a three-day period of mourning was ordered.[27] The entire schedule of programs was changed for several days to fit the Stalingrad propaganda line.[28]

Hitler saw to it that the German High Command's Special Announcement of February 3 on Stalingrad's fall conformed to the myth. It praised General Paulus, and his forces, and conveyed the distinct impression that the Army, "true to its oath," had gone down fighting to the last man. "The sacrifice of the Army was not in vain," since it had served as the "bulwark of the European mission." By its steadfast resistance, the Sixth Army was said to have tied down strong enemy forces and to have enabled the High Command to mount countermeasures. Indeed, the fate of the entire eastern campaign depended upon this sacrifice. The Sixth Army had proudly rejected two offers of surrender, and the swastika had flown until the very end. The men of Stalingrad "died that Germany might live . . . Generals, officers, NCO's and common soldiers fought shoulder to shoulder to the last bullet . . . Their example will have an effect upon generations in the most distant future."[29] The announcement concealed not only the fact that Paulus and several other generals had surrendered to the Russians, but that 90,000 men of the Sixth Army had followed them into captivity.

Martin Sommerfeldt, a liaison officer between the High Command and the Propaganda Ministry, showed his disdain for this Special Announcement when he wrote, "On February 3 a special conference of the foreign press was called once more. I gave the Special Announcement to Brauweiler, because I refused to read a document which lied more vulgarly than the message that the eastern campaign had been decided."[30]

But most officials were troubled by no such scruples. Alfred Rosenberg experienced no difficulty in linking the new myth with traditional Nazi ideology. His two lead articles in the *Völkischer Beobachter* (January 30, February 4) eulogized the Sixth Army's role in the forefront against the "Jewish-Bolshevik underworld." German soldiers, he asserted, had fulfilled their mission to protect not only the Reich, but all of Europe. An entire army had sacrificed itself "for all of us" and, indeed, for Western civilization. Goethe and Beethoven, Augustus and Pericles were being defended in the wilds of the east. In his radio analysis of the campaign, Major General Kurt Dittmar, the Army's chief spokesman and propagandist, emphasized the military significance of the Sixth Army's sacrifice at Stalingrad, thereby lending the prestige of the Army to the support of the official propaganda line.

Hitler realized that as a result of Stalingrad he might well face a crisis in morale on the home front. For that reason, in February 1943 he ordered that all military commentaries on Stalingrad be discontinued, while an official interpretation of the battle was to be prepared and presented for his approval.[31]

Heinz Schröter of the war correspondents staff of the Sixth Army was commissioned to write the account, intended for wide circulation. He refers to this project in *Stalingrad,* published several years after the war: "When my account of the twenty-two divisions which never returned was laid before the Minister for Public Enlightenment and Propaganda, he was aghast. His comment: 'Intolerable for the German people.' "[32] No such brochure, written by Schröter or anyone else, ever appeared. However, a painting by Friedrich Eichhorst entitled "Memory of Stalingrad" was shown in a major art exhibition at the Haus der Kunst in Munich later in the year, and a sculpture by Ernst Hinkelday was included in the 1943 Heroes Memorial Day exhibit at the Berlin Armory.

Since Hitler's prestige could not afford the disclosure of his bungling at Stalingrad, he at length forbade all references to Stalingrad and to the winter campaign of 1942–1943. Repeated directives told propagandists not to discuss the battle. For example, as the German and Italian troops went down to defeat in Tunisia in May 1943, a directive to the press ordered that "under no circumstances are references to Stalingrad to be made in the commentaries." Hitler's chief military historian, Colonel Walter Scherff, in a letter to General Jodl dated June 25, 1943, reported on his recent conversation with the Führer: "Hitler said there was no reason to refer publicly to the winter campaign of 1942–1943 . . . especially regarding Stalingrad."[33] In February 1944, the first anniversary of Stalingrad, strict orders were issued forbidding any discussion of the debacle. Throughout the war the authorities made every effort to conceal the facts of the campaign, and much of the material on the battle which was submitted to the official censors was denied publication. They also attempted to confiscate letters from veterans of Stalingrad. An entry in a section of Goebbels's diary for this period, which has recently been discovered, sheds a good deal of light on this question. On February 14, he noted that the Führer had sent Keitel to him to discuss a matter of grave import, i.e., the confiscation of the Stalingrad letters. Keitel reported that 1900 had come into the Reich, and that of these only forty-five had been delivered. But these forty-five letters enabled a number of people to learn the truth about Stalingrad. Goebbels observed that it was best not to do anything at the moment, but to await subsequent developments. "The Führer is also of this opinion."[34] Goebbels was aware that any publicity on the matter would cause a good deal of trouble; nevertheless, giving no explanation at all led to equally grave problems of morale.

The Stalingrad crisis presented German propagandists with one of their most delicate wartime assignments. The SD reports reflected a general feeling of relief in mid-January, when it was admitted that the Sixth Army was surrounded. But the enemy news broadcasts, the few letters from the Volga that were delivered, and the meager information disseminated from the Führer headquarters only whetted the appetites of the Germans to get at the real truth. As the facts about Stalingrad came gradually to light, there was increasing criticism of the manner in which the entire campaign had been handled. The SD recorded evidence of a deep depression following the announcement of the fall of Stalingrad, but that no serious crisis was developing on the home front.[35] People clamored for news about the prisoners taken at Stalingrad, because they were not convinced by the official assertion that the entire Army had "fought to the last cartridge." A rumor spread that 90,000 prisoners had surrendered to the Soviets at Stalingrad, including twenty-three generals.[36] These figures were in fact quite accurate. Naumann has observed that he and Goebbels were of the opinion that Stalingrad affected the Wehrmacht to a greater degree than the home front.[37]

The Soviets made use of the opportunities that Stalingrad afforded their psychological warfare efforts. One of their favorite methods was to announce over Moscow radio at well-timed intervals the names of German prisoners of war, an artifice which attracted a wide listening audience in Germany. Countless people waited evening after evening for mention of their loved ones. The enemy tactics included mailing postcards and letters to persons in Germany whose relatives had been killed in action or taken prisoner on the eastern front. Bona fide letters were interspersed with fraudulent ones. This effective Soviet propaganda led to the circulation of the wildest rumors, and the various ministries and the OKW and OKH received many letters inquiring about the fate of individual soldiers captured at Stalingrad and elsewhere on the eastern front. This correspondence became a source of embarrassment to the High Command and to the Party, and on May 28, 1943, Martin Bormann sent a circular letter to Party functionaries on the subject, describing the clever Soviet propaganda which threatened to expose the official German war news policy as a fraud. He included a copy of the form letter which the OKW had prepared to answer inquiries from relatives of German prisoners.[38] It contained the charge that the Soviets' handling of the question of prisoners' affairs was a breach of international law, since the enemy had neither published a list of the captives' names nor allowed teams of neutrals to inspect their prison camps. Therefore, the High Command concluded, all the men in question would have to be regarded as "missing" unless subsequent information proved the contrary. The OKW regretted not being in a position to give reassuring answers to the inquiries, but Moscow's actions precluded its doing so. In his instructions, Bormann pointed out the dangers involved in this agitation and instructed his Party subordinates to approach the troubled families and treat them "warm-heartedly and tactfully."

The "Heitz Affair" showed that there was little the Party members could do to relieve the tension caused in Germany by the obscurity which shrouded Stalingrad. A rumor spread during the summer of 1944 that General Heitz, a prisoner of war in the Soviet Union, was able to act as a contact between the home front and the German captives. According to the story, relatives had merely to complete a form which was available and dispatch it to the commander of Soviet prisoner-of-war camp number 27. Apparently Heitz actually did have contacts with several of the prisoner-of-war camps, and evidence points to his having been able to get scattered bits of news back to Germany.[39]

The rumor circulated that the official form in question had been prepared by the OKW and that the High Command would indeed help to establish contacts. This was partly the result of an indiscretion by a Dr. Dränger of Chemnitz, who misinterpreted an answer to an inquiry he received from the Saalfeld, Thuringia, office of the OKW.[40] Hundreds of letters began to pour into the offices of the

High Command in connection with Heitz, with postmarks ranging from Vienna to Flensburg.[41] For some time, even the Reich propaganda offices were uncertain if the questionnaire was a "refined agitation trick of enemy elements or whether the Wehrmacht Information Office actually was carrying out this function."

The Heitz Affair seemed so serious that one Nazi functionary speculated in a report to the Reich Propaganda Office at Essen "that the appearance of these questionnaires was a part of the planned putsch of the clique of generals."[42] Before the affair had died down, the Party chancellery, the OKW, the Propaganda Ministry, and the SS had all become involved. Goebbels ordered a propaganda counteroffensive through his whisper propaganda channels, and the Party chancellery admitted that the Heitz Affair was a refined Soviet swindle. The OKW had never established contact with Heitz.

Not the least embarrassing result of the Stalingrad disaster was the periodic pronouncements of the "National Committee for a Free Germany," the Seydlitz committee composed of prominent prisoners of war in the Soviet Union. The Wehrmacht was subjected to a barrage of counterpropaganda concerning the "committee of traitors," even though it was given no attention in German home propaganda. To attack the Seydlitz propaganda dropped by the Russians over the German lines, the chief of the Army General Staff, General Heinz Guderian, issued a statement to the troops at the front that the committee consisted of Communist émigrés and that the soldiers involved had been drugged. But German officialdom in general acted upon the sensible conviction that the less attention paid to this committee the better.

The home front was never really convinced by the Stalingrad propaganda. To the German people Stalingrad spelled disaster, and as a result Hitler lost much of his prestige as a strategist. The situation was quite unlike that of the previous winter after the reversal at Moscow, because in this case he could not escape blame for the tragedy by sacking the commander in chief and his generals, for now he was himself commander in chief and had personally directed the operations in Russia. His boasts of 1942 had proved empty, as had those of 1941.

Hitler's reaction to the defeat at Stalingrad was one of contempt for his officers and men. After promoting Paulus to field marshal only hours before the end, the Führer fully expected him to commit suicide. When he chose captivity instead, Hitler was beside himself with rage: the Sixth Army had "fallen short at the threshold of immortality"; Paulus and the others were disgraced by their craven clinging to life. Hitler made matters worse by attempting to conceal the fact that some 90,000 German soldiers had surrendered. When all was lost, he expected that every last man would die a hero's death there, and later generations would be able to look back on Stalingrad and feel that the men who gave their lives were fulfilling Germany's mission to protect the west from a "Jewish-Bolshevik-Mongol inundation."

The men at Stalingrad took a rather dim view of Nazi rhetoric on their fate. It was clear to them that they had been betrayed, as the following quotation from a letter written by a German soldier in the Stalingrad pocket during the final days of the battle reveals: "When you receive this letter, listen intently to it, perhaps you will hear my voice then. They tell us that our struggle is for Germany. But there are only a few here who believe that this meaningless sacrifice could be of use to our country."[43]

Yet nothing short of total victory or total defeat was acceptable to Hitler, and it followed that the entire Sixth Army had to perish in an act of self-immolation. Whatever he did had to be done in the most forceful, epic manner. Defeat, if defeat it was to be, should have the style of a great military triumph, in the "brave manner of the National Socialist." The myth of Stalingrad was an attempt to turn defeat into victory, to replace an unfortunate reality with a "new reality," and it was consonant with Hitler's world view which was based on race, violence, and struggle to the death.

XII Postlude to Stalingrad: Goebbels's Anti-Bolshevik Campaign

Stalingrad marked a turning point in German war propaganda that featured a rising tide of emotion which culminated in a nearly total surrender to the mythical and irrational in 1945. Oddly enough it was the Allied demand for "unconditional surrender," conceived by Roosevelt, sanctioned by Churchill, and announced at the Casablanca Conference in January 1943, that gave an impetus to this development. Stalingrad and "unconditional surrender" were the two pillars of the myth promulgated in the winter of 1943.

The demand for an "unconditional surrender" of Germany provided Goebbels with a dramatic issue, and he used it to conjure up frightening images of slavery and liquidation should the Allies prevail.[1] According to Goebbels this was the issue he had been looking for:

What he [Churchill] together with Roosevelt . . . hatched there at Casablanca with the formula of "unconditional surrender" was one of the worst cases of stupidity in world history. I would have never been in the position to conceive an inflammatory slogan of this kind for my propaganda . . . By their demand for an unconditional surrender, Churchill and Roosevelt have succeeded in achieving what my propaganda alone could have done only with the greatest difficulty: to weld the German people together in a solid block which will be victorious or go down to destruction. He who today might

191

still think of opposition against us or of peace with the enemy is
a hopeless fool and should have his head chopped off for his stupidity.[2]

The myth of the danger to Western civilization posed by the
"Jewish-Bolshevik-Mongol" drive for total continental power took
the tactical form of the exaggerated propaganda of doom following
Stalingrad. Goebbels sounded the keynote of the campaign in his
notorious "total war" address in the Berlin Sports Palace on February
19 which was a demagogic tour de force. The thrust of the speech
was that only the Wehrmacht stood between the survival of Western
culture and racial chaos:

Bolshevization of the Reich would bring the liquidation of our entire
intelligentsia and leadership class . . . and our working masses . . .
[would be forced to become] Bolshevik-Jewish slaves . . .

Behind the flooding Soviet divisions we already see the Jewish
liquidation squads, and behind these arises the terror, the ghost
of hungering millions, and absolute anarchy. Here international Jewry
again shows itself to be the devilish ferment of decomposition,
enjoying a cynical satisfaction at throwing the world into horrible
disorder and thereby causing the downfall of a culture thousands
of years old, to which it has never contributed. Thus we know what
job lies ahead of us.[3]

The German nation was fighting for its very existence, for its most
precious possessions, for its families, women, and children, for the
beauty of its countryside, for its cities and villages, indeed for
"everything that makes life livable." Total war was the only alternative
to total destruction.[4]

Goebbels's "Ten Questions to the German Nation," touted as a
"plebiscite for total war," summarized the issues: Did they believe
in ultimate victory and were they willing to follow the Führer "through
thick and thin" until this victory was theirs? Would they work the
longer hours necessary, even up to seventeen hours per day? Were
the English correct in saying that the Reich did not want total war
but capitulation? Did the nation want total war, "more total and
radical" than they could even imagine? Was their trust in the Führer
firmer than ever before? "Are you prepared from now on to use
all of your strength to make available the men and weapons needed
on the eastern front in order to strike the death blow to Bolshevism?"

Did they agree that the government should liquidate a small clique of war shirkers? Should all citizens be treated the same and share in the job at hand? The handpicked audience ecstatically roared its approval.

It has become clear that Goebbels's address was not in fact directed to his audience in Berlin; instead it was delivered to convince Hitler that he should take decisive steps to introduce a concentrated total war effort on the home front.[5] Goebbels had been upset about the war production effort, and he proposed stringent measures to ensure every last citizen's participation in strengthening the nation. In mid-January Hitler had ordered Keitel, Bormann, and Lammers to explore the question of total war. Goebbels was increasingly provoked because the committee did next to nothing except to announce later in January that all men from sixteen to sixty-five and all women from seventeen to forty-five were expected to report by March 31 for defense work. But Goebbels envisioned a radical departure from the previous lax standards; it was his contention that the total war program needed direction and he intended to see that it was provided. The Sports Palace address, he thought, would yield the necessary incentive.[6]

Goebbels was to fail in his effort, however, even though Hitler was very impressed with the recording of the mass meeting which was rushed by courier plane to his headquarters in Vinniza immediately after the address.[7] Naumann offers the following reason for Hitler's decision not to bend to Goebbels's requests for mobilizing the home front. The Führer was haunted by the vision of a restaging of a "stab in the back betrayal" like that of 1918; as a result, he would take no steps which in any way might lead to unnecessary unrest in the Reich. In 1918 this had meant strikes, starvation, and revolution; he would avoid reoccurrence of this trauma at all costs. What Goebbels felt to be a criminal dereliction of duty continued on the home front; the scandalous Berlin restaurants for Party *Bonzen,* the hairdresser salons operating at full capacity, and the hundreds of thousands of private maids employed were but the worst examples of luxuries which he wanted curtailed.

Goebbels continued to hammer away at the question of total war, arguing that only a 100 percent involvement would prevent the Reich's enslavement.[8] The enemy, he pointed out, had long before instituted total mobilization. The only alternative was for every German man and woman to contribute to the common effort and to summon the resources and energy necessary for the final victory. Heroic thought and action were the command of the hour, and Goebbels belabored this theme in two *Reich* articles to further that end.[9] Hitler, nevertheless, refused to give way to Goebbels's prodding, and this would trouble the minister until the end of the war.

Goebbels's Sports Palace tour de force was motivated by a second consideration: to launch a major propaganda campaign based on gloom and fear of bolshevism, which was to become the leitmotiv of the winter of 1943. Its most appropriate catchphrase was "Western Civilization in Danger," a conviction reinforced by the discovery of the Katyn massacre in February. The campaign was very persuasive because it accurately mirrored German opinion at that point in the war. Fear of the "Mongol hordes" of the Red Army was intensified as a result of Stalingrad. Furthermore, Goebbels's appeal struck a responsive chord because he enjoyed the distinct advantage of capitalizing on a theme which was consistent with Nazi ideology and yet which also complemented the German's traditional fear of the unknown east. The irony of the situation was that in the opinion of both the propaganda minister and Naumann, the campaign ultimately was too successful in that the soldiers of the Wehrmacht themselves came to believe the extraordinarily exaggerated accounts of the nature of the Bolshevik beast-man. Naumann contends that the campaign had deleterious effects at the front, although back in the Reich Goebbels found the response he desired.[10]

Goebbels used every available means to carry his message to the nation, and Propaganda Directive Nr. 49 enjoined the Nazi leaders to mobilize the Party in an effort to spread the truth to every last village in the Reich.[11] The entire Berlin and provincial propaganda apparatus concentrated its work almost exclusively on the anti-Bolshevik campaign during this period. Every public medium was admonished to draw variations on the theme "Victory or Bolshevik Chaos" to the end that the nation would "stand solid with Europe" in a common anti-Jewish, anti-Bolshevik front.

The Reich as well as the eastern military zone was saturated with anti-Bolshevik propaganda. Wall posters proclaimed impending doom, with slogans such as "Victory or Bolshevism," "Hard Times,

Hard Work, Hard Hearts," and "Total War—the Shortest War."[12] Over a million copies of Goebbels's address were distributed, and the Postal Service contributed to victory with the letter stamp "Our Führer Will Banish Bolshevism." The Nazis went to great lengths to spread fear of the Soviets by constant allusions to the terror that would follow a "Jewish-Bolshevik" victory in the war. The message was simple enough: either Europe must unite behind the Reich to achieve victory or the entire continent would sink into Bolshevik chaos. The fate of Western civilization hung in the balance.

Goebbels was shrewd enough to play on the fear of the Russians in the Allied camp, an appeal lent more credence in London than in Washington. He observed in his diary that even the enemy press was admitting the propaganda victories that he was winning in the anti-Bolshevik campaign, and he pointed to tensions in Britain and the United States to support his case: "There can no longer be any talk that we are merely standing on the defensive in the propaganda war. We have seized the offensive now and are making a good deal of trouble for the English and Americans with our anti-Bolshevik releases. This proves the point that cleverly directed propaganda can make gains in an unpromising military situation. One only needs the power of imagination."[13]

In his editorial of March 7, 1943, Goebbels denied attempting to influence opinion among the enemy nations, asserting that what he had to say was directed only to the German people. How the foreign countries interpreted it was their own business. Nonetheless, he charged that although the British government might deny it, "they cannot deceive us about the fact that widespread elements of the English public are also already realizing the danger which Bolshevism poses for the Western world."[14]

The question of international Jewry's role in the "conspiracy" against the Reich was given bold play in the anti-Bolshevik campaign. Hitler's proclamation on the anniversary of the founding of the NSDAP, which was read by State Secretary Esser in the Hofbraühaus in Munich on February 24, 1943, was little more than an anti-Semitic tirade. Hitler outlined once again the part being played by the Wehrmacht in the struggle against the "Jewish Bolsheviks" of Moscow, who were supported by the Jewish bankers of London and New York. He promised that the Reich would destroy the power of the world Israelite coalition and assured the nation that the war would not result in the annihilation "of the Aryan race, but will end with the destruction of European Jewry."[15]

In many respects, the entire propaganda campaign following Stalingrad was as much an anti-Jewish as an anti-Bolshevik crusade. The two themes were interchangeable; for example, in the reporting on the massacres at Katyn, the Jewish "blood guilt" was stressed to an even greater extent than the Bolshevik.

In commenting to the journalists at the daily press conference at the Propaganda Ministry on May 10, 1943, Ministerial Counsel Fischer took the following line: "A great political task will be fulfilled with the anti-Semitic campaign . . . The Jewish question might ostensibly be solved in Germany, but do not forget that Jewry has expanded its position more than ever in the world, occupies the strongest bastions and stands ready to wring our necks . . . Within a short time the whole German press [must] become an anti-Semitic fighting press."[16]

Goebbels was elated with the success his campaign enjoyed. His assistant Rudolf Semmler observed that the minister took account of every foreign writer who showed concern about the spread of bolshevism and the complications which could result from a Soviet victory. Goebbels felt that these fears could be traced directly to his own propaganda campaign. Semmler commented that "Goebbels is as proud as a general would be of his successful operations."[17] As the minister himself wrote, "Let Europe be frightened to death; all the sooner will it become sensible."[18]

Fear was a major component of home propaganda as well, and Goebbels painted a bleaker picture of the military situation on the eastern front than the facts warranted. Following the defeat at Stalingrad, the Wehrmacht set out to stabilize the front, which had been threatened with catastrophe. By mid-March the German forces held the same line in the Donetz and Mius area as they had during the winter of 1941–1942.[19]

The directives to the press stressed that the newspapers were not to make the error of commenting optimistically on the course of the war in Russia because this would tend to arouse a false sense of security.[20] A case in point was the treatment of the German recapture of Kharkov in March 1943. Goebbels noted in his diary that initially Hitler wanted to play up the success at Kharkov but that he had finally conceded that this would conflict with his current propaganda orchestration. Goebbels found it very difficult to explain Kharkov at the height of his anti-Bolshevik propaganda campaign, and he did his best to camouflage the victory. Beyond a Special Announcement, it did not receive much attention. Instead, the *Völkischer Beobachter* diverted the public's attention to naval engagements off the coast of South America.[21]

Goebbels was displeased by the Russian reverses: "We were just gathering momentum in injecting a real fear of Bolshevism in the world. We cannot do that now with as much success as we have in the past weeks." At another point he wrote that he would prefer "that we hold on to the rather pessimistic interpretation . . . for it will be that much easier to push through total mobilization decrees." Above all, Goebbels wished to avoid conveying the mistaken impression that the Wehrmacht was launching a grand offensive and that the country could expect news of many more such victories.[22] Through SD channels he learned that many people realized they were being deceived by his campaign of "functional pessimism." In his *Reich* article of March 14, 1943, the minister categorically denied that he had exaggerated the situation on the eastern front and declared that anyone who believed that he had was guilty of "wanton self-deception."[23]

Under these conditions, the release of the news on the discovery of the Katyn massacres was a timely, felicitous contribution to the propaganda of pessimism. The allegation that the Soviets had liquidated the flower of the Polish officer corps in the Katyn Forest had the most serious implications, confusing the Allies' relations among themselves as well as with the Polish government-in-exile in London. This is not the place to assess guilt for Katyn, although J. K. Zawodny makes a persuasive case that Stalin was responsible for this crime.[24] Goebbels made the most of the opportunity it presented. He commented at the time that "we are now using the discovery of 12,000 Polish officers, murdered by the GPU, for anti-Bolshevik propaganda in a grand style. We sent neutral journalists and Polish intellectuals to the spot where they were found. Their reports now reaching us from abroad are gruesome. The Führer has also given permission for us to hand out a dramatic news item to the German press. I gave instructions to make the widest possible use of this propaganda material. We shall be able to live on it for a couple of weeks."[25]

Headlines such as "GPU Murder of 12,000 Polish Officers" and "Judas Blood Guilt Grows to the Unfathomable" decried the crime as one of the most hideous aberrations of the human soul. The Nazis charged that Jewish officers of the Red Army were responsible for the murders, and a documentary film was promptly released entitled *In the Forest of Katyn*. The Foreign Ministry published its *Official Material on the Mass Murders at Katyn* as well.[26]

The Allies were taunted with references to their "embarrassed silence" about the Russian mass murders. When were the nations which earlier had shouted protests whenever "some Hebrew had his window kicked in" going to take a stand? The answer was simple, they asserted. It was because the Jews controlled the Allied press. The "Jewish" story that Katyn was some archaeological burial ground was too absurd for comment, they held.[27]

Ironically, Himmler saw the value of Katyn for German propaganda. He wrote to von Ribbentrop after the discovery was announced, asking whether it would not be a good opportunity to embarrass the Warsaw government-in-exile by inviting the Polish premier Sikorski to fly to Katyn and view the mass graves.[28] Ribbentrop answered on April 26, 1943, that although the idea had a good deal of merit as a propaganda measure, any contact with the head of the émigré regime was out of the question.[29]

Having achieved his goals, Goebbels ordered an end to the propaganda of doom in April 1943. Determination to slay the Bolshevik had been intensified and at least some measures for total war had been instituted. Goebbels had endeavored to strengthen the nation's will to resist, to see that war production rose, to raise morale, and to assure the Reich of Hitler's genius and the inspired character of his mission. In his Sports Palace address of June 5, 1943, Goebbels officially declared that the crisis had ended.[30]

XIII Italy Leaves the War

Major Nazi propaganda campaigns in World War II followed one of two patterns. Either they reported news of victory with appropriate fanfare or they shrouded defeat in the reassuring fog of myth. The Axis loss of North Africa in May 1943 and the subsequent fall of Mussolini fit neither of these models, and Goebbels was forced to assign the reversals the role of peripheral propaganda motifs. The result was one of the worst propaganda defeats of the entire war. Even though Stalingrad was a tragedy without parallel, Goebbels made of it a propaganda rallying cry. But after the Axis surrender of 252,000 troops at Cape Bon in Tunisia, he did not have the raw material to write a scenario like the one devised for Stalingrad. There was to be no official myth of Rommel, El Alamein, or the Africa Corps.

News from the African front worsened the already depressed public morale. Once General Eisenhower had launched "Operation Torch" by landing 107,000 troops in Casablanca, Oran, and Algiers in November 1942, the German-Italian position in the African theater became untenable. Now Rommel faced the enemy on two fronts. Initial German reaction to the Allied landing took the form of the preposterous claim that England and the United States had violated international law by illegally entering Vichy's North African provinces in a brutal "gangster operation" inspired by the "forces of international

Jewry" in league with Franklin and Eleanor Roosevelt.[1] Goebbels's assertion met a cold response at home where people did not want to be lectured on points of international law when the war "obviously was a struggle for world power."[2] Nor were they impressed by the continuous reports of German "planned withdrawals"—news accounts of the fall of Tobruk a few days after the Allied landing were the most blatant example of this technique. What made the situation worse was that although the city was in Allied hands on November 12–13 the OKW did not announce the loss until November 14. This was very agitating to Goebbels who learned that ever growing numbers of people were turning to the German broadcasts of the BBC which often reported news hours, sometimes even days, before Berlin made the identical announcements. Goebbels complained to the Führer headquarters about this problem, pointing out that the trust of the people could not be misused in such a way. He received the unsatisfactory reply that the Wehrmacht communiqués for Africa had to await the Italian initiative.[3]

A good many people were convinced that the long-awaited second front had begun in earnest in North Africa, and they found the situation disturbing. Neither Hitler's claims in his November 9 Munich address nor Pétain's alleged announcement that Vichy would resist an Allied landing because the "honor of France was at stake" was particularly reassuring. The propaganda from Rome was more bombastic and unconvincing than ever.[4] Although the state of affairs gave little cause for confidence, many people still believed that the strategic genius of Rommel would yet turn the tide—references were made to his remark in October 1942 that he would take Egypt.[5] There was some speculation that the field marshal was not in Africa at all, but "was in a hospital in Berlin." Rommel did in fact return to the Reich for medical treatment in 1943, but the earlier rumors resulted from the official silence on the "Desert Fox" which Goebbels demanded in order to protect the general's reputation. Rommel was a friend of his who frequently visited the Goebbels family at Schwanenwerder and Lanke when he returned to Berlin.

News from the African front was scarce for several months following the Allied landing. One theme, however, was repeatedly aired—the "world imperial threat of the U.S.A.," a spinoff from Hitler's November 8 address in which he answered Roosevelt's announcement that the Allies were opening up a second front in North Africa in support of their "heroic allies in Russia":

If Roosevelt began his attack on North Africa with the observation that he must protect it from Germany and from Italy, then you don't have to waste words describing the lies of this old gangster. Without a doubt he is the most hypocritical member of this entire club opposed to us. But Mr. Roosevelt can be sure that he won't have the last say . . . no attack which the enemy has launched against us has yet been successful.[6]

The lesson to be learned was clear: the Africa Corps would drive the Allied forces into the sea. No second "miracle of Dunkirk" would ensue. Helmut Sündermann published an article entitled "Roosevelt against Europe—Europe against Roosevelt" in which he predicted that the combined striking force of the Navy's U-boat fleet and the Africa Corps would write an end to Roosevelt's drive for world power.[7] The Nazis also attempted to spread dissension among the Allies by conjuring up the claim that the "Jewish-driven Roosevelt" not only meant to make a cipher of Germany, but most assuredly would devour England's world empire as well. Not being inspired by a Weltanschauung delivered by Providence, the Yankee merchants of death knew no true and enduring values; they respected only the almighty dollar. Hitler and the Wehrmacht would be forced to teach them some, the *Völkischer Beobachter* boasted.[8]

Roosevelt was accused of pursuing perfidious and sinister aims. One day he allegedly was about to invade Spain; the next he was staging a reign of terror in North Africa against his supposed French "ally"; on another occasion he was accused of "opening the gates of South America to Bolshevism." Roosevelt also served as a convenient racial symbol now that most of European Jewry had either emigrated or been transported to the death camps. The theme of Jewish control over the president lent some sense of cohesion to the otherwise poorly organized anti-American propaganda campaign, and it was easily merged with the Nazis' anti-Bolshevik appeal which, as has been seen, assumed growing importance after Stalingrad. Although Goebbels charged that Roosevelt intended to "deliver Europe to the Bolsheviks," he made no attempt to reconcile the German occupation of Vichy France in November 1942 with the propaganda claim that the Reich's mission was to spread *Kultur* and social justice in contrast to the enemy's sole interest in conquest.

During the long months of the Stalingrad debacle, the African front was very much in the background, where it remained throughout March and much of April 1943. When news from Africa did appear, it offered little hope for the German cause. But pessimism outran the objective military situation by several months. Some people had expected the entire front to collapse by February.[9] Rommel, who had returned to Germany on sick leave, was ordered to remain in Europe and to take a rest cure; after mid-March his command was assigned to General von Arnim who, unlike Rommel, was considered expendable in the Africa Corps' hopeless situation. For all practical purposes the Africa Corps was cut off from its sources of supply across the Mediterranean, and the end came at Tunis in May. The German and Italian troops, totaling some 252,000 men, then began their long months of Allied captivity, a situation which not a few of them welcomed, in contrast to their counterparts on the eastern front, many of whom preferred death to Soviet captivity. Goebbels was clearly pleased to learn that so many German troops had safely fallen into Allied captivity and that a second massacre on the Stalingrad model was avoided.

Nothing came of Hitler's boast to Mussolini that "with your support, Duce, my troops will make Tunis the Verdun of the Mediterranean."[10] Yet during the final weeks before the end in Africa, German propaganda made a great play of Mussolini's will to fight to the final victory side by side with the Führer. As respect for the Duce and the Italian military fell to a new low, the propagandists whistled another tune. Theodor Seibert wrote a gratuitous article in the *Völkischer Beobachter* claiming that the German and Italian soldiers had come to know each other better than at any other time in their history. Each had learned to respect the other, and the Wehrmacht had learned to forget earlier prejudices about the skill of its neighbors to the south. The Italians had proved to be the best of comrades and were the worthy heirs of the traditions of the Roman Empire.[11]

There was a wide divergence between Goebbels's public and private posture on the Italian question, and his diary notations at this point in the war were devastating. Speculating why Rommel had fallen ill in North Africa, he cited the tense relations between Mussolini and Rommel. Such a situation, he decided, would make anyone sick: "The North African operation has cost us a tremendous price in both equipment and blood. We can thank the Italians for that. In the final analysis, they should have carried out their war preparations so that at least they could have held their overseas territories. But that isn't the worst of it; they aren't even able to defend Italy itself. Without a doubt our allies are the worst to be found in the whole world."[12]

The quiet on the news front from Africa was foreboding, and those who could read between the lines knew how to interpret a cover story, complete with photographs, which was headlined "The Atlantic Wall Stands Impregnable."[13] The message was clear: once the Allies had wiped out resistance in North Africa, they would undergo a vain attempt to gain a foothold on the continent. When the Führer headquarters and Nazi propagandists began to employ the familiar Stalingrad language about "heroic resistance" in Tunisia, it became obvious that the game was up in North Africa. As the first pocket surrendered, the OKW's jargon was pregnant with meaning: "In the area of Bizerta several fighting units clung to their positions to the last bullet."[14] Finally, the headlines on May 14 carried the message, "Heroic Battle in Tunisia Ended."[15] A letter from Hitler to General von Arnim, commander of the Africa Corps, praised him highly:

I am grateful to you, and congratulate you and your heroic fighting troops who loyally defended every last meter of African soil with our Italian comrades.

All the German people have followed the heroic campaign of their soldiers in Tunisia. It will play a vital part in our final victory in this war. Your fight to the finish and the exemplary conduct of your troops is an inspiration for the Wehrmacht of the Greater German Reich and will remain a glorious chapter in German military history.[16]

At length the German people were informed about the whereabouts of Field Marshal Rommel in language which left his heroic image unsullied. The history of his ill health was detailed, and a very carefully worded communiqué indicated that he had left his comrades behind in Africa only after the Führer had ordered him to do so. On March 11 Hitler had awarded Rommel yet another medal in recognition of his distinguished service as commander of the Africa Corps, adding the Swords and Diamonds to his Knights Cross of the Iron Cross.[17] The nation was reassured that "after his complete recovery the Führer will give him a new assignment."[18]

Even before the campaign had ended Goebbels and his staff had begun the challenging assignment of softening the blow of the German defeat. The minister wrote in his diary at that time:

The fighting is over in Tunisia. I write these lines with a heavy heart. I can't read the English-American braggadocio any more . . . I find it unbearable to become enraged every day with these reports and to sit here in a stew. . . . Naturally the end of the fighting in Tunisia is very depressing. Sometimes I have the feeling that we are not taking the initiative as much as we should in this war. In the past five months, the enemy has assumed the upper hand almost everywhere. They are smashing us in the air war, and have opened severe wounds in the east, they trounced us in North Africa and even the U-boat war is not now bringing the successes which we had expected from it.[19]

As the battle came to an end Fritzsche took a line in his weekly newscast which was intended to conceal the real significance of the reversal, but which demonstrated instead the weakness of Nazi propaganda on North Africa. Fritzsche unleashed his sarcasm on London where "Big Ben rang out for victory" and where "a Negro march was played to honor the colonials." In the North African theater, he pointed out, a most unequal struggle had pitted an "unbelievably small German and Italian force against the elite troops of England and the United States," who had planned to link up with the Soviet hordes moving in from the east and together storm the continent. They had failed because the six months that the Africa Corps held out enabled the Axis to complete the Atlantic Wall and the other defenses of "Fortress Europe." Fritzsche climaxed his remarks with the contention that the enemy's victory in Africa had come six months too late. Europe was now impregnable: "The great chance which fate bid the enemy is past." Their success was due to the bravery of the Stalingrad fighters and "to the German and

"The Eternal Jew": Advertisement for an
anti-Semitic exhibition. (Bundesarchiv.)

"The aim of bolshevism: To drown the world in blood." Poster of
the Anti-Bolshevik Fighting Alliance, Berlin. (Bundesarchiv.)

A war poster: "Adolf Hitler Is Victory." (Bundesarchiv.)

Goebbels in a characteristic platform pose. (Bundesarchiv.)

Goebbels greets Wilhelm
Haegert, former head of the
Publications Section in the
Propaganda Ministry, on the
square of reoccupied
Lauban/Silesia in 1945.

The radio commentator
Hans Fritzsche, famous for
his witty and sarcastic
reports on war news.

Werner Naumann after the war. (Personal collection.)

Günther d'Alquen at the front.
(SS Kriegsberichter.)

Helmut Sündermann,
deputy Reich press chief.
(Personal collection.)

Eberhard Taubert.
(Personal collection.)

Hans Schwarz van Berk.
(Personal collection.)

Rudolf Hess prepares for flight to Scotland. Willi Messerschmitt
at left. (Courtesy of Josef Platzer, far right.)

Comrade among comrades. (*Mit Hitler in Polen.*)

Italian troops who held out in Tunisia until the hour of danger had passed."[20]

When the weary Axis forces surrendered at Cape Bon, Goebbels outlined a tactical propaganda operation which embraced the following points:

1. The two-year campaign in North Africa proved the superiority of the Axis troops both in morale and as a fighting force.
2. North Africa assured the completion of "Fortress Europe."
3. North Africa tied down most of the English imperial forces for more than two years.
4. Plans of the enemy for a second front are now out of the question.
5. By holding down the British and American troops in Africa, Japan assumed the initiative in the Pacific.
6. The danger to enemy shipping in the Mediterranean remains a serious threat.
7. The bravery our troops demonstrated will always be a source of pride for the German people.
8. Mutual German-Italian comradeship and loyalty were the key-notes of the campaign, which was ended only because of the difficulties we faced in supplying our troops, and which gave the enemy an overwhelming superiority in both men and matériel.[21]

The thrust of the propaganda line was that the African campaign "had been a complete strategic success."[22] For obvious reasons no comparisons to Stalingrad were to be made.[23]

The impression this propaganda made on most people was poor. Goebbels simply did not master the task facing him, and even his *Reich* article at the time of the surrender did not treat the subject at hand, but was devoted instead to the Jewish question. The Germans were uninterested in being deceived about the nonexistent powers of the so-called international Jewish conspiracy. Instead, they wanted straight talk on Africa, which was not forthcoming.

An SD report at the end of May summarized the problem in words which irritated Goebbels. SD Chief Ohlendorf's office offered an objective assessment of the morale situation which left no doubt that the newspaper and radio propaganda was receiving scant attention. The real questions on people's minds—about the duration of the war, the damage to German industries, and the Reich's chances for victory—were not being answered. Under such circumstances, it was very difficult for any propaganda to come across successfully. The SD summarized the state of affairs with the remark that public opinion and the content of German propaganda were poles apart.

The North African propaganda, especially the coverage on the Tunisian campaign, brought the crisis in public confidence to a head. There were several reasons for this development. Despite the fact that Eisenhower had landed in North Africa, creating a completely new strategic problem, there was no mention of this in the German news media. And although Hitler and Mussolini realized that they ultimately would be forced out of Africa, they failed to prepare the nation for this development. Instead, some people continued to conjure up images of Rommel capturing Egypt and carrying the war against the English to the Near East, India, and Asia, while others were unable to reconcile earlier boasts of alleged German supply deliveries, U-boat successes, and tactical air operations in the African theater with subsequent reports of enemy superiority in men and matériel. Furthermore, it was obvious that the initiative in the war now belonged to the Allies. But Hitler and Goebbels did not choose to admit the objective military-strategic situation until they were forced to; had they done so, they would have attained a much higher level of credibility in 1943 than was the case.[24]

Following "Tunisgrad," as the surrender in North Africa was popularly referred to in Germany, there was very little coverage of the Mediterranean front. Criticism of Italy continued to spread throughout the Reich. The general opinion was that the fighting spirit of the Italians was negligible. One *Volksgenosse* summed up the people's view succinctly: "Perhaps we can trust Mussolini, but you can be sure that one day he will land here as an Italian immigrant."[25] Bormann felt that the situation was getting out of hand, and he ordered the Party stalwarts to move against the complainers. His contention was that German distrust would have effects far beyond Italy; the Reich would forfeit the loyalty of all its allies fighting in the east to defeat Soviet Russia.[26]

The communiqué of July 19 covering the final meeting between the Führer and the Duce before the fall of the Italian dictator reflected Hitler's low estimate of Mussolini's performance: "The Führer and the Duce met on Monday July 19 in a city in Upper Italy. They discussed the military situation."[27] The meaning behind this pallid communiqué was unmistakable: the Duce's prestige had fallen to a new low, and for all intents and purposes the truncated remains of the Roman Empire were now but another province of the Greater German Reich.

The sands of time were running out for Mussolini. For some time dissatisfaction with him had been growing in Italy, and the surrender in Tunisia made his position even more precarious. The final blow came in response to the Allied landing in Sicily in July 1943 when Mussolini's enemies in the army and the Party joined forces with the crown to topple him from power.[28]

On July 26, Victor Emmanuel named Marshal Badoglio as prime minister. Badoglio proceeded to build a cabinet with non-Party members, declared the Fascist Party dissolved, and initiated negotiations with the Allies to take Italy out of the war. He made a public declaration that Italy would continue to fight loyally side by side with Germany, a stratagem to avert the immediate occupation of Italy by the Wehrmacht.

The news of the fall of Mussolini sent a shock wave throughout Germany. The mood in the Führer headquarters was devastating, and the Allied raids over Hamburg and Hannover which followed the revelation only made matters worse. Hitler reacted in a rage characteristic of him when he felt betrayed, and he conceived of several alternative plans to handle the situation. The boldest of these was to dispatch a parachute division to Rome to arrest the conspirators and the king and to clean out the Vatican, which he long had suspected was a nest of intrigue.[29] But he too had to await the developing events. Goebbels's first reaction was to wail "Duce . . . Duce . . . Duce!" in a falsetto mockery of the Italian crowds in the Palazzo Venezia.[30]

Goebbels mirrored in his diary the extremely difficult circumstances in which he found himself in those days:

Clearly there is a great deal of unrest and exasperation among the German people, and the situation is made worse by the fact that at the moment we are unable to detail the background of the crisis in Italy. What can we say as of now? We cannot say what we think personally much less write it. And what we are able to write will not give anyone a clearer picture of the Italian crisis . . . The country demands the facts and more than anything wants to hear from the Führer. But of course he cannot do that at this time; it is out of the question. The reason for this is that we ourselves are waiting to see how things develop; and the people must wait as well.[31]

The German public first heard the news about the fall of Mussolini on the BBC, a full day before that extraordinary event was announced from Berlin. Subsequent Nazi propaganda on Italy followed the inept pattern established at the outset. At no time during the war was German propaganda more equivocal than during the Italian crisis of 1943. The weekly radio address of Hans Fritzsche, delivered as usual on July 31, was a shallow performance which exasperated those who even bothered to listen to it. The German people wanted facts, not a virtuoso rhetorical performance with no flesh and blood.

During the following weeks, ad hoc measures characterized German propaganda regarding Italy. From the fall of Mussolini until the Allies captured Sicily on August 18, coverage on the Duce and the southern front was paltry except for some low-keyed biographic sketches of his career remarkable for their obscurity. There was no mention of the fact that Mussolini was a captive of the Badoglio regime, and understandably the Nazis did not speculate about the real intentions of the new government. The best that they could do was to offer the rididulous palliative that Mussolini had stepped down "due to ill health" and that Badoglio would fight on nobly in the great tradition of the Roman Empire and Italian fascism.[32] As the crisis continued to unfold Goebbels's position became more embarrassing by the day because he, like the German people, learned of Italian developments over the radio.[33] His opportunity for maneuver was narrowed to the limit.

Goebbels tried vainly to protect Berlin's vulnerable position by cleverly worded staff and media directives. "The fact that the Reich Government has kept its counsel does not mean that we are embarrassed or perplexed. We have kept quiet solely for our own national interest. This theme is to be avoided wherever possible."[34] As he often did in times of stress when the objective situation could not be faced squarely, he fell back on the myth that the presence of the Führer guaranteed victory.

All of this did not go down well with the people, and an intolerable credibility gap resulted. The first reaction in Germany was one of shock that a twenty-year-old regime could topple within a matter of hours. German propaganda had long emphasized the theme that the Duce and the Fascist Party were one with the life stream of Italy; the one could not exist without the other. But in the clinch there were no spontaneous uprisings in support of either the Duce or the Fascist Party in Italy.

The next concern abroad in the Reich was to obtain the facts about the state of affairs in Rome and on the Sicilian front. When these were not forthcoming, discontent spread with each passing day of the news block. Germans felt uneasy about being completely defenseless in the face of new disasters. A word from the Führer would have been reassuring as tension waxed in August 1943, and there was widespread hope that he would speak during the current crisis; under the circumstances, however, such an address was out of the question. Probably a majority of Germans intuitively sensed the gravity of the situation, and it was not uncommon for SD informers to hear that "we have a right to learn what the hell is going on," or "What good does it do our propaganda if we never learn the truth? In the end we will have to get the facts, just like at Stalingrad."[35]

The combined effects of a prolonged war, the defeats at Stalingrad and in Africa, the air raids, and the fall of Mussolini further demoralized the public and encouraged the spread of defeatism and open hostility to the Nazi regime. This was expressed in many ways. Some critics simply stated facts: "This is the beginning of the end for Fascism and National Socialism." Others cursed the Party *Bonzen,* the high-living "Golden Pheasants," and the corruption which pervaded the power structure of the Third Reich. Still others publicly demanded the end of the regime. An informer reporting from Braunschweig heard two women at the farmers market bemoaning the fact that there seemed to be no way out of Germany's desperate plight. Some railway workers close by shouted, "There is a way out all right; we've got to get rid of our Government."[36]

Some Germans were bold enough to insult Nazi Party officials publicly, a situation which created several bizarre incidents. For example, the mayor of Göttingen was harassed by his fellow Aryans during the course of a train ride from Hannover to his home in the late summer of 1943. When some passengers noticed the mayor's Party lapel badge, they began to whisper ominously. Soon someone pointed to the Nazi and affirmed that there sat another who would have to be dealt with at the proper time. One woman went so far as to threaten him with her fist. Such occurrences were not uncommon, and they tended to encourage the boldness of others. Gradually one did not see so many Party badges being worn; and by mid-1943 there was a certain risk associated with the practice. This was indicative of the reaction of one sector of the public to the declining fortunes of the Nazis.

Another symptom was the spread of rumors based on fear during this phase of the war, a situation which the news block on Italy only intensified. According to one of them, Göring, von Ribbentrop, and von Schirach had all gone into hiding. Another bore the traumatic scars of the devastating fire storm raids over Hamburg in late July 1943. Allegedly Roosevelt had demanded that Hitler be replaced with another chancellor by August 15; if he were not, then Berlin, Munich, Leipzig, and the remaining larger cities of Germany would be pulverized as Hamburg had been before them. Many rumors were traced to the BBC, which cleverly exploited the embarrassing situation in which Goebbels found himself.

Another effect of the news block was the increasing evidence of hangman's wit in the Reich. Hitler, it seems, had left the government to write yet another book; his next major work was entitled *Mein Irrtum.* According to another story, Hitler and Goebbels were both killed in a U-boat which was sunk. Although neither of them was saved, the German people were rescued. Another popular joke concerned the Party's gradual demise; any Party member bringing in five new converts to the NSDAP would be allowed to quit himself. And if he brought in ten new members, he would receive a document attesting that he himself never belonged. One wit conceived of an advertisement offering a Golden Party Honor Badge in trade for some good running boots.[37]

The fall of Mussolini was just the beginning of the troubles to come in Italy. Hitler's suspicion that Badoglio's assurances of loyalty to Berlin were a façade proved to be correct. For weeks both the Germans and the Badoglio regime unsuccessfully tried to deceive one another. Badoglio began negotiations with the Allies to take Italy out of the war, while at the same time he gave his "word of honor as a Marshal of Italy" that he would remain loyal to Berlin.

For his part, Hitler was also playing a game of deception by preparing contingency plans to occupy Italy, to intern all the Italian troops, and to rescue Mussolini.[38]

General Castellano signed the unconditional surrender of Italy in the name of the Badoglio government on September 3 at Cassibile, Sicily, although the Germans had to wait until September 8 to learn of the dramatic turn of events over the wires of the BBC. Hitler was enraged and began the German occupation of Italy. Goebbels wrote that "the Italians have left us in a critical hour. But they had better know that they have committed the most accursed political deed ever recorded in history. They have lost their sense of balance. A country simply cannot go back on its word twice in the course of a quarter of a century without cloaking the honor of Italy in disgrace and defamation."[39] He referred to Badoglio's radio appeal to the Italian people to lay down their arms with the caustic remark that they had done that long ago and the Germans hardly needed a "Freemason traitor with a Jewish mistress" in Rome to belabor the obvious.

The first propaganda reports on the Italian defection resounded in the vituperative tone characteristic of nazism in crisis. No holds were barred, and the radio, press, and speakers corps were ordered to blast away with their full complement of invective, which they had been forced to repress during the previous five weeks. The *Völkischer Beobachter* sounded the betrayal motif, asserting that eternal suffering and shame awaited the guilty in that special circle which Dante had reserved for traitors. While taking care to avoid attacks on the Italian national character, the propagandists were to launch a campaign reviling the "aristocrats, Freemasons, Jews, opportunists, and fair weather allies (Glücksritter)" responsible for timing the news of the surrender with the landing of the Americans at Salerno and the British in Calabria. Not only would the campaign in the south continue, but the Nazis would guarantee that the Italians would not be able to "harvest the fruit of their treachery."[40] German countermeasures were in progress which had led to the capture of Rome and the disarming of all Italian troops in Italy, southern France, and the Balkans.

Goebbels, joining the Party elite which hurried to the Führer headquarters at Rastenburg, implored Hitler to speak to the German people. Göring echoed this plea and added that the men at the front wanted to hear his voice as well. The Reichsmarschall, in a characteristic gesture of flamboyance, affirmed that a speech at this juncture in the war would be equivalent to the fighting strength of ten divisions.[41] Hitler finally gave his assent and recorded a speech which Goebbels first released to the public a day later on Friday evening at 5 over all the Reich networks. It was repeated several times over the various military and local stations so that as many people as possible would be exposed to the tranquilizing effects of a message from the Führer.

Hitler's recorded talk, brief and to the point, was at once a violent attack on the "Badoglio clique," a warning to the Italians who might resist German occupation, a paean of flowery praise for the Duce, and an appeal to the German home and fighting fronts to make the *Endsieg* a reality. "Mussolini," he said, "was one of the most significant men . . . in modern history, the greatest son of the Italian soil since the fall of antiquity." His overthrow would remain a source of "deep shame for future generations in Italy . . . Now as always I am happy to call this great and loyal man my friend."[42]

Then, with a remark calculated to steel the nation, Hitler claimed that "the fall of Italy has very little military significance," because with few exceptions it was the blood of German soldiers which had been shed to protect the soil of Europe and Italy. Now the Wehrmacht was free to continue the campaign without interference from any side, and the nation could rest assured that harsh measures were being taken to secure German interests in Italy. Hitler concluded his talk with the strangely prophetic remark that "a July 25th" (the date of Mussolini's overthrow) would never occur in Germany. Fate missed this particular little irony by only five days: the attempt on his life was made on July 20, 1944. Hitler did not predict victory for 1943; he promised only the nation's determination to fight until the Reich's enemies were destroyed.

The melodramatic rescue of Mussolini from "high atop a mountain" in Italy on September 12 was heralded as one of the most heroic exploits in world history, which featured the adventurous folk hero Otto Skorzeny and his SD Special Command who piloted several gliders to the mountain resort chosen by Badoglio's staff to hide the Duce—the Hotel Campo Imperatore on the Gran Sasso, the highest peak in the Apennine range. Hitler was certain that the world would marvel at Skorzeny's bold action, which he considered the quintessence of *Nibelungentreue*.[43]

The media celebrated the rescue as if it were one of the great victories of the war. The weekly newsreel featured dramatic shots of Skorzeny and Mussolini in which the Duce, clad in a black overcoat and hat, resembled more a shady rug dealer with Mafia contacts than the heroic figure of yore. Skorzeny, back at the Führer headquarters, accepted the laurels due a Siegfried figure—the Knights Cross of the Iron Cross from the Führer himself. The sequence was highlighted by coverage of the reunion of Hitler and Mussolini two days later. Goebbels was very gratified with the reaction to the freeing of Mussolini: "We can celebrate a moral victory of the first order," he wrote.[44]

At length, on September 19, Goebbels broke his long silence on the Italian question. Following the news that Mussolini had been overthrown on July 25, the minister could not bring himself to write the lead editorial for *Das Reich*. Finally, one month later, he returned to his customary editorial, although he did not choose to treat the chaotic situation south of the Alps. But on September 19 he took up the theme with a vengeance: "Let us spare ourselves running through the long story of Badoglio's treachery. Nausea wells up in our throats when we even think about it. There has never been a more contemptible betrayal in history." Hitler, he asserted, had acted brilliantly under the circumstances; his clear thinking had saved one of the most dangerous situations of the war.

Goebbels, not a little embarrassed by the Italian crisis, gave himself a vote of confidence as well:

At the time it caused some excitement that the writer of these lines skipped his weekly article on the Friday following the 25th of July. Some evil-wishers even believed that they could draw the conclusion that the events related to the fall of the Duce and that the take-over of the Badoglio regime in Rome might have left him something at a loss for words. That there could be no discussion of such a thing hardly needs more proof today. Obviously it would have been possible to speak during the week in question just as in all others . . . But respect for our national interests kept us quiet. What we could say, we did not want to, and what we wanted to say, we could not . . . This then was the classical example for the necessity of keeping silent during a war.

Goebbels concluded with the affirmation that such a turn of events as those in Italy was impossible in Germany, because the Reich had the Führer and furthermore the Party would guarantee the nation's integrity. Goebbels ended his remarks with a homily based on an Alpine metaphor. The nation, he said, had passed a precipice along a narrow and dangerous path: "Not everyone saw the danger; but all continued along the path more firmly united and following the Führer . . . Today this great man guards our life and future."[45]

The proclamation of the founding of a rejuvenated Fascist Party and the formation of the puppet Salo Republic in the German and Italian controlled regions of the country brought about a situation which was not without serious disadvantages for both Hitler and Mussolini. With the Duce overthrown, Hitler had been able to act according to his will, entirely unrestrained by considerations of how a particular decision would be received in Italy. But now he had Mussolini to deal with once again.

Goebbels attempted to make the most of a very difficult and trying state of affairs. Accordingly he stressed the themes that the Fascist Party had been reborn and was stronger than ever, the Italians were rallying to the Duce, and the Führer and Mussolini held all the trump cards for a military decision in Italy, now that the "traitorous King Victor Emmanuel" had been "expelled from the country." As the weeks of 1943 gave way to the new year, German propaganda concerning the Italian front gradually shifted to the more important anti-Semitic and anti-Bolshevik motifs. Never again did the Duce enjoy the prominence which he did following the Skorzeny episode. The Führer-Duce "loyalty of the Nibelungen" theme brought a measure of substance to a campaign which otherwise was a propagandist's nightmare. Hitler sounded the loyalty to the death motif in his Munich address two months later: "I am happy that we succeeded in saving the man who himself did everything possible to make his people great, strong, and happy and who also gave them a part in an historic struggle which will decide the future and culture of this continent."[46]

A chart registering German morale in the autumn of 1943 would show a post-Stalingrad low, followed by a moderate rise attributable to the general sense of relief subsequent to Goebbels's doom propaganda campaign. With the fall of Mussolini morale dipped precipitously, but with his rescue, the occupation of Rome, the internment of most of the Badoglio forces, and the flight of Victor Emmanuel and Badoglio spirits improved once more, despite the incessant pounding the Reich was taking from the air. The fact that Rommel and Kesselring were in command in the south lent confidence as well.

Contempt for Italy and the Italians reached a new low throughout the Reich, and some people called for the capture and execution of the king and Badoglio. The general feeling was that Italy's days of having a voice in the affairs of the continent were gone forever. One wag summed up the opinion by saying that "the Italians from now on will at best be sidewalk chestnut salesmen and donkey drivers." There was some sympathy for the German "protection of the Vatican," which allegedly would terminate its role in espionage circles as the Lisbon of Italy. One officer observed that "now the pope is closer to Himmler than he is to heaven" (dem Himmler näher als dem Himmel).

As for Mussolini, there was little hope for him either. First, he might well tie the Führer's hands when severity was in order. Furthermore, his Fascists were "cowards and intriguers" who left him in the lurch when he needed them most on July 25. Instead of storming the Badoglio power centers out of loyalty to the Duce, they sat on their hands. Now these same "cowards" and "corrupt Fascist leaders" had been returned to power. The Germans placed little faith in them, preferring to put their trust in the Wehrmacht instead. They saw the Duce for what he was after his rescue and for what he would remain until his death in 1945—a man totally dependent on Hitler, a man who would follow his orders "like a *Reichsstatthalter*."

There was not a little cynicism following Mussolini's "return to power." Some Germans wanted something tangible as repayment for Hitler's loyalty. At the very least they expected that after years of subjection to Italy the South Tyrol would be incorporated into the Greater German Reich. Some overzealous visionaries conjured up dreams on the model of the Renaissance princelings and cast their eyes to the south, arguing that the entire province of Venitia should be annexed. Mussolini's speech upon reassuming his functions as Duce did not have the desired effect.

The Italian troops interned in Germany following Badoglio's armistice were often subjected to humiliation both in prison camps and on the job in German war industries. They were spat upon, mocked, threatened, and denounced. One German worker had this to say: "This pack at least will learn what work is here in Germany, even if they were cowards on the battlefield. We'll see to that, even if they croak as a result of it." A businessman from Schwerin remarked that "this nation by betraying us and thereby all humanity should be excluded from the human race. They should be treated like the Jews, who never were part of the human family."[47]

German contempt for their Italian "ally" became so pervasive that Keitel and Bormann felt compelled to dispatch an order to combat it, fearing that those Italians who continued to fight alongside the men of the Wehrmacht would soon turn against a nation which demonstrated its derision for them in such an obnoxious manner.[48] Several months later Hitler ordered all criticism of Italian Fascists to cease, since they were the last bulwark against communism in Italy.[49] During the summer of 1944 when 600,000 Italian military internees were being transferred for work in the Reich's industries, Bormann warned the Party that the German attitude toward the Italians had to change immediately, lest it endanger the war effort.[50] The Italian question gradually faded away in favor of propaganda on the air war, the Allied invasion of France, and the "Jewish-Bolshevik danger." Nazi Italian propaganda had been a consummate failure from the beginning, and it was never to improve. German arrogance and Italian bungling had made for a rather infelicitous wartime marriage.

XIV The Long Retreat, 1943–1944

Throughout 1943 and 1944 the emphasis in Nazi propaganda was placed on the merits of Germany's inner lines and the advantages of defensive warfare. In this way Goebbels minimized the public's expectations, and he made a concerted effort to conceal German offensive operations and counterattacks. For example, when Hitler launched his final major offensive in Russia, "Operation Citadel"—the Kursk offensive of July 1943—no mention was made of this maneuver.[1] Consequently, Berlin did not lose face when the attack failed. Again, stress was laid on the German "elastic defensive."

Following this line, the Nazis rationalized the loss of Orel on August 5 as part of a "carefully prepared evacuation" that came as a result of a "shortening of the front." This was supposed to explain the loss of Bjelgorod on the next day "in the course of this elastic defense" and in addition the withdrawal from ruined Kharkov, which was carried out "according to plan" on August 22. On September 25, Smolensk was evacuated "after total destruction and ruin of all points of military importance . . . without any hindrance whatsoever from the enemy."[2] Baron Christoph von Imhoff reported in an interpretive article on German strategy that during the struggle for the Kursk salient in July 1943, the enemy had thrown everything they had into the battle, including millions of Chinese coolies.[3]

Fritzsche boasted in his radio broadcast of August 7, 1943, that

the enemy had gained only a pile of ruins when they took Orel:
"The destroyed city of Orel, however, that name which has become
meaningless even by Bolshevik calculations, was bought at much,
much too high a price."[4] With his characteristic sarcasm, Fritzsche
observed later in the month of August that the enemy had not
reached its real goal of regaining the lost grain areas. He declared
that in their vainglorious celebrations after retaking ruined cities
the Bolsheviks were overlooking the fact that the Wehrmacht was
now "playing with the tremendous areas which we have already
conquered in the East."[5]

More and more people looked to Hitler for a message of reassurance. But the Führer was awaiting news of a significant victory before
speaking once more to the nation, and his silence was a cause of
widespread concern. A letter from Berger to Himmler dated July
30, 1943, made this quite plain:

Reichsführer: I should like to bring something to your attention
at the risk of your getting mad at me.

We cannot go on much longer through thick and thin the way things
are going now. The German people must be spoken to. The Reichsmarschall of the Greater German Reich has no following at the
moment, not only on account of the notorious superiority of the
enemy air force but above all because he has avoided going into
those areas which have suffered heavy attacks and speaking to the
people there. Reich Minister Dr. Goebbels is not believed much any
more. Reich Organization Chief Dr. Ley is not convincing enough
at the moment to do the job necessary. It seems entirely inadvisable
that the Reichsführer SS speak to the nation at the moment; it is
not yet the proper time for that. In my opinion the Führer must
go before the nation, so that the common man who is doing his
duty faithfully and bravely right along and has remained loyal to
him, can see a way out of our problems.[6]

If people did not hear from Hitler, they were given a liberal
exposure to Goebbels who took up the slack with a propaganda
campaign of primary importance which lasted throughout the period
from 1943 to 1945—the miracle weapons propaganda.[7] The charge
has been made that Goebbels simply manufactured this propaganda
in order to convince a war-weary, desperate nation to hold on until
the bitter end in hope of a final victory. Prince Schaumburg-Lippe

has written that the miracle weapons propaganda proved that Goebbels was unable to distinguish between illusion and reality, indeed
that he became the victim of his own propaganda.[8] But this interpretation does not square with the facts. Goebbels and some of his
top staff members believed in the miracle weapons precisely because
Albert Speer—his denials in his memoirs notwithstanding—gave them
cause for such conviction.[9] There were several occasions when
Goebbels witnessed rocket launches either in person or on film, and
he was in close contact with Speer who kept him informed about
the latest breakthroughs in weapons innovation. Naumann observed
that after viewing one such rocket launch both he and Goebbels
"believed that we were seeing a weapon which in a short time would
bring us substantial relief in the air war."[10] Realizing the potential
of miracle weapons propaganda, Goebbels appointed Schwarz van
Berk as his coordinator in the Ministry for its dissemination. Thereafter Schwarz van Berk directed a vigorous campaign in the public
media which culminated in an all-out whisper propaganda campaign
in 1945.[11]

Goebbels launched his miracle weapons campaign in a Sports Palace
rally on June 5, 1943, where he shared the podium with Speer.
The meeting was devoted to the air war which cast a dark and
ominous shadow on prospects for a German victory. Acutely aware
of the widespread suffering caused by the Allied air fleets which
were roaming German skies with little opposition from Göring's
Luftwaffe, Goebbels assured the nation that the Reich would answer
terror with counterterror. He placed great store in the development
of new weapons which would avenge the country for its suffering:

I have recently made several trips to the bombed areas of the west
and northwest to gain a clear picture of conditions on the spot.
The average citizen in the Reich does not know at all what the
people have to put up with there, under what primitive conditions
they often have to live to begin their destroyed lives anew, what
high morale and discipline they constantly manifest under the
conditions. Anybody living elsewhere who thinks he has a complaint
to raise about something connected with the war should take a look
at Essen, Dortmund, Bochum, Wuppertal or at the other cities of
the bombed area and redden with shame . . . One day the hour
of revenge will come . . .[12]

He promised that the ruined cities would be rebuilt in the future and that children would look with pride to their parents who "by their heroism have placed a wreath of unforgettable glory on the coat of arms of their proud cities."[13] An SD report on this Goebbels rally stated that the country welcomed his announcement of the counterterror, but that as one person said, "There's lots of talk already but the revenge doesn't seem anywhere in sight. We would all like to experience this announced revenge."[14]

Goebbels's declaration set off a wave of rumors on the nature of the revenge. People who had come to expect all sorts of extraordinary things from the Führer let their imaginations run away with them. There was talk of new rockets, revolutionary howitzers to bomb England, and six-motored bombers. There were stories of a new type of bomb which was of such great power that it took one huge airplane to deliver only one of them. The Reich would need but twelve bombs of this type, "constructed on the principle of atom splitting," to destroy a city of a million people.[15] According to yet another rumor, Hitler had spoken to the soldiers and had asked "that God might forgive him if he should be forced to use the new weapons."[16]

Expectations reached a fever pitch, and Schwarz van Berk reports that an article he published in *Das Reich* in December 1943 devoted to the new weapons had a greater impact than anything he ever wrote. It had been inspired by a conference he had with Speer in which the armaments minister assured him that he had realized some exceptional breakthroughs in weaponry which might well change the course of the war. The repercussions could be predicted because the article which resulted from this meeting was not standard wartime Nazi journalism. Instead Schwarz van Berk merged the practical effect of miracle weapons propaganda with a more convincing and compelling topic: technology and human survival. The thrust of the article was that the Führer already had the new weapons at his disposal, but he was awaiting the most propitious political-strategic moment to deploy them. The time had come, he said, when half the world might be blown up: "The last great duty of Western civilization is to harness technology to reason. Today's weapon innovators can be tomorrow's life innovators."[17]

Miracle weapons propaganda reached a new threshold in the spring of 1944, but disappointment was widespread when the Nazis did not deliver on their promises. When the V-1 and V-2 rockets were deployed after July 1944, they fell far short of expectations. Yet from the summer of 1944 until the end of the war Goebbels indulged in what even to him must have seemed miracle weapon fantasies. Speer reacted ever more angrily to the campaign, and after what he deemed a particularly indiscreet article by Schwarz van Berk in December 1944 he forbade the latter's attendance at the subsequent closed sessions of the weapons seminars held at the Armaments Ministry periodically for the Party and military elite, meetings which Schwarz van Berk had regularly attended.[18] He also implored Goebbels to halt the campaign, and the latter responded by substituting his theme of the "great turning point" for the prior emphasis on weaponry.[19]

Throughout the fall and winter of 1943–1944, German morale continued to deteriorate. The SD reported on November 4, 1943, that worry about the eastern front weighed heavily upon the country and that all the other fronts were of secondary interest.[20] But the Nazis had little to offer in the way of reassurance. As one SD report observed, most people were happy if the country got through another day of the war without something disastrous happening.[21]

The German propagandists were burdened with a nearly impossible job. An SD report of May 28, 1943, pointed to the fact that it was exceedingly difficult to be convincing under the present conditions. The masses felt helpless with all the problems of the war besetting them, and this manifested itself in apathy and skepticism about propaganda.[22] At the same time that there was less and less reason to believe in the final victory, the Party stepped up its demand for fanaticism, which was symbolized by Goebbels's "30 War Articles for the German Nation."[23] According to Article I, "Everything is possible in this war except that we would ever surrender and weaken as a result of the blows of the enemy." Those who did not agree and who might even conceive of a "cowardly betrayal of the nation's right to live . . . must be expelled with ignominy and outrage from the fighting and working German community." The nation must defend its freedom, and the way was through discipline, "the most important of all war virtues." Those who would not sacrifice for the racial community were branded materialists without the "slightest inkling of their historic duties." Goebbels admonished the nation to be ever mindful of its German racial background. "Believe faithfully and firmly in the Führer and in victory," he demanded.[24]

Hitler echoed this refrain in his Munich address on November 9 in which he called for heroism, and issued a warning that he would not hesitate to execute a few slackers on the home front. The only chance for these people was not to reveal themselves, because the minute they did, "they would lose their heads."[25] The Reich, he promised, would never capitulate, no matter how long the war might last. This, clearly, was a demand for an unreasoning surrender to Hitler's "either-or" world view which knew only victory or death.

Those who refused to believe and who showed any outward signs of resistance to the Nazi line were, as Hitler threatened, in real danger for their lives. The Führer headquarters and the SS issued orders to the Party leaders that it was their responsibility to take action against the pessimists and complainers. Kaltenbrunner's directive of December 22, 1943, ordered his subordinates in the Security Police and the SD to take action against the "complainers and troublemakers."[26] He pointed out that every German citizen had the right under Paragraph 127 of the Penal Code to apprehend anyone he saw violating any law and to turn him over to the nearest police station. It was the duty of the political leaders to follow this policy. He commanded his subordinates to help all Party offices involved in stamping out the enemies of the state.[27]

Propaganda in 1944 conformed to the tactical guidelines which Goebbels summarized in his address to the Reichsleiters and gauleiters at a meeting in Munich in late February 1944. The most reassurance that he could offer was the assertion that the military situation had to be viewed in perspective. The Russians, he said, had not suddenly become superior soldiers and the Germans weaker ones. In order to realize its strategic goals, the Wehrmacht had pulled back to a "more favorable position on a new, shortened front, which could be held under all conditions." As a result he cautioned his Party colleagues not to speak "of the Führer losing the initiative or his operational freedom in the east . . . These are armies of rats who rush obediently against our protective dam in confused packs."[28]

This accounts for the deception in the reports about the eastern front in home propaganda. The OKW wrote off the loss of Sevastopol and the Crimea as only a "local undertaking."[29] The confidential instructions to the press ordered the newspapers to point out that the real goal of the Crimean campaign had been to hold down as many units of the enemy as possible and that the withdrawal from Sevastopol had been planned long in advance.[30]

Attention was deflected from the destruction of the Fourth Army in the pocket to the east of Minsk by the dramatic coverage of the Allied landing in France. As a result the public never learned that 350,000 men had been lost there. Instead, they were told that the battle units in the area of Bobruisk had "fought their way back to our main lines."[31] There was really little to be said as German troops were gradually forced westward. By September 1944 the Russians had occupied Bulgaria and Rumania, had crossed the Danube, and had joined with Tito's partisan forces. In the north the way to Poland stood open, and Finland left the war.

For the time being all eyes were focused on the coast of France, and the invasion was the most dramatic news event of the year. Nazi propagandists had spent much of the winter and spring of 1944 assuring the nation that German defenses were ready to turn back the "invaders." Imposing photographs of Rommel walking along the beaches of France inspecting the fortifications left the impression that only the best commanders were in charge. Goebbels taunted the Allies: "That it is coming we take for granted. It is really of little interest to us when and where it will come. . . . We are prepared for it everywhere and at all times."[32] To the German people it seemed as if the campaign would never get under way.[33] Wilfred von Oven attests that the air was "laden with an unbearable tension all the time."[34] The result was that when the invasion finally began, it came as a relief to a people who had borne their anxiety and fears about the landing for months. The SD reported that the invasion "is almost the only topic of discussion," and it had raised morale immediately.[35] Banner headlines trumpeted the event: "The Battle Has Begun in the West."[36]

Goebbels took the position that the invasion was really the work of the Kremlin, and he cited Eisenhower's message to the people of western Europe that the landing was taking place in cooperation with their "great Russian allies." In no case were the propagandists to use the term "second front," a phrase which many Germans equated with defeat; instead they were to demand brave demeanor and confidence in the final victory, while avoiding all prophecies on the outcome of the operations.[37]

Goebbels did his best to cause dissension among the Allies by asserting that English and American soldiers were dying for the Jews and profiteers of London and New York. He ridiculed their battle cry of "freeing the continent." Freeing it from what? he queried. "From its solidarity, from its steps towards unity, from its growing feeling of a common purpose, from feelings of responsibility of all to all? Such a liberation would be Europe's greatest disaster," he declared.[38]

The nation was urged to look to the Führer for leadership in those days of stress: "The German people are united in this fateful hour in their firm belief in the triumph of their just cause, united with the Führer, our guarantee of victory and of a future worthy of our nation . . ."[39]

Such unreasoning trust seemed temporarily vindicated with the announcement that one of the long-awaited miracle weapons, the V-1, a gift to the Reich from the Führer and his brilliant technicians and scientists, was now being deployed against England. The OKW communiqué of June 16, 1944, brought the news that London had been blanketed "with a new type of explosive projectile of the heaviest caliber."[40] Although this was the blow that the nation had been expecting for months, the Nazis were careful not to build up hopes which might lead to more disappointment.

As the Wehrmacht was rolled back in the west, the propaganda strategists found themselves in a dilemma. For some time they had taken the position that the German Army was holding in the east in order to ensure success on the invasion front. It took relatively little time for the Allies to make a mockery of this propaganda. However, under the circumstances the Nazis saw no alternative but to call the withdrawals on both fronts an "intermittent phase" of the war and to hold to Goebbels's blanket tactical directive for 1944.[41]

As Germany's fortunes declined, the propaganda minister found himself in a nearly hopeless situation. People had tired of Nazi clichés, and there was a good deal of criticism of Nazi propaganda. The OKW communiqué was singled out for disapproval. When a communiqué used the words "in the area of" such and such a place, most people drew the conclusion that the Army had already pulled back from the city or town in question. Timeworn phrases like "shortening of the front" had long since lost any effectiveness.[42] Such headlines as "All Chances for Victory Ours" more often than not evoked contempt. Radio programs which were eagerly followed early in the war now were derided. Several Army officers and some Waffen-SS commanders complained that many of the programs on the "Ost Soldaten Sender" were overly sentimental "tingel-tangel."[43]

The SD reports of spring 1944 referred to a "Stalingrad mood" on the home front, and people in the bombed areas charged that things could not be worse even if the Reich lost the war. They had nothing more to lose. Many people were horrified with the prospect of a Russian invasion, and German victory seemed less and less possible. They wondered whether all the death and sacrifices were worth it.[44] But as the SD editors noted, German opinion during the period was far from unified: "Morale at this time is diverse. People waver between the fear that terrible times are ahead, and the hope that everything could change in our favor suddenly. Many are really insecure and desperate because of the military situation today."[45] Not a few hoped that a "great miracle," which they associated with the long promised "revenge," would change the whole picture overnight.[46]

Goebbels did have what he considered to be an ace in the hole—the possible disintegration of the Allied coalition—and he consistently applied pressure to further that end during the last years of the war. A landmark in his campaign to exploit intra-Allied hostilities was the Soviets' "goodwill gesture" of dissolving the Comintern on May 22, 1943, which he characterized as merely a tactical maneuver.[47]

Late in 1943 Goebbels began a concerted effort to heighten tensions among the Allies by his comments on the Moscow and Teheran meetings. It was his contention—quite correct in retrospect—that the only thing which was holding the Allies together was their common desire to defeat Germany; the closer the enemy came to realizing this goal, the more strained would its alliance be.[48] Should Germany one day actually be defeated, then a "horrible Third World War" would be unavoidable. He believed that Teheran was but the first step in Soviet plans to bolshevize Europe.

Goebbels emphasized the theme that the United States and Great

Britain were under the control of the Bolsheviks and that the west had bowed to the will of Stalin. He pointed to the very sensitive question of the postwar western boundaries, and called the Moscow Conference a total victory for Stalin, since there was no mention in the Allied communiqué of Poland, Finland, the Baltic states, the Dardanelles, or the Balkans.[49]

Goebbels often repeated the point that the Allies were being tricked by Stalin, realizing that readers among the neutral and enemy states would take notice of what he was saying. He taunted the west, dropping hints here and there that the Soviets were not conquering territory in order to turn it over to their coalition partners or to the inhabitants, but to annex it themselves. He warned that "the English and Americans have lost their influence on our continent and if conditions remain as they are they will never regain it."[50] In effect, Goebbels was daring the west to make demands on the Soviets, demands which might well lead to the dissolution of the coalition.

In his *Reich* article which appeared only three days after the Allied landing in France, Goebbels warned Great Britain and the United States that they might well have to fight another war to free the buffer states from the Stalinist yoke. He gave notice that if the Bolsheviks should fight their way to the Elbe and to the Rhine, they would be in a position to make short shrift of the Allies, since they would hold all the cards. As a result they would dominate Eurasia from the Atlantic to the Pacific, without being in danger of having to fight a two-front war. Indeed, they would be in a position to force all of Europe to fight for them. "What possibilities would still be open to London and Washington in such a conflict?" he asked.[51]

The Nazis also hammered away at the sensitive questions of the future of Poland, the status of the Polish government-in-exile in London, and the Soviet-Polish borders, all of which were serious points of contention among the Allies. Goebbels taunted the west by querying whether the English really believed that the Bolsheviks would stop at the Curzon Line, just to hand over the remainder of Poland, including East Germany, to the Polish émigrés in London. With his characteristic sarcasm, the minister observed that "if history once more might be turned back to August 1939, the Poles, knowing what they do today, would probably come bearing the key to the city of Danzig to us upon a golden plate amid a festive procession."[52]

The Warsaw uprising exacerbated tensions among the Allies, because of the suspicion that Stalin purposely stood by while the Polish Home Army was wiped out by the Germans in a sixty-three-day battle. Allied attempts to fly supplies in to aid the rebels failed, as did their entreaties to Stalin to move into Warsaw and join forces with the defenders. When the Russians finally took Warsaw, there was no Polish Home Army to contend with. The Nazis made much of this situation. Following the capitulation on October 2, 1944, headlines read "Warsaw as a Warning," and the accompanying stories demonstrated how the Kremlin had washed its hands of the insurgents in Poland.[53] They charged that one of the reasons why the Poles had not been helped from the west was that Stalin refused to allow them to use the airports under their control. The Nazis called the Allied attempt to aid the defenders a tragic farce.[54]

Poland was to cause considerably more tension among the coalition powers. Russia's puppet Lublin Committee made allegations against the Polish government-in-exile in London that were answered in kind. Stalin unilaterally recognized his own Lublin Committee as the provisional government of Poland on December 31, 1944, and Goebbels warned that only trouble lay ahead for Poland, Finland, Hungary, Rumania, Bulgaria, and Czechoslovakia—and for any nation which submitted to the enemy.[55]

XV The Twentieth of July and Beyond

The abortive assassination attempt on the life of Hitler on July 20, 1944, offered Goebbels dramatic confirmation of a central tenet in his mythical panoply—that the Führer was sent by Providence to lead the Reich across the abyss to greatness. This is not the place to recount the history of the German resistance movement, which culminated in the ill-fated bomb plot that was calculated to kill Hitler and much of his staff during a military situation conference at his headquarters in Rastenburg in East Prussia. Peter Hoffmann has given the definitive account of that ominous series of events in his *Widerstand, Staatsstreich, Attentat: Der Kampf der Opposition gegen Hitler.*[1]

The attempt on the life of the leader of the nation at war was a theme which competed with unconditional surrender as compelling propaganda.[2] Goebbels perceived the value of the near miss on the Führer's life for his propaganda, and the events of the subsequent weeks profoundly reflected his elasticity in both leading and reacting to spontaneous demonstrations of support for Hitler.

Within a matter of hours after the failure of the *Attentat* Hitler dictated a message of reassurance to the German people, which was phoned to the Propaganda Ministry between 2 and 3 P.M.[3] The Führer ordered the message to be broadcast with the greatest possible speed, but a circumspect Goebbels, having extricated himself from the hands of the resistance in Berlin, awaited the proper moment to make the announcement. As he told Fritzsche, "We cannot afford any propagandistic extravaganzas considering the great tension among our people today. The announcement itself must therefore carry some thoughtful commentary, its shock effect must be watered down, and the whole day's programming must be unified."[4]

Hitler was disturbed when he learned that the news had not yet been broadcast that he was alive and in full control of affairs. Late that afternoon he got through a call to Goebbels and reprimanded him for not carrying out his order.[5] Thereupon Goebbels announced over the air that the Führer was alive and would soon be speaking to the nation. The tension was heightened as the *Deutschlandsender* broadcast at intervals that the Führer would be speaking presently. Bormann wired the gauleiters at 8:40 P.M. that Hitler planned to address the nation by radio that night.[6]

The series of teletyped messages from Hitler that were dispatched by Bormann through the Party chancellery channels to the gauleiters on July 20 reflect the confusion and chaos of that day. They document the Nazis' attempts to stop the rumors about the movement of troops in Berlin's Government Quarter and to gain control of the situation by countering the orders of the conspirators. Directive Nr. 4, issued by the Führer headquarters at 9:20 P.M. on the evening of July 20, charged that the "traitorous" National Committee for Free Germany under General von Seydlitz and Count Einsiedel had staged the coup from Moscow and that once the plot had succeeded, they planned to sign an armistice.[7] In fact the Moscow group had nothing at all to do with the plot, since it had been excluded from all the workings of the resistance cells within Germany.[8]

It was not until 1 A.M. on July 21 that Hitler was heard to say:

I do not know how many times now my assassination has been planned and attempted. If I speak to you today it is really for two special reasons:

1. So that you might hear my voice and know that I am uninjured and safe.
2. So that you might learn of a crime which is unparalleled in German history.

A very small clique of egotistical, criminally stupid officers without conscience concocted a plot to kill me and at the same time to liquidate the German Wehrmacht Operations Staff. The bomb which was placed by Colonel Count von Stauffenberg exploded two meters to my right. It seriously wounded several of my faithful colleagues, and one has died. I myself am completely uninjured except for some minor superficial burns and bruises. I view this as confirmation of the duty which Providence has placed upon me to continue to fulfill my life's goal just as I have up to now . . . Thus in an hour in which German armies find themselves in the most difficult struggle— as in Italy now too in Germany—a very small group has arisen who believed that now as in the year 1918 they could plunge a dagger into our back. But they were very much deceived this time. The belief of these usurpers that I was killed is now proved false, this very moment in which I speak to you, my dear fellow Germans. The circle of usurpers is very, very small. It does not have anything to do with the German Wehrmacht and above all nothing to do with the German Army. It is a very small clique of criminal elements, who are now being mercilessly liquidated.

Therefore I now order

1. That no civilian office accept any directive at all from any post arrogant enough to follow these usurpers.
2. That no military unit, no troop commander, and no soldier should obey any order of these criminals, and on the contrary, all are duty bound to arrest immediately those who have given or transmitted the order or, if they resist, to shoot them on the spot.

Hitler then announced that he had appointed Himmler as commander of the Reserve Army and General Guderian as chief of the General Staff. He did not mention the fall of Fromm, whom Himmler was replacing, nor did he refer to Zeitzler, except to say that the latter had been sick. The Führer stated:

Nothing at all has changed in the other offices of the Reich. I am confident that with the fall of this very small clique of traitors and conspirators, we can now provide the atmosphere we need behind us in the homeland, which the soldiers need at the front. Because it is impossible that up front hundreds of thousands and millions of brave men give everything they have, while at home a very small clique of egotistical, miserable creatures constantly try to nullify this self-sacrifice. This time we are going to settle accounts in the way we best know how as National Socialists.

I am convinced that every decent officer and every brave soldier will understand that in this hour.

What Germany's fate might have been if the plot had succeeded today is something that everyone should consider. I myself do not thank Providence and my creator because he has saved me. My life is really only care and work for my people, and I thank him only because he has given me the opportunity to be able to continue in my work . . .

I especially want to greet most warmly you my old battle comrades, that I was once more permitted to escape a fate, which really did not save me from something horrible, but might have brought something horrible for the German people.

I see in this the direction of Providence, that I must continue my work and that therefore I shall continue it.[9]

Directly following Hitler's talk Göring and Dönitz delivered short, emotional messages to the men of the Luftwaffe and Navy respectively. They thanked Providence for saving the Führer and admonished their men to be faithful to the oath they had taken to Hitler personally. Their bitterness and hatred for the "traitorous clique of generals" were unbounded, and they promised their liquidation forthwith.

A DNB newscast following Hitler's message announced that the plot of the traitorous officer clique had completely failed. Some of them had already committed suicide, while Army units had shot others, including Colonel Count von Stauffenberg.[10] Finally, at 3:40 A.M. on July 21, Bormann wired a report on the events of the day to all the gauleiters which included a brief discussion of the parts played by von Stauffenberg, Olbricht, Fromm, and Beck. He declared, "This case of state treason can now be considered closed."[11]

Hitler's radio message was well timed to evoke the propaganda effect he desired; it was clear, forthright, and to the point. Anyone wavering between going over to the resistance or remaining faithful to Hitler would give serious second thoughts to the dangers involved. Time and time again he referred to the officers as a "very small clique" of traitors in an attempt to conceal the wide extent of opposition to the regime.

In an effort to convince the Army officers and soldiers in the field that he had complete faith in them, Hitler drafted an "Order of the Day" of July 21 to the Army which was read over the radio by General Guderian. In fact Hitler did not have faith in most of his officers but he had to conceal his distrust. His "Order of the

Day" reiterated most of the points of his radio address of the night before, but he concluded by urging the Army to continue to fight with exemplary obedience and faithful fulfillment of their duty until the final victory. Guderian ended his brief commentary with a spirited appeal: "Loyalty is the mark of honor! Long live Germany and our Führer, Adolf Hitler! And now, the nation to arms!"[12] Within a few days it was announced that the Führer had agreed to a request from Göring, Keitel, and Dönitz to introduce the Hitler salute throughout the Wehrmacht as an outward sign of allegiance to the commander in chief.[13]

It took a day to coordinate all the various directives which had been issued in the excitement of July 20. The newspapers of July 21 contradicted Hitler's own radio message because the directives delivered at the special press conference following the news of the assassination attempt were very misleading. This explains why the newspapers at first put the blame for the bomb plot on a "world conspiracy of Plutocrats and Bolsheviks"—criminals, cowards, and murderers who had to turn to the basest trickery because they could not win the war on the battlefield.

It was not until July 22 that the editors caught up with the events. The *Völkischer Beobachter* carried a banner headline underscored in red: "Answer of the Nation: Unconditional Loyalty."[14] The *Deutsche Allgemeine Zeitung* was headlined "With the Führer to Victory."[15] Both featured photographs of Hitler. The editors carried out their directive to make the putsch a rallying cry in the nation's drive toward final victory.[16]

The events of July 20 left many Germans in a state of shock. They were enraged that a group of officers would attempt to strike down Hitler at the height of the war, and many suspected that traitors were to blame for the rapid retreat in the east. The SD observed that even in areas which did not support Hitler, such as North Berlin, there was a good deal of evidence that people were relieved that the Führer had lived, because they did not know how the war could go on without him. Many attributed his narrow escape to divine intervention. When they heard the Führer's voice once more, many felt that a better day was at hand.[17] But the intelligence reports show that following the initial relief and joy over Hitler's stroke of good fortune, the hard realities of the war and the bad news from the two fronts led once more to widespread depression. Nevertheless, there is a good deal of evidence supporting the contention that following the 20th July many of those who found Hitler distasteful rallied around his banner. A Lüneburg SD man reported, "The attempt on the Führer's life . . . has been discussed like no other event for a long time . . . Citizens who bother with politics only seldom or not at all, and who complain and gripe about everything, are now complaining to a much greater degree about Stauffenberg and his followers. Some of these individuals admit that often they have been critical and hostile towards this or that measure or even of the Führer himself. But what has now happened is a lot worse and they cannot condone it under any conditions. Therefore these people are really experiencing the meaning of the Führer more or less for the first time."[18]

The wave of mass meetings held by the Party evoked genuine enthusiasm for the Führer's cause. For example, 350,000 people swarmed into the Schwarzenberg Square in Vienna on the evening of July 21 to attend a loyalty rally. Gau Lower Danube reported that such enthusiasm had not been seen since the *Ostmark* rejoined the Reich in 1938. Hamburg, Stuttgart, Kassel, Weimar, Breslau, Münster, Frankfurt-am-Main, and other cities reported spontaneous mass meetings.[19]

Some of the reports from the gaus were surprisingly candid. For example, Dr. Meyer-Hertmann of the Münster Propaganda Office observed that the Nazis of Catholic Paderborn were satisfied that 20 percent of the population attended the Hitler rally, a figure which "according to the *Kreisleiter* has not yet been reached for any rally." Meyer-Hertmann went on to point out that in a purely Catholic area like Salzkotten in the Paderborn district, the attendance of about a thousand people should be judged a great success, "since after all . . . many people attended this rally who had not taken part in anything of a political nature for years."[20]

Admittedly many of these reports from the other gaus were exaggerated. The response in Berlin itself was disappointing. In a letter dated August 4, 1944, an official of the Deutsche Propaganda Atelier, GMBH (an independent business concern that did a good deal of work for the Propaganda Ministry) made the following observations in a letter to a functionary of the RMfVP: "Looking over the Berlin material you can see for yourself once more that in no way does it correspond to what one would expect from a loyalty mass meeting of the capital city of the Reich, and . . . it cannot even be compared with the material from Vienna . . . We are sorry to report that under these conditions we shall not be able to prepare a really complete and effective portfolio on the loyalty mass meeting."[21]

The Party contrived "enthusiasm" where it was not spontaneous. On July 23 Naumann issued orders to all gauleiters and leading gau propaganda officials that they were to stage mass demonstrations and rallies in support of the Führer down to the *kreis,* or county, level. Naumann observed that this was to be a "spontaneous expression of the will of the people at the nefarious coup d'etat against the Führer."[22] It is significant that the state secretary ordered his propagandists to cooperate with the local Wehrmacht in the rallies. In addition to these public mass meetings, Naumann arranged for rallies to be held in local shops and factories. All means of public communication were coordinated in the campaign.

To carry out Naumann's directive, the head of the Propaganda Staff, Wächter, teletyped instructions to the gau propaganda chiefs.[23] Only Nazis with proven ability were to be charged with organizing the meetings. Block leaders were to "invite" the people of their areas to attend the mass meetings, and loudspeakers urging their attendance were to be stationed at appropriate points. Store owners were to decorate their windows with photographs of Hitler. Party officials were advised to be aware of possible air raids to avoid embarrassment.

Wächter ordered that banners with slogans such as "Down with the Traitors" were to be avoided. Instead they were urged to take a more positive approach, using phrases such as "Long Live the Führer," "Führer Command, We Follow!" or "Adolf Hitler Means Victory." Speakers were to avoid the "pastoral and pathetic." Should pro-Nazi officers be available, they were to deliver short messages to affirm the faith of the Wehrmacht in the Führer. The meetings were to be closed with a "show of strength." After all, he added, National Socialist rallies were not bourgeois club gatherings.[24]

The Nazis had a great deal of success with their propaganda campaign following the 20th July, and the Reich propaganda offices worked as seldom before to carry Hitler's message to the people.

By July 24 Gau Lower Silesia alone (Breslau) had held two hundred mass meetings attended by between 350,000 and 400,000 people.[25] Even allowing for bureaucratic padding of these figures, it is clear that Goebbels's team carried out an important assignment, in cooperation with many pro-Nazi officers who were anxious to redeem the Army and the Wehrmacht.

Goebbels was to experience some difficulty in orchestrating the July 20 propaganda in the face of the understandably overzealous rhetoric after that traumatic day. He had to take steps to mitigate divisive intraclass hostility following Reich Organization Chief Ley's bitter attack on the aristocracy during the course of an address to Berlin factory workers which was carried over all the radio networks.[26] Ley deliberately played on the class jealousies of his audience by vilifying the "reactionary gentlemen" who had betrayed the Führer to whom they owed their uniforms, power, and prestige. "Thank God that it was not a worker!" he said, and furthermore "today the German people demand that the Revolution finish what it has not completed. These creatures must be annihilated. Every German must know that his entire family will be liquidated should he betray Germany."[27] The SD reports show a generally negative reaction to Ley's address. Hitler took steps to stop this type of divisive propaganda and ordered that Party men not attack the officer corps or aristocracy as a whole.[28]

Goebbels in his radio address of July 26 gave a dramatic review of the events of July 20 that was heavily weighted with an explanation of his own role in suppressing the uprising. The putschists, he said, had forgotten that the Berlin Guard Battalion was strongly National Socialist and that its commander, Major Remer, "saw that his best move was to come to me and report on the course of events. Thereby the whole rascally trick (Schurkenstreich) had been practically quelled in the course of one short hour."

Goebbels related that Remer's telephone conversation with the Führer "belongs among the most exciting memories of my life":

A young officer of the German Army, who had proved his worth at the front and was decorated with the Oak Leaf Cluster to the Knight's Cross, had the honor to receive direct orders from the Führer and Commander-in-Chief . . .

The orders were to strike down the clique of traitors immediately
. . . In a few minutes the Guard Battalion returned from its post
in the Government Quarter and took up positions in my garden.
At the request of Major Remer I spoke to the men gathered there,
gave them the straight facts and experienced an outbreak of rage
and indignation such as I had never before witnessed. I will never
forget this moment.

Immediately after my speech was over the officers and soldiers took
up their machine guns and rifles to be prepared to settle accounts.
I was stormed from all sides not to allow any other unit have the
honor of washing away in their own blood the shame which the
clique of traitors tried to bring to the German uniform.[29]

Without naming any of the officers involved except von Stauffenberg, Goebbels derided them one by one, hinted at who they were,
and told that they had been executed. Then he turned to an old
trick that he used only when he was not in a position to give more
specific information: "Spare me from reporting more details to you.
They cast so much shame on the plotters that they would only
complicate the facts of the case."[30]

Goebbels charged that the conspirators were creatures of the enemy,
aristocrats related by blood to the English, who seriously misjudged
"the German people, German soldiers, and above all the National
Socialist movement." One cannot "play Badoglio" with such forces.
And, he said, "whatever concerns the Führer is really in the hands
of God." Just as Providence saved the Führer, so most assuredly
would he lead the German nation to victory.[31] Following Goebbels's
speech, the press was directed to drop the theme of July 20, since
"further comment on it would be superfluous."

Finally the daily press directive of July 31, 1944, stated that the
theme of the 20th July had been closed with the announcement
of the names of the leaders (Rädelsführer) of the assassination
attempt.[32] But this was unrealistic. Goebbels dealt with the putsch
in his *Reich* editorials during the month of August. Photographs
of Goerdeler were published along with an offer of 1 million
reichsmarks for information that would lead to his capture.[33] The
daily directive of August 5 raised the issue once more, ordering
the press to stress the fact that the Army had cleansed itself of
the criminals of July 20.[34] The press directive of August 8 demanded
that the editors devote an entire issue to Freisler's trial of the

conspirators before the People's Court.[35] With the headlines "Sentenced by the Nation," the *Völkischer Beobachter* printed Freisler's judgment:

In the name of the German people!
Honorless little ambitious people, oathbreakers!
    Erwin von Witzleben,
    Erich Hoeppner,
    Hellmuth Stieff,
    Paul von Hase,
    Robert Bernardis,
    Peter Graf York von Wartenburg,
    Albrecht von Hagen,
    Friedrich Karl Klausing,
betrayed the sacrifices of our soldiers, our nation, our Führer, and our Reich in a manner without parallel in our entire history, instead of bravely fighting on to victory like the whole German nation, following the Führer . . . Cowardly, they thought they could deliver our nation to the mercy of the enemy, even to enslave it in dark reaction. Traitors to everything for which we are living and fighting, they are all sentenced to death. Their property goes to the Reich.[36]

Rommel's suicide following the 20th July, which was forced on him by the Nazis, was a personal blow to Goebbels, because his relations with the field marshal were very close. According to Naumann, during the war both men spoke quite frankly with one another and they aired grievances which they would admit to few others. One of Goebbels's men, Alfred Ingemar Berndt, was assigned to cover his African campaigns, and he wrote stirring and noteworthy accounts on Rommel the man and the strategist. Rommel was a central figure in Goebbels's propaganda, in every sense *ein Volksgeneral*. As a result, word of his death troubled Goebbels deeply; furthermore he was faced with a difficult problem in deciding how to release the news. To overplay the drama of the state funeral might arouse suspicion that Hitler was responsible for Rommel's demise. As a result Goebbels issued instructions through Naumann that the coverage was to be in low key. The ruse was successful, and the great majority of people believed that Rommel had indeed died as the result of wounds received on the invasion front in France.[37]

There is no question that Goebbels gained considerable power as a result of the putsch attempt. Even on July 20 Hitler ordered the chief of the Party chancellery Bormann to take the initial moves toward a stepped-up total war effort.[38] In two very important Führer directives countersigned by Göring and Bormann, Hitler named Goebbels to a new post with far-reaching powers, which carried the resounding title of Reich Plenipotentiary for Total War Deployment.[39] Goebbels was overjoyed with this new position, which he had wanted since Stalingrad. Von Oven reported that when he went to pick up Goebbels at the Silesian Railway Station in Berlin, even as the minister was descending the ramp he called out to him, "The Doctor has won his greatest victory!"[40]

Now that Goebbels had assumed the powers he wanted in order to lead the total war effort, he served simultaneously as a policy maker and the Reich's propaganda minister. On August 24, 1944, he announced new total war measures including the introduction of the sixty-hour week, and he put many categories of people whom he considered war slackers to work.[41] At the same time that he pushed for total war, he stepped up his propaganda of hate directed against the Allies, and the Morgenthau Plan provided him with an excellent issue for focusing attention on the theme of unconditional surrender. At Quebec Roosevelt and Churchill had signed a modified version of Morgenthau's plan for "converting Germany into a country primarily agricultural and pastoral in character." Although the two heads of state withdrew their support within a matter of weeks, the damage had already been done.[42] Following an American press leak on the Morgenthau Plan, German newspapers carried such headlines as "The Threat of Annihilation from the West," "Wipe Out Germany as an Industrial State," "Roosevelt and Churchill Agree to the Morgenthau Plan." They charged that the plan would put Versailles in the shadows, and the themes were merged with the anti-Bolshevik propaganda both at home and abroad.[43]

Goebbels declared in his radio address of October 27, 1944, that the Wehrmacht provided the last breakwater against the storm from the east. Look to the Balkans, he said, where the "Bolshevik poison" was destroying the newly captured areas: a Bolshevization of Europe, which would most assuredly follow a German defeat, would at the same time write the end to "Western civilization." The Balkan leaders who had proved cowardly and betrayed the Reich had really delivered their people for deportation to Siberia. Goebbels proclaimed, "God will be with us if we exert all our national potential in guarding our country and thereby all of Europe from a fate which would be worse than hell."[44]

In his article dated October 22, 1944, entitled "For Our Children," Goebbels charged that the enemy planned to liquidate "thirty to forty million people" through a combination of blood terror, mass deportations, economic slavery, and starvation. Never before, he asserted, had there been "such devilish plans for the systematic butchering of a great, cultured people, than these which the enemy side conjured up here with such cynicism."[45]

But German morale was rapidly deteriorating and it suffered another blow when it was announced that an emergency home defense force, the *Volkssturm,* was being formed. Hitler declared in his *Volkssturm* directive that in order to counter the "will to annihilation of our Jewish international enemies" the nation had to deploy all its manpower in the war.[46] Every man between the ages of sixteen and sixty was ordered to join the forces of the *Volkssturm* and to defend the homeland. The new units were given a noisy buildup. Himmler delivered an address to several of them "in an East Prussian city" on October 18, the anniversary of the Battle of the Nations at Leipzig. He compared the emergency forces with the *Landsturm* men who had served under "Blücher, Scharnhorst, Gneisenau, and Clausewitz" and had united to defeat Napoleon. Against such troops, he maintained, the enemy could really not hold out much longer. "We look to the future with confidence and trust," he said.[47]

Another new propaganda theme was provided by General Vlasov and the "Committee for the Liberation of the Peoples of Russia" (KONR) late in 1944. Goebbels made use of what seemed to be an excellent propaganda motif—Russian nationals fighting side by side with the Wehrmacht, united in the goal of destroying the "Jewish-Bolshevik regime" in control of their homeland. A good deal of emphasis was placed on Vlasov's "Army of Liberation," which the Nazis lauded as an important reinforcement of the Wehrmacht's eastern front. In the Prague Manifesto the committee attacked bolshevism as a "system of slavery" and pledged itself to the task of destroying Stalin's tyranny and establishing the rule of law in their mother country once more. They looked forward to signing an "honorable peace" with Germany.[48]

The telegrams of mutual admiration which passed between Vlasov and several top Nazis are noteworthy, because they add to the mystique about KONR. Himmler wired congratulations to the committee on its founding, wishing it "complete success in our common struggle." In his communication to von Ribbentrop, Vlasov requested the foreign minister to "express to the Führer of the German nation my assurance that the people of Russia are filled with a valiant determination to see this struggle through to its victorious end and not to lay down its weapons until the Bolshevik tyranny is destroyed."[49]

In December 1944, General Guderian wired his appreciation for the work Vlasov was doing and assured him that his troops would receive full support from the High Command. Guderian declared his conviction that, with these determined comrades-in-arms against bolshevism, "victory in this common struggle will most assuredly be ours."[50] However, the Vlasov propaganda proved to be ephemeral, and with the coming of 1945 discussion of Vlasov and his troops all but disappeared from German propaganda.

The Vlasov affair and the *Volkssturm* were further signs of the disintegration of the Third Reich. By late 1944, Germany's chances of turning the tide were slim indeed. Complaining, defeatism, and pessimism were widespread, and the Nazis turned increasingly to terror as a complement to their propaganda. As Bormann observed in his communication to Party leaders on October 10, 1944, "Many of these rumor-spreaders can yet be brought to reason by showing them just how dangerous such irresponsible behavior can be for them personally. These thoughtless and stupid babblers are very easily distinguished from the known enemies, from the real saboteurs, the common scamps and traitors who are attempting systematically to tear down our power as a nation. There is only one method to treat these incorrigible evil meaning defeatists, no matter how few they might be, and that is to handle them mercilessly."[51]

XVI The Twilight of the Gods

The year 1945 offers many insights into the behavior of a totalitarian power apparatus in a defeat situation. In the Nazi context this took the form of Goebbels's gradual retreat from the use of objective propaganda to a complete dependence on myth. By 1945 nazism had come full circle, returning to its irrational core once more.

The cult of the Führer was intensified during the final months of the war, reaching its apogee in Goebbels's *Reich* article entitled "Der Führer," published on the last day of 1944 as the Battle of the Bulge raged. Hitler was portrayed as being superior to any other leader in the world not only in will power, but also in character. He was alleged to be an absolute master of military strategy, the classic war leader, who, following the dictates of Providence, would lead the nation in the "birth of a new epoch" which lay over the horizon.[1] It became commonplace for the Nazis to capitalize on the prestige of military men during the final months of the Third Reich. A few generals and junior officers, who in no way represented the feelings of the majority of the military, offered extravagant statements of devotion to the Führer which took on heightened flamboyance with Colonel-General Dietl's affirmation that "I believe in the Führer. The more trying the situation, the more I trust him."[2]

The long-awaited Russian winter offensive, which began on January 12, 1945, made rapid headway. By the end of February, East Prussia had been cut off and the Russians had achieved their goal of reaching the Oder River from Frankfurt to the sea.[3] The defenders of several besieged cities continued to offer bitter resistance. Breslau fought on, and Graudenz held out for several weeks. Poznan surrendered on February 23 after a twenty-eight-day siege, following which General Gonell shot himself rather than go into Russian captivity. Danzig held out until March 27, and Königsberg was not overrun until April 9, after a heroic defense by General Lasch. The Russians finally subdued Küstrin on the Oder at the end of March, which brought them one step closer to Berlin.[4]

Helmut Sündermann set an example followed by many other propagandists with his lead article in the *Völkischer Beobachter* entitled "Let Us Force the Turning Point: We Can Do It."[5] He listed the Reich's advantages in the crisis. Besides its leadership, which was second to none in world history, the nation had a socialistic ideal that fulfilled a century-long hope as well as the advantage of a racial unity unparalleled in German history. Furthermore, the German people could reflect on a 2000-year-old military tradition and look forward to an "eternally peaceful future." Thus, in that decisive hour, Sündermann called upon the nation to "crown all the sacrifices already made" and to "force the turning point."[6] But several confidential reports reveal that many Germans were critical of Hitler's sending battalions of young boys and old men to the front.[7] Many Wehrmacht veterans were also resentful of the *Volkssturm*. In one incident in the area of Schwiebus in January 1945, Army officers tore medals and insignia from the uniforms of the *Volkssturm* men who were marching by and yelled insults at them.[8] At the direction of the Reich chancellery, directives ordered a press campaign backing the *Volkssturm*.[9] Youth's role in the struggle for Germany's existence was also stressed. On more than one occasion Hitler received groups of Hitler Youth in his headquarters, where he was photographed awarding them medals for acts of heroism in combat. At one such ceremony the Führer was quoted as saying: "You know the struggle now from your own experience and realize that we are engaging in a battle for the very existence of the German people. Despite all our troubles today I am firmly convinced that we shall win the victory in this fight, above all because of German youth and especially because of you, my young men!"[10]

Quite understandably no propaganda could veer public opinion to a positive assessment of Germany's chances to turn the tide. Goebbels paid close attention to the "Activity Reports" of his Ministry which reflected public sentiment, but those of early 1945 were most distressing. One such report, dated February 21, made clear that German morale could hardly fall any lower.[11]

Some echoes from the provinces demonstrated outspoken popular criticism of Hitler and the entire Nazi hierarchy. In March 1945, Gau Propaganda Leader Weise summed up the opinion prevailing in Halle: "The Führer once said that the last battle-worthy Russian divisions had been annihilated. Who can be offended, if we no longer believe what the Führer says."[12] The propaganda situation, understandably, was equally as critical as the military one.

Goebbels's strategy for the final war year was outlined in a ministerial directive to the gau propaganda chiefs dated early February 1945.[13] "The great hour has arrived for German propaganda," he declared, since it is only in difficult times that the worth of leadership can be proved. The functionaries were to be ready with the proper arguments to counter "a small minority of negative elements" that might cause difficulties for the nation. Doubters were to be answered with plain talk, not slogans. Therefore, he ordered, in the future the propaganda tone should be that of "manly encouragement" and reassurance that Germany would be ultimately victorious.

The propaganda minister then listed some motifs that he wanted to be used, including "our reserves in men and matériel," "a nation of 90,000,000 cannot be conquered," "heroic individual deeds," and "the limited political and material possibilities of our enemies." He noted that leading political and military figures would soon be speaking on these subjects. For the areas where war damage made many of the older propaganda methods technically impossible, he appealed for improvisation and listed as possibilities records, leaflets, whisper propaganda, and impromptu radio broadcasting.[14]

Bormann dispatched a directive from Hitler's headquarters which urged the gauleiters to support Goebbels's propaganda campaign in every way possible. He reiterated the minister's plea for sincere, manly propaganda, free of clichés, since the Party could evoke fanatical resistance on the part of the German people only by illustrating the seriousness of the threat. Bormann enjoined the Party to mobilize its entire apparatus in an untiring effort to spread the Nazis' message to every household.[15]

It took a prodigious effort to keep the propaganda machine functioning under the invasion conditions of 1945. As might be imagined, throughout the last months of the war the lines of communication between the Propaganda Ministry in Berlin and the forty-odd local propaganda offices were often broken. Chaos and disorganization resulted. Often telephone and teletype connections were out for days at a time, forcing the local functionaries to depend on courier service for their news, directives, and other official business.[16]

The extreme conditions called for improvisation. As a result, Goebbels stepped up the person-to-person "Whisper Propaganda Campaign" and the "Special Deployment Berlin" in 1945. Whisper propaganda had proved effective in Vienna in late 1943 as well as in Berlin and Breslau in 1944, and it was being extended during the current campaign to Dresden, Leipzig, Stuttgart, Munich, Weimar, Erfurt, Hamburg, Hannover, Mainz, Wiesbaden, and Nuremberg.[17] Goebbels himself decided what the nature of the directives of the whisper campaign should be, and Naumann worked out the details.[18]

The operation was a cooperative effort of both the Propaganda Ministry and the OKW/WPr, and it was intended to raise morale by convincing the Germans that their chances for ultimate victory in the war were excellent. They had only to trust in their leaders. The men involved, who had all seen service at the front, were detailed by the OKW/WPr.[19]

Their methods were simple. Operating in groups of two, one dressed as a civilian and the other in an army uniform, they moved into areas where crowds gathered, on streetcars and subways, on squares, and in bomb shelters. Pretending not to know one another, the propagandists engaged in conversations among themselves or countered the defeatism of strangers. All the while they made the most of their countrymen's respect for veterans. As one directive worded it, "The soldiers must always be prepared to convince the dissatisfied with words of reason, to quiet the doubters, to encourage the wavering."[20]

The meeting of the Allied leaders at the Yalta Conference, which sat from February 7–12, 1945, afforded the deflated Nazi propaganda effort a much needed boost for several weeks. The daily directive to the press laid clear lines for the attack on the Allies' "coarse agitation swindle." The editors were ordered to quote the hateful speeches and declarations of the enemy, to reveal its aim to destroy Germany and to annihilate its people. The "Wilson swindle" was suggested as a historical parallel.

The propagandists were directed to stress the atrocities committed by the Red Army in the occupied German territories as an illustration of the true meaning of Yalta and to demonstrate that bolshevism allied with plutocracy would bring about permanent world war. Therefore the Reich must turn the tables and destroy its enemies. By thus linking a traditional propaganda motif with German patriotism, the Nazis hoped to raise the fighting spirit of the nation to a fever pitch.[21] The maneuver did prove to be very successful and was employed repeatedly.

Throughout this period Stalin was portrayed as a crass imperialist, a sinister man who intended to destroy Germany and rule Europe. Should these plans remain unfulfilled, he would attempt to bring about the end of the world. If Germany no longer survived, then "the world would die a horrible death." Admittedly this took some imagination but it was no less believable than the time-honored "Protocols of the Elders of Zion" motif. Besides, the mood of 1945 was peculiarly suited to cataclysmic predictions.

The charges against world Jewry, the historical target of nazism, offered the propaganda of 1945 the cohesion and unity it needed. In his *Reich* article entitled "The Year 2000," Goebbels warned that if the Germans should end their resistance, then the Soviets would add eastern and southeastern Europe as well as a sizable part of Germany to their empire.[22] Stalin's agreements with Churchill and Roosevelt would not deter the Red dictator from this goal, because the eternal Jew was the source of this treachery. Goebbels charged that international Jewry stood behind the Allied coalition of plutocrats and Bolsheviks; indeed they had succeeded in unifying the entire world in opposition to Germany. Goebbels warned that "every Russian, English, and American soldier is a mercenary of this race of parasites and their world conspiracy, and in this war, not Europe but the Jews will go to their destruction."[23]

The Reich press chief told a press conference in Berlin that the

Allied leaders meeting at Yalta were not fit to comment on peace at all, since they themselves were three of the most despicable war criminals in world history. Dietrich reported that the Allies were striving to achieve two goals: to bring about the surrender of the German people through deception, and to promise peace to the naïve. Needless to say, the Nazis did not release the official Yalta communiqués of the Allies.

One report in the German press reviewed the gains that the Russians made at Yalta and outlined what lay in store for Germany and Europe should they be able to implement their goals:

The Crimea Conference at Yalta has ended with a communiqué . . . [that] is nothing but a command from the Soviet dictator to his plutocratic satellites. Moscow has completely triumphed at this conference . . . This was to be expected . . . The Bolshevization of Poland was not resisted at all, and everything was made ready for the Bolshevization of eastern Europe, and even of the entire continent . . . It is the most unscrupulous and all-encompassing plan for murder against a nation and against a continent ever concocted. In this case the enemy does not even try to conceal its plans with misleading rhetoric. Their goal in this war . . . is . . . the biological extermination of the whole German race.[24]

To emphasize the extent of the Soviet victory at Yalta, the Nazis charged that any Germans who fell into captivity on the western front were to be turned over to the Russians.[25] Germans feared nothing more than falling into the hands of the Bolsheviks.

After the Red Army had crossed the German frontier, frightening accounts of murder, rape, and pillage became commonplace. Hitler reacted with his characteristic emotionalism: "Several areas in the east of our Reich are now discovering at first hand the real nature of Bolshevism. The way this Jewish pest is handling our women, children, and men is the most abominable fate which the human mind can concoct. There is only one answer for this Jewish-Bolshevik genocide and its west-European and American allies: to employ our full energies with the most extreme fanaticism and dogged steadfastness which a merciful God affords humans in difficult times for the defense of their lives."[26]

An example of the techniques used in the 1945 atrocity campaign was the appeal to the nation by the chief of the General Staff, Heinz

Guderian, in a press conference that he devoted to Soviet barbarism. General Guderian stated that he had come before the press to counter the enemy propaganda that the tales of Russian atrocities were fantasies:

The sight of murdered women, and of the butchered children and old people has made a deep impression in the hearts of German soldiers . . . They shall never forget the tears and suffering of the women and girls who were raped, tortured, and harassed . . . The peoples of the east, brought together in the Soviet Army, have been subjected for years to propaganda systematically developed by Jews and have been . . . prepared for the day in which they would be able to force their way onto German soil . . . At the beginning of the Soviet winter offensive, the men of the Red Army were given orders to murder and to plunder . . . We want to free the German territory in the east from the bloodstained clutches of the Bolshevik beasts . . . With passionate determination we are working toward that time when we can move once more from the defensive to the offensive on the eastern front . . . We are striving with all the ardor of our souls and the passion of our hearts for the reconstitution of a German east, as we look beyond our present time of troubles.[27]

Following Guderian's statement, two officers listed the horrors which they had witnessed, emphasizing the suffering of German women. They had not heard of any woman under fifty-five years of age who had not fallen victim to the Red Army men, since resistance meant certain death. Finally, the sworn statement of a German mother was read, in which she described her own suffering as well as the murder of her child.

Realizing that many Germans were more receptive to the Wehrmacht veterans than to the ordinary Nazi functionary or propagandist, Goebbels arranged to have many other well-known officers speak.[28] The press and radio dealt extensively with the subject of Russian atrocities, as did the Party speakers.[29] The propagandists had a good deal of success with their appeals to the retreating Wehrmacht as well, and one Army document carried the assertion that "during the withdrawals in the west and east, the appeals to the soldiers by women and children have proved extremely effective."[30]

The Nazis charged that the Soviets would not stop with atrocities alone, for their goal was the total destruction of the German race. This was a central propaganda theme in 1945, and it was very important in Party indoctrination material as well.[31] In the first press conference he had held in more than a year, Reich Press Chief Dietrich instructed the journalists to stress this motif. For his part, Goebbels warned repeatedly in his speeches and in his newspaper editorials that the Allies planned to exterminate the German race. Even Himmler's SS, experts on such matters, had their say in *Das Schwarze Korps*: "The allies and Russia are united on one thing, to annihilate and destroy the German people totally . . . It is the same everywhere with the Bolsheviks: they destroy what they cannot assimilate."[32] In an address before the Reichsring for National Socialist People's Enlightenment and Propaganda on February 20, 1945, State Secretary Naumann asserted that "the goal of the enemy is to take unyielding control of Germany to the year 2000. They speak less about reparations than about the biological destruction of a nation . . ."[33]

Goebbels declared in a major address to the country at the end of February 1945 that the people of the world had gone deaf from hearing about the Soviet atrocities perpetrated throughout Europe.[34] This was not the product of the imagination of the propagandists, he asserted, but was a horrible truth. International Jewry would have no success with its denials of this, Goebbels observed, and he warned that the Bolsheviks would have to pay dearly for their crimes. After conjuring up images of German women being ravished like animals by monsters in human form from the steppes, he exclaimed that no German now dared to beg the government for peace.

In order to increase the credibility of the stories of Soviet atrocities as well as the alleged plans for the destruction of the Teutonic race, Goebbels was forced to drop other propaganda lines that conflicted with these charges. One example of this reformulation of strategy was illustrated by the instructions delivered to the press on January 11, 1945. On that occasion Fischer outlined the reasons for Germany's not being in a position to make the most of the troubled relations among the Allies. To do so would presumably have neutralized the atrocity campaign, which was based on the charge that the enemy was united in its aim to destroy totally Germany and its people.[35]

But the atrocity propaganda was not well received in some quarters. Many people felt that Goebbels was greatly exaggerating the situation in his attempt to evoke the bitterest resistance.[36] The campaign was even resisted by some Party functionaries, such as Gauleiter Eggeling of Gau Halle-Merseburg, who complained to Bormann about the matter. Eggeling was concerned about feeding and housing the refugees who had already overcrowded his gau, and he predicted that if the fighting spread to the area between the Elbe and the Oder, another 1,500,000 would pour in. He warned, "Our peoples' nerves are already at the breaking point, and it is dangerous to continue frightening them with accounts of atrocities."[37]

The atrocity propaganda was calculated to reinforce the Nazis' demand for fanatical resistance in Germany's darkest hour in order to gain the final victory. Goebbels went before the nation on February 28, 1945, with what turned out to be his final major address of the war. He described the military situation as critical, but claimed that the tide was turning in Germany's favor:

As our forefathers have done so often in the past, we too shall stop the thrust of the Mongols into the heart of Europe . . . We would rather die than capitulate . . . Our struggle will bring victory in the end, and if that were not the case . . . then history itself does not possess a higher morality and the world . . . would no longer have any justification for existing, since life in it would be worse than that in hell, and I would no longer find it worth living . . . nor my children . . . nor any of them whom I have loved.[38]

Goebbels launched into a discussion of one of his heroes, Frederick the Great. If only Germany would fight as Prussia had fought for its existence under Frederick II, victory would surely be the reward. He quoted a letter from Frederick to his sister Amalia written in March 1757, in which the king commented that victory or death were the only alternatives. Goebbels promised that just as victory had been the result of Frederick's determination, "Adolf Hitler will do the same thing for the German people."[39]

The response to Goebbels's address was disappointing. Von Oven regarded it as a miscalculation of the first order and called it "a real graveside address." It was his contention that any propaganda whatsoever would have struck the wrong note.[40] According to the Special Deployment Berlin report for the period February 28–March 6, 1945, the great majority of the citizens of the capital found the speech depressing. The general feeling was that "the Doctor had to speak . . . What does the period of Frederick have to do with us?"[41]

Still the Nazis had no choice but to call for bitter resistance, and Hitler used the OKW communiqué to dramatize the allegedly fanatical fighting that took place for every town and fortress. "Sacrifice" and "heroism" often appeared in the communiqués and were reminiscent of the propaganda that followed the loss of Stalingrad. For example, after the battle for Küstrin there was no mention of a surrender. Instead, the OKW reported that "the fortress of Küstrin fell to enemy superiority in men and matériel after a bitter struggle."[42]

The case of Königsberg was unusual. The city had been encircled since the end of January, and the Nazis had made several appeals to the defenders. At one point District Chief Wagner exhorted his men to "fight like Indians and strike out like lions." He issued a warning at the same time that those who did not resist to the last would be executed.[43] Throughout March the Nazis featured reports on the courage shown by the defenders. Finally, on April 9, the OKW affirmed that the heavily outnumbered garrison of Königsberg was unable to stop the enemy from forcing its way into the inner ring of the fortress. As a result, heavy street fighting was in progress. Following this announcement, there was no mention of Königsberg in the communiqué for two days. The reason for this was that Hitler had refused the request of General Lasch to break out of the city, and in desperation Lasch had surrendered it on the night of April 8–9.[44] Hitler was outraged, and the communiqué reported on April 12 that "the fortress of Königsberg was surrendered to the Bolsheviks by the Fortress Commandant, General of the Infantry Lasch, after heavy attacks lasting several days . . . Some of the garrison who are true to their duty are still offering bitter resistance to the Bolsheviks in isolated defense pockets. General of the Infantry Lasch was sentenced to death by hanging by the court-martial because of the cowardly surrender to the enemy. His family has been arrested."[45] Hitler appended to the communiqué a stern warning that cities must be defended to the last. Should commandants not carry out these orders they would be sentenced to death.

The defense of Breslau met Hitler's expectations. Gauleiter Hanke, speaking from the Fortress of Breslau on March 5, promised that the city would fight "as long as there was an iota of strength left among the defenders of the Fortress."[46] The city was praised as the symbol of German determination. There men of the Wehrmacht, the *Volkssturm*, and the Hitler Youth, united with the city's inhabitants, had been able to ward off the enemy for months. The Nazis asserted that their loyalty had provided the Führer with the time necessary to take new countermeasures.

As a tribute to Hanke's performance, Hitler awarded him the "Golden Cross of the German Order." The Fortress of Breslau did not surrender until the general capitulation of Germany on May 7, 1945, but by that time Hanke had fled to safety. In late January he himself had ordered the execution of Breslau's vice mayor, Dr. Spielhagen, for attempting to flee.[47]

The Nazis invariably used terror when other methods of persuasion failed. For example, Hitler administered drumhead justice as an antidote to cowardice. He authorized the gauleiters to establish military courts in areas threatened by the enemy, and he ordered that they be merciless in their judgments.[48] The jurisdiction of these courts was almost unlimited. Cowardice and defeatism were punishable by death. Throughout the Reich the bodies of victims of courts-martial dangled from trees and lampposts as warnings to the rest of the population.

Inspired by Goebbels, the Werewolves added to the atmosphere of fear and terror with their first message to the nation on Easter Sunday 1945. In a "Proclamation to the German People" that they broadcast from their own radio station, the Werewolves solemnly promised never to halt their resistance to the invaders and declared that the "German Freedom Movement" had become the standard for all Germans. They warned that those who did not continue the fight would be hunted down and dealt with mercilessly. "Hate is our prayer, and revenge our battlecry!" they exclaimed.[49]

This was a people's war, and every citizen was encouraged to learn how to fire the single-man weapon called the "Panzer Fist." The newspapers carried explanations on its use, in picture format, and posters and leaflets were circulated with the caption "What Everyone Must Know about the Panzer Fist." Every German should consider it his duty to assume his place in the "Front of the Panzer Fists."[50]

Hitler expected his Party comrades to organize the common

defensive effort courageously, and to this end he broadened the powers of the gauleiters by appointing them Reich defense commissars of the various provinces.[51] Although he rewarded them with this extensive power, he demanded in return a devotion which knew no fear. Nazi officialdom was not exempt from terror, as the Hitler-Bormann orders to the Party functionaries reveal. The gauleiters were expected to make themselves useful where the people most needed them, to radiate confidence in the Führer, and to convince the population that the Party was in control of the situation. This was no mean assignment under the conditions. Should they fail to offer resistance to the last, Nazi officials would have to face the consequences.[52] Bormann's directive of February 24, 1945, warned that those who weakened were "traitors to the nation and murderers of our women and children . . . There is only one way to stay alive: to be ready to die fighting and thereby to force the victory."[53]

To prove that the government would ruthlessly punish any misbehavior, Himmler announced the execution of the SS colonel and police director von Salisch for deserting Bromberg as well as the court-martial and execution of Colonel von Hassenstein for an unauthorized retreat.[54] The worse the military situation became, the more unrestrained were the threats. In a directive dated April 1, 1945, Bormann ordered all gauleiters and other Nazi officials to remain in their provinces and to die fighting for the final victory.[55] The farther the Russians advanced toward Berlin, the more intense German propaganda and resistance became.

On April 15, Hitler struck up the "Jewish-Bolshevik" motif once again in his final appeal to his troops and to the nation just before the Battle of Berlin:

Soldiers of the eastern front!
For the last time the deadly Jewish-Bolshevik enemy is going over to the attack with his hordes. He is trying to destroy Germany and exterminate our people. You soldiers of the east already know yourselves. . . what fate is threatening. . . The old men and children are murdered, the women and girls are reduced to army camp whores. The remainder go to Siberia.

We knew about this attack in advance, and since January of this year everything has been done to build up a strong front. The enemy is confronted by a tremendous amount of artillery. Losses in our infantry have been replaced with countless new units. Alarm units, newly organized units, and the Volkssturm are reinforcing our front. This time the Bolshevik will experience the old fate of Asia, that is, he must and shall bleed to death before the capital city of the German Reich.

Whoever does not do his duty at this moment is a traitor to our people . . . Whoever commands you to retreat, without your knowing him well, is to be taken prisoner at once and if necessary killed on the spot, no matter what his rank may be.

Berlin will remain German, Vienna will become German once more, and Europe will never become Russian . . . In these hours the whole German people is looking to you, my warriors in the east, and is hoping . . . that the Bolshevik onrush will be drowned in its own blood because of your steadfastness, your fanaticism, your weapons, and your leadership. At the moment when fate has removed the greatest war criminal of all times from the earth [Roosevelt] the turning point of this war will be decided.[56]

With this appeal ringing in their ears, the German people prepared for the onslaught. Goebbels as gauleiter of Berlin and Reich defense commissar prepared for a ruthless defense of the capital and warned his subordinates that should white flags appear in the streets he would barricade the blocks involved and have the whole area blown up.[57] He and the new commandant of Berlin, General Weidling, prodded the defenders, who consisted of the remainder of the Fifty-seventh Panzer Corps, the Eighteenth Panzergrenadier Division, scattered army and SS units, the *Volkssturm,* and units of Hitler Youth. Even whitebearded men from the capital's old peoples homes were called out to dig trenches around the city, and they were promptly referred to by the Berliners as the "Father Christmas Club." A newspaper for the defenders of Greater Berlin entitled *Der Panzerbär* was published daily, demanding self-sacrifice for the Fatherland.

Goebbels urged that everyone, including women and children, join in the struggle, and revolutionize warfare through their example. If anyone felt that success was impossible, then he should "buy a rope at once, and execute upon himself the work of destruction which in his opinion has become inevitable for the nation."[58] In a broadcast on April 21, Goebbels declared Berlin "a front line city": "Defenders of Berlin, the eyes of your women, your mothers, and your children are fixed on you. They have entrusted to you their lives, their happiness, . . . and their future. You are now aware of your task . . . The hour of the supreme test has come."[59]

There is conflicting evidence regarding what Goebbels said when he met the representatives of the press for the last time on April 21, speaking by candlelight in the film room of a mansion on Hermann Göring Street. According to Hans Fritzsche, the minister gave vent to his wrath and reproached the German people just as Hitler was to do, charging that "they had earned the fate which was imminent." He allegedly ended his last press conference by shouting, "If we fall, we will make the earth quake in the process."[60]

Naumann has challenged this account, and his recollection of Goebbels's message is more plausible because Goebbels would hardly berate the nation at the same time that he was calling for defense to the death. According to Naumann, "He spoke in deadly earnest about the coming end, that all attempts to turn the tide had failed, and concluded 'May God be merciful to the German people, because I fear the worst. But gentlemen, you can be assured that neither I nor my family will be captured alive by the Russians.' "[61]

On April 24, the German High Command launched its final battle plan. General Wenck's Twelfth Army, deployed against the Americans on the Elbe and Mulde rivers, was to rush westward to meet the Ninth Army wheeling from the south toward Berlin. Then, should Steiner be able to make progress, the three armies were to check the Soviet drive to surround Berlin. But this was a vain hope, since the Soviets soon closed the ring around the capital at Potsdam and Brandenburg.

The battle for Berlin raged in several sectors of the city. The Reich chancellery itself lay under artillery fire, and on April 28 the Russians raised the red banner over the Reichstag. Berlin's last chance for relief was lost when units of Wenck's Twelfth Army were beaten back in their push from the southwest of the city.[62]

Throughout those final days, the German High Command continued to report devastating Soviet losses, claiming in the communiqué of April 20 that 2,807 Russian tanks had been destroyed since April 1. The communiqués stressed the gravity of the situation and the self-sacrifice of the combatants:

In the battle for Berlin every foot of ground is contested. (April 25)

In the struggle for Berlin which is of decisive importance for the future of the Reich and for the existence of Europe, both sides yesterday threw reserves into the battle. (April 26)

Fanatical house-to-house fighting for the center of Berlin raged day and night. In a severe struggle, the gallant garrison defended itself against Soviet masses attacking ceaselessly. Nevertheless a further enemy advance in individual districts could not be prevented. (April 29)

Much was made of the fact that Hitler remained in Berlin to command its defense: "The news was passed from foxhole to foxhole. It was radioed to every tank, however heavily engaged, to every gun crew, to every headquarters, to every runner hurrying through the enemy fire—wherever there were German soldiers—the same news was discussed: The Führer is in Berlin."[63] *Der Panzerbär* trumpeted, "Where the Führer is, victory is!"[64]

The Hitler cult continued unabated until the last. Goebbels gave his customary message on the occasion of Hitler's birthday, affirming that "I . . . am convinced that fate will award the laurel wreath to him and his people after the last hard test. I can only say that these times with all their sombre majesty have found their only worthy representative in the Führer."[65]

Nazi zealots went to every length to raise the spirits of the defenders. The arrival of "reserves from the west" early on April 23 allegedly brought "marked relief and great joy" to the Berliners and caused "real outbursts of joy" at the troop command posts.[66] Naumann promised in a speech delivered on April 26 that a German army which would "grab victory from the hands of the Bolsheviks"[67] was moving rapidly toward the capital. Further, he had the Propaganda Ministry print and distribute handbills addressed to the soldiers of General Wenck's army; but in fact they were meant to influence the defenders within Berlin itself. The flyers urged Wenck's army to "hurry, come quickly, help us."[68]

Throughout the battle the Werewolf radio warned that death awaited the cowardly. Never would Germany surrender to the Bolshevik scourge: "There will be no peace in Europe until the German people are certain that they will keep their freedom. Before that the German people will not lay down their arms, even if we have to fight at the North Pole."[69] Every man, woman, and child was expected to do his "duty." Bodies of "cowards" were hung from lampposts in Berlin to act as deterrents to surrender and defeatism. A sign attached to one such unfortunate offender read, "I, Cpl. Höhne, of Berlin, was too cowardly to defend my wife and children."[70]

As the battle drew to a close, Goebbels's mission as a National Socialist had for all intents and purposes been concluded. He had proclaimed the Party's myths, he had buttressed them with tactical propaganda, and now as the Reich lay in the death throes, he had surrendered to the irrational as a propagandist and had left the success or failure of the Nazi war gods entirely in the hands of fate. Providence would judge the currency of his mythical structure. Naumann relates that he had several conversations with Goebbels during the last days of the Battle of Berlin, because time lay heavy on his hands. Having moved to the Führer bunker with his family, he no longer directed a vast propaganda network, and he no longer had a real function. Curiously, Goebbels ended his career as he had begun it, as a writer. Naumann recalls that "he put his final thoughts to paper knowing full well that the manuscript would be lost and that there was little chance that it would ever be read after the war."[71]

Goebbels was named Reich chancellor and Naumann propaganda minister on Hitler's final appointment list before he and his bride, Eva Braun, committed suicide on April 30. Goebbels served but one day in his new post, and when it became clear that the Russians were about to storm the bunker, he prepared to meet his fate. Once more Naumann is our guide: "After we had said our last goodbyes, he went arm and arm with his wife up the steps of the bunker to his death. He had buckled his belt, and put on his gloves and hat. This is my last memory of these two people with whom I had spent so many years of my life."[72] In order to protect the myth of the Viking fight to the death in Berlin, the new Reich chancellor Admiral Dönitz did not reveal that either the Führer or his propaganda minister had committed suicide. Instead, he arranged a ghoulish ritual in the Goebbels tradition.

Late on the evening of May 1, three separate announcements warned that news of the utmost importance was about to be broadcast. Excerpts from Wagner set the mood for what was to follow. The adagio of Bruckner's Third Symphony was then played, which

Bruckner had composed as a tribute to Wagner after learning of the master's death. The brief message that the Führer had died "fighting Bolshevism to the last breath" was followed by three rolls of the drums, the German national anthem, and the Horst Wessel song.[73]

Finally Dönitz addressed the nation. He described Hitler as a man who had dedicated himself to the struggle against bolshevism and had sacrificed his life for that cause. Dönitz stated that in his capacity as the new chief of state, he would continue the war for one reason only—"to save the German people from Bolshevism"—and he charged that the United States and Great Britain had surrendered any interests of their own and were fighting solely for the spread of bolshevism in Europe.[74]

The faithful spoke out to honor Hitler. Gauleiter Hanke called on the nation to "do everything which is still in our power so that we may save as many German people as can still be saved from Bolshevism."[75] The Luftwaffe ace Hans Rudel declared that the "death of our Führer is the most terrible blow that could have fallen on us at this moment. We soldiers . . . lost our great idol . . . there is only one thing to do, . . . to go on fighting."[76]

In Field Marshal Schörner's Order of the Day of May 2, he wrote that Adolf Hitler had died a hero's death, "as a martyr to his ideal . . . and as a soldier of Europe's mission . . . fighting to the last breath against Bolshevism . . . the Führer's heroic death imposes a supreme obligation on every decent soldier. Your actions must be such that you can fearlessly face the judgment of the dead Führer. Heil Adolf Hitler!"[77]

On May 2, General Weidling surrendered the city. Nevertheless, some minor pockets of German resistance remained, and many of these fought to the last man.[78] One radio newscast announced, "Even now, when the heroic struggle in the Reich capital is drawing toward a close, the enemy is met by murderous resistance from the ruins and rubble."[79] The High Command did not admit that the capital had fallen until May 4.

Before the unconditional surrender of Germany on May 7, the anti-Bolshevik theme dominated the official messages of the Dönitz government. In one radio report the newly appointed foreign minister Count Schwerin von Krosigk attacked the United Nations meeting at San Francisco, charging that the Soviets would sabotage the idle, internationalist dreams of peace and world order which held sway there.[80]

All attention was focused on the east, and the battle fronts against the Reich's enemies in the west were hardly mentioned in the news. On May 4, Dönitz once more urged the German people to continue the fight, pointing out that the "struggle against the Western powers has become senseless . . . the only purpose for which we still have to fight is to save as many Germans as possible from Bolshevization and enslavement."[81]

Finally, as further resistance to the invaders appeared hopeless, Dönitz announced on May 8 that he had ordered the unconditional surrender of all the German fighting forces.[82] The final OKW communiqué, which was written by Jodl, paid tribute to the living and the dead:

The struggle has ceased on all fronts since midnight. The Wehrmacht has stopped the hopeless fight on the orders of the Grand Admiral . . . True to his oath the German soldier has given his utmost for the nation in this struggle, and this shall always be remembered. At great sacrifice the home front supported him to the last with all its resources . . .

Therefore, every soldier can lay down his weapon proudly and with his head high, and in the saddest hours of our history can undertake work for the life of our people both bravely and with confidence in the future.

In this dark hour the Wehrmacht pays tribute to its comrades killed in action.

The dead obligate us to absolute fidelity, obedience, and discipline towards our Fatherland which is bleeding from countless wounds.[83]

The limited propaganda success which Goebbels enjoyed in 1945 was due only in part to his ingenuity. Instead, it resulted from the fact that traditional Nazi propaganda overlapped and merged with traditional German patriotism and the people's intuitive response to defend the Fatherland in danger. Propaganda claims about "Jewish-Bolshevism" and the Reich as the protector of Western civilization—which some Germans questioned as late as the debacle at Stalingrad and even during the long retreat of 1944—suddenly took on credibility when Russian troops began pouring out of Poland into Germany's eastern provinces. At that time even the most convinced anti-Nazis were ready to respond to the Party's propaganda motifs, a situation which Goebbels fully appreciated.

By 1945 the German people had surrendered themselves to the clique of forceful and determined Nazis who ultimately led them to defeat. True to form, Goebbels directed his propaganda during the Third Reich's last days in a manner which lent coherence and unity to Hitler's ideological posture. For decades the Führer had based his ideology on race, and he died fighting "Jewish-Bolshevism" as Aryan man's leader in its "life or death struggle against the racial underworld."

Hitler put an entirely new and sinister twist on the death myth. When he realized that he and his followers were themselves about to be destroyed, his will was that Germany itself should be annihilated. Defeat, if defeat it had to be, was to be forged in the epic National Socialist manner. The result was his scorched earth policy and his recriminations in the last days against the German people who, he maintained, had proved themselves weak in the face of a stronger force represented by "Jewish-Bolshevism." The Reich as he knew it should not survive. This demonstrated nazism's marriage with nihilism at its death, signaled by Germany's cataclysmic funeral pyre. For his part, Goebbels was less concerned that the nation be destroyed than that Germans in the distant future would regard his conduct at the time of the Reich's direst need as both noble and heroic.

NOTES

Notes

Chapter I. The Mythical World of
Nazi Propaganda

1. Frederick C. Barghoorn, *Soviet Foreign Propaganda* (Princeton, N.J.: Princeton University Press, 1964), pp. 8–9.

2. Robert T. Holt and Robert W. van de Velde, *Strategic Psychological Operations and American Foreign Policy* (Chicago: University of Chicago Press, 1960), pp. 26–27.

3. Harold D. Lasswell, "The Strategy of Soviet Propaganda," in Wilbur Schramm, ed., *The Process and Effects of Mass Communication* (Urbana: University of Illinois Press, 1954), p. 538.

4. Helmut Heiber, *Joseph Goebbels* (Berlin: Colloquium Verlag, 1962), and Z. A. B. Zeman, *Nazi Propaganda* (London: Oxford University Press, 1964).

5. Ernest K. Bramsted, *Goebbels and National Socialist Propaganda 1925–1945* (East Lansing: Michigan State University Press, 1965).

6. Marlis G. Steinert, *Hitlers Krieg und die Deutschen: Stimmung und Haltung der deutschen Bevölkerung im Zweiten Weltkrieg*, 2 vols. (Düsseldorf: Econ, 1970).

7. Wilfred von Oven, *Mit Goebbels bis zum Ende*, 2 vols. (Buenos Aires: Dürer Verlag, 1949), I, 32–33.

8. Karl Dietrich Bracher, *Die deutsche Diktatur* (Cologne and Berlin: Kiepenbeuer and Witsch, 1969), p. 198.

9. Hannah Arendt, *The Origins of Totalitarianism* (New York: Meridian, 1958), p. 361.

10. Ernst Nolte, *Der Fascismus in seiner Epoche* (Munich: R. Piper, 1963), p. 354.

11. Franz Neumann, *Behemoth* (New York: Oxford University Press, 1942), p. 125.

12. Fritz Stern, *The Politics of Cultural Despair* (Berkeley: University of California Press, 1961), pp. xiii, xx, 61–62, 86, 90–91, 201–2, 263, 295.

13. Walter Laqueur, *Russia and Germany* (Boston: Little, Brown, 1965), pp. 93–104.

14. Göring, address for "Erntedankfest," October 6, 1942, VB-ND, p. 1. Hans Jenker, in a work on the Wagner festivals entitled *Bayreuth* (Berlin: Kintzel Verlag, 1943), likened the role of the Jews in the war with the behavior of the legendary anti-hero Hagen who killed Siegfried with a cowardly thrust of a spear into his back.

264   NAZI PROPAGANDA

15. *Der ewige Jude*, vintage 1940, directed by Fritz Hippler and written by Goebbels's expert on Jewish questions Eberhard Taubert. The butchering scenes were so shocking and had such a poor reception that a shortened version was released. See Joseph Wulf, *Theater und Film im Dritten Reich* (Gütersloh: Sigbert Mohn Verlag, 1964), pp. 410–12. Taubert mentioned to me that his anti-Semitic work at that time was a "peripheral activity" (Nebentätigkeit), an assertion which hardly squares with the truth. Interview with Eberhard Taubert, Cologne, August 4, 1970.

16. *Jud Süss*, directed by Veit Harlan, with Ferdinand Marian, Kristina Söderbaum, Heinrich George, Werner Krauss, and Eugene Klöpper. For an account of Goebbels's directives to Harlan for this production, see Veit Harlan, *Im Schatten meiner Filme* (Gütersloh: Sigberg Mohn Verlag, 1966), pp. 89–130. In his autobiography, Harlan claims rather unconvincingly that his interpretation of the film was not anti-Semitic at all and that Goebbels was entirely responsible for this interpretation. *Ibid.*, p. 127.

17. *Ibid.*, p. 130.

18. Goebbels, directive of September 25, 1940, in Willi A. Boelcke, *Kriegspropaganda 1939–1941: Geheime Ministerkonferenzen im Reichspropagandaministerium* (Stuttgart: Deutsche Verlags-Anstalt, 1966), p. 526. It is true that many of the actors were forced to play in *Jud Süss*, and Goebbels's "lex Harlan" set a precedent binding actors to accept ministerial commands to play roles and to take orders like common soldiers. State Secretary Leopold Gutterer, interview with author, Aachen, August 5, 1970.

19. Hitler, address, January 30, 1939, in Max Domarus, ed., *Hitler: Reden und Proklamationen 1932–1945*, 2 vols. (Würzburg: Verlagsdrückerei Schmidt, 1963), II, 1058.

20. "Europäische Judendämmerung," November 1940, in Helmut Sündermann, *Die Entscheidungen reifen* (Munich: Franz Eher, 1943), pp. 57–60.

21. "Du bist die Kette ohne Ende," *Lieder zur Hochzeit*, NSDAP, Munich, 1937.

22. Ufa studios, directed by Gustav Ucicky. See also commentary by Siegfried Kracauer in *From Caligari to Hitler* (Princeton, N.J.: Princeton University Press, 1947), pp. 269–70.

23. Baldur von Schirach, "Die Fahne ist mehr als der Tod," *Schulungsdienst der Hitler Jugend*, Issue 6, March 1941.

24. The lines are from the "Stukalied." *Stukas*, Karl Ritter director, 1941.

25. *Wunschkonzert*, Eduard von Barsody director, 1940.

26. *Kolberg*, Veit Harlan director, 1945.

27. Adolf Hitler, *Mein Kampf* (Munich: Franz Eher, 1943), pp. 53–70.

28. *Ibid.*, p. 751.

29. Adolf Hitler, *The Testament of Adolf Hitler* (The Hitler-Bormann Documents, February–April 1945) (London: Cassell, 1961), p. 46.

30. Von Oven, *Mit Goebbels* I, 181, January 27, 1944.

31. The "plutocrats" were defined as some two hundred leading Jewish or Jewish-controlled families who sought to rule the world in their own interests. Goebbels, rally at Münster, February 28, 1941, in Joseph Goebbels, *Die Zeit ohne Beispiel* (Munich: Franz Eher, 1941), pp. 248–49.

32. "Denn wir fahren gegen Engelland," *Schulungsdienst der Hitler Jugend, BDM-Werk Glaube und Schönheit*, Issue 3, November 1940.

33. Goebbels felt more deeply about the Führer than even his grossly fawning statements reveal. He was convinced that Hitler's career was even more important than that of Christ, although he could not say that to the public "without being horribly misunderstood." He was certain that Hitler had performed actual miracles. Prinz Friedrich Christian zu Schaumburg-Lippe, *Dr. G.* (Wiesbaden: Limes Verlag, 1963), pp. 125–26, 131–32.

34. "Mitteilungen für die Truppe," December 1944, MGRC, Roll 160, 1527669, NA.

35. Lev Bezymenski, *The Death of Adolf Hitler: Unknown Documents from Soviet Archives* (New York: Harcourt, Brace & World, 1968), pp. 35–51.

Chapter II. *The Nazi Propaganda Machine and World War II*

1. Gustav Le Bon, *The Crowd*, 5th ed. (London: T. Fischer Unwin, 1908), p. 45.

2. Schaumburg-Lippe, *Dr. G.*, p. 15.

3. Dr. Werner Naumann, interview with author, Klingenberg-am-Main, July 11, 1970.

4. *Ibid.*

5. Colonel Martin, the liaison officer from the OKW to the Propaganda Ministry, was also present at the Lanke meeting on May 11, 1942. Eberhard Taubert, interview with author, Cologne, August 4, 1970.

6. Wolfgang Diewerge, interview with author, Düsseldorf, July 12, 1970.

7. Magda had turned down Herbert Hoover's son's proposal of marriage before finding her spiritual home in the movement. E. Ebermeyer and H. Roos, *Gefährtin des Teufels: Leben und Tod der Magda Goebbels* (Hamburg: Hoffmann und Campe, 1952), p. 27.

8. Bramsted, *Goebbels and National Socialist Propaganda*, pp. 49–87.

9. Gutterer, interview, August 5, 1970.

10. The action was directed by the National Socialist People's Welfare League. Gutterer claims that the men and women involved became convinced National Socialists from that point forward, a contention difficult to prove. Interview, August 5, 1970.

11. Le Bon, *The Crowd*, p. 37.

12. Hitler, *Mein Kampf*, pp. 193–204, 650.

13. Eugen Hadamovsky, *Propaganda und nationale Macht* (Oldenburg: Verlag Gerhard Stalling, 1933), p. 43.

14. Goebbels, *Rede vor der Generalität: Der Krieg als Weltanschauungskampf, Posen, January 25, 1944* (Berlin: NS-Führungsstab des Oberkommandos der Wehrmacht, 1944), OKW/WPr, T-77, Roll 852, 558135, NA.

15. Diewerge, interview, July 12, 1970.

16. Naumann, interview, July 11, 1970.

17. Dr. Werner Naumann, interview with author, Lüdenscheid/Westphalia, August 6, 1970.

18. Chief of the Security Police and the SD Reinhard Heydrich was very complimentary about Gutterer in a letter he wrote to Himmler dated October 30, 1940, requesting the Reichsführer SS to approve his promotion to Brigadeführer. Relations between the Propaganda Ministry and the SS had never been closer now that Gutterer had assumed a leading role there, Heydrich affirmed. He was seeing to it that the SD's "Meldungen aus dem Reich" were given every consideration in the Ministry's propaganda. Furthermore, he was demonstrating his loyalty to the SS publicly by wearing the SS black to all the recent Hitler rallies in the Sports Palace. See Heydrich to Himmler, Leopold Gutterer NSDAP Personnel File, Berlin Document Center. Of the several propaganda officials interviewed for this book, only Taubert argued that Gutterer had been underrated by his former colleagues and historians. Taubert, interview with author, Cologne, August 4, 1970.

19. Günter d'Alquen, interview with author, Mönchen-Gladbach, July 13, 1970; also Naumann, interview, July 11, 1970.

20. Hans Schwarz van Berk, interview with author, Munich, July 28, 1970.

21. *Ibid.* Compare Naumann, interview, July 11, 1970.

22. Diewerge, interview, July 12, 1970; compare Naumann, interview, July 11, 1970.

23. Taubert, interview, August 4, 1970; see also the privately published manuscript by Taubert entitled *Der antisowjetische Apparat des deutschen Propagandaministeriums*.

24. Naumann, a seventeen-year-old SA man at the time, first attracted Goebbels's attention at a rally in Görlitz in 1928. Naumann, interview, July 11, 1970.

25. Letter, Himmler to Berger and von Herff, August 2, 1942, in Helmut Heiber, ed., *Reichsführer! Briefe an und von Himmler* (Stuttgart: Deutsche Verlags-Anstalt, 1968), pp. 142–43. Compare Naumann's own views on his relationship with Hitler, interview, August 6, 1970.

26. Schwarz van Berk asserts that he saw Naumann risk his life on several occasions at the front while they were serving in the *Leibstandarte*. Interview, July 28, 1970.

27. Gutterer, interview, August 5, 1970. Boelcke makes the undocumented charge in *Kriegspropaganda* that Naumann was keeping a file on Goebbels so that he could overthrow him and become the propaganda minister. There is no evidence to prove this contention which probably stems from an unnamed informant from the Propaganda Ministry whom Naumann had offended. Naumann himself answers this charge by denying it and offering the more plausible contention that he was hoping to replace Lammers as head of the Reich chancellery, a position which would have brought him into the closest proximity to Hitler. Although Naumann was a trusted SS man, a Bormann-Naumann power rivalry would probably have resulted from such an arrangement. See Boelcke, *Kriegspropaganda*, pp. 54–57, and transcript of interview with Naumann, August 6, 1970.

28. *Hitler's Secret Conversations 1941–1944*, trans. N. Cameron and R. H. Stevens (New York: Farrar, Strauss, and Young, 1953), pp. 388–90.

29. Domarus, *Hitler*, I, 973.

30. Wilhelm Treue, ed., "Rede Hitlers vor der deutschen Presse," November 10, 1938, *Vierteljahrshefte für Zeitgeschichte*, VI (April 1958), 175–91.

31. See Boelcke, *Kriegspropaganda*, pp. 35–119.

32. Von Oven, *Mit Goebbels*, I, 14–20.

33. "Richtlinien für die Durchführung der Propaganda der NSDAP," sent to all gauleiters and gau propaganda chiefs, NSDAP, T-81, Roll 84, 95625, NA. Compare "Reichspressechef Dr. Dietrich vor der deutschen Presse am 3. September 1939," VI Nr. 213/39, SO, ZSg 109/3, BA. Dietrich struck a characteristically pedestrian note in a basic war directive to the press in which he called on the reporters to produce "a psychological West Wall" among the German people to support their soldiers in the Polish campaign.

34. Schaumburg-Lippe, *Dr. G.*, pp. 243–44.

35. Two examples of such themes were Julius Streicher's fall from power and complaints about the great numbers of Party men to be seen on the home front. Diewerge, interview, July 12, 1970.

36. *Ibid*.

37. *Ibid*.

38. Taubert, interview, August 4, 1970.

39. Naumann, interview, July 11, 1970.

40. Gutterer, interview, August 5, 1970.

41. Schwarz van Berk, interview, July 28, 1970.

42. Even before the war, Hitler had signed three directives outlining Dietrich's functions. Besides the 1937 order naming Dietrich state secretary and Reich press chief, he also signed the following documents: "Befügnisse des Reichspresschefs," February 28, 1934, NSDAP, Partei Kanzlei, *Verfügungen/Anordnungen/Bekanntgaben*, 5 vols. (Munich: Franz Eher, 1941–1943), I, 442. A Hitler directive of February 16, 1939, read: "Die Veröffentlichung von amtlichen Nachrichten jedweder Art aus dem Bereich der Reichsministerien und sämtlicher übrigen Dienststellen des Reiches

erfolgt ausschliesslich auf dem Wege über die Presseabteilung der Reichsregierung im Reichspropaganda-ministerium." OKW/WPr, T-77, Roll 984, 4474812, NA. See also Boelcke, *Kriegspropaganda*, p. 147.

43. Helmut Sündermann, interview with author, Leoni/Starnberger See, November 12, 1969. Compare Dietrich, Nuremberg testimony, October 30, 1947, 1948/56, IfZ. The clippings Dietrich gathered were edited specifically for Hitler and, according to Dr. Schmidt of the Foreign Office, they represented one of his main reading sources during the war. The impressions that Hitler culled from this news formed the basis of daily directives to Dietrich. Furthermore, Dietrich controlled the important news agency "Deutsches Nachrichtenbüro," and it was his function to transmit the official High Command communiqués and Special Announcements for publication. Erich Murawski, *Der deutsche Wehrmachtbericht* (Boppard: Harold Boldt Verlag, 1961), pp. 135–37; testimony by Hans Fritzsche, June 27, 1946, International Military Tribunal, *Trial of the Major War Criminals before the International Military Tribunal*, November 14, 1945–October 1, 1946, 42 vols., Blue Series (Nuremberg, 1947–1949), XVII, 154; testimony by Dr. Paul Karl Schmidt, "Leiter der Presse und Nachrichtenabteilung des Auswärtigen Amtes," Archive des Centre de Documentation Juive Contemporaire, CXXVa-74, cited in Leon Poliakov and Josef Wulf, *Das Dritte Reich und seine Diener* (Berlin: Arani, 1959), pp. 448–49. See as well Otto Dietrich, *12 Jahre mit Hitler* (Munich: Isar Verlag, 1955), pp. 130–31, 154–55, 251.

44. Hans Fritzsche, interrogation at Nuremberg, translation of Document NG-172, Office of U.S. Chief of Counsel, IfZ. Heinz Lorenz, a member of Dietrich's staff, testimony at Nuremberg, July 28, 1948, Document NG-4331, Office of U.S. Chief of Counsel, IfZ.

45. Naumann, interview, July 11, 1970.

46. *Ibid.*

47. RMfVP, T-70, Roll 3, 3505763, NA.

48. Dietrich, Nuremberg testimony, October 30, 1947, 1948/56, IfZ.

49. Sündermann, interview, November 16, 1969.

50. Naumann, interview with author, Bad Homburg, November 17, 1969.

51. Sündermann claims that Dietrich refused to transmit Hitler's directives regarding alleged atrocities committed by Allied troops in occupied western Germany, an act of insubordination leading to his dismissal. Sündermann, interview, November 16, 1969. See also Dietrich, Nuremberg testimony, October 30, 1947, 1948/56, IfZ. Dietrich complained in his memoirs that "my official high-sounding title was 'Pressechef der Reichsregierung,' but the title did not carry with it corresponding powers." Hans Fritzsche, in testimony offered at Nuremberg on June 27, 1946, observed that "Dietrich and Amann [who headed the organization of publishers] were nominally subordinate to him [Goebbels]; actually both had the same authority as he had and I always had to adjust differences or co-ordinate among these three authorities." International Military Tribunal, *Trial of the Major War Criminals*, VII, 154. See also Oron J. Hale, *The Captive Press in the Third Reich* (Princeton, N.J.: Princeton University Press, 1964), pp. 320–21.

52. In his "Basic Order on Military Reporting in the Wehrmacht" of December 26, 1941, Hitler demanded absolutely accurate reports from every military sector. Hitler to the Wehrmacht, Bormann to the Reichsleiter, gauleiter, and unit chiefs, T-580, Roll 15, NA.

53. Walter Hagemann, *Publizistik im Dritten Reich* (Hamburg: Hansischer Gilden Verlag, 1948), pp. 412–14; Murawski, *Deutsche Wehrmachtbericht*, pp. 39–67.

54. For one example among many see SD report, April 28, 1940, R 58/150, BA.

55. Ohlendorff, chief SD, to Berndt, RMfVP, November 25, 1943, RMfVP, T-580, Roll 683, NA.

56. Jodl, Der Chef des Wehrmachtführungsstabes im Oberkommando der Wehrmacht, Nr. 4210-41 geheim, to the OKH, OKM, ObdL, WFSt (WPr), and WFSt

(Ausl./Abw.), June 18, 1941, in Murawski, *Deutsche Wehrmachtbericht*, pp. 701–2.

57. Jodl, Chef, WFSt/OKW, "Betrifft: Abfassung des Wehrmachtberichts," with notation F(ührer) hat Kenntnis 4/5. 11, October 25, 1944, in Murawski, *Deutsche Wehrmachtbericht*, pp. 757–59. The chief of the OKW/WPr, General Hasso von Wedel, noted in his account of the history of his office that, although "absolute truth" was the guiding principle in formulating the communiqués, still "the security of the war effort and of our German soldiers took precedence." This meant not listing items which "might possibly endanger our own troops or home population." Hasso von Wedel, *Die Wehrmachtpropaganda 1939–1945*, vol. I: *Die Abteilung für Wehrmachtpropaganda im Oberkommando der Wehrmacht (OKW/WPr)*, Dokumentation in Maschinenschrift (Koblenz, 1957), p. 50, BA. See also vol. II of this work entitled *Die Propagandatruppe* (Koblenz, 1958), BA.

58. Von Oven, *Mit Goebbels*, II, 217–18.

59. Von Wedel, *Die Wehrmachtpropaganda*, I, 10. See also Murawski, *Deutsche Wehrmachtpropaganda*, p. 137.

60. Kurt Hesse, *Der Feldherr Psychologos* (Berlin: Mittler, 1922).

61. See the "Weisungen für die militärische Zensur," OKW/WPr, Berlin, 1941, T-77, Roll 1040, 6513902, NA; compare "Tätigkeit der Zensoren im Kriege," February 4, 1939, T-77, Roll 1036, 6508817, NA. For organizational charts of the OKW/WPr, see von Wedel, *Wehrmachtpropaganda*, I, 31.

62. Murawski, *Deutsche Wehrmachtbericht*, pp. 130–32.

63. Keitel to Goebbels, January 15, 1940; Goebbels to Keitel, January 18, 1940; RMfVP, T-70, Roll 7, 3510913, NA.

64. Führer order, February 10, 1941, WFSt Nr. 75/41g, released by Keitel on February 17, 1941. "Durchführungsbestimmungen zum Erlass des Führers und Obersten Befehlshabers der Wehrmacht vom 10.2.41," OKW/WPr, Roll 1040, 6513424, NA.

65. Goebbels, diary fragment, February 14, 1943, Archiv 2771/61, ed 83, IfZ.

66. Murawski, *Deutsche Wehrmachtbericht*, p. 140.

67. The Germans had in fact registered some successes at Salerno, but Goebbels did not want this fact reported. Goebbels, diary entry, September 18, 1943, MGRC, T-84, Roll 265, NA.

68. Goebbels, diary entry, September 23, 1943, *ibid*. It did not help matters when von Wedel moved his OKW/WPr staff office to the Führer headquarters in September 1943. Von Wedel, *Wehrmachtpropaganda*, I, 33–45.

69. Naumann, interview, July 11, 1970. See also "Arbeitsabkommen zwischen dem Auswärtigen Amt und dem Reichsministerium für Volksaufklärung und Propaganda," October 22, 1941, files of Auswärtiges Amt, Deutsches Zentralarchiv, Potsdam.

70. Goebbels, "General-referat Ostraum," *Nachrichtenblatt des Reichsministeriums für Volksaufklärung und Propaganda*, November 18, 1941, RMfVP, T-70, Roll 31, 3537340, NA. There was a long history to the Goebbels-Rosenberg rivalry. One notorious feud concerned their dispute over the direction of Nazi policy toward modern art, a controversy which raged during the early years of the Third Reich. Rosenberg sided with the *völkisch* interpretation, while Goebbels was aligned with the National Socialist liberals on this question. Their mutual problems were attributable to Hitler's predilection for dividing power among his subordinates. Goebbels, as president of the Reich Culture Chamber, was threatened by Rosenberg, whom the Führer had charged with the "Überwachung der gesamten geistigen und weltanschaulichen Schulung und Erziehung der NSDAP." Rosenberg, for his part, detested Goebbels. See Hildegard Brenner, "Die Kunst im Politischen Machtkampf der Jahre 1933/34," *Vierteljahrshefte für Zeitgeschichte*, X (January, 1962), 17–42.

71. Goebbels, diary fragment, February 16, 1943, Archiv 2771/61, ed 83, IfZ.

72. During the course of a meeting Goebbels had with Hitler, he had complained about Rosenberg and Hitler allegedly had replied, "But I've given Rosenberg a free

hand. Why doesn't he use it?" Berger to Himmler, January 29, 1943, SS, T-175, Roll 124, 2599596, NA. See also Taubert's memorandum to Gutterer revealing that Bormann and Lammers had to deal once more with a Goebbels-Rosenberg jurisdictional dispute. Taubert to Gutterer, April 3, 1944, CGD, T-580, Roll 941, NA.

73. According to Tiessler, not long after the beginning of the offensive against Russia, Goebbels held a conference with Gutterer and himself and gave them "Narrenfreiheit" on the "subhuman" policy. According to the minister's strategy, he could take the credit for the good his men accomplished but they must answer for any trouble which ensued. Walter Tiessler, "Leiter des Reichsring für nationalsozialistische Propaganda und Volksaufklärung innerhalb der Reichspropagandaleitung der NSDAP; Verbindungsmann zum 'Stabe des Stellvertreters des Führers' und zum Leiter der Parteikanzlei" (Hess and Bormann), interview, Munich, July 30, 1970.

74. Hitler, Reichstag address, September 1, 1939, in Domarus, Hitler, II, 1317. See also Bormann, Rundschreiben Nr. 198/42, "Stimmungsberichte," December 18, 1942, T-580, Reel 15, NA.

75. "Tätigkeitsbericht," RPA Bochum, Kränzlein to Schaeffer, January 20, 1943, T-580, Roll 683, BA. Naumann to Kränzlein, Berlin, April 17, 1943, T-580, Roll 683, NA.

76. MGRC, T-580, Roll 660, NA.

77. Goebbels, "Verordnung über ausserordentliche Rundfunkmassnahmen von 1. September 1939," T-77, Roll 1015, 2482728, NA.

78. Gürtner to Goebbels, September 1, 1939, Vierteljahrshefte für Zeitgeschichte, XI (October 1963), 419–20.

79. Goebbels, "An die obersten Reichsbehörden," September 21, 1939, OKW/WPr, T-77, Roll 1015, 2482736, NA. The Wehrmacht was among the worst offenders, and Goebbels's complaint to Keitel resulted in the latter's order to the armed forces forbidding the practice: "The main weapon of the enemy against the spirit of resistance of our Volk is the radio. Whoever, as a German soldier, exposes himself and his spirit to this enemy propaganda, commits spiritual self-mutilation. This is no less contemptible than cowardly physical self-mutilation." Keitel order, WNV/Abw III/WPr (IIc), January 26, 1940, OKW/WPr, T-77, Roll 1015, 2482742, NA. Although Goebbels had some success with Keitel, there were other gaps in foreign propaganda which he could not seal off: Ribbentrop's Seehaus Dienst continued to circulate daily reports on foreign propaganda to a subscriber list numbering in the hundreds. Although Goebbels was able to trim down the number, the problem continued to gall him.

80. Naumann, interview, July 11, 1970.

81. Ibid.

82. Gutterer, interview, August 5, 1970. There is a good deal of disagreement over the value of the SD reports as a scientific indicator of public opinion. Dr. Heinz Boberach of the German Federal Archives, Koblenz, argues that they were excellent for this purpose. Meldungen aus dem Reich: Auswahl aus den geheimen Lageberichten des Sicherheitsdienstes der SS 1939–1944 (Berlin: Luchterhand, 1965), pp. ix–xxviii. Naumann contends that he and Goebbels found them very unsystematic, unscientific, and unreliable, and their usefulness to Goebbels declined year by year during the course of the war. However, they remain the best source on public opinion within the Reich for World War II. See the Ph.D. dissertation by David Kitterman, "National Diary of German Civilian Life during 1940: The SD Reports," University of Washington, 1972, which contains an analysis of the administration, content, and value of the reports (pp. 1–37).

83. Boberach, Meldungen aus dem Reich, pp. xvii–xxviii.

84. Ibid., p. xxvi; see also Naumann, interview, July 11, 1970. On April 17, 1943, Goebbels wrote in his diary: "The SD report is causing a stink again. I have not been happy with it at all of late. It is entirely unpolitical and is sent to the offices taking it completely unedited. There is a certain danger in this; because most of

the readers . . . don't have the insight to distinguish the important from the unimportant." Louis Lochner, ed., *The Goebbels Diaries 1942–43* (New York: Doubleday, 1948, incomplete), p. 333.

85. See "Goebbels vor Offiziere im Juli 1943," in Hildegard von Kotze, ed., *Vierteljahrshefte für Zeitgeschichte*, XIX (January 1971), 94.

Chapter III. The Battle of Poland

1. Hitler elaborated on this point in May 1942: "[W]hen the Russo-German Pact was signed, we had the task of converting to a completely reverse opinion these whom we had originally made into fanatical opponents of Russia—a maneuver that must have appeared to be a rare old muddle to the older National Socialists. Fortunately, the spirit of Party solidarity held firm, and our sudden about-turn was accepted by all without misgiving. Then, on June 22, 1941, again 'About turn!' Out shot the order one fine morning without the slightest warning! Success in an operation of this nature can only be achieved if you possess the press and know how to make tactical use of it." *Hitler's Secret Conversations 1941–1944*, p. 390.

2. William Shirer, *Berlin Diary* (New York: Knopf, 1942), p. 183.

3. *Keesing's Archiv der Gegenwart*, 1939, p. 3702.

4. VB-MA, August 28, 1939, p. 1.

5. VB-ND, August 26, 1939, p. 1.

6. *Ibid.*, August 31, 1939, p. 1.

7. Reichstag speech, September 1, 1939, in Domarus, *Hitler*, II, 1312–1317. Directives for the press treatment of the "counterattack" in VI. 197/39, SO, ZSg 109/3, BA.

8. Domarus, *Hitler*, II, 1341.

9. Alfred-Ingemar Berndt and Hasso von Wedel, eds., *Deutschland im Kampf*, 58 vols. (Berlin: Otto Stollberg, 1939–1944), I/II (September 1939), 15–16.

10. *Ibid.*, pp. 7–8.

11. Karl Dönitz, *Zehn Jahre und zwanzig Tage* (Bonn: Athenäum, 1958), p. 45.

12. VI. 199/39, September 3, 1939, SO, ZSg, 109/3, BA.

13. Wolfgang Diewerge and Leopold Gutterer, interviews, July 12 and August 5, 1970, respectively; VI. 199/39. September 3, 1939, SO, ZSg 109/3, BA.

14. Hitler, "Aufruf an das deutsche Volk," in Domarus, *Hitler*, II, 1339–1341.

15. Hitler, "Aufruf an die Soldaten der Ostarmee," in *ibid*.

16. Dönitz, *Zehn Jahre und zwanzig Tage*, p. 59.

17. *Ibid*.

18. OKW/WPr, "Fernschreiben an Führerzug," "Entwurf für das vom Führer gewünschte amtlich Dementi zur angeblichen Versenkung des britischen Dampfers 'Athenia' durch ein deutsches U-Boat," OKW/WPr, T-77, Roll 1035, 6507269, NA.

19. Notes taken by Fritz Sänger at press conference of September 4–5, 1939, Sammlung Sänger, ZSg 109/19, BA.

20. VB-MA, October 21, 1939, pp. 1–2. See also Sammlung Sänger, October 19, 1939, ZSg 102/19, BA, and the transcript of Goebbels's speech over all radio networks on the evening of October 22, 1939, "Aussage von Charles Eric Wakeham," D/912, IfZ.

21. William Shirer, *The Rise and Fall of the Third Reich* (New York: Simon & Schuster, 1960), pp. 636–38.

22. *Ibid.*, p. 637.

23. Boelcke, *Kriegspropaganda*, p. 254.

24. This faux pas was mentioned in Goebbels's press conference of October 16, 1939. VI Nr. 235/39, ZSg 102/19, SO, BA. Goebbels modestly gave his *Athenia* propaganda high marks when he addressed a group of officers from the OKW/WPr at the ministry in November 1939. It was clear, he said, that the sinking of the

Athenia would be of use to the British, no matter who sank her. The great danger was to prevent them from exploiting the affair as they had the *Lusitania*. It was the success of one's propaganda that really counted, he noted, not the truth or falsehood that it might convey objectively.

25. "Göring vor den Arbeitern der Rheinmetall-Borsig-Werke in Berlin-Tegel," September 9, 1939, in Domarus, *Hitler*, II, 1350.

26. *Rheinsische Landeszeitung*, Wuppertal, September 12, 1939, p. 1.

27. Hitler address in the "Artushof am Langen Markt," Danzig, in Domarus, *Hitler*, II, 1365.

28. Joint German-Soviet communiqué of September 17 in VB-MA, September 18, 1939, p. 2.

29. VB-MA, September 19, 1939, p. 1.

30. Von Ribbentrop to press, Moscow, VB-MA, September 30, 1939, p. 1.

31. Statement by Dr. Kausch, press conference, RMfVP, October 9, 1939, Sammlung Brammer, ZSg 101/34, BA. For press directives of September 17, 20, and 29, 1939, on the eastern settlement, see Sammlung Sänger, ZSg 102/19, BA.

32. Hitler, Reichstag address, October 6, 1939, in Domarus, *Hitler*, II, 1383. In his Reichstag address of October 6 Hitler felt compelled to speak to the question of resettlement, declaring that the Reich and the Soviet Union were cooperating to foster stability, peace, and prosperity for the Poles: "In the age of national and racial principles it is utopian to believe that these . . . people can be assimilated. Germany and the Soviet Union are agreed to support one another to carry out an extensive resettlement of these people . . . to end once and for all one of the major issues of conflict in the world." At the same time Hitler reaffirmed his friendship with the Soviets, pointing out that German and Russian interests completely overlapped. Yet the German public, like the Nazis themselves, were unimpressed.

33. John W. Wheeler-Bennett, *The Nemesis of Power* (London: Macmillan, 1964), pp. 381–82.

34. Gerd Brausch, "Der Tod des Generalobersten Werner Freiherr von Fritsch," *Militärgeschichtliche Mitteilungen*, VII (1/1970), 95–112.

35. Hitler, "Tagesbefehl an die Wehrmacht," September 23, 1939, OKW/WPr, T-77, Roll 1014, 2480761, NA.

36. Hitler, telegram to Freifrau von Fritsch, "Persönliche Dokumente Gen. Ob. v. Fritsch," September 23, 1939, F 10, IfZ.

37. Goebbels, press conference, September 22, 1939, Sammlung Sänger, ZSg 102/19, BA. Historic symbolism was employed in the form of a photograph of Field Marshal von Mackensen offering his final salute over the casket of von Fritsch, and a fleeting glance of the statue of Frederick the Great along the route of the funeral cortege. VB-MA, September 27, 1939, p. 1; Ufa newsreel Nr. 474/1939, BA, released during the last week of September 1939.

38. VB-MA, September 27, 1939, p. 1.

39. Scheller, Wehrkreiskommando X, Hamburg, to OKW/WPr III, Berlin, September 23, 1940. Scheller's letter reported on the directive of the Propaganda Ministry forbidding the memorial article on the grounds that there was "no need to raise this specter again." OKW/WPr, T-77, Roll 972, 4459793, NA; see also VI 225/40, September 23, 1940, SO, ZSg 109/15, BA.

40. Scheller to OKW/WPr, T-77, Roll 972, 4459793, NA.

41. Letter from NCO's and men, Third Infantry Regiment, Poland, to von Brauchitsch, September 27, 1939. Grosscurth Collection, MGRC, T-84, Roll 229, NA.

42. *Frankfurter Zeitung*, October 2, 1939, p. 1.

43. Domarus, *Hitler*, II, 1384.

44. *Ibid.*, pp. 1385–1393.

45. Shirer, *Berlin Diary*, pp. 199–202.

46. SD report, October 11, 1939, in Boberach, *Meldungen aus dem Reich*, pp. 8–9.

47. Naumann and Gutterer, interviews, July 12 and August 5, 1970, respectively.
48. "Bestellungen aus der Pressekonferenz," October 4, 1939, Sammlung Brammer, ZSg 101/14, BA.
49. "Vertrauliche Informationen," October 9, 1939, Sammlung Brammer, ZSg 101/34, BA. See also Martin Broszat, *Nationalsozialistische Polenpolitik 1939–1945* (Stuttgart: Deutsche Verlags-Anstalt, 1961), pp. 19–20.
50. Pressedienst der NSDAP, "Kriegssonderdienst der NS Partei Korrespondenz," *Die Innere Front*, March 24, 1940.
51. *Ibid.*
52. Notes of press conference, October 20, 1939, Sammlung Sänger, ZSg 102/19, BA.
53. Der Reichsführer SS, SS Hauptamt-Schulungsamt, *Grenzkampf Ost* (Berlin: Nordland, undated).
54. Germany Auswärtiges Amt, *Dokumente zur Vorgeschichte des Krieges* (Berlin: Reichsdruckerei, 1939). See also VB-MA December 13, 1939, pp. 1–5.
55. Otto Dietrich, *Auf den Strassen des Sieges* (Munich: Franz Eher, 1940), pp. 180–81.

Chapter IV. The Phony War

1. For a complete text of the Shirer interview see OKW/WPr, T-77, Roll 1015, 2482220, NA. The fleet visit is described in Shirer, *Berlin Diary*, pp. 265–70. For a description of the Sommerfeldt-Lochner affair, see Martin Sommerfeldt, *Das Oberkommando der Wehrmacht gibt bekannt* (Frankfurt-am-Main: Westdeutsche Verlag, 1952), pp. 38–43. Sommerfeldt left the general unnamed.
2. VI 235/39, October 16, 1939, ZSg 109/4, BA; see also notes of press conference, October 16, 1939, Sammlung Sänger, ZSg 102/19, BA.
3. Fritzsche, *Hier spricht Hans Fritzsche* (Zurich: Interverlag, 1948), p. 85. Cartoon by Girod, October 26, 1939.
4. Goebbels, press conference, December 23, 1939, in Boelcke, *Kriegspropaganda*, p. 250.
5. Reichspropagandaamt Berlin, Sonderrundschreiben VI., Nr. 39, December 30, 1939, Sammlung Nadler, ZSg 115/19, BA.
6. Dönitz, *Zehn Jahre und zwanzig Tage*, pp. 68–71.
7. Winston Churchill, *The Gathering Storm* (Boston: Houghton Mifflin, 1948), pp. 489–92. "U-Boat Kommandant Prien berichtet über den erfolgreichen Angriff im Kriegshaven Scapa Flow," VB-ND, October 19, 1939, p. 2.
8. "Sonderpressekonferenz," October 17, 1939, Sammlung Sänger, ZSg 102/19, BA.
9. Ufa Ton Woche, 476/39, October 1939.
10. VB-ND, October 19, 1939, pp. 1–2. See also FZ, September 16, p. 1, September 19, p. 1; *Kölnische Zeitung*, October 14, 1939, p. 1.
11. Günter Prien, *Mein Weg nach Scapa Flow* (Berlin: Deutscher Verlag, 1940), p. 188.
12. *Ibid.*, pp. 188–89.
13. Dönitz, *Zehn Jahre und zwanzig Tage*, p. 175.
14. Churchill, *Gathering Storm*, pp. 520–26; Friedrich Ruge, *Der Seekrieg* (Stuttgart: Koehler Verlag, 1954), p. 310.
15. Ruge, *Seekrieg*, p. 54.
16. Churchill, *Gathering Storm*, pp. 520–26.
17. "Führer Conferences on Naval Affairs," in H. G. Thursfield, ed., *Brassey's Naval Annual 1948* (London: Clowes & Sons, 1948), p. 68.
18. Text of Captain Langsdorff's telegram in "Report of the C.-in-C. Navy to the Führer on December 16, 1939, at 1300," in *ibid.*, p. 68.

19. Raeder to Langsdorff, radiogram 1347/16 of December 16, 1939, in *ibid.*, p. 69.

20. Langsdorff to German ambassador in Buenos Aires, December 19, 1939, in *ibid.*, p. 69.

21. Boelcke, *Kriegspropaganda*, p. 244.

22. *Ibid.*, p. 245.

23. VB-MA, December 15, 1939, pp. 1–2. The *Preussische Zeitung* went so far as to carry a headline declaring that the "Admiral Graf Spee Didn't Suffer a Scratch."

24. *Reichsrundfunk* report from Montevideo, December 15, 1939, VB-MA, December 16, 1939, p. 5.

25. "Die Kreuzfahrt des Panzerschiffes 'Admiral Graf Spee': Ein Besuch an Bord im Hafen von Montevideo," VB-MA, December 17, 1939, p. 1.

26. VB-MA, December 18, 1939, p. 2.

27. Domarus, *Hitler*, II, 1433.

28. VI 292/39, December 21, 1939, SO, ZSg 109/6, BA.

29. Illegible, OKM to OKW/WPr and OKW/Ausl., "Material für die Steuerung der deutschen Propaganda," December 20, 1939, OKW/WPr, T-77, Roll 1036, 6509210, NA.

30. SD report, November 29, 1939, R58/144, BA.

31. SD reports, October 18, 1939, and November 29, 1939, R58/144, BA.

32. SD report, October 23, 1939, R58/144, BA. Not all Germans were deceived by prospects of an easy victory. The population of western Germany, which was more vulnerable to enemy air attacks, was generally more skeptical. Businessmen there were hesitant about investing capital in enterprises which might be bombed out at any time, and farmers saw no reason to exert themselves planting extensive fields of crops which might be destroyed in a future German western offensive. SD report, October 18, 1939, R58/144, BA.

33. See Anton Hoch, "Das Attentat auf Hitler im Bürgerbräukeller," *Vierteljahrshefte für Zeitgeschichte*, XVII (October 1969), 383–413, and Johann Georg Elser, *Autobiographie eines Attentäters: Aussage zum Sprengstoffanschlag im Bürgerbräukeller, München am 8. November 1939*, ed. Lothar Gruchmann (Stuttgart: Deutsche Verlags-Anstalt, 1970).

34. VB-MA, November 10, 1939, p. 1.

35. SD report, November 10, 1939, in Boberach, *Meldungen aus dem Reich*, pp. 18–19.

36. *Ibid.*

37. VB-MA, November 10, 1939, p. 1.

38. VB-MA, November 11, 1939, p. 1.

39. Ufa Ton Woche 480/39, November 1939.

40. VB-MA, November 12, 1939, pp. 1–2.

41. VI Nr. 256/39, November 9, 1939, SO, ZSg 109/5, BA.

42. Notes of Goebbels's press conferences, November 10, 16, and 20, 1939, in Boelcke, *Kriegspropaganda*, pp. 222, 226, 229.

43. See VB-ND, November 23, 1939, p. 1; VI Nr. 267/39, November 22, 1939, SO, ZSg 109/5, BA.

44. Shirer, *Berlin Diary*, p. 251. See also SD report, November 22, 1939, in Boberach, *Meldungen aus dem Reich*, pp. 19–20.

45. Hoch, "Attentat auf Hitler," pp. 383–413. Hitler had received a warning on November 2 that his life was to be in danger between November 7–9, 1939, in the form of a letter from the astrologer Earl Ernst Krafft who lived in the Black Forest. Hitler handed this letter to Goebbels during luncheon at the Reich chancellery on November 9, the noon following the bombing. See Boelcke, *Kriegspropaganda*, pp. 223–24.

46. Shirer, *Berlin Diary*, p. 251.

47. Walther Koerber, Hermann Wanderscheck, and Hans Zugschwert, *Mord! Spionage! Attentat! Die Blutspur des englischen Geheimdienstes und der Münchner Bomben-Anschlag* (Berlin: Verlag Wehrfront Alfred Becker, 1940), pp. 56–93.

48. See Goebbels, notes of press conferences, December 2–5, 1939, Sammlung Sänger, ZSg 102/20, BA.

49. VB-MA, December 8, 1939, p. 1. According to Max Domarus, the article was a repetition of the themes which Hitler had elaborated to Sven Hedin in a conversation he had with the poet on October 16, 1939. Domarus, *Hitler*, II, 1429.

50. Sven Hedin gave an account of his meeting with Goebbels in March 1940 when the minister revealed his true feelings about the Finns. Hedin, *Ohne Auftrag in Berlin* (Buenos Aires: Dürer, 1949), pp. 104–9.

51. The *Lokalanzeiger* had printed such a headline, thereby provoking this directive. Notes of press conference of December 3, 1939, Sammlung Sänger, ZSg 102/20, BA.

52. VI Nr. 62/40, February 13, 1940, SO, ZSg 109/9, BA.

53. SD report, December 4, 1939, in Boberach, *Meldungen aus dem Reich*, p. 22. For directives on treatment of the Finnish war see VI Nr. 292/39, December 21, 1939, SO, ZSg 109/5, BA, as well as the notes taken by Karl Brammer at the press conference on the same day, "Das deutsch-russische Verhältnis basiert auf der historischen Tatsache, der jahrhunderte langen Zusammenarbeit beider Völker," SB, ZSg, 102/20, BA.

54. Ufa Ton Woche, 484/39, BA.

55. "Der Führer bei seinen Soldaten an der Westfront," VB-MA, December 27, 1939, p. 1.

56. Former Radio Section Chief Diewerge has observed that his staff analyzed the mail like a Gallup poll to meet the requests. Diewerge, interview, July 12, 1970. Naumann, interview, July 11, 1970. See also Heinz Gödecke and Wilhelm Krug, *Wir beginnen das Wunschkonzert für die Wehrmacht* (Berlin and Leipzig: Nibelungen Verlag, 1940).

57. Propaganda Company to OKW/WPr, December 7, 1939, T-77, OKW/WPr, Roll 1036, 6509214, NA.

58. Complaint from W. Allg. to WPr, December 14, 1939, OKW/WPr, T-77, Roll 968, 4453950, NA.

59. VI Nr. 283/39, December 11, 1939, SO, ZSg 109/6, BA.

60. Von Brauchitsch, "Der friderizianische Soldat und die Gegenwart," VB-MA, January 24, 1940, pp. 1–2.

61. Von Rundstedt, "Zum Heldengedenktag 1940: Opfer für Deutschland," VB-ND, March 10, 1940, pp. 1–2.

62. Goebbels, *Das Reich*, February 9, 1940, pp. 1–2.

63. Domarus, *Hitler*, II, 1441–1481.

64. Goebbels, press conferences of April 5 and May 6, 1940, in Boelcke, *Kriegspropaganda*, pp. 313–14, 341. Rudolf Hess also ordered Party members to limit their discussion of war aims to living space, work, bread, and a lasting peace. Hess, order of May 14, 1940, *Reichsverfügungsblatt der NSDAP*, Ausgabe A, A58/40, in *ibid.*, p. 341.

65. For examples see VB/MA, January 14 and March 18, 1940, pp. 1–2.

66. Goebbels, press conference, May 27, 1940, in Boelcke, *Kriegspropaganda*, p. 366.

67. NSDAP, Gau Hessen-Nassau to all Party speakers, February 20, 1941, NSDAP, T-81, Roll 117, 137944, NA.

68. Beginning in the fall of 1939, almost every SD report noted that English planes or balloons were dropping leaflets. See SD report, October 23, 1939, R58/144, BA. For Goebbels's instructions on the leaflets see press conference, December 11, 1939, in Boelcke, *Kriegspropaganda*, p. 239.

69. NSDAP, T-81, Roll 119, 139544, NA.

70. SD report, January 1940, R58/149, BA; see also OKW/WPr, T-77, Roll 1033, 6504759, NA.

71. Naumann relates that on more than one occasion Goebbels cited this quotation, which he attributed to Goethe. Naumann, interview, July 11, 1970. For Goebbels's views on the artist in wartime, see his speech of February 15, 1941, delivered in Berlin in connection with the "Kriegstagung der Reichsfilmkammer," in Gerd Albrecht, *Nationalsozialistische Filmpolitik* (Stuttgart: Enke Verlag, 1969), pp. 465–79. See also the interview with Gustav Gründgens, the famed interpreter of Mephistopheles, who at the time was director of the Berliner Theater, VB-MA, October 19, 1939.

72. SD report, August 1940, "Zu den Bayreuther Festspielen 1940," R58/153, BA.

73. SD report, January 8, 1940, economic special report entitled "Kohlenmangel beeinflusst stark die Stimmung der Bevölkerung," in Boberach, *Meldungen aus dem Reich*, pp. 34–36.

74. SD report, April 1940, "Schwierigkeiten der Kartoffelversorgung," in *ibid.*, p. 57.

75. SD report, March 18, 1940, "Klagen der Bevölkerung über die Abgabe von Mangelware," in *ibid.*, pp. 55–56.

76. Hitler's activities at Christmas inspired such rumors because people misinterpreted his statement to the soldiers along the West Wall that 1940 would bring the final victory. Yet another rumor had it that the Führer had given Winifred Wagner the go ahead to prepare next year's Bayreuth Festival, "since the war will be over this year [1940]." Ribbentrop's visit with the pope in March led some to believe that the Vatican was about to serve as a peace mediator, and the rumors climaxed later in the month at the conclusion of the Finnish war and in connection with the European trip of American Under Secretary of State Sumner Welles. See SD report, January 15, 1940, R58/147, BA, and SD report, March 18, 1940, R58/149, BA.

Chapter V. Blitzkrieg 1940: "The Reich Rescues Scandinavia"

1. Walter Ansel, *Hitler Confronts England* (Durham, N.C.: Duke University Press, 1960), pp. 57–58.

2. Ruge, *Seekrieg*, p. 66.

3. Walter Hubatsch, *Weserübung* (Göttingen: Musterschmidt Verlag, 1960), p. 35.

4. Hitler, "Weisung für 'Fall *Weserübung*,'" Berlin, March 1, 1940, in *ibid.*, pp. 439–40.

5. VB-MA, February 19, 1940, p. 1. For orders to the press on handling the events, see VI Nr. 41/40, February 18, 1940, SO, ZSg 109/8, BA as well as the account "Der Bericht des Kapitäns der 'Altmark,'" VB-MA, February 19, 1940, p. 2.

6. SD report, February 25, 1940, in Boberach, *Meldungen aus dem Reich*, p. 52; Presserundschreiben II/221/40, Sammlung Nadler, ZSg 115/19, BA. The *Altmark* was given only passing reference in the newsreels the week after the incident, UTW 501/16/1940, BA. It was never reported in the OKW communiqués.

7. "Wilfred" was the name of a popular comic strip character in England at the time. The connotation of "Wilfred" was that the operation was weak, second-best, and poorly timed, but better than nothing. See Churchill, *Gathering Storm*, pp. 226–28.

8. Hubatsch, *Weserübung*, p. 35.

9. VB-MA, April 10, 1940, p. 1.

10. Ruge, *Seekrieg*, pp. 66–69; compare Dönitz, *Zehn Jahre und zwanzig Tage*, pp. 77–89.

11. Goebbels, press conferences, April 9 and 10, 1940, in Boelcke, *Kriegspropaganda*,

pp. 315–17; VI Nr. 84/40, April 10, 1940, SO, ZSg 109/10, BA. Goebbels himself doubted the credibility of the propaganda line, and his staff was told that "der Minister erwartet von Angehörigen des Ministeriums, dass diese These der Inschutznahme auch von ihnen selbst nicht etwa angezweifelt oder gar lächerlich gemacht wird." Boelcke, *Kriegspropaganda*, p. 316.

12. UTW 502/17/1940, April 1940, BA.

13. Von Ribbentrop, press conference, Berlin, April 9, 1940, VB-MA, p. 1.

14. "Memorandum der Deutschen Reichsregierung an die Regierung von Norwegen und Dänemark," VB-MA, April 10, 1940, p. 2.

15. Ruge, *Seekrieg*, pp. 70–73.

16. Boelcke, *Kriegspropaganda*, pp. 316–17.

17. The OKW communiqué of April 10 carried the news of the sinking of the *Blücher* and the *Karlsruhe*. The OKW kept silent about the loss of the cruiser *Königsberg* which went down on the 10th. Goebbels forbade the publication of photographs of the *Blücher* and *Karlsruhe*. See Boelcke, *Kriegspropaganda*, p. 316.

18. VI Nr. 87/40, April 14, 1940, SO, ZSg 109/10, BA.

19. OKW communiqué, April 17, 1940.

20. SD report, April 18, 1940, R58/150, BA.

21. SD report, April 28, 1940, R58/150, BA.

22. SD report, April 26, 1940, R58/150, BA.

23. See Boelcke, *Kriegspropaganda*, pp. 706–7.

24. Goebbels, press conference, May 7, 1940, in *ibid.*, p. 341.

25. Hubatsch, *Weserübung*, p. 215.

26. Boelcke, *Kriegspropaganda*, pp. 367–69; see also "Ein dummes Ablenkungs-manöver," VB-MA, June 1, 1940, p. 1.

27. OKW communiqué, June 10, 1940.

28. General Dietl was in fact a native of Bad Aibling, Bavaria. VB-MA, June 11, 1940, p. 3. The coverage devoted to General Dietl and Norway was forced off the front pages by an even more dramatic news story. On that day Mussolini announced the Italian declaration of war against France.

29. "Abschlussbericht über die Aktionen im Norden," in Domarus, *Hitler*, II, 1522.

30. Dönitz, *Zehn Jahre und zwanzig Tage*, p. 93.

31. Hubatsch, *Weserübung*, pp. 221–27.

32. *Ibid.*, p. 226.

33. Goebbels, news conference, January 13, 1941, in Boelcke, *Kriegspropaganda*, p. 126.

34. Joseph Goebbels, *Die Zeit ohne Beispiel* (Munich: Franz Eher, 1941).

35. Goebbels, press conference, April 26, 1940, in Boelcke, *Kriegspropaganda*, p. 331.

36. SD report, April 29, 1940, in Boberach, *Meldungen aus dem Reich*, p. 63.

Chapter VI. *Victory in the West: The Battle of France*

1. Goebbels, press conference, April 3, 1940, in Boelcke, *Kriegspropaganda*, p. 310.

2. Hans-Adolf Jacobsen, *Fall Gelb* (Wiesbaden: Franz Steiner, 1957), pp. 140–41.

3. VI 102/40, Boelcke, *Kriegspropaganda*, p. 339.

4. "Bewegtes Mittelmeer," FZ, May 5, 1940, p. 1. See also "Anhaltende Spannung auf dem Balkan," FZ, May 9, 1940, p. 1.

5. "Achtung! An alle die es angeht: Termin 20. Mai—Die Pläne der Aggressoren entschleiern sich," VB-MA, May 7, 1940, p. 1.

6. VI Nr. 106/40, May 8, 1940, SO, ZSg 109/11, BA.

7. SD report, May 14, 1940, in Boberach, *Meldungen aus dem Reich*, pp. 64–65.

8. Boelcke, *Kriegspropaganda*, pp. 342–43.

9. SD report, May 14, 1940, in Boberach, *Meldungen aus dem Reich*, pp. 64–65.

10. Boelcke, *Kriegspropaganda*, p. 344.

11. VI Nr. 109–110/40, May 10, 1940, SO, ZSg 109/11, BA.

12. Goebbels, press conference, May 11, 1940, in Boelcke, *Kriegspropaganda*, p. 346.

13. Domarus, *Hitler*, II, 1502–1503.

14. Von Ribbentrop, press conference, Berlin, May 10, 1940, VB-MA, May 11, 1940, p. 3.

15. "Memorandum der Reichsregierung an die Königlich Belgische und Königlich Niederländische Regierung," May 9, 1940, VB-MA, May 11, 1940, p. 3.

16. "Der Bericht des Oberkommandos der Wehrmacht an die Reichsregierung," *ibid.*, pp. 4–5.

17. "Bericht des Reichsministers des Innern an die Reichsregierung," March 29, 1940, *ibid.*, pp. 5–6.

18. SD report, May 14, 1940, in Boberach, *Meldungen aus dem Reich*, pp. 64–65.

19. *Ibid.* Goebbels was not certain how his charge that the Belgians and Dutch had violated their rights as neutrals would be received and he had taken precautions before the attack to put the damper on any sympathy which might be evoked for the two countries (see VI Nr. 106/40, May 8, 1940, SO, ZSg 109/11, BA). On the morning of May 10 he took steps to assure that the new line would be credible by ordering that "the whole nation must become convinced that Holland and Belgium in fact have violated their neutrality." See Goebbels, press conference, May 10, 1940, in Boelcke, *Kriegspropaganda*, p. 345.

20. "Richtlinien für die Presseberichterstattung über die Operationen im Westen," cited in Boelcke, *Kriegspropaganda*, pp. 344–45.

21. Goebbels, press conference, May 10, 1940, in *ibid.*, p. 344.

22. Words by Heinrich Anacker, music by Herms Niel, cited in *ibid.*, p. 359.

23. Alfred Rosenberg, "Die Revolution Europas," VB-MA, May 12, 1940, pp. 1–2.

24. "Oberkriegshetzer Churchill Premierminister," VB-MA, May 12–13, 1940, p. 1. Compare "Das Kabinett der Kriegstreiber," FZ, May 14, 1940, p. 1.

25. VI Nr. 110/40, May 11, 1940, SO, ZSg 109/11, BA.

26. Goebbels, press conference, May 13, 1940, in Boelcke, *Kriegspropaganda*, p. 348.

27. *Ibid.*

28. "Der Schwerpunkt muss jedoch bei allen Betrachtungen auf den deutschen rechten Flügel, auf die Vorgänge in Holland und Belgien und damit die Bedrohung Englands gelegt werden," VI Nr. 111/40, May 15, 1940, SO, ZSg 109/11, BA.

29. Goebbels, press conference, May 14, 1940, in Boelcke, *Kriegspropaganda*, p. 350.

30. Goebbels, press conference, May 11, 1940, in *ibid.*, p. 347.

31. Hitler, "Rückgliederung von Eupen, Malmedy und Moresnet," in Domarus, *Hitler*, II, 1513.

32. Wilhelm Weiss, *Der Krieg im Westen dargestellt nach den Berichten des "Völkischen Beobachters"* (Munich: Franz Eher, 1940), pp. 19–21.

33. UTW 507/22/1940, UTW 508/23/1940, UTW 509/24/1940, BA.

34. Wilhelm Weiss, "Nach der Kapitulation," VB-ND, May 16, 1940, pp. 1–2. See also VI Nr. 110/40, May 14, 1940, and VI Nr. 111/40, "Richtlinien für die Behandlung und Kommentierung der gegenwärtigen militärischen Ereignisse und Lage," May 15, 1940, SO, ZSg 109/11, BA.

35. "Bei seinen Soldaten schlägt Deutschlands Herz," VB-MA, May 16, 1940, pp. 1–2. See also Otto Dietrich, "Der Feldherr," in OKW, *Die Wehrmacht: Der Freiheitskampf des grossdeutschen Volkes* (Berlin: Verlag Die Wehrmacht, 1940), pp. 206–11.

36. Goebbels, press conference, May 15, 1940, in Boelcke, *Kriegspropaganda*, p. 351.

37. Goebbels, press conference, May 16–18, 1940, in *ibid.*, pp. 352–55.

38. *Ibid.*
39. Goebbels, press conference, May 21, 1940, in *ibid.*, p. 359.
40. Kurt Hesse, "Panzerschlacht bei Cambrai," VB/MA, May 21, 1940, p. 1.
41. Goebbels, press conference, May 20, 1940, in Boelcke, *Kriegspropaganda*, p. 358.
42. Boelcke, *Kriegspropaganda*, p. 349.
43. OKW release of May 13, 1940, VB-MA, May 14, 1940, p. 1.
44. *Ibid.*
45. Goebbels, press conference, May 14, 1940, in Boelcke, *Kriegspropaganda*, p. 349.
46. "Hermann Göring über die deutsche Kriegführung," press conference, May 20, 1940, Berlin, in Weiss, *Krieg im Westen*, pp. 53–54.
47. Erhard Klöss, ed., *Der Luftkrieg über Deutschland* (Nördlingen: Deutscher Taschenbuch Verlag, 1963), p. 29. See also Anton Hoch, "Der Luftangriff auf Freiburg am 10. Mai 1940," *Vierteljahrshefte für Zeitgeschichte*, IV (October 1956), 138.
48. Deutsche Wochenschau, 506/21/1940, BA.
49. SD report, May 23, 1940, in Boberach, *Meldungen aus dem Reich*, pp. 70–71.
50. For Goebbels's reaction, see his press conference of May 20, 1941, in Boelcke, *Kriegspropaganda*, p. 358.
51. SD report, May 27, 1940, in Boberach, *Meldungen aus dem Reich*, pp. 70–71.
52. Goebbels in his press conference of May 21, 1940, ordered that "Herr Fritzsche should do everything possible to provide special material for the periodical *Das Reich*, so that it has a great impact abroad from the beginning." See Boelcke, *Kriegspropaganda*, p. 359.
53. "Die verpassten Gelegenheiten," *Das Reich*, June 2, 1940. Goebbels's weekly articles all appeared on pp. 1–2 of *Das Reich*, and were read over the radio on Friday evenings.
54. Goebbels, press conference, May 30, 1940, in Boelcke, *Kriegspropaganda*, pp. 369–70. For the corresponding directives to the press of May 29–30, see VI Nr. 123–24/40, SO, ZSg 109/11, BA.
55. *Das Schwarze Korps*, May 30, 1940, p. 1.
56. *General Anzeiger* (Wuppertal), June 1–2, 1940, p. 1.
57. Alfred Rosenberg, "Der Zusammenbruch des französischen Nationalismus," VB-ND, June 2, 1940, pp. 1–2.
58. SD report, June 10, 1940, in Boberach, *Meldungen aus dem Reich*, pp. 74–75.
59. *Ibid.*, p. 75.
60. SD report, June 3, 1940, R58/151, BA.
61. VI Nr. 120/40, May 26, 1940, SO, ZSg 109/11, BA.
62. VI Nr. 122/40, May 28, 1940, SO, ZSg 109/11, BA.
63. OKW communiqué, May 30, 1940.
64. Wilhelm Weiss, "Vom Durchbruch bis zur Katastrophe," VB-MA, May 31, 1940, pp. 1–2.
65. Major Carl Cranz, "Der Totentanz von Dünkirchen," VB-ND, June 4, 1940, pp. 1–2.
66. VB-MA, June 5, 1940, p. 2. The Germans claimed "total air superiority," and the newsreels depicted the Stukas' reign of terror over the fleeing enemy on the sands of the beach below. UTW 510/25/1940, BA.
67. "Zusammenfassender Wehrmachtbericht aus dem Führerhauptquartier vom 4. Juni 1940 nachts," in Erich Murawski, *Der Durchbruch im Westen: Chronik der holländischen, belgischen, und französischen Zusammenbruchs* (Oldenburg: Gerhard Stalling, 1940), pp. 198–203.
68. Hitler, "An die Soldaten der Westfront," June 5, 1940, in Domarus, *Hitler*, II, 1521.
69. Günter d'Alquen, "Auf dem Kemmel," VB-ND, June 5, 1940, p. 3.

70. Domarus, *Hitler*, II, 1518.

71. SD report, May 16, 1940, in Boberach, *Meldungen aus dem Reich*, p. 69.

72. Fritzsche took this opportunity to advise Goebbels to end the press's use of the teletype channels once and for all. Goebbels decided that he could not hamstring the world press just as Germany was winning one of its greatest victories; such a ruling would do more harm than good. Instead, he ordered tighter censorship controls over the foreign reporters. Goebbels, press conference, June 1, 1940, in Boelcke, *Kriegspropaganda*, p. 374.

73. VI Nr. 134, June 10, 1940, SO, ZSg 109/12, BA.

74. Domarus, *Hitler*, II, 1523.

75. Von Prentzel, lead article, VB-MA, June 13, 1940, pp. 1–2.

76. "Mittelmeer—Die Neue Front," *Das Reich*, June 16, 1940, pp. 8–9.

77. *Ibid.*, p. 1.

78. SD reports Nr. 96–98, June 1940, R58/151, BA.

79. Goebbels, press conference, June 16, 1940, in Boelcke, *Kriegspropaganda*, p. 392.

80. Cynics north of the Alps referred to this as a "Treppenwitz der Weltgeschichte." SD report, June 27, 1940, in Boberach, *Meldungen aus dem Reich*, pp. 81–82.

81. Goebbels, press conference, June 23, 1940, in Boelcke, *Kriegspropaganda*, p. 402.

82. Goebbels, press conference, June 26, 1940, in Boelcke, *Kriegspropaganda*, p. 407.

83. SD report, June 17, 1940, R58/151, BA.

84. Theodor Seibert, "Paris," VB-ND, June 15, 1940, p. 1.

85. Frank Götz, "So marschierten unsere Truppen in Paris ein," June 15, 1940, in Weiss, *Krieg im Westen*, pp. 167–68.

86. Domarus, *Hitler*, II, 1534.

87. Albert Speer, *Erinnerungen* (Berlin: Propyläen Verlag, 1969), pp. 87–93, 166–75.

88. Murawski, *Durchbruch im Westen*, p. 268.

89. Domarus, *Hitler*, II, 1528.

90. Goebbels, press conferences, June 17–28, 1940, in Boelcke, *Kriegspropaganda*, pp. 393–411. Major Murawski's radio commentary on the OKW communiqué for June 18 stressed that in World War I it took over a month between the original German note requesting negotiations and the actual signing of the armistice. See Murawski, *Durchbruch im Westen*, pp. 275–79.

91. "Reynauds Trümmerhaufen," VB-ND, June 18, 1940, pp. 1–2. See also Goebbels, press conference, June 18, 1940, in Boelcke, *Kriegspropaganda*, p. 396.

92. Shirer, *Berlin Diary*, p. 422.

93. Domarus, *Hitler*, II, 1528–1529.

94. "Präambel zu den Waffenstillstandsbedingungen," in Domarus, *Hitler*, II, 1529–1530.

95. Hitler's spite at seeing the French monuments commemorating the victory in 1918 at Compiègne was so bitter that he ordered them to be blown up. Only the statue of Field Marshal Foch was to remain. Domarus, *Hitler*, II, 1530. The railway car used in the ceremonies was sent to Berlin where it was displayed in the Lustgarten. Curious Germans, taking a Sunday stroll down Under den Linden during the coming winter, would be reminded in this way of Hitler's day of triumph. The reminiscence of fleeting glory would be all they had to sustain them through another night in the bomb shelters when the grandeur of June 1940 and the warmth of summer were but pale memories. See Ernst Braeckow, Propaganda Ministry, ed., *Grossdeutschland im Weltgeschehen: Tagesbildberichte 1941* (Berlin: Verlag Joh. Kasper, 1942, no pagination, photograph in caption for March 21–31, 1941).

96. Shirer, *Berlin Diary*, pp. 428–92.

97. Hitler took several steps to downgrade Italian participation in the Battle of

France. Following the signing of the German terms in the railway car at Compiègne on June 22, the French delegation flew to Rome to sign the Italian conditions. The Battle of France did not officially terminate until six hours after the signing of the Italian-French armistice. Domarus, *Hitler*, II, 1533. See also VI, Nr. 144/40, June 22, 1940, SO, ZSg 109/12, BA.

98. Goebbels, press conference, June 24, 1940, in Boelcke, *Kriegspropaganda*, p. 404.

99. June 24, 1940. Domarus, *Hitler*, II, 1533.

100. Goebbels, press conference, June 25, 1940, in Boelcke, *Kriegspropaganda*, p. 406.

101. Goebbels ordered that the hatred of England theme must be rigorously and mercilessly pursued. By taking this step, he was merely returning to the central theme of the war which had been developed intensively since 1939 and which had been interrupted only for tactical reasons at the climax of the Battle of France.

102. *Das Reich*, June 30, 1940, pp. 1, 2, 6.

103. Goebbels, press conference, July 10, 1940, in Boelcke, *Kriegspropaganda*, p. 422. Editors had to be warned that they were being too good to Pétain; Goebbels was especially disturbed about articles which made it appear that German and French interests completely overlapped. One such example was headlined "Pétain Turns Thumbs Down on the Parliamentary Cesspool." VI 162/40, July 13, 1940, SO, ZSg 109/13, BA.

104. VI Nr. 173/40, July 26, 1940, ZSg 109/13, BA.

105. *Ibid.*

106. Kurt von Raumer, *Das Reich*, June 30, 1940, pp. 8–9.

107. Goebbels, *Das Reich*, June 9, 1940, p. 1.

108. Boelcke, *Kriegspropaganda*, p. 346. *Sieg im Westen* was a Noldan Production directed by the Army Press Group of the OKW/WPr in cooperation with the Film Section of the Propaganda Ministry. According to the head of the Army Press Group, Dr. Hesse, the Army commander in chief von Brauchitsch ordered the production. See the brochure which accompanied the film, OKW/WPr, ed., *Sieg im Westen: Der Kriegsfilmbericht des Heeres* (Berlin, 1941). Goebbels, whose sensitive ego caused him to be suspicious of all propaganda which he did not control, was very critical of *Sieg im Westen*. On the other hand, the SD reports reveal that the film was very well received indeed. The overall impression one gains from viewing it is that its effectiveness is second only to *Triumph des Willens* of 1934 vintage. For Goebbels's press conference directive on the film which he issued on February 1, 1941, see Boelcke, *Kriegspropaganda*, p. 610. The SD report of March 13, 1941, deals with its reception in Germany. See R58/158, BA.

Chapter VII. The Battle of Britain

1. Martin Dibelius, *Britisches Christentum und britische Weltmacht* (Berlin: Junker und Dünnhaupt, 1940); Giselher Wirsing, *100 Familien regieren England* (Berlin: Deutsche Informationsstelle, 1940). See also Peter Aldag, *Juden beherrschen England* (Berlin: Nordland, 1939), Ferdinand Gral, *Englands Kriege: Die Geschichte der britischen Kriege in 5 Erdteilen* (Berlin: Verlag der deutschen Arbeitsfront, 1940), Wilhelm Ziegler, *Ein Dokumentenwerk über die englische Humanität* (Im Auftrag des Reichsministeriums für Volksaufklärung und Propaganda) (Berlin: Deutscher Verlag, 1940).

2. See "Warum uns England überfallen hat," "Englands einziges Ziel: Die Vernichtung des deutschen Volkes," *Aufklärungs und Redner-Informationsmaterial der RPL der NSDAP und des RPA des DAF*, No. 1/46 (January 1940), and "Plutokratischer Despotismus," and "England will die Welt beherrschen," *ibid.*, No. 30/75 (May 1940), IfZ.

3. "Volkssozialismus oder Plutokratie," VI 291/39, December 12, 1939, SO, ZSg, 109/6, BA.

4. Goebbels, "Von der Gottähnlichkeit der Engländer," *Das Reich*, June 16, 1940. Goebbels had defined the "plutocrats" in his rally at Münster on February 28, 1940, as a political clique composed of a few hundred families who were attempting to rule the world in their own financial interest. The group allegedly controlled vast territories and was trying to keep Germany from its rightful place in the sun. Goebbels, *Die Zeit ohne Beispiel*, pp. 248–49.

5. *Das Reich*, June 23, 1940.

6. When Hitler stepped off the train bringing him home from a meeting with the Duce at the Brenner Pass in March 1940, he had been particularly gratified by the warmth of the reception which greeted him, highlighted as it was by the singing of the *Englandlied*. Domarus, *Hitler*, II, 1486.

7. Keitel to Düring, Drahtlosen Dienst, OKW/WPr, T-77, Roll 1015, 2483046, NA.

8. NSDAP, T-81, Roll 677, 4714649, NA. See also Ansel, *Hitler Confronts England*, pp. 3–4.

9. See SD reports, May 27, June 20, and July 4, 1940, R58/151-2, BA.

10. SD report, June 24, 1940, R58/151, BA.

11. See Goebbels's press conference of July 4, 1940, in Boelcke, *Kriegspropaganda*, p. 413, and VI Nr. 154/40, July 4, 1940, SO, ZSg 109/13, BA.

12. Domarus, *Hitler*, II, 1540–1559. The evening before Hitler delivered this address, he read it to Goebbels and Naumann at Schwanenwerder, the minister's estate on the Wannsee. Hitler was convinced that his rhetoric would have the desired effect and that England would sue for peace, but Goebbels disagreed adamantly. Naumann, interview, July 11, 1970. For a description of the events attendant on Hitler's Reichstag address, see Shirer, *Berlin Diary*, pp. 452–57.

13. Domarus, *Hitler*, II, 1560.

14. VI Nr. 168/40, July 20, 1940, SO, ZSg 109/13, BA. VI Nr. 170/40, July 23, 1940, *ibid*. See also Goebbels, press conference, July 24, 1940, in Boelcke, *Kriegspropaganda*, p. 435.

15. Hitler, OKW/WFA/L Nr. 33160/40, "Weisung Nr. 16 über die Vorbereitungen einer Landungsoperation gegen England," July 16, 1940, in Hubatsch, *Weserübung*, pp. 61–65.

16. Hitler, OKW/WFA/L Nr. 33210/40, August 1, 1940, "Weisung Nr. 17 für die Führung des Luft-und Seekrieges gegen England," in *ibid*., pp. 65–66.

17. Basil Collier, *The Defense of the United Kingdom* (London: Her Majesty's Stationery Office, 1957), pp. 147–282.

18. SD report, "Auswirkungen und Aufnahme der allgemeinen Propaganda, Presse und Rundfunklenkung in der Zeit vom 6.–8. August 1940," SO, R58/153, BA.

19. VB-MA, August 12, 1940, pp. 1–2.

20. "Des 'Horst-Wessel-Geschwaders' grösster Tag," VB-ND, August 20, 1940, p. 2.

21. SD report, August 19, 1940, SO, R58/153, BA.

22. Goebbels, staff conference, July 24, 1940, in Boelcke, *Kriegspropaganda*, p. 477.

23. *Ibid*. See also VI Nr. 199/40, August 24, 1940, SO, ZSg 109/14, BA.

24. At his press conference of August 3, 1940, Goebbels ordered, "Make a big thing of the announcement that Hamburg was 'pulverized' by an English bombing attack, which was widely quoted especially in 'America.' " See Boelcke, *Kriegspropaganda*, pp. 444–45. Compare Shirer, diary entry, August 5, 1940, in *Berlin Diary*, pp. 463–65.

25. VB-MA, August 4, 1940, p. 1. See also VI Nr. 186/40, August 9, 1940, SO, ZSg 109/14, BA.

26. Goebbels, press conference, August 17, 1940, in Boelcke, *Kriegspropaganda*, p. 465.

27. *Ibid.*

28. Goebbels, press conference, September 11, 1940, in Boelcke, *Kriegspropaganda*, p. 499. See also VI Nr. 215/40, September 11, 1940, SO, ZSg 109/15, BA.

29. Goebbels, press conference, September 19, 1940, in Boelcke, *Kriegspropaganda*, pp. 514–15.

30. VI Nr. 182/40, August 5, 1940, SO, ZSg 109/14, BA.

31. SD report, late August 1940, R58/154, BA. Royal Air Force raids on Berlin set tongues wagging. According to Nazi propaganda, not a single enemy aircraft could penetrate the capital's defensive girdle. "Without any question, we must annihilate England" and "London must be pulverized" were the reactions of two *Volksgenossen* overheard by SD informers. See SD report, September 2, 1940, R58/154, BA.

32. Domarus, *Hitler*, II, 1577–1580.

33. Ansel, *Hitler Confronts England*, p. 299.

34. With the headlines "Der Reichsmarshall an der Kanalküste," the *Völkischer Beobachter* of September 14, 1940, devoted over two-thirds of page one to photographs of fighting Hermann Göring.

35. Goebbels, staff conference, September 17, 1940, in Boelcke, *Kriegspropaganda*, p. 510.

36. Herbert Menzel, "Auf einen Frühvollendeten: Dem Freiherrn von Richthofen," *Des Reich*, August 18, 1940, p. 17.

37. Goebbels, press conference, September 12, 1940, in Boelcke, *Kriegspropaganda*, p. 502. See also VI Nr. 212/40, September 8, 1940, SO, ZSg 109/15, BA.

38. Boelcke, *Kriegspropaganda*, p. 502.

39. *Das Reich*, September 15, 1940.

40. "Vertraulicher Informationsbericht," September 9 and 10, 1940, Sammlung Brammer, ZSg 101/36, BA.

41. SD report, September 23, 1940, R58/154, BA.

42. *Das Reich*, September 29, 1940. The quotation is rather more humorous in the original Berlinese: "Nachtigal, ick hör dir tropsen."

43. Boelcke, *Kriegspropaganda*, p. 572.

44. OKW/WPr, T-77, Roll 972, 4458932, NA.

45. Goebbels, staff conference, April 14, 1941, in Boelcke, *Kriegspropaganda*, pp. 678–79.

46. Goebbels, press conference, October 7, 1940, in *ibid.*, p. 539; SD report, October 21, 1940, R58/155, BA.

47. SD report, October 7, 1940, in Boberach, *Meldungen aus dem Reich*, p. 106.

48. Baldur von Schirach, *Ich glaubte an Hitler* (Hamburg: Mosaik, 1967), pp. 269–70. The NS Volkswohlfahrt undertook the evacuation of children between the ages of three and fourteen.

49. See Chef der Parteikanzlei, R. 188/42, December 7, 1942, "Kinderlandverschickung"; V.I. 39/428, September 9, 1941, "Kinderlandverschickung"; V.I. 60/727, December 3, 1941, "Erweiterte Kinderlandverschickung," *Verfügungen/Anordnungen/Bekanntgaben*, II, 34–35.

50. See Goebbels, staff conferences, July 26 and October 3, 1940, in Boelcke, *Kriegspropaganda*, pp. 438, 537.

51. Major Kietzell to Colonel Martin, October 24, 1940, OKW/WPr, T-77, Roll 971, 4457889, NA. This letter analyzed the "poor execution of a well meant policy of State and Party."

52. Goebbels, press conference, October 3, 1940, in Boelcke, *Kriegspropaganda*, p. 537.

53. Adolf Schmidt, *Jugend im Reich* (Berlin: Junge Generation, 1942), p. ii.

54. SD report, October 7, 1940, in Boberach, *Meldungen aus dem Reich*, pp. 104–9.

55. SD report, August 1940, R58/153, BA. Goebbels, press conference, August 7, 1940, in Boelcke, *Kriegspropaganda*, p. 448.

56. SD report, November 21, 1940, in Boberach, *Meldungen aus dem Reich*, pp. 111–14.

57. Hitler address, January 30, 1941, in Domarus, *Hitler*, II, 1666. The SD report of September 9, 1940, noted that most people thought that the war would be over before the coming of winter. R58/154, BA.

58. Domarus, *Hitler*, II, 1612–1613.

59. Hitler was enraged that the English would have the temerity to attack Munich on the evening of his annual November pilgrimage to the holy places. *Ibid.*, p. 1601.

60. The SD reported that as a result of Hitler's speeches in mid-winter the general feeling was that victory was assured in 1941. SD report, February 27, 1941, R58/157, BA.

61. Andreas Hillgruber, *Hitlers Strategie: Politik und Kriegführung 1940–1941* (Frankfurt-am-Main: Bernard & Graefe, 1965), p. 501.

62. See Goebbels, press conferences, October 21, 28, 1940, and January 7, 1941, in Boelcke, *Kriegspropaganda*, pp. 551, 559, 597.

63. Theodor Seibert, "Am Kanal," VB-MA, October 22, 1940, p. 1.

64. "So hat Winston Churchill noch nie gelogen," VB-MA, November 18, 1940, p. 2.

65. Goebbels, *Das Reich*, October 13, 1940.

66. "Weihnachtsansprache Rudolf Hess an alle Deutsche in der Heimat, an der Front, jenseits der Grenzen und im Übersee," VB-MA, December 27, 1940, pp. 1–2.

67. Goebbels, *Das Reich*, December 22, 1940.

68. See James Douglas-Hamilton, *Motive for a Mission: The Story behind Hess's Flight to Britain* (London: St. Martin's, 1971), pp. 129–30.

69. Hans Baur, *Ich flog Mächtige der Erde* (Kempten: Albert Pröpster, 1962), pp. 202–4.

70. For further details see text of author's interview with Josef Platzer who served on the staff of Rudolf Hess, Munich, July 24, 1970.

71. Goebbels, press conference, May 13, 1941, in Boelcke, *Kriegspropaganda*, p. 728.

72. Domarus, *Hitler*, II, 1715–1716.

73. Rudolf Semmler, *Goebbels—The Man Next to Hitler* (London: Westhouse, 1947), pp. 32–33.

74. Goebbels, staff conference, May 19, 1941, in Boelcke, *Kriegspropaganda*, p. 740.

75. Goebbels's directive of July 13, 1941, to all Reichsleiter, gauleiter, and Verbändeführer ordered that all photographs of Hess be removed and that books and other materials dealing with him were to be taken from the bookstores, NSDAP, T-81, Roll 675, 5484243, NA. Some Party men with publishing interests objected, and "Professor" Heinrich Hoffmann sent a special request to the Propaganda Ministry asking for special permission to continue traffic in Hess material (Verlag Heinrich Hoffmann to NSDAP, Reichspropagandaleitung, October 29, 1941, *ibid.*, 5484240). He was refused, and Goebbels had Tiessler answer Hoffmann with the admonition that all discussion about Hess must stop and that he "was not to be mentioned in any connection whatsoever." Tiessler to Verlag H. Hoffmann, November 13, 1941, *ibid.* Hoffmann did manage to keep Hess's photograph in Braeckow, *Grossdeutschland*. See also Goebbels, press conference, May 19, 1941, in Boelcke, *Kriegspropaganda*, p. 740, and Semmler, *Goebbels*, pp. 32–33.

76. SD report, May 15, 1941, in Boberach, *Meldungen aus dem Reich*, pp. 145–46.

77. Paul Schmidt, *Statist auf diplomatischer Bühne 1923–1945* (Bonn: Athenäum Verlag, 1954), p. 538. To the delight of the film audiences, some theaters inadvertently

continued to show newsreels of the reception for Hess at the Messerschmidt complex in Augsburg which had been held in early May. "Zur Aufnahme der Wochenschau vom 9.–16. 5., 1941," SO, R58/160, BA.

78. Personal interview with Karl Hauck, SA Politischer Leiter, and Hans Baur, Hitler's pilot, November 2, 1969. Baldur von Schirach contends that Hess was not insane: "What he did was a desperate act of an illusionist obsessed with an idée fixe." Schirach, *Ich glaubte an Hitler*, pp. 277–78. Goebbels on the other hand could not forgive the embarrassment Hess caused Hitler and the Party, and he wrote in his diary on February 13, 1942, that "Hess has written a letter to his wife. The letter is disarmingly naïve. He still believes that he has done the country a great service, and that the dream of Professor Haushofer that he will return with a peace settlement will yet be fulfilled. . . . He still holds to his quackery. He simply is not in the condition that we supposed. He is a hopeless case ("An ihm ist Hopfen und Malz verloren"). Goebbels's diary, IfZ. Albert Speer contends that Hess wanted to contribute something of great value to the war effort, after being on the periphery for so many years, and that he was also motivated by the urge to diminish Bormann's influence with Hitler. Speer, *Erinnerungen*, pp. 189–90. Hitler felt that Hess had betrayed him, and his remark the day after the attempt on his life in July 1944 reveals just how deeply Hess's act had hurt him: "Hess will be mercilessly strung up, just like these pigs, these criminal officers. He started it all then, he provided the example for treachery." *Ibid.*, p. 400.

Chapter VIII. Balkan Interlude: Spring 1941

1. Ruge, *Seekrieg*, p. 102.

2. *Ibid.*, pp. 100–1. Jürgen Rohwer, "Der U-Bootkrieg und sein Zusammenbruch 1943," in H. A. Jacobsen and Jürgen Rohwer, eds., *Entscheidungsschlachten des zweiten Weltkrieges* (Frankfurt-am-Main: Bernard & Graefe, 1960), p. 333. For orders on the press release of the unrestricted submarine campaign see VI Nr. 14/40, August 17, 1940, SO, ZSg 109/14, BA.

3. "Grossadmiral Raeder sprach zu den deutschen Werftarbeitern," VB-MA, January 29, 1941, pp. 1–2. Headlines read "British Empire Crumbling: Two Islands in the Bermudas Leased to the USA," VB-MA, January 24, 1941, p. 1.

4. VI Nr. 6/41, January 8, 1941, SO, ZSg 109/18, BA; VB-MA, January 9, 1941, p. 2.

5. Goebbels, "Britannia Rules the Waves," *Das Reich*, March 30, 1941. "The Battle of the Atlantic," radio address, March 26, 1941, T-314, Roll 1652, IX B41, NA.

6. Jacobsen and Rohwer, *Entscheidungsschlachten*, p. 333; Ruge, *Seekrieg*, p. 128; compare Dönitz, *Zehn Jahre und zwanzig Tage*, pp. 174–75.

7. Whereas Prien and Schepke were killed, Kretschmer went into captivity along with most of his crew. He had been the darling of the headline writers. In December 1940 after he had reached the 250,000-ton kill mark, he was celebrated as the nation's leading submarine ace who at the age of twenty-nine had written a glorious chapter in the Reich's history. VB-MA, December 17, 1940, p. 1.

8. VB-MA, May 28, 1941, p. 1; VI Nr. 131/41, May 27, 1941, SO, ZSg 109/21, BA.

9. SD report, May 26–28, 1941, R58/160, BA.

10. Gruchmann, *Der Zweite Weltkrieg*, pp. 110–11; Domarus, *Hitler*, II, 1677–1678. Hitler's Directive Nr. 25 of March 27, 1941, laid the military plans for the attack on Yugoslavia.

11. VI Nr. 73/41, March 25, 1941; VI 83-4/41, April 4–5, 1941, SO, ZSg 109/19–20, BA; Goebbels, staff conference, April 3, 1941, in Boelcke, *Kriegspropaganda*, pp. 654–55.

12. Domarus, *Hitler*, II, 1687–1689.

13. Goebbels, staff conference, April 6, 1941, in Boelcke, *Kriegspropaganda*, pp. 658–65; see also SD report, April 10, 1941, R58/178, BA; VI Nr. 85/41, April 6, 1941, SO, ZSg 109/20, BA.

14. Goebbels, "Das alte Lied," VB-MA, April 9, 1941, pp. 1–2.

15. Kurt von Tippelskirch, *Geschichte des zweiten Weltkrieges* (Bonn: Athenäum Verlag, 1951), pp. 147–50; Domarus, *Hitler*, II, pp. 1692–1693. Even before the fighting ended, Hitler had established the Croatian separatist "Ustasha State" under Dr. Ante Pavelic, and annexed the area in the Slovenian north around Marburg to the Reich.

16. VI Nr. 98/41, April 19, 1941, SO, ZSg 109/20, BA; VB-MA, April 20, 1941, p. 2.

17. Goebbels, *Das Reich*, May 25, 1941.

18. Goebbels celebrated the occupation of Crete with an article entitled "The Heroization of the Retreat" which mocked the themes of his London counterparts Lindley Fraser and Sefton Delmer. *Das Reich*, June 8, 1941.

19. VI Nr. 135/41, May 31, 1941, SO, ZSg 109/21, BA.

20. Karl Richard Ganzer, "Zwischen Leistung und Traum: Zum Tode Wilhelm II," *Das Reich*, June 15, 1941, p. 23.

Chapter IX. The Soviet War: From Minsk to Moscow

1. SD report, October 23, 1939, R58/144, BA.

2. According to the secret protocols of the German-Soviet agreements, Stalin was promised not only the Baltic states but Bessarabia and North Bukovina as well. According to Weinberg, there was a confidential protocol appended to their agreement on the Polish borders "providing for the return of Germans to Germany and Ukrainians and Belorussians to the Soviet Union." Gerhard L. Weinberg, *Germany and the Soviet Union 1939–1941* (Leiden: E. J. Brill, 1954), pp. 48, 59–60, 99–103.

3. VI 138/40, June 16, 1940, Sammlung Sänger, ZSg 109/12, BA.

4. SD report, July 4, 1940, in Boberach, *Meldungen aus dem Reich*, pp. 82–83.

5. SD report, September 9, 1940, R/58/154, BA.

6. *Das Reich*, October 13, 1940. See also the SD report of September 30, 1940, which read, "Über die Auswirkungen des Paktes gegenüber Russland ist sich die Bevölkerung grösstenteils nicht im klaren. Das Misstrauen, das man schon immer und gerade in letzter Zeit in besonderen Masse der Sowjetunion entgegenbrachte, ist keinesfalls geschwunden." The SD report of October 3, 1940, noted that there were rumors "über Verschiebungen von Truppen in den Osten, den Bau eines Ostwalls und über Verhandlungen Ribbentrops in Moskau gemeldet." See Boberach, *Meldungen aus dem Reich*, pp. 100–2.

7. Naumann, interview, July 12, 1970.

8. VI Nr. 267/40 and 271/40, November 11 and 14, 1940, SO, ZSg 109/16, BA.

9. Hubatsch, *Weserübung*, pp. 84–92.

10. See VI Nr. 52/41, SO, ZSg 109/19, BA, and SD report, March 17, 1941, R58/158, BA.

11. Keitel directive, February 12, 1941, OKW/WPr, T-77, Roll 792, 5521114, NA.

12. *Ibid.*; Dr. Heinrich Gerlach, Sixth Army Stalingrad veteran, interview with author, Brake/Unterweser, July 27, 1959.

13. Keitel directive, OKW/WFSt/Abt 1 (I Op.), Nr. 44699/41, g. Kdos. Chefs., Fu. H. Qu., May 12, 1941, OKW/WPr, T-77, Roll 792, 5521256, NA.

14. *Ibid.* Compare the Keitel directive to OKW-Gen. Qu. and WPr, OKW/WFSt. May 25, 1941, OKW/WPr, T-77, Roll 792, 5521313, NA. See also Keitel to Rosenberg,

OKW/WFSt/Abt. I (IV/Qu), Nr. 00400/41, g. Kdos, March 9, 1941, OKW/WPr, T-77, Roll 792, 5521135, NA.

15. Keitel to Todt, under general heading "Schreiben an zivile Dienststellen über Feindtäuschung," Geheime Kommandosache, March 9, 1941, OKW/WPr, Roll 792, 5521131, NA.

16. Goebbels, press conference, June 5, 1941, in Willi A. Boelcke, ed., *"Wollt Ihr den totalen Krieg?" Die geheimen Goebbels-Konferenzen 1939–1943* (Stuttgart: Deutsche Verlags-Anstalt, 1967), p. 180. Compare Gutterer, interview, August 5, 1970.

17. *Das Reich*, June 13, 1941. This article was not included in the appropriate volume of Goebbels's writings and speeches, *Die Zeit ohne Beispiel*. Hans Fritzsche, *Hier spricht Hans Fritzsche* (Zurich: Interverlag, 1948), p. 84.

18. Heiber, *Joseph Goebbels*, p. 297. In the end, only those informed by Hitler's chancellery could be certain of what was to take place. Many higher officials of the various ministries in Berlin were told only at the last minute, or learned of the attack at the time of its official announcement. Hans Fritzsche, for example, had no official word about the coming attack. In his memoirs he related how Goebbels gathered all his section chiefs together at his Schwanenwerder estate on the evening of June 21, 1941, where he at last informed them of the momentous event. None of the officials were permitted to leave the minister's villa before 5 A.M. in order to maintain the secrecy of the attack. Fritzsche, *Hier spricht Hans Fritzsche*, p. 84.

19. Boelcke, *"Wollt Ihr den totalen Krieg?"* p. 180.

20. SD reports, March 27, April 10, and May 12, 1941, in Boberach, *Meldungen aus dem Reich*, pp. 127–29, 133–35, 143–45; see also SD report, "Russlandgerüchte und ihre Auswirkungen," R58/160, BA.

21. Berndt and von Wedel, *Deutschland im Kampf*, XLIII/IV (June 1941), 73–79. Three months later Hitler made the following statement to his inner circle: "The spirit of decision consists simply in not hesitating when an inner conviction commands you to act. Last year I needed great spiritual strength to take the decision to attack Bolshevism. I had to foresee that Stalin might pass over to the attack in the course of 1941. It was therefore necessary to get started without delay, in order not to be forestalled—and that was not possible before June. . . . I couldn't start a campaign of propaganda to create a climate favorable for the reverse situation; and innumerable lives were saved by the fact that no newspaper or magazine article ever contained a word that could have let anyone guess what we were preparing . . . But at the moment of our attack, we were entering upon a totally unknown world—and there were many people among us who might have reflected that we had, after all, a pact of friendship with the Russians!" Evening of September 17–18, 1941, *Hitler's Secret Conversations*, in Cameron and Stevens, eds., pp. 26–27.

22. "Note des Auswärtigen Amtes an die Sowjetregierung," in Berndt and von Wedel, *Deutschland im Kampf*, XLIII/IV (June 1941), 80–92.

23. For the general directive to the press on the position to be taken regarding the Russians, see "Presse-Rundschreiben Nr. II/98/41," RPA Berlin, June 25, 1941, OKW/WPr, T-77, Roll 1045, 6519099, NA.

24. *Münchner Neueste Nachrichten*, June 23, 1941, p. 1; compare VB-ND, June 23, 1941, pp. 1–2, as well as the "Sonderausgabe," *Berliner Morgenpost*, June 22, 1941, p. 1, headlined "Russlands Verrat an Europa entlarvt."

25. For orders to the periodical press, see *Zeitschriftendienst*, August 15, 1941, and September 24, 1941. The OKW contended that a Russian attack had been imminent in the summer of 1941 and that the enemy's assault was timed to coincide with Germany's all-out campaign against Great Britain. OKW, *Die Wehrmacht: Um die Freiheit Europas* (Berlin: Verlag die Wehrmacht, 1941), p. 9.

26. Oberkommando der Wehrmacht, *Die Berichte des Oberkommandos der Wehrmacht* (Berlin: Verlag die Wehrmacht, 1941), June 29, 1941, pp. 229–33. The daily directive

of June 29, 1941, read: "The German press will . . . express appreciation to the German soldiers in a way worthy of them." Also, it noted that "the great Special Announcements of the High Command taken together are a serious documentation of the danger which threatened . . . Europe from the East." VI Nr. 164/41, ZSg 109/22, SO, BA.

27. SD Report Nr. 198, June 30, 1941, "Aufnahme und Auswirkung der allgemeinen Propaganda-Presse und Rundfunklenkung in der Zeit vom 27.–30.6.41," CGD, Roll 963, Folder 121, NA.

28. Dietrich, *12 Jahre*, p. 104. See also Semmler, *Goebbels*, p. 45, and Murawski, *Der deutsche Wehrmachtbericht*, pp. 60–61.

29. Goebbels, undated diary fragment, MGRC, T-84, Roll 267, NA.

30. In Goebbels's directive "An die obersten Reichsbehörden," of August 11, 1941, he ordered that the fanfares were to be followed immediately by the Special Announcements, just as the Badenweiler March was immediately followed by the entrance of the Führer. RMfVP, T-70, Roll 6, 3509483, NA.

31. VI Nr. 156/41, June 22, 1941, ZSg 109/22, SO, BA. For other important directives to the press during this period, see the following: VI Nr. 162/41, June 27, 1941, ZSg 109/22, SO, BA, which included the directive "Kreuzzug gegen den Bolschewismus"; VI Nr. 164/41, June 29, 1941, ZSg 109/22, SO, BA; "Bestellungen aus der Pressekonferenz," June 23, 1941, ZSg 101/20, Sammlung Brammer, BA.

32. "Der Schleier Fällt," *Das Reich*, July 6, 1941. Goebbels observed in his diary, "We perhaps do not yet really know in what a precarious position we were in in June of this year. Fall would surely have brought the explosion." He wrote further that Russia and England had as their goal the destruction of the Reich and that it would have been impossible to describe the result of the Bolshevik hordes pouring into highly civilized central and western Europe. He observed as well that the great danger would serve as a warning to German intellectuals who felt that the eastern campaign was not necessary, and that he would ask Hitler's permission to take large groups of them on visits to Soviet concentration camps "so that they . . . can see there what constitutes the Bolshevik man." Undated fragment, MGRC, T-84, Roll 267, NA.

33. *Berliner Illustrierte Zeitung*, July 17, 1941; "Vertrauliche Mitteilungen," Reichspropagandaamt Berlin, June 30, 1941, SO, ZSg 109/22, BA; VI Nr. 162/41, June 27, 1941, and VI Nr. 165/41, June 30, 1941, SO, ZSg 109/22, BA; "Presse Rundschreiben" Nr. II/99/41, OKW/WPr, Roll 1045, T-77, 6519101, NA. See also Alfred Rosenberg's article "Europas Wiedergeburt," VB-B, "Die germanischen Kameraden," VB-B, September 2, 1941, p. 8, which carried photographs of the graves of SS men from Norway, Denmark, Flanders, the Netherlands, and the Reich, lying side by side.

34. Goebbels, "Das Tor zum neuen Jahrhundert," *Das Reich*, September 28, 1941. See also the undated fragment in Goebbels's diary in which he wrote that "even former communists are greatly shocked by what they see." MGRC, T-84, Roll 267, NA.

35. Wolfgang Diewerge, *Deutsche Soldaten sehen die Sowjetunion* (Berlin: W. Limpert, 1941). Diewerge states that these were bona fide letters and that this could be proved by checking the serial numbers of the men who wrote them. He contends that the letters from former German Communists were the most bitterly disappointed of them all. Diewerge, interview, July 12, 1970.

36. MNN, July 12, 1941, p. 1. Compare "Vor neuen Zielen," FZ, July 12, 1941, p. 1. The commentary to the Wehrmacht communiqué, which as usual was incorporated in the directives to the press, had included the observation on July 11 that "Cannae was always our model for the battle of encirclement and annihilation." VI Nr. 177/41, ZSg 109/23, SO, BA.

37. Boberach, *Meldungen aus dem Reich*, pp. 155–66.

38. See statement by Reich Press Chief Dietrich, "Ergänzung zum zusammenfassenden Informationsbericht," August 2, 1941, ZSg 101/40, SB, BA.

39. John Huizenga, "Yosuke Matsuoka and the Japanese-German Alliance," in *The Diplomats: 1919–1939*, ed. Gordon A. Craig and Felix Gilbert (Princeton, N.J.: Princeton University Press, 1953), pp. 641–45. For an excellent study on many facets of the Matsuoka problem, consult Paul W. Schroeder, *The Axis Alliance and Japanese-American Relations: 1941* (Ithaca, N.Y.: Cornell University Press, 1958), pp. 126–67. Compare Yale C. Maxon, *Control of Japanese Foreign Policy: A Study of Civil Military Rivalry 1930–1945* (Berkeley, Calif.: University of California Press, 1957), pp. 164–66.

40. Telegram, Ribbentrop to Ott, June 28, 1941, IMTFE, Exhibit No. 1096; telegram, Ribbentrop to Ott, July 1, 1941, printed in *Department of State Bulletin*, June 16, 1946, p. 1040. Both documents cited in Craig and Gilbert, *Diplomats*, pp. 644–45.

41. This position is documented in the "Outline of National Policies in View of the Changing Situation," presented before the Imperial Conference of July 2, 1941. It was clear that the Konoye government would continue to walk the tightrope between its 1940 Tripartite Pact with the axis and its Neutrality Pact negotiated with the Soviet Union in April 1941. The statement read as follows: "Our attitude with reference to the German-Soviet war will be based on the spirit of the Tripartite Pact. However, we will not enter the conflict for the time being. We will secretly strengthen our military preparedness vis à vis the Soviet Union, and we will deal with this matter independently. In the meantime, we will conduct diplomatic negotiations with great care. If the German-Soviet war should develop to the advantage of our Empire, we will, by resorting to armed force, settle the Northern Question and assure the security of the northern borders." Nobutaka Ike, ed., *Japan's Decision for War: Records of the 1941 Policy Conferences* (Stanford, Calif.: Stanford University Press, 1967), p. 79.

42. BOKW, 1941, pp. 268–73, 313, 318; VB-B, September 24, 1941, p. 1.

43. Alexander Dallin, *German Rule in Russia: 1941–1945* (London: St. Martin's Press, 1957), pp. 8–11, 42–49.

44. *Ibid.*, p. 49.

45. *Ibid.*, p. 56; Georg Leibbrandt, state secretary in the Rosenberg Ministry, interview with author, Bonn, July 23, 1966.

46. An excellent study on the manner in which Hitler went about resettlement in the east is Broszat, *Nationalsozialistische Polenpolitik*. For documentation on the "Commissar Order," see Jodl, Kriegstagebuch, Wehrmachtführungsstab L, March 3, 1941; Keitel, "Richtlinien auf Sondergebieten zur Weisung Nr. 21" (Fall Barbarossa), Führer headquarters, March 13, 1941; Oberkommando des Heeres, Gen. St. d. H./Gen. Qu., "Die Durchführung besonderer sicherheitspolizeilicher Aufgaben ausserhalb der Truppe . . ." March 26, 1941. For complete copies of the orders above see Walter Warlimont, *Im Hauptquartier der deutschen Wehrmacht 1939–1945* (Frankfurt-am-Main: Bernard & Graefe, 1962), pp. 166–87. The actual order for Himmler's SS to move in with its liquidation squads was prepared long in advance, although the secret command from Hitler to the Reichsführer came only with the outbreak of hostilities.

47. *Hitler's Secret Conversations*, entries for July 27, September 17, and October 26–27, 1941, and April 5, August 6, 1942, pp. 13–15, 26–30, 76–77, 325–30, 500–3.

48. "Rede Heinrich Himmlers bei der SS-Gruppenführertagung in Posen am 4. Oktober 1943," IMT, XXIX, 122.

49. Dallin, *German Rule in Russia*, pp. 426–27. According to Dallin's figures, approximately 5,160,000 Russian prisoners of war were captured. Of these, only 1,053,000 survived the war. Dallin observes that even these figures are a conservative estimate of the number of captured Russians who were exterminated.

50. CGD, T-580, Roll 16, Folder 177, NA.

51. "Richtlinien für die Behandlung des Themas 'Die Ernährung der Front und der Heimat,'" OKH, Gen. St. d. H./H. Wes. Abt. (II) to OKW/WPr, November 1, 1941, OKW/WPr, T-77, Roll 1023, 2494687, NA.

52. XLIII AK, "Behandlung von Bevölkerung, Banden und Wirtschaftsgütern," March 14, 1943, Document NOKW-515, in Dallin, German Rule in Russia, p. 550.

53. Gehlen Report, "Fremde Heere Ost," "Dringende Fragen des Bandenkrieges und der 'Hilfswilligen' Erfassung," November 25, 1942, H3/191, Captured Records Section, Departmental Records Branch, Adjutant General's Office, U.S. Army, Alexandria, Virginia, in Dallin, German Rule in Russia, p. 546.

54. Dallin, German Rule in Russia, pp. 545–46.

55. Ibid., pp. 428–53. For an account of conditions in the camps for the eastern workers, see the anonymous "Fremde Heer Ost" document in NSDAP, T-81, Roll 219, 369453, NA. See Göring and Sauckel's instructions for employers to stress German superiority in organization and ability in the document "Merkblatt Nr. 1 für Betriebsführer über den Einsatz von Ostarbeitern," CGD, T-580, Roll 15, Folder 176A, NA.

56. Oberst Martin, "Verbindungsoffizier des OKW zum RMVP," Berlin, July 30, 1943, "Notiz zur Unterrichtung des Herrn Obergruppenführers," SS, T-175, Roll 29, 2537005, NA.

57. Goebbels, diary entry, June 4, 1942, MGRC, T-84, Roll 267, NA.

58. Taubert and Tiessler, interviews, August 5, 1970, and July 30, 1970, respectively.

59. Reichsführer SS, SS Hauptamt, Der Untermensch (Berlin: Nordland, 1942).

60. Brandt to Ohlendorf, date illegible, in reply to Ohlendorf's communication of August 31, 1942, Himmler Files, Box VIII, Folder 286, HL. See also Ohlendorf to Himmler, September 2, 1942, Himmler Files, Box VIII, Folder 286, HL.

61. d'Alquen, interview, Mönchen-Gladbach, July 13, 1970. d'Alquen first revealed the details of his initial discussion on The Subhuman to Jürgen Thorwald in May 1953, ZS2, IfZ. See also Heinz Höhne, The Order of the Death's Head, trans. R. Barry (New York: Coward-McCann, 1970), pp. 506–8.

62. Gutterer to Himmler, March 5, 1943, Himmler Files, Box VIII, Folder 286, HL.

63. Himmler to Gutterer, March 12, 1943, Himmler Files, Box VIII, Folder 286, HL.

64. Brandt to Berger, April 14, 1943, Himmler Files, Box VIII, Folder 286, HL. The Subhuman affair made remarkably little impression on Gutterer who in an interview in 1970 could not recall anything about it. This illustrates not only his rapid decline in influence at the Ministry, which he readily admits, but also that Taubert was indeed Goebbels's vehicle in his attempt to penetrate Himmler's armor. Gutterer, interview, August 5, 1970.

65. Brandt to Naumann, March 16, 1943, Himmler Files, Box VIII, Folder 286, HL.

66. Berger to Brandt, April 17, 1943, Bezug: Schreiben von 14.4. 1943–tgb. nr. 49/7/43g, Himmler Files, Box VIII, Folder 286, HL.

67. Ibid.

68. Von Kielpinski to Brandt, September 16, 1943, Himmler Files, Box VIII, Folder 286, HL.

69. Tiessler and Taubert, interviews, July 30 and August 4, 1970, respectively. For the Goebbels directive, see RMfdbO, T-454, Roll 80, 000478, NA.

70. For an analytical catalogue of the failures of Nazi Ostpolitik and its effects on the propaganda front, see Taubert, "Querschnitt durch die Tätigkeit des Arbeitsgebiets Dr. Taubert des R.M.V.P. bis zum 31.12.1944," G PA 14, Yivo Institute for Jewish Research, New York City.

71. To analyze the degree to which Goebbels recognized the extent of the problem, see "Aufzeichnung über die deutsche Pressepolitik hinsichtlich der Sowjetunion,"

unsigned and undated, but probably written by Brammer, Sammlung Brammer, ZSg 101/42, BA.

72. Günter d'Alquen described the problem rather clearly: "We don't know where we're going to put our asses down out there at the front and we're supposed to believe that . . . mere subhumans are responsible for it? We must be miserable supermen." d'Alquen, interview with Jürgen Thorwald, May 1953, ZS2, IfZ.

Chapter X. The Battle of Moscow

1. *Berliner Börsenzeitung*, October 10, 1941, p. 1.

2. *Ibid.*, p. 1. Consult Sommerfeldt, *Oberkommando*, p. 100, and "Bestellungen aus der Pressekonferenz vom. 8. Oktober 1941," ZSg 101/22, SB, BA. For additional documentation on Dietrich's historic press conference see "Bestellungen aus der Pressekonferenz vom 9. Oktober 1941," ZSg 101/22, SB, BA, as well as the "Tagesparolen des Reichspressechefs," VI Nr. 265/41, October 9, 1941, ZSg 109/26, SO, BA.

3. Dietrich, *12 Jahre*, pp. 101–3. Hans Fritzsche has written that he knew at the time that Hitler had ordered the Dietrich press conference. Fritzsche, *Hier spricht Hans Fritzsche*, p. 219. There is further evidence to support Dietrich's case. Erich Murawski has written that the communiqué of October 9 differed in tone and style from the previous releases, and he contends that Hitler either wrote it himself or had General Jodl do so. Murawski, *Deutsche Wehrmachtbericht*, p. 61.

4. VI Nr. 265–6/41, October 9–10, 1941, ZSg 109/26, SO, BA; Murawski, *Deutsche Wehrmachtbericht*, p. 62; Peter Bor, *Gespräche mit Halder* (Wiesbaden: Limes Verlag, 1950), p. 23.

5. According to the records of the 47th Liaison Conference of the highest Japanese government and military officials meeting on August 16, 1941, Foreign Minister Toyoda would not admit this to the German ambassador Ott, but instead preferred to cloak his true intentions in the vain assurance that "the present state of our war preparations against the Soviet Union represents the first step in future operations against the Soviets; and I believe that this is in keeping with the spirit of the Tripartite Pact." Ike, *Japan's Decision for War*, pp. 121–22.

6. Records of Japanese Imperial Conference of September 6, 1941, in Ike, *Japan's Decision for War*, pp. 158–59.

7. Johanna M. Meskill, *Hitler and Japan: The Hollow Alliance* (New York: Atherton, 1966), pp. 41–42. The records of the 67th Liaison Conference in Tokyo on November 13, 1941, confirmed the Japanese refusal to strike against the Soviet Union. Ike, *Japan's Decision for War*, p. 242.

8. Rudolf Semmler, diary entry, October 9 and 11, 1941, *Goebbels*, pp. 54–56.

9. Goebbels, undated directive, "Propagandaaktion Parole: Deutschlands Sieg-Brot und Freiheit für unser Volk und Europa," NSDAP, T-81, Roll 673, 5481696, NA. Official Nazi statistics reported that from October 15, 1941, to March 31, 1942, some 74,684 rallies were held, with attendance at 18,511,990. Reichspropagandaleitung "Rundschreiben Nr. G 8/42," a report sent to all Party Speakers, RMfdbO, T-454, Roll 69, 000184, NA.

10. Some of Goebbels's colleagues advised a radical shift in propaganda which would entail a more realistic interpretation of the war. Berndt, the chief of the Propaganda Section in the Ministry, took this position in his memorandum "Propaganda Plan for the War Winter 1941–1942." Berndt warned that German morale was sagging, and he deprecated the propaganda concerning the Soviet war. He advised that Berlin must assume a harder line in order to strengthen the German people for crises, to instill courage, and to avoid weakness and fear. "To victory through sacrifice" must be the battle cry during the long winter which lay ahead, he urged. Berndt,

RMfVP, "Propagandaplan für den Kriegswinter 1941–1942," undated, NSDAP, T-81, Roll 673, 5481672, NA.

11. Hitler's address to the Old Guard was defensive in tone. Instead of declaring that the campaign was won, he spoke about the goals of the campaign having already been won, i.e., "the annihilation of the enemy's power" and "the occupation of the enemy's basic industrial and agricultural areas." He was not "concerned with motives of prestige," because "we alone . . . determine the speed of our advance." To the doubters and complainers he had this to say: "If our enemies say, 'Yes,' then, the battle will surely last until 1942—it can last as long as necessary—but the last battalion on the field will be German!" Berndt and von Wedel, *Deutschland im Kampf*, LIII/IV (November 1941), 84–99.

12. RMfVP, "Vorlage," "Übersicht über die augenblickliche Propagandalinie," November 10, 1941, NSDAP, T-81, Roll 672, 5480996, NA.

13. Wächter and Berndt, RMfVP. "Propaganda-Parole Nr. 10" to all gauleiters, chiefs of the Reich propaganda offices, and gau propaganda chiefs, "Notwendigkeit, das Volk noch widerstandsfähiger gegen alle Anfälligkeiten des Krieges zu machen," December 16, 1941, quoting Goebbels's dispatch to the gauleiters, NSDAP, T-81, Roll 672, 5480897, NA. Compare the directive included in the "Sonderdienst der Reichspropagandaleitung," December 2, 1941, which warned the propagandists not to awaken any hopes that the war would be concluded by some specific date in the future. NSDAP, T-81, Roll 158, 318988, NA.

14. Wächter and Berndt, RMfVP, "Propaganda-Parole Nr. 10" to all gauleiters, chiefs of the Reich propaganda offices, and gau propaganda chiefs, December 16, 1941, NSDAP, T-81, Roll 672, 5480897, NA.

15. Goebbels, "Wann oder Wie," *Das Reich*, November 9, 1941.

16. VB-B, November 25, 1941, p. 1.

17. Tippelskirch, *Geschichte des zweiten Weltkrieges*, pp. 208–9.

18. VB-B, December 5, 1941, pp. 1–2.

19. Saul Friedländer, *Prelude to Downfall: Hitler and the United States 1939–1941*, trans. A. Werth (New York: Knopf, 1967), p. 49.

20. Hitler address, in Domarus, *Hitler*, II, 1661.

21. For directives on covering Lend-Lease see VI Nr. 57–66/41, March 7–17, 1941, SO, ZSg 109/19, BA; for the Atlantic Charter, VI Nr. 211/41, August 15, 1941, SO, ZSg 109/24, BA; for the *Greer* incident, VI Nr. 235–39, September 8–12, 1941, SO, ZSg 109/25, BA. For a sampling of press reports on the United States during the period see Theodor Seibert, "Das Rätsel Amerika: Acht Jahre Roosevelt," VB-ND. February 24, 1941. p. 34, and the following Goebbels articles: "Im Gelächter der Welt," "Fleisszensuren von USA," "Aus dem Lande der unbegrenzten Möglichkeiten," and "Marathonlauf hinter dem Kriege," *Das Reich*, February 16, May 4, May 25, and September 21, 1941, respectively.

22. Speer, *Erinnerungen*, p. 319.

23. *Das Reich*, May 25, 1941.

24. Goebbels, diary entry, January 30, 1942, IfZ.

25. "Die Fortsetzung der Operationen und die Art der Kampfführung im Osten sind von jetzt ab durch den Einbruch des russischen Winters bedingt. Auf weiten Strecken der Ostfront finden nur noch örtliche Kampfhandlungen statt." *BOKW*, 1941, p. 382. To further the credibility of the new line, Dietrich ordered that the press was to give a good deal of space to the war correspondents' reports which shed light on the severity of the winter months in the Soviet Union.

26. See the "Bestellungen aus der Pressekonferenz vom 8. Dezember 1941," ZSg 101/22, SB, BA; VI Nr. 322/41, December 8, 1941, ZSg 109/28, SO, BA; VI Nr. 323/41, December 9, 1941, ZSg 109/28, SO, BA.

27. Berndt and von Wedel, *Deutschland im Kampf*, LV/VI (December 1941), 70–99.

28. Warlimont, *Im Hauptquartier der deutschen Wehrmacht*, pp. 225–37; Gert Buchheit,

Hitler der Feldherr (Rastatt: G. Grotesche Verlag, 1958), pp. 243–48; *BOKW,* 1941, p. 401.

29. SD report, January 5, 1941, SS, T-175, Roll 262, 275520, NA.

30. Dietrich, *12 Jahre,* pp. 104–5.

31. Boelcke, *Wollt Ihr den totalen Krieg?* pp. 195–96.

32. *Ibid.*

33. Göring warned that such "gossiping" only upset the home front; it was enough for the homeland to know that the SS was backing up the Wehrmacht by taking merciless revenge for the enemy's barbarism. Partei-Kanzlei, "Vertrauliche Informationen," Article 98, "Feldpostbriefe aus dem Osten," January 31, 1942, NSDAP, T-81, Roll 2, 63395, NA.

34. Goebbels, radio address, December 21, 1941, "Ruf zur Gemeinschaftshilfe: Aufruf zur Sammlung von Wintersachen für unsere Front," Goebbels, *Das Eherne Herz* (Munich: Franz Eher, 1943), pp. 131–37.

35. Wächter and Berndt, RMfVP, "Propaganda Parole Nr. 12" to all gauleiters, chiefs of the Reich propaganda offices, and gau propaganda chiefs, "Die Bedeutung der Sammlung von Woll-Pelz-und Wintersachen für die Front," undated, NSDAP, T-81, Roll 672, 5480990, NA. Wächter and Berndt ordered the functionaries to carry out the collection "in a grand style," and they emphasized the political importance of the campaign. See the corresponding directive to the press, VI Nr. 342/41, December 29, 1941, ZSg 109/28, SO, BA.

36. Goebbels, "Ein Volk hilft sich selbst: Rundfunkrede zum Abschluss der Sammlung von Woll-Pelz-und Wintersachen für die Front," January 14, 1942, in Goebbels, *Das Eherne Herz,* pp. 176–79; Bramsted, *Goebbels and National Socialist Propaganda,* pp. 248–49. Naumann gave his former chief low marks for the Christmas collection performance, citing it as an example of Goebbels's predilection for "overdoing a good thing, for throwing too much fat on the fire." He contends that it was a failure and caused as much unrest as the "Kristallnacht" in 1938. I disagree and feel that Schwarz van Berk was closer to the mark with his observation that the campaign was a "Ventil Aktion" calculated to keep people busy in the way one keeps workers busy peeling potatoes. To Germans at home, the thought of their men freezing in Russia was even worse than their being wounded; as a result they wanted to feel that they personally had taken part in the campaign and had helped to alleviate the suffering of the troops. Schwarz van Berk cited this as an example of the German people's willingness to sacrifice for victory. Naumann and Schwarz van Berk, interviews, July 11 and July 28, 1970, respectively.

37. Goebbels, diary entry, June 5, 1942, MGRC, T-84, Roll 267, NA.

Chapter XI. The Myth of Stalingrad

1. Wächter and Berndt, RMfVP, Propagandaparole Nr. 32, "Keine Illusionspropaganda," May 22, 1942, NSDAP, T-81, Roll 672, 5480798, NA.

2. Rundschreiben Nr. 177/42/IX, Presseabteilung des Reichspropagandaamtes, September 11, 1942, MGRC, T-84, Roll 164, 1530990, NA.

3. Dietrich, *12 Jahre,* p. 109.

4. VI Nr. 237/42, ZSg 109/38, SO, BA.

5. Berndt and von Wedel, *Deutschland im Kampf,* LXXIII/IV (September 1942), 81–83.

6. *Ibid.,* LXXVII/VIII (November 1942), 63.

7. Fritzsche, *Hier spricht Hans Fritzsche,* p. 220.

8. Murawski, *Deutsche Wehrmachtbericht,* p. 121.

9. VI Nr. 302/42, November 23, 1942, SO, ZSg 109/39, BA.

10. Sommerfeldt, *Oberkommando,* p. 112.

11. SD reports, November 26, December 3, 1942, SS, T-175, Roll 264, 2758190, NA.

12. *Frankfurter Zeitung*, December 9, 1942.

13. *Kessing's Archiv der Gegenwart*, 1942, p. 5744. See also "Notiz für Reichsleiter Bormann," January 6, 1943: "Concerning the problem of defensive propaganda . . . Goebbels gave the Section Chiefs instructions to avoid anything in their propaganda which would appear to be a retreat from our aggressive posture." NSDAP, T-81, Roll 672, 5480895, NA.

14. Berndt and von Wedel, *Deutschland im Kampf*, LXXIX/LXXX (December 1942), 77–83.

15. Goebbels, diary entry, December 8, 1942, MGRC, T-84, Roll 262, NA. The minister observed that he could speak on the problem of winter supplies publicly, but that such favorable conditions were best handled through person-to-person propaganda.

16. SD report, Abschnitt Linz, January 4, 1943, NSDAP, T-81, Roll 7, 14436, NA.

17. Gutterer, interview, August 5, 1970.

18. Goebbels, diary entry, December 12, 1942, MGRC, T-84, Roll 262, NA. For further evidence of the public's concern over the news policies, see the "Anlage zum Tätigkeitsbericht vom 8. Dezember 1942," RMfVP, CGD, T-580, Roll 963, Folder 131, NA.

19. Bormann, Rundschreiben Nr. 198/42, December 18, 1942, CGD, T-580, Roll 15, Folder 176A, NA.

20. Alfred Philippi and Ferdinand Heim, *Der Feldzug gegen Sowjetrussland 1941 bis 1945* (Stuttgart: W. Kohlhammer, 1962), pp. 199–200.

21. H. Schröter, *Stalingrad*, trans. Constantine Fitzgibbon (New York: Dutton, 1958), pp. 174–75.

22. Philippi and Heim, *Feldzug gegen Sowjetrussland*, pp. 192–93.

23. Sommerfeldt, *Oberkommando*, p. 114.

24. Berndt and von Wedel, *Deutschland im Kampf*, LXXXI/II (January 1943), 87–89.

25. *Ibid.*, pp. 59, 73.

26. "Tagesparolen des Reichspressechefs," February 3, 1943, MGRC, T-84, Roll 164, 1531187, NA.

27. Ernst Kris and Hans Speier, *German Radio Propaganda: Report on Home Broadcasts during the War* (London: Oxford University Press, 1944), pp. 431–32.

28. Hinkel to Goebbels, "Rahmen Programm um die Meldung Stalingrad," CGD-RMfVP, T-580, Roll 682, Folder 562, NA. Beethoven's "Eroica" was included in many broadcasts.

29. Berndt and von Wedel, *Deutschland im Kampf*, LXXXIII/IV (February 1943), 52–53.

30. Sommerfeldt, *Oberkommando*, p. 118.

31. An OKW directive conveyed Hitler's orders barring lectures on Stalingrad. OKW/WPr, T-77, Roll 1036, 6508208, NA. For the order on the Stalingrad news block see Rundschreiben Nr. II/3/43, "Vertrauliche Mitteilungen," February 15, 1943, OKW/WPr, T-77, Roll 1045, 6519221, NA.

32. Schröter, *Stalingrad*, p. 9. The author noted, "This book has already been written once, in 1943, making use of all the open and secret material and documents in the possession of the German Supreme Command. This was done on Goebbels's instructions, and in Adolf Hitler's name." VI Nr. 38/43, February 11, 1943, ZSg 109/41, SO, BA, reported that an official brochure on Stalingrad was being prepared.

33. OKW/WPr, T-77, Roll 1035, 6507945, NA.

34. Goebbels, diary entry, February 14, 1943, Archiv 2771/61, ed. 83, IfZ.

35. SD reports, "Meldungen aus dem Reich," January 25, 28, February 4, 1943, T-175, Roll 264, 2758535, 2758564, NA.

36. RPA Koblenz to Dr. Schäffer, RMfVP, February 11, 1943, CGD, T-580, Roll 683, Folder 563, NA.

37. Naumann, interview, July 11, 1970.

38. Bormann, "Leiter der Partei-Kanzlei," Rundschreiben Nr. 83/43, to all Reichsleiter, gauleiter, and kreisleiter, CGD, T-580, Roll 16, Folder 180, NA.

39. "Der Chef der Sicherheitspolizei und des SD," IV A 1 a-B. Nr. 1386/44, Berlin, July 9, 1944, to RMfVP, "Betrifft: Stalingradkämpfer," in answer to RMfVP document Pro VS 2426A/5.4.44/231A–2, 3, May 5, 1944, CGD, T-580, Roll 650, Folder 426, NA.

40. Sondermann, RMfVP, "An die Kanzlei im Hause," "Entwurf für einen Schnellbrief an alle RPA," Pro VS 2426A/14.9/44 202–3, 12, Berlin, September 14, 1944, CGD, T-580, Roll 650, Folder 426, NA.

41. For samples of this correspondence as well as a copy of the "Fragebogen an General Heitz," see CGD, T-580, Roll 850, Folder 426, NA.

42. NSDAP, Gau Essen, Kreisleitung Duisburg; Kreisstabsamt Bg./Sch, Duisburg, July 25, 1944, to "Reichspropagandaamt z.Hd. Pg. Oberheiden, Essen/Ruhr," "Betrifft: Nachforschung nach Kriegsgefangenen und Vermissten in der Sowjetunion," CGD, T-580, Roll 650, Folder 426, NA.

43. Last Letters from Stalingrad, trans. Franz Schneider and Charles Gullans (New York: William Morrow, 1962), p. 22.

Chapter XII. Postlude to Stalingrad: Goebbels's Anti-Bolshevik Campaign

1. In the view of General Adolf Heusinger, the "unconditional surrender" demand was the most powerful weapon in Goebbels's arsenal. Interview with author, the Pentagon, Washington, D.C., November 27, 1962. This was the view of most German officers including Kesselring, Manstein, von Witzleben, Blumentritt, Guderian, von Manteuffel, Warlimont, and Westphal. See Anne Armstrong, Unconditional Surrender: The Impact of the Casablanca Policy upon World War Two (New Brunswick, N.J.: Rutgers University Press, 1961), pp. 137–47.

2. Von Oven, diary entry, February 19, 1944, in Mit Goebbels, I, 202; compare Naumann, interview, August 6, 1970.

3. Berndt and von Wedel, Deutschland im Kampf, LXXXIII/IV (February 1943), 83–84.

4. Ibid., pp. 88–106. Reaction to Goebbels's address was on the whole very favorable. See for example the SD report from Linz, February 19, 1943, NSDAP, T-81, Roll 6, 13346, NA. As always, the reports from the provincial Reich propaganda offices gave the minister unqualified praise. Typical was that from RPA Bochum: "The speech of the Minister has exploded like a bomb." CGD, T-580, Roll 672, Folder 514, NA, February 19, 1943. The newspapers and periodicals were directed to give central attention to Goebbels's speech. See the secret Memorandum Nr. II/4/43 of Reich Propaganda Office Berlin, February 23, 1943, OKW/WPr, T-77, Roll 1045, 6519223, NA.

5. Goebbels's diary entry for February 19, 1943, included the following passage: "This evening many people are of the opinion that this mass meeting is really a type of quiet coup d'etat. But we are simply jumping over the many hurdles which the bureaucracy has built in our path. Total war is now no longer just a question on the minds of a few perceptive men, but the whole nation is concerned with it." Archiv 2771/61, Ed. 83, IfZ.

6. Naumann, interview, August 6, 1971. See also Günter Moltmann, "Goebbels's Rede zum totalen Krieg," Vierteljahrshefte für Zeitgeschichte, XII (January 1964), 15, 22. Semmler's diary entry of January 29, 1943, included the observation that "Goebbels is brooding over a daring plan. He will try to bring pressure on Hitler by putting forward radical demands in a speech at the Sports Palace. The crowd will applaud

wildly. In this way he may be able to force Hitler to put an end to half measures. If his demands are not met then the government will be compromised. The Führer could not afford that at the moment." Semmler, *Goebbels*, p. 68.

7. Hitler commented to Naumann very favorably about the address. Naumann, interview, August 6, 1971. The Sports Palace address acted as a red flag to Goebbels's enemies. Rosenberg wrote a scathing letter to both Bormann and Göring complaining that Goebbels's theatrics had done great damage to the Party and the war effort. He could not "imagine that the Führer read the whole speech, if he ever saw it at all." Letter dated March 2, 1943, RMfdbO, T-454, Roll 8, 4914655, NA. Hitler personally congratulated Goebbels on his address and referred to it as a "psychological and propaganda masterpiece." Goebbels, diary entry, March 9, 1943, MGRC, T-84, Roll 260, NA.

8. NSDAP, Reich Propaganda Command, "Rednerschnell-information," "Antibolschewistische Propaganda," February 22, 1943, NSDAP, T-81, Roll 23, 20711; "Vertrauliche Informationen," Press Memorandum Nr. II/7/43, March 16, 1943, MGRC, T-84, Roll 168, 1534966, NA.

9. Goebbels, "Die Winterkrise und der totale Krieg," *Das Reich*, March 14, 1943. Goebbels, "Ein offenes Wort zum totalen Krieg," *Das Reich*, April 4, 1943. See also Bormann, Directive Nr. 37/43, Führer headquarters, March 1, 1943, "Mobilisierung der deutschen Heimat," CGD, T-580, Roll 15, Folder 177, NA. See also Bormann's order, "Anordnung A 43/43," June 24, 1943, "Haltung der Parteigenossen im Kriege," CGD, T-580, Roll 15, Folder 177, NA. The latter directive warned that those Party members who did not meet the standards or who showed the least doubt about the final victory would be expelled from the Party.

10. Naumann, interview, November 21, 1969.

11. Wächter, RMfVP, "Propagandaparole Nr. 49," to all gauleiters, gau propaganda chiefs, and chiefs of the Reich propaganda offices, February 17, 1943, NSDAP, T-81, Roll 672, 5480700, NA. Compare the "Anweisung für antibolschewistische Propagandaaktion," from Fröhlich of the Reich Propaganda Command, February 20, 1943, which in effect was a reiteration of the main theses of Goebbels's address of February 19, 1943. The directive also instructed the gau propaganda leaders to call a conference of all their Party speakers in order to orient them to the anti-Bolshevik campaign. The Propaganda Ministry noted that it was dispatching Reich speakers to these provincial conferences who would brief the lower echelon speakers on the current propaganda line. The Reich speakers had had a conference of their own in Berlin on February 15–16, 1943. NSDAP, T-81, Roll 24, 22074, NA; *Deutscher Wochendienst*, February 5, 1943. See also NSDAP, Reich Propaganda Command, "Rednerschnellinformation," Issue 51, "Antibolschewistische Propaganda," February 22, 1943, NSDAP, T-81, Roll 23, 20711, NA. The latter document included the order that "all speeches at meetings and rallies from now on are to be based on anti-Bolshevik propaganda . . . The speakers must follow the guidelines given here . . ."

12. RMfVP, Rundschreiben Nr. 138, to all Reich propaganda offices, NSDAP, T-81, Roll 24, 21916, NA.

13. Goebbels, diary entry, March 8, 1943, MGRC, T-84, Roll 263, NA. See the front page article in the March 7, 1943, issue of the *Völkischer Beobachter* (Berlin) headlined "Herrschaft des Bolschewismus auf den Ruinen der Westmächte," which made it clear that not only Germany but Stalin's western allies would share the same unhappy fate. The living hell that awaited Germany in case of defeat was a major theme of the Wehrmacht propaganda as well. See the "Mitteilungen für das Offizierkorps," undated Special Issue, which spread the fear that a Bolshevik victory would be the signal for a European catastrophe, in which Europe stood the chance of becoming a province of the Soviet Union and its revolutionary herd. In such an event mass deportations and slavery would become the order of the day. OKW/WPr, T-77, Roll 1040, 6514285, NA.

14. Goebbels, "Damals und Heute," *Das Reich*, March 7, 1943. In his diary entry of March 14, 1943, Semmler quoted Goebbels as having said, "I shall now try by every means to stimulate this fear, until at last there comes a breach between East and West. That is the great long-range object of my work, which I hope to attain by this summer." Semmler, *Goebbels*, pp. 76–77.

15. Berndt and von Wedel, *Deutschland im Kampf*, LXXXIII/IV (February 1943), 78. Goebbels dealt with the theme of international Jewry in his *Das Reich* article of February 28, 1943, entitled "Die Krise Europas," as well as in the May 9 issue entitled "Der Krieg und die Juden."

16. MGRC, T-84, Roll 164, 1531089, NA.

17. Semmler, diary entry, March 13, 1943, Semmler, *Goebbels*, p. 76.

18. Goebbels, diary entry, March 9, 1943, MGRC, T-84, Roll 260, NA.

19. Von Manstein, *Lost Victories* (Chicago: Henry Regnery, 1958), pp. 393–442; von Tippelskirch, *Geschichte des Zweiten Weltkrieges*, pp. 320–27.

20. DW, March 5, 1943. According to Goebbels, Hitler endorsed his anti-Bolshevik campaign as well as the tone of exaggerated pessimism characterizing German propaganda at that time. Goebbels, diary entry, March 9, 1943, MGRC, T-84, Roll 260, NA.

21. See "Case Study Nr. 13.6.: Inferences about the Nazi Propaganda Effort to Influence Domestic and Foreign Opinion by Manipulating the Presentation of Military Developments," in Alexander George, *Propaganda Analysis: A Study of Inferences Made from Nazi Propaganda in World War II* (White Plains: Roe Peterson, 1959), pp. 237–40.

22. Goebbels, diary entries, March 1, 9, 12, 15, 1943, MGRC, T-84, Roll 263, NA.

23. Goebbels, "Die Winterkrise und der totale Krieg," March 14, 1943, in Joseph Goebbels, *Der Steile Aufstieg* (Munich: Franz Eher, 1944), p. 222. Goebbels noted in his diary on March 2, 1943, that "our present portrayal of the situation at the front is not really believed any more; it is assumed that functional pessimism lurks behind it . . . an assumption which is really not entirely erroneous." MGRC, T-84, Roll 263, NA.

24. J. K. Zawodny, *Death in the Forest* (Notre Dame, Ind.: University of Notre Dame Press, 1962).

25. Goebbels, diary entry, April 14, 1943, in Lochner, *The Goebbels Diaries*, p. 328.

26. RMfVP, *Im Walde von Katyn*, 1943; Auswärtiges Amt, *Amtliches Material zum Massenmord von Katyn* (Berlin: Franz Eher, 1943); Press Section of the Reich Propaganda Office, Directive Nr. 68/iv/43, April 16, 1943, MGRC, T-84, 1531100, NA; "Special Information for Periodicals," April 17, 1943, MGRC, T-84, Roll 168, 1534952, NA; VI Nr. 94/43, April 14, 1943, ZSg 109/42, SO, BA; Goebbels, diary entries, April 9, 14, 18, 1943, MGRC, T-84, Roll 263, NA.

27. VB-B, April 14, 1943, p. 1; April 15, p. 1; April 16, pp. 1–3; April 17, pp. 1–3; April 18, p. 2; *Deutsche Allgemeine Zeitung*, April 15, 1943, pp. 1–2; April 16, pp. 1–2; April 17, pp. 1–2; April 18, pp. 1–2. See also the radio address by Hans Fritzsche, May 6, 1943, which was devoted to the theme of the allied "counter-offensive against Katyn." RMfVP, T-70, Roll 123, 365536, NA.

28. Himmler to von Ribbentrop, date illegible, April 1943, Feld-Kommandostelle, Himmler Files, Box VII, Folder 277, HL.

29. Von Ribbentrop to Himmler, Fuschl, April 26, 1943, Himmler Files, Box VII, Folder 277, HL.

30. When Goebbels decried the "Jewish-Bolshevik" danger, he spoke from the heart. On April 16, 1943, after seeing a showing of the newsreels on Katyn, he wrote, "One hardly dares to imagine what would happen to Germany and Europe if this Asiatic-Jewish flood were to inundate our continent." Goebbels, diary entry, April 16, 1943, in Lochner, *The Goebbels Diaries*, p. 331.

Chapter XIII. Italy Leaves the War

1. VI Nr. 288/42, November 8, 1942, VI Nr. 293/42, November 13, 1942, VI Nr. 294/42, November 14, 1942, VI Nr. 299/42, SO, R58/166, BA

2. See SD reports of November–December 1941 in Boberach, *Meldungen aus dem Reich*, pp. 316–28.

3. Goebbels, press conference, November 14, 1942, in Boelcke, *Wollt Ihr den totalen Krieg?* pp. 302–3.

4. VB-MA, November 9, 1942, pp. 1, 4.

5. Boberach, *Meldungen aus dem Reich*, p. 323.

6. Hitler address, Munich, November 8, 1942, in Domarus, *Hitler*, II, 1940–1941.

7. Original in the *Nationalsozialistische Partei Korrespondenz*, reprint in VB-MA, December 13, 1942, p. 3.

8. Headlines of the *Völkischer Beobachter* (MA), December 9, 1942, "Die neuesten Erkenntnisse aus USA," "Grossbritannien passt nicht mehr ins Weltbild der Zukunft," "Britische Abwehrversuche gegen den nordamerikanischen Imperialismus."

9. SD reports, January 11, 28, 1943, R58/179, BA.

10. F. W. Deakin, *The Brutal Friendship* (New York: Harper & Row, 1962), p. 274.

11. Theodor Seibert, "Africa," VB-MA, May 14, 1943, pp. 1–2.

12. Goebbels, diary entry, April 11, 1943, in Lochner, *The Goebbels Diaries*, p. 294.

13. VB-MA, April 13, 1943, p. 1. According to the report, "Bauinspektor Speer" had arranged a visit of the German and foreign press corps to the recently completed bastions along the Atlantic coast.

14. OKW communiqué, May 9, 1943.

15. VB-MA, May 14, 1943, p. 1.

16. Domarus, *Hitler*, II, 2013–2014.

17. DNB text of May 11, 1943, in Domarus, *Hitler*, II, 2014–2015. See also VB-MA, May 5, 1943, p. 3, and Goebbels's assessment of the Rommel propaganda, May 10, 1943, in Lochner, *The Goebbels Diaries*, p. 369.

18. Domarus, *Hitler*, II, 2014–2015.

19. Goebbels, diary entry, May 14, 1943, in Lochner, *The Goebbels Diaries*, pp. 378–79.

20. Fritzsche, radio address, May 8, 1943, RMfVP, T-70, Roll 123, 3651546, NA.

21. VI Nr. 118/43, May 13, 1943, SO, ZSg 109/43, BA.

22. Seibert, "Africa," VB-MA, May 14, 1943, pp. 1–2.

23. *Reichsrednerschnellinformation*, May 18, 1943, NSDAP, T-81, Roll 683, 4721691, NA.

24. SD report, May 28, 1943, R58/183, BA.

25. SD report, July 19, 1943, R58/186, BA.

26. Bormann to the Reichsleiters, gauleiters, and unit chiefs, Directive Nr. 58/43, CGD, T-580, Roll 15, NA.

27. Communiqué, July 19, 1943, in Domarus, *Hitler*, II, 2023.

28. Ivone Kirkpatrick, *Mussolini: A Study in Power* (New York: Hawthorn, 1964), pp. 545–67; Deakin, *The Brutal Friendship*, pp. 357–488.

29. Goebbels, diary entry, in Lochner, *The Goebbels Diaries*, pp. 370–81.

30. Von Oven, diary entry, July 27, 1943, *Mit Goebbels*, I, 68–69.

31. Lochner, *The Goebbels Diaries*, pp. 406–16.

32. See VB-MA and FZ, July 27, 1943, p. 1.

33. Goebbels, diary entry, July 26, 1943, in Lochner, *The Goebbels Diaries*, pp. 405–6.

34. For a copy of Goebbels's orders farther down the chain of command, see NSDAP, Gau Hessen-Nassau, Frankfurt-am-Main, August 2, 1943, Rundschreiben Nr. 42/43, NSDAP, T-81, Roll 117, 137458, NA. Also see the text of radio address

by Hans Fritzsche, July 31, 1943, RMfVP, T-70, Roll 123, 3651566, NA, and VI Nr. 181-3, July 27–29, 1943, SO, ZSg 109/43, BA.

35. For complete coverage on public opinion during this period, see SD reports, August 2, 16, 1943, R58/187, BA.

36. *Ibid.*

37. *Ibid.*

38. Deakin, *The Brutal Friendship*, pp. 528–30.

39. Lochner, *The Goebbels Diaries*, p. 427.

40. VB-MA, September 9–11, 1943, pp. 1–2. VI 220–21, September 9–10, 1943, SO, ZSg 109/44, BA. Reichspropagandaleitung, Chef des Propagandastabes, Redner-Schnellbrief Nr. 1, September 10, 1943, NSDAP, T-81, Roll 41, 38953, NA.

41. Goebbels, diary entry, September 10, 1943, in Lochner, *The Goebbels Diaries*, pp. 440–41.

42. Hitler, recorded radio address from the Führer headquarters, September 10, 1943, in Domarus, *Hitler*, II, 2035–2039; VI Nr. 222/43, September 11, 1943, SO, ZSg 109/44, BA.

43. Hitler especially wanted the English to be impressed by this expression of his loyalty, and he told his servant Linge that "it will show the English that I never leave a friend in the lurch, that I am a man of honor. I keep my word. England will say 'He is a true friend.'" Domarus, *Hitler*, II, 2040.

44. Goebbels, diary entry, September 15, 1943, in Lochner, *The Goebbels Diaries*, p. 452. Compare Fritzsche's radio address of September 18, 1943, RMfVP, T-70, Roll 123, 361590, NA. Following the rescue the chief of the unit guarding Mussolini ran up to Skorzeny with a glass of red wine and offered the greeting, "To the victor!" This anecdote cited by Skorzeny reflects the kind of resistance the Germans met atop the Gran Sasso. SS Kriegsberichter Robert Krötz, "Gespräch mit dem Duce Befreier," VB-MA, September 17, 1943, p. 3.

45. Goebbels, "Das Schulbeispiel," *Das Reich*, September 19, 1943. Ursula von Kardorff of the *Deutsche Allgemeine Zeitung* has written that the press directives from the Propaganda Ministry were characterized by a desperation which could not be concealed. Ursula von Kardorff, *Berliner Aufzeichnungen* (Munich: Biederstein Verlag, 1962), p. 59.

46. Hitler address, November 8, 1943, Löwenbräukeller, Munich, in Domarus, *Hitler*, II, 2052.

47. See SD reports of September–October 1943, R58-188-91, BA.

48. Bormann, Rundschreiben Nr. 152/43, October 15, 1943, "Behandlung der bündnistreuen italienischen Soldaten," CGD, T-580, Roll 16, NA.

49. Bormann, Bekanntgabe 69/44, March 23, 1944, "Italien: Verbot der Kritik am Faschismus," CGD, T-580, Roll 16, NA.

50. Bormann, Bekanntgabe 203/44, August 26, 1944, "Behandlung der in das zivile Arbeitsverhältnis überführten italienischen Militärinternierten," CGD, T-580, Reel 17, NA.

Chapter XIV. The Long Retreat, 1943–1944

1. The High Command communiqués reported on "Operation Citadel" as if it were a Soviet offensive. See the OKW communiqués of July 14–20, 1943. For a sample of news in this theater see VB-B, July 9, 1943, which was headlined "Hohe Sowjetverluste bei schweren Panzerschlachten."

2. OKW communiqué, September 25, 1943, Berndt and von Wedel, *Deutschland im Kampf*, XCVII/C (September–October 1943), 71–72.

3. "Krieg ohne Sondermeldung: Überdimensionale Schlacht im Osten," *Das Reich*, January 23, 1944, p. 5.

4. Fritzsche, radio address, August 7, 1943, Reel 5, HL.

5. Fritzsche, radio addresses, August 21, 28, 1943, CGD, Reel 5, HL. See as well the instructions to the periodical press, ZD, August 13, 1943.

6. Berger, chief, Reichssicherheitshauptamt, to Himmler, July 30, 1943, SS, T-175, Roll 124, 2599100, NA.

7. For a comprehensive account of Goebbels's public references to the miracle weapons, see Bramsted, *Goebbels and National Socialist Propaganda*, pp. 316–25.

8. Schaumburg-Lippe, *Dr. G.*, p. 223.

9. Wehrmachtpropaganda, Vortragsnotiz 75/42, November 11, 1942, "Rüstungspropaganda," cites Speer requesting Goebbels to begin a propaganda campaign on the German weapons, OKW/WPr, T-77, Roll 1006, 2470161, NA; see also Schwarz van Berk to Lt. Krause, OKW/WPr, October 26, 1942, citing Goebbels's wish for "eine lebhafte Propaganda Aktion über neue Waffen und Waffenwirkungen um der amerikanischen Rüstungspropaganda entgegenzutreten," OKW/WPr, T-77, Roll 1006, 2470169, NA.

10. Naumann, interview, August 6, 1970. According to Naumann, "Ich was dabei, als in Peenemünde Herrn Goebbels der Start einer Braun'schen Rakete vorgeführt wurde. Wir standen wenige Meter vor dieser Waffe und sahen, wie sich die später berühmte VI oder V2 ganz langsam erhob . . . rauf in den Himmel stieg und in Richtung Ostsee verschwand. Das war für mich und uns Beteiligte ein ganz tiefer Eindruck . . . Diese Vorführung fand im Frühjahr 1943 statt." See also Gregor Janssen, *Das Ministerium Speer* (Berlin: Ullstein, 1968), pp. 189–207.

11. Schwarz van Berk, interview, July 28, 1970.

12. "Reichsminister Speer und Dr. Goebbels im Berliner Sportpalast, 5. Juni 1943; Kundgebung der NSDAP anlässlich der Verleihung von Ritterkreuzen des Kriegsverdienstkreuzes" in Joseph Goebbels, *Goebbels Reden*, 2 vols., ed. Helmut Heiber, vol. II: *1939–1945* (Düsseldorf: Droste Verlag, 1972), pp. 225–28.

13. *Ibid.*, p. 228.

14. SD report, "Meldungen aus dem Reich," June 10, 1943, SS, T-175, Roll 265, 2759632, NA.

15. *Ibid.*, July 1, 1943, SS, T-175, Roll 265, 2759632, NA.

16. "Tätigkeitsbericht," RMfVP, September 25, 1944, CGD, Reel 4, HL.

17. The article in question was entitled "Die ungeahnten Folgen," *Das Reich*, December 5, 1943, p. 3. The other material is based on Schwarz van Berk, interview, July 28, 1970.

18. Speer, *Erinnerungen*, pp. 418–19, 579; compare Schwarz van Berk, interview, July 28, 1970.

19. Speer, *Erinnerungen*, p. 418.

20. SD report, "Meldungen aus dem Reich," November 4, 1943, SS, T-175, Roll 266, 2760825, NA.

21. *Ibid.*, May 28, 1943, SS, T-175, Roll 265, 2759542, NA.

22. *Ibid.*

23. Goebbels, "Die 30 Kriegsartikel für das deutsche Volk," *Das Reich*, September 26, 1943.

24. *Ibid.*

25. Hitler address, Munich, November 9, 1943, VB-ND, November 10, 1943, pp. 1–4.

26. Kaltenbrunner, chief of the Security Police and the SD, Directive IV-Nr. 3080/43, December 22, 1943, "Unterstützung politischer Leiter durch Polizeikräfte beim Einschreiten gegen Meckerer und Unruhestifter," sent to all "Staatspolizei-leitstellen" by way of information to "Die Inspekteure der Sicherheitspolizei und des SD," and all "SD-Leit-Abschnitte." CGD, T-580, Roll 644, Folder 393, NA.

27. *Ibid.* On the subject of Party leadership and responsibility in wartime, see the following documents, all from the chief of the Party Chancellery Martin Bormann

at the Führer headquarters: A.55/43, August 29, 1943, "Generalmitgliederappelle zum verstärkten Führungseinsatz der gesamten Parteigenossenschaft"; A.56/43, August 30, 1943, "Aktivierung der Parteimitglieder—Durchführung von Propagandamärschen"; V.I. 25/305, May 21, 1943, "Merksätze der NSDAP für den Parteigenossen im Kriege"; VI 31/400, June 23, 1943, "Sprechabende—Hausbesuche, Mundpropaganda." All the latter documents are to be found in NSDAP, Parteikanzlei, *Verfügungen/Anordnungen/Bekanntgaben,* IV, 8–12, 17–18, 28–29.

28. *Rede des Reichsministers Dr. Goebbels auf der Reichs-und Gauleiter Tagung in München, February 23, 1944* (Munich: Franz Eher, 1944).

29. Berndt and von Wedel, *Deutschland im Kampf,* CXIII/XVI (May–June 1944), 15.

30. VI, Tagesparole des Reichspressechefs, May 13, 1944, HL.

31. Murawski, *Deutsche Wehrmachtbericht,* pp. 178–79.

32. Goebbels, *Das Reich,* January 23, 1944.

33. SD report, "Meldungen aus dem Reich," May 18, 1944, SS, T-175, Roll 266, 2762030, NA. The SD report of May 25, 1944, noted that there was widespread disappointment and concern that the battle had not been joined. SS, T-175, Roll 266, 2762052, NA.

34. Von Oven, diary entry, May 13, 1944, *Mit Goebbels,* I, 260.

35. SD report, "Meldungen aus dem Reich," June 8, 1944, SS, T-175, Roll 266, 2762085, NA.

36. VB-B, June 7, 1944, p. 1.

37. RMfVP, Propagandaparole Nr. 66, June 6, 1944, Reel 4, HL.

38. Goebbels, "Solange wir atmen," *Das Reich,* June 25, 1944.

39. VB-ND, June 7, 1944, p. 1. For more on the Hitler cult of this period, see VI, April 17, 1944, "Tagesparole des Reichspressechefs," HL; Goebbels's directive, "Der Reichspropagandaleiter an alle Gauleiter, Geburtstag des Führers 1944, Meldung Nr. 307, Reichspropagandaleitung," Berlin, March 17, 1944 (sic), MGRC, T-84, Roll 164, 1531095, NA; compare DAZ, April 30, 1944, headlined "Mit dem Führer zum Sieg," p. 1.

40. Berndt and von Wedel, *Deutschland im Kampf,* CXIII/VI (May–June 1944), 109–10.

41. VI, "Tagesparole des Reichspressechefs," "Nachkonferenz," June 26, 1944, HL.

42. SD report, "Meldungen aus dem Reich," January 27, 1944, SS, T-175, Roll 266, 2761523, NA.

43. RMfVP, Hinkel, "Dem Herrn Reichsminister über den Herrn Staatssekretär," Berlin, January 10, 1944. In this document Hinkel asked Goebbels to get the Ministry in contact with the OKW so that the same ground rules for home broadcasting would be put into effect by the stations under the Wehrmacht's control. CGD, T-580, Roll 682, Folder 562, NA.

44. SD report, "Meldungen aus dem Reich," April 20, 1944, SS, T-175, Roll 266, 2761969, NA.

45. *Ibid.,* April 6, 1944, SS, T-175, Roll 266, 2761879, NA. See this issue for a complete report on opinion about various questions concerning the eastern front, e.g., on the loss of the Balkans with its rich oil-producing areas, or the implications of the Crimean debacle.

46. RMfVP, "Tätigkeitsbericht," July 17, 1944, RMfVP, Reel 2, HL. For a full report on public opinion about various phases of the air war, see SD report, "Meldungen aus dem Reich," May 4, 1944, SS, T-175, Roll 266, 2762005, NA.

47. See the article "Warum Stalin die Komintern ausschaltete," VB-B, July 5, 1943, p. 1. For a press directive on the question consult DW, May 28, 1943.

48. Von Oven, diary entry, November 25, 1943, *Mit Goebbels,* I, 155.

49. Goebbels, "Die Zwangsläufigen Schlüsse," *Das Reich,* November 14, 1943.

50. Goebbels, "In der Bereitschaft," *Das Reich,* March 12, 1944.

51. Goebbels, "Der Krieg in der Sackgasse," *Das Reich*, June 9, 1944.
52. Goebbels, "Die Stunde der höchsten Bewährung," *Das Reich*, January 30, 1944.
53. DAZ, October 4, 1944, p. 1. See also "Zankapfel Warschau," DAZ, August 30, 1944, p. 1.
54. William Hardy McNeill, *America, Britain, and Russia: Their Cooperation and Conflict 1941–1946 (Survey of International Affairs*, Arnold Toynbee, ed., London: Oxford University Press, 1953), pp. 430–33. Herbert Feis, *Churchill-Roosevelt-Stalin* (Princeton, N.J.: Princeton University Press, 1957), pp. 378–90.
55. "Mundparole Nr. 29," September 7, 1944, "Wer Deutschland untreu wird, verfällt dem Bolschewismus," Reel 2, HL. See also Goebbels's *Reich* article of November 9, 1944, entitled "Lautlose Methode des Kreml," in which he spoke of the Kremlin's Trojan horse methods of infiltration.

Chapter XV. The Twentieth of July and Beyond

1. Munich: Piper & Co., 1969, pp. 466–571.
2. Naumann has remarked that the goals he and Goebbels were working toward were immensely furthered by the popular reaction to the attempted assassination. See Naumann, interview, August 6, 1970.
3. Von Oven, diary entry, July 23, 1944, *Mit Goebbels*, II, 59–60.
4. *Ibid.*, p. 60. There is a discrepancy in the sources on the reason for the delay in broadcasting. Naumann contends that it was due to technical difficulties in the Führer headquarters. Naumann, interview, August 6, 1970.
5. Von Oven, diary entry, July 23, 1944, *Mit Goebbels*, II, 75–76. See also Constantine Fitzgibbon, *20 July* (New York: William Norton, 1956), p. 206, and Bramsted, *Goebbels and National Socialist Propaganda*, pp. 335–57.
6. Bormann to the gauleiters, "Fernschreiben Nr. 4," Führer headquarters, July 20, 1944, CGD, T-580, Roll 22, 44545B, NA.
7. Bormann to the gauleiters, "Rundschreiben Nr. 4," Führer headquarters, July 20, 1944, MGRC, T-84, Roll 21, NA.
8. For an excellent account of the events of July 20 and the Seydlitz group, see Bodo Scheurig, *Freies Deutschland* (Munich: Nymphenburger, 1960), pp. 137–56.
9. Hitler, radio address from the Führer headquarters, DNB, July 21, 1944, MGRC, T-84, Roll 165, 1532547, NA.
10. Göring and Dönitz, addresses from the Führer headquarters, DNB, July 21, 1944, MGRC, T-84, Roll 165, 1532550, NA.
11. Bormann, "Rundschreiben Nr. 6," July 21, 1944, MGRC, T-84, Roll 21, NA.
12. VB-B, July 24, 1944, p. 1. For the handling of the events of July 20 in the Wehrmacht, see "Rücksichtslose Säuberung des Heeres," a report from the Führer headquarters announcing that Hitler had accepted the Army's demand that he establish a special Honorary Tribunal of senior officers to purge the nest of traitors from their ranks and thereby restore the Army's honor. "The Führer has responded to this wish," the report stated, and had appointed Keitel, von Rundstedt, Guderian, Schrot, Specht, Kriebel, and Kirchhain to the tribunal, MGRC, T-84, Roll 165, 1532514, NA. See Guderian's tract "Führer befiehl, wir folgen!" which was distributed at the front to counter enemy leaflets on the 20th July. MGRC, T-84, Roll 165, 1532496, NA.
13. VB-B, July 24, 1944, p. 1. See Bormann's communication to the Reichsleiters and gauleiters on this matter, July 23, 1944, MGRC, T-84, Roll 21, NA.
14. VB-B, July 22, 1944, p. 1.
15. DAZ, July 22, 1944, p. 1.
16. VI, "Aus der Nachkonferenz, July 21, 1944"; "Tagesparole vom 22. Juli 1944"; "Informationen der PK vom 23. Juli 1944," HL.
17. SD report, July 21, 1944, "Erste stimmungsmässige Auswirkungen des Anschlags

auf den Führer," "SS Obergruppenführer, Chef der Sicherheitspolizei Kaltenbrunner to Reichsleiter Bormann," MGRC, T-84, Roll 19, Folder 20, NA.

18. SD subsection report, Lüneburg to SD Leitabschnitt Hamburg, July 23, 1944, CGD, T-580, Roll 22, 44566, NA.

19. Frauenfeld, RPA Vienna to Wächter, RMfVP, July 25, 1944, "Treuekundgebung für den Führer," CGD, T-580, Roll 675, Folder 528, NA; Kaufmann, RPA Lower Danube to PM/RPL, Krämer, July 22, 1944, ibid.; RPA Graz to PM Abteilung Pro, July 22, 1944, ibid.; Wimmer, gau propaganda chief, Weimar, to Naumann, RMfVP, July 21, 1944, ibid.; Kassel, "KSL an PM Abt Pro," July 21, 1944, ibid.; "Gauleiter, Gau Süd-Hannover-Braunschweig," to Goebbels, July 22, 1944, ibid.; Müller, Stuttgart, to PM Abt Pro, July 22, 1944, ibid.; Schulz, RPA Nieder-Schlesien, Breslau, to Goebbels, July 24, 1944, ibid.; Weinheimer, Frankfurt, to Sondermann, RMfVP, August 8, 1944, ibid.

20. Meyer-Hertmann, RPA Münster, to Sondermann, RMfVP, August 8, 1944, CGD, T-580, Roll 675, Folder 528, NA.

21. CGD, T-580, Roll 675, Folder 523, NA.

22. Naumann, RMfVP, to all gauleiters, chiefs of the Reich propaganda offices, and gau propaganda chiefs, "Rundspruch Nummer 195," "Treuekundgebungen anlässlich des misslungenen Attentats auf den Führer," July 23, 1944, CGD, T-580, Roll 675, Folder 528, NA. To exert pressure on his subordinates, Naumann requested that press reports and photographs of the most impressive meetings were to be rushed to the Propaganda Section of the Ministry.

23. Wächter, RMfVP, "Fernschreiben an alle Gaupropagandaleiter," "Durchführung der Treue-Kundgebungen für den Führer," July 23, 1944, CGD, T-580, Roll 675, Folder 528, NA.

24. Ibid.

25. Schulz, RPA Lower Silesia, to Goebbels, July 24, 1944, CGD, T-580, Roll 675, Folder 528, NA.

26. Naumann, interview, August 6, 1970.

27. Dr. Ley, "Treuebekenntnis der Werktätigen," Berlin, July 22, 1944, VB-B, July 23, 1944, pp. 1–2.

28. Bormann, Führer headquarters, July 24, "Fernschreiben," to all Reichsleiters, gauleiters, and unit chiefs, "Behandlung der Ereignisse des 20.7.1944 in der Öffentlichkeit," MGRC, T-84, Roll 21, NA. Goebbels himself was guilty of implicating the aristocracy. In the course of a radio address delivered on the evening of July 26, he said that upon hearing the news on July 20, he immediately knew that one of the laborers who had worked in the conference room could not be involved: "What interest would a worker . . . have to raise his hand against the Führer, the hope of our nation . . . This sneaky attack could only have been committed by a totally evil and depraved person, and I knew in what circles to find him." Goebbels, radio address, evening of July 26, 1944, Goebbels Reden, II, 343–44. Himmler's address to the gauleiters' meeting at Poznan on August 3, 1944, violated Hitler's order that the officer corps was not to be attacked. He called the whole General Staff reactionary, defeatist, and unheroic. The army could not compare to the SS. He went so far as to charge that there were cases in which army officers had deliberately caused great losses to Waffen SS units. The 20th July was just an "outward expression of a situation which has been developing for a long time," he asserted. Vierteljahrshefte für Zeitgeschichte, I (October 1953), 357–94. Also see Himmler's address delivered at Bitsch on July 26, 1944, Die Lage, "Zentralinformationsdienst der Reichspropagandaleitung der NSDAP and RMfVP," Special Edition, July 27, 1944. Compare Himmler's "Tagesbefehl des Reichsführers SS an das Heimatheer," August 1, 1944, DAZ, August 3, 1944, p. 1.

29. VB-B, July 27, 1944, pp. 1–2.

30. Ibid. Goebbels was prepared to die defending himself barricaded in his office.

NOTES 303

Late on the night of July 20, after Himmler and the other investigators and well-wishers had left the Propaganda Ministry, Goebbels told Naumann that "aber das können Sie mir glauben, verhaftet hätte mich niemand. Hier mit dieser Pistole hätte ich jeden, der versucht hätte, mich zu verhaften, zunächst einmal über den Haufen geschossen." Naumann, interview, August 6, 1970.

31. See Goebbels's articles treating the events of July 20: "Der Befehl der Pflicht," *Das Reich*, August 6, 1944; "In den Stürmen der Zeit," *Das Reich*, August 20, 1944.

32. "Tagesparolen des Reichspressechefs," July 31, 1944, HL.

33. DAZ, August 3, 1944, p. 1.

34. Tagesparole des Reichspressechefs," August 5, 1944, HL.

35. *Ibid.*, August 8, 1944, HL.

36. VB-ND, August 10, 1944, pp. 1–3.

37. According to Naumann, Goebbels kept few secrets from Rommel. The field marshal in turn aired his disappointments about Hitler to the minister. Shortly before his death he complained to Goebbels that Hitler provided for a dual command in France between himself and von Rundstedt. Rommel was adamant on the point that a single man should have been given full command power. See Naumann, interviews, July 11 and August 6, 1970.

38. Hitler, "Verfügung 10/44," July 20, 1944, CGD, T-580, Roll 18, Folder 182, NA.

39. Hitler, "Erlass des Führers über den totalen Kriegseinsatz vom. 25. Juli 1944," CGD, T-580, Roll 17, Ordner 179, NA.

40. Von Oven, diary entry, July 25, 1944, *Mit Goebbels*, II, 94–96.

41. "Informationen aus der PK," August 24, 1944, "Inform. Nr. 395," HL; "Die Parole der Woche," ZD, August 25, 1944.

42. Feis, *Churchill-Roosevelt-Stalin*, p. 370.

43. Armstrong, *Unconditional Surrender*, pp. 69–77; DAZ, September 26, 1944, p. 1; for documentation on the Propaganda Ministry's foreign campaign against bolshevism see Dr. Kurtz, RMfVP, to Verhouz, Propaganda Section Lemberg, in which he reported on details for handling a special campaign which Goebbels ordered so that "the terror of the Bolsheviks in the regions which they are occupying can be exposed to the European public." Berlin, April 26, 1944, CGD, T-580, Roll 648, Folder 411, NA; Taubert to Naumann, RMfVP, on long-range strategy in the anti-Bolshevik campaign, April 3, 1944, CGD, T-580, Roll 841, Folder 9, NA; Laber, RMfVP, to Taubert, June 20, 1944, concerns von Oven's discussion with Geobbels on this campaign, CGD, T-580, Roll 648, Folder 411, NA; Kurtz to Taubert, June 14, 1944, deals with problems involved in the campaign in Latvia and shows how facts and figures were juggled by certain overzealous Nazi propagandists and Kurtz's complaints about this, CGD, T-580, Roll 648, Folder 411, NA; "Protokol über die Besprechung Sonderaktion 'Wiederbesetzte Gebiete' am 22.5.1944," CGD, T-580, Roll 648, Folder 411, NA.

44. Goebbels, radio address, October 27, 1944, DAZ, October 28, 1944, pp. 1–2.

45. Goebbels, "Für unsere Kinder," *Das Reich*, October 22, 1944.

46. Hitler, directive announcing the formation of the *Volkssturm*, DAZ, October 19, 1944, p. 1.

47. Himmler address, October 18, 1944, DAZ, October 19, 1944, pp. 1–2. See also DAZ, October 20, 22, 24, 1944, p. 1.

48. VB-B, November 15, 1944, p. 1; "Communications on the Eastern Policy of the Reich Ministry for the Occupied Eastern Territories," December 11, 1944, RMfdbO, T-454, Roll 17, 000632, NA.

49. VB-ND, November 16, 1944, p. 1. In his famous Poznan address on October 4, 1943, Himmler had declared that men like Vlasov come cheap just as long as you keep them supplied with money, whisky, cigarettes, and women. Himmler felt that there was danger in the Vlasov movement: "At that moment in which we say

to our own infantry that we cannot conquer the Russians and that the Russian can be defeated only by Russians, at that moment we begin to destroy ourselves . . . For that reason it [the Vlasov movement] must be destroyed. The Führer has strictly forbidden it." SS, T-175, Roll 85, 2610152, NA. For directives to the press on handling the Vlasov material, see the records of the press conference of November 22, 1944, RMfdbO, T-454, Roll 102, NA. For material on Vlasov directed to the Wehrmacht, see MGRC, T-84, Roll 160, 1527237, NA.

50. VB-ND, December 9, 1944, pp. 1–2.

51. Bormann to gauleiters, Reichsleiters, kreisleiters, unit chiefs, "Unterstützung Politischer Leiter durch Polizeikräfte beim Einschreiten gegen Meckerer und Unruhestifter sowie ehrenamtliche Tätigkeit von Parteigenossen in der Sicherheitspolizei," October 10, 1944, CGD, T-580, Roll 17, Folder 180, NA. For reports on morale, consult Tätigkeitsbericht, RMfVP, September 18, 1944, T-580, Roll 682, Folder 563, NA; ibid., October 3, October 9, October 16, November 14, 1944, Reels 3 and 4, HL; SD report, "Meldungen aus dem Reich," November 20, 1944, SS, T-175, Roll 267, 2762267, NA.

Chapter XVI. The Twilight of the Gods

1. Goebbels, "Der Führer," Das Reich, December 31, 1944. For Nazi reports on the reaction to the Hitler and Goebbels appeals see CGD, T-580, Roll 672, NA.

2. General Dietl had perished in an airplane accident in June 1944. Nevertheless, this quotation was referred to on more than one occasion during the last months of the Third Reich. "Mitteilungen für die Truppe," December 1944, MGRC, T-84, Roll 160, 1527669, NA.

3. Von Tippelskirch, Geschichte des zweiten Weltkrieges, p. 547.

4. For representative guidelines to the propagandists for this period see VI, January 17, 22, and February 1, 1945, ZSg 109/56, SO, BA. The article "Countermeasures" appeared in the Deutsche Allgemeine Zeitung on January 21, 1945. See as well war correspondent Günter Heysing, "The Meaning of the Eastern Campaign," VB-ND, February 15, 1945, p. 1. Compare similar propaganda distributed to the troops, such as the flyer "How Much Longer Can the Soviets Advance?" charging that the enemy was moving forward with only a few tanks and trucks to carry infantry. CGD, T-580, Roll 675, Folder 530, NA.

5. VB-ND, February 11, 1945, p. 1.

6. Ibid.

7. For example, Reichspropagandaamt Lüneburg reported to Schäffer of the RMfVP on February 19, 1945, that "an extremely strong opposition has arisen regarding the enrollment in the Volkssturm-Batl." CGD, T-580, Roll 656, Folder 448, NA.

8. Von Oven, diary entry, January 23, 1945, Mit Goebbels, II, 216.

9. VI, January 1, 1945, ZSg 109, SO, BA. SS War Correspondent Eschenhagen, "Thus Fought Upper Silesia's Volkssturm," VB-ND, January 25, 1945, p. 1. The Germans tired of the propaganda involving the Volkssturm in which such clichés as "every single Volkssturm man had the fighting power of a company" were poorly received. Morale Report, "Sondereinsatz Berlin," February 14, 1945, OKW/WPr, T-77, Roll 1037, 6509332, NA.

10. "20 bewährte Hitlerjungen beim Führer," VB-ND, March 21, 1945, p. 1. Compare "Die jungen Soldaten," VB-ND, March 10, 1945, p. 1.

11. RMfVP, "Tätigkeitsbericht," February 21, 1945, CGD, T-580, Roll 682, NA. Compare the Activity Report of March 22, 1945, from Hamburg regarding morale in that city. In generalizing on the morale there, the propagandists of the Whisper Propaganda Campaign (Mundpropaganda Aktion) characterized it as "continuing to fall, fatalistic, 'it doesn't matter what comes, only put an end to it.'" OKW/WPr, T-77, Roll 1037, 6509579, NA.

12. The quotation is taken from information gathered through SD channels, March 28, 1945, CGD, T-580, Roll 660, NA. See also the Activity Report of January 24, 1945, addressed to Goebbels, CGD, T-580, Roll 682, NA.

13. Goebbels, "Der Reichspropagandaleiter der NSDAP an alle Gaupropagandaleiter," February 5, 1945, NSDAP, T-81, Roll 23, 20755, NA.

14. *Ibid.* For an example of the response to Goebbels's appeal, see the document "Bericht über die Versammlungswelle des Gaues Westmark im Februar 1945," submitted to the Propaganda Ministry by the chief of the "Active Propaganda Section" in the Gau Propaganda Office Westmark. It was stated in the report that during the month of February 1945, 135 public propaganda meetings were held which were attended by 70,000 to 80,000 people. CGD, T-580, Roll 683, Folder 563, NA.

15. Bormann, Rundschreiben 131-45, "Aktivierung der Aufklärungsarbeit," March 3, 1945, CGD, T-580, Roll 18, Folder 180, Na.

16. A typical example of this chaos was the plea sent to the Party chancellery in Berlin for delivery to the Propaganda Ministry, from Diewerge, the chief of the Reich Propaganda Office Danzig-West Prussia: "Wireless message of 2.5.45 . . . Since 2.3.45 without any connection and information. Urgently request call RPA Danzig. Confirmation requested. Request further sending material via courier." CGD, T-580, Roll 682, NA.

17. RMfVP, "Tätigkeitsbericht," October 24, 1944, CGD, T-580, Roll 682, Folder 563, NA. Goebbels's order to increase the whisper-propaganda effort included the request that the propaganda offices ascertain what rumors were current and to take immediate steps to counter them. RMfVP, "Rundspruch Nr. 205," October 24, 1944, CGD, T-580, Roll 657, Folder 450, NA. Consult the "Vortragsnotiz für Chef WFSt," Berlin, February 22, 1945, OKW/WPr, T-77, Roll 1037, 6509327, NA.

18. Wächter, chief of the Propaganda Staff, RMfVP, "Rundschreiben an alle Gaupropagandaleiter," December 17, 1944, CGD, T-580, Roll 672, Folder 516, NA.

19. "Wehrmachtfürung Stab/AgWPr/W" to Army District Command X and XI, February 19, 1945, OKW/WPr, T-77, Roll 1037, 6509329, NA. "Durchführung der Mundpropaganda-Aktion," "Befehl Chef AgWPr vom 27.3. 1945," OKW/WPr, T-77, Roll 1037, 6509311, NA.

20. OKW/WPr, to the several participating military districts, March 20, 1945, OKW/WPr, T-77, Roll 1037, 6509320, NA. A great number of the "Reports on the Special Deployment Berlin" have survived, and they provide a comprehensive coverage on morale in the capital during this period. OKW/WPr, T-77, Roll 1037, 6509356, NA.

21. VI, February 2–16, 1945, ZSg 109/56, SO, BA.

22. Goebbels, "Das Jahr 2000," *Das Reich*, February 25, 1945.

23. *Ibid.* See as well Goebbels's lead article in *Das Reich* of January 21, 1945, entitled "The Jews."

24. DAZ, February 15, 1945, p. 1. For an example of the propaganda directed to the troops concerning the meaning of Yalta, see "Das Todesurteil von Jalta," "Arbeitsunterlage für den Nationalsozialistischen Führungs-Offizier und Kompanieführer," March 12, 1945, MGRC, T-84, Roll 159, 1526101, NA.

25. RMfVP, "Chef des Propagandastabes," "Mundpropaganda-parole Nr. 21," March 27, 1945, CGD, T-580, Roll 672, Folder 516, NA.

26. "Address of the Führer on the 25th Anniversary of the Announcement of the Party Program," delivered by Hermann Esser in Munich, February 24, 1945, VB-ND, February 27, 1945, p. 1. The *Völkischer Beobachter* (ND) featured the following headline on March 8, 1945: "Murder, Plunder, Desecrate, Burn; Soviet Army Commanders Gave This Order to Their Hordes!"

27. VB-ND, March 8, 1945, p. 1.

28. See the text of a radio address on Russian atrocities delivered by Major-General Remer on March 6, 1945. OKW/WPr, T-77, Roll 1039, 6512709, NA.

29. RMfVP, chief of the Propaganda Staff, "Material für Propagandisten Nr. 25; Bolschewistische Greuel," January 16, 1945, CGD, T-580, Roll 673, Folder 516, NA. See also VI, March 7–8, 1945, ZSg 109/56, SO, BA.

30. Stellv. Generalkommando XAK, Gruppe Nationalsozialistische Führung, Hamburg, "Sprachregelung," March 16, 1945, OKW/WPr, T-77, Roll 1039, 6512684, NA. Compare "Greuel Aufklärung, NS Führung, Generalkommando LXXXII A. K., March 3, 1945, MGRC, T-84, Roll 159, 1525945, NA.

31. For an example of this see Bormann to the gauleiters, "Rundschreiben 131/45," "Aktivierung der Aufklärungsarbeit," March 8, 1945, CGD, T-580, Roll 18, Folder 180, NA.

32. Das Schwarze Korps, February 15, 1945, pp. 1–2.

33. Naumann, address before the "Reichsring für nationalsozialistische Volksaufklärung und Propaganda," February 20, 1945, MGRC, T-84, Roll 160, 1527251, NA. The idea that the Allies were preparing to "biologically exterminate" the German people once they had won the war appeared so preposterous that I queried each official of the Propaganda Ministry whom I interviewed whether he really believed the charge. Helmut Sündermann was offended that an interviewer could be so naïve as to conceive of this being merely tactical propaganda. He referred to the exportation of German labor to the Soviet Union after the fall of Hitler as "biological extermination." Naumann asserts that Roosevelt and Morgenthau harbored sinister plans for occupied Germany, a fear which most Nazis held. Sündermann, interview, November 16, 1969. Naumann, interview, August 6, 1970.

34. Goebbels, radio address, "Zur Lage," February 28, 1945, VB-ND, March 1, 1945, pp. 1–2.

35. VI, January 11, 1945, ZSg 109/56, SO, BA.

36. For example see the "25. Bericht über den 'Sondereinstaz Berlin' für die Zeit vom 30.3.–7.4. 1945," OKW/WPr, T-77, Roll 1037, 6509356, NA.

37. Gauleiter Eggeling to Bormann, "Beleg Nr. 5," February 10, 1945, CGD, T-580, Roll 660, Folder 461, NA.

38. Goebbels, radio address, "Zur Lage," February 28, 1945, VB-ND, March 1, 1945, pp. 1–2.

39. Ibid., pp. 1–2.

40. Von Oven, diary entry, March 3, 1945, Mit Goebbels, II, 261–62.

41. "Bericht über den Sondereinsatz Berlin für 28.2–6.3. 1945," OKW/WPr, T-77, Roll 1037, 6509397, NA. "Old Fritz" continued to be a favorite of Goebbels, and he referred to him often in both his speeches and articles. See Goebbels, "Die Lehre der Beharrlichkeit," Das Reich, March 18, 1945. Frederick the Great was often referred to in Wehrmacht propaganda as well. One flyer featured a picture of the king with the caption "The Spirit of Resistance Then Was Frederick the Great." MGRC, T-84, Roll 160, 1527619, NA.

42. OKW communiqués, March 29, 30, 31, 1945.

43. See the article headlined "Der Geist von Königsberg; Festung der Waffen und Herzen; Ein Beispiel für das ganze Volk," VB-ND, March 2, 1945, p. 1.

44. Von Tippelskirch, Geschichte des zweiten Weltkrieges, pp. 550–51.

45. OKW communiqué, April 12, 1945. To be sure, Hitler had long before outlined what he expected of the commandants and the men defending German fortresses. In an order dated October 1944, he declared that their honor as soldiers depended on their offering resistance to the death, and under no circumstances were soldiers to enter into a "cowardly and ignominious capitulation." The Führer, the Führer's headquarters, October 1944 (sic) OKW/WRSt/Qu2, Nr. 0012743/44, OKW/WPr, T-77, Roll 782, 5508769, NA. In yet another Hitler directive dated November 28, 1944, the commander in chief ordered that should a troop commander be ready to give up the fight, he was to pass the command on to someone who would continue the struggle, no matter what his rank. OKW/WPr, T-77, Roll 782, 5508812, NA.

46. DAZ, March 6, 1945, p. 1, headlined "Gelöbnis der Schlesischen Hauptstadt; Gauleiter Hanke über den unerschütterlichen Kampfwillen der Verteidiger"; DAZ, April 12, 1945, p. 1; VB-ND, April 13, 1945, p. 1.

47. DAZ, January 31, 1945, p. 1.

48. See the Bormann order of February 2, 1945, "Anordnung Nr. 79/45g," which dealt with the drumhead courts-martial. Included in the directive was a copy of Reich Minister of Justice Thierack's order regarding the composition and jurisdiction of the courts: "The courts-martial have competence for all criminal offenses which endanger the German fighting power or determination to fight." The only sentences were release, death, or referral to another court. CGD, T-580, Roll 18, Folder 180, NA.

49. VB-ND, April 3–4, 1945, p. 1; Hans Fritzsche testified at Nuremberg that Goebbels personally dispatched the Werewolf appeals to the broadcasting stations. See testimony of November 3, 1945, International Military Tribunal, *Nazi Conspiracy and Aggression, Opinion and Judgment* (Washington, D.C.: Government Printing Office, 1947), Supplement B, pp. 1512–1513. Many Germans found the Werewolf movement absurd. See the "Special Deployment Berlin" reports for March and April 1945 (that of April 10, 1945, is of special interest), OKW/WPr, Roll 1037, 6509356, NA. Helmut Sündermann contended that the Werewolf propaganda was really for foreign consumption and that as a result he limited domestic coverage of it to an absolute minimum, attesting that he never would have mentioned it at home except that the enemy might thereby become suspicious that it was a hoax. It seemed absurd to Sündermann for the Party to claim that the war would be fought to the bitter end while at the same time it began a propaganda campaign dealing with a postwar guerrilla effort. Sündermann, interview, November 16, 1969.

50. See article "Die Front der Panzerfäuste," DAZ, March 22, 1945.

51. See the "Second Führer Order Concerning Cooperation between the Party and the Armed Forces in an Operations Area within the Reich," September 19, 1944, and the "Second Führer Order Concerning Command Authority in an Operations Area within the Reich," September 20, 1944, OKW/WPr, T-77, Roll 774, 5500444, NA. See also Bormann, "Anordnung 190/44g," "Einsatz der NSDAP zur Durchführung unmittelbarer Reichsverteidigungsaufgaben und sonstiger Grosseinsätze," August 23, 1944, CGD, T-580, Roll 17, Folder 179, NA.

52. Bormann, "Rundschreiben 242/44," August 15, 1944, "Totaler Kriegseinsatz," CGD, T-580, Roll 17, Folder 179, NA. Bormann, Directive, December 12, 1944, "Persönlicher Einsatz der Hoheitsträger," CGD, T-580, Roll 18, Folder 180, NA. Bormann, "Rundschreiben 43/45," January 30, 1945, "Einsatz der Parteiführerschaft," CGD, T-580, Roll 18, Folder 181, NA.

53. Bormann, "Zur 25. Wiederkehr des Jahrestages der Programmverkündung," CGD, T-580, Roll 18, Folder 181, NA.

54. Described in Bormann, "Bekanntgabe 61/45," "Verhalten der Dienststellen bei Feindannäherung," February 8, 1945, CGD, T-580, Roll 18, Folder 180, NA.

55. Bormann, "Anordnung," April 1, 1945, MGRC, T-84, Roll 169, 1536475, NA. Bormann demanded that credit be given to the Party men when it was due them. On April 4, 1945, he wrote a scathing protest to Chief of the Reich Central Security Office Kaltenbrunner concerning the latest SD report, which had been critical of the Party leadership. Bormann held that his Party functionaries were demonstrating bravery down the line, and he cited several cases of misrepresentation in Kaltenbrunner's report. Bormann to SS Obergruppenführer Dr. Kaltenbrunner, April 4, 1945, NSDAP, T-81, Roll 5, 13047, NA.

56. "Der Führer an seine Ostkämpfer," DAZ, April 17, 1945, p. 1. See also VI, April 17, 1945, ZSg 101/42, SB, BA.

57. Semmler, *Goebbels*, p. 190.

58. Goebbels, "Resistance at All Costs," *Das Reich*, April 21, 1945. Goebbels had

been very impressed by captured Russian films covering the defense of Leningrad. Gutterer, interview, August 5, 1970.

59. Goebbels, radio address, April 21, 1945, Records of the Foreign Broadcast Intelligence Service, 1941–1945, Federal Communication Commission, Daily Report (hereinafter cited as FBIS-FCC-DR), April 23, 1945, RG 262, NA.

60. Fritzsche, *Hier spricht Hans Fritzsche*, pp. 27–30.

61. Naumann, interview, August 6, 1970.

62. Görlitz, *Zweite Weltkrieg*, II, 562–64.

63. Report on North German Home Service, April 24, 1945, FBIS-FCC-DR, April 24, 1945, RG 262, NA. According to Naumann, Goebbels was gratified that Hitler had decided to remain in Berlin. Naumann, interview, August 6, 1970.

64. *Der Panzerbär: Kampfblatt für die Verteidiger Gross-Berlins*, April 29, 1945, p. 2.

65. Goebbels address, April 19, 1945, in Semmler, *Goebbels*, pp. 197–98.

66. Report of North German Home Service, April 23, 1945, FBIS-FCC-DR, April 24, 1945, RG 262, NA.

67. *Der Panzerbär*, April 27, 1945, p. 1.

68. Fritzsche, *Hier spricht Hans Fritzsche*, p. 44. See also testimony of Fritzsche, delivered at Nuremberg, June 27, 1946, IMT, XVII, 156.

69. FBIS-FCC-DR, April 19, 1945, RG 262, NA.

70. Front Report, April 23, 1945, FBIS-FCC-DR, April 24, 1945, RG 262, NA.

71. Naumann, interview, August 6, 1970.

72. *Ibid.*

73. FBIS-FCC-DR, May 1, 1945, RG 262, NA.

74. *Ibid.*

75. *Ibid.*, May 3, 1945, RG, 262, NA.

76. *Ibid.*

77. *Ibid.*

78. Görlitz, *Zweite Weltkrieg*, II, 572.

79. FBIS-FCC-DR, May 3, 1945, RG 262, NA.

80. Count Schwerin von Krosigk, radio address, May 2, 1945, FBIS-FCC-DR, May 3, 1945, RG 262, NA.

81. Dönitz, address, May 4, 1945, FBIS-FCC-DR, May 5, 1945, RG 262, NA.

82. Joachim Schultz, *Die Letzten 30 Tage: Aus dem Kriegstagebuch des Oberkommando der Wehrmacht*, ed. Jürgen Thorwald (Stuttgart: Steingruben, 1951), pp. 90–92.

83. OKW communiqué, May 9, 1945.

SELECTED BIBLIOGRAPHY

Selected Bibliography

Personal Interviews

Günter d'Alquen: editor, *Das Schwarze Korps*; commander, SS Kriegsberichterabteilung; SS Standartenführer; attached to Goebbels's office in 1940.

Flugkapitän Hans Baur: Hitler's pilot; lt. general, Waffen SS.

Karl Baur-Callwey: director of Munich publishing house Verlag D. W. Callwey; senator, Reichskulturkammer; SA Obersturmbahnführer.

Hans Schwarz van Berk: editorial staff, *Das Reich*; SS Obersturmführer; attached to SS Regiment "Kurt Eggers," 1945.

Wolfgang Diewerge: director, Radio Section, Propaganda Ministry; director, Radio Danzig; chief of Reich Propaganda Office, Danzig-West Prussia; Oberregierungsrat; SS Standartenführer.

Dr. Heinrich Gerlach: Stalingrad veteran, author of *Die verratene Armee* (Munich: Nymphenburger Verlagshandlung, 1957).

Dr. Leopold Gutterer: state secretary, Propaganda Ministry; SS Brigadeführer.

Karl Hauck: Munich "Old Fighter"; SA Politischer Leiter.

General Adolf Heusinger: chief, Operations Staff, OKH.

Dr. Georg Leibbrandt: state secretary, Reich Ministry for the Occupied Eastern Territories.

Dr. Werner Naumann: chief of the Ministeramt and state secretary, Propaganda Ministry; service in I. SS Panzer Korps and Leibstandarte SS "Adolf Hitler"; SS Brigadeführer; member "Freundenkreis Himmler."

Josef Platzer: personal staff, Rudolf Hess.

Helmut Sündermann: deputy Reich press chief; Reichshauptamtsleiter; writer for *Völkischer Beobachter* and other publications.

Dr. Eberhard Taubert: director, Abteilung Ost und Anti-Bolschewismus, Propaganda Ministry; Oberregierungsrat.

Walther Tiessler: director, Reichsring für nationalsozialistische Propaganda und Volksaufklärung, Reichspropagandaleitung der NSDAP; liaison man, Goebbels to Hess and Bormann.

Documentary Sources

Captured German Documents Deposited at the National Archives, Washington, D.C.

Records of the National Socialist German Workers Party.
Records of Headquarters, Supreme Command of the Armed Forces.
Records of Headquarters, Army High Command.
Records of the Reich Ministry for Public Enlightenment and Propaganda.
Records of the Reich Ministry for the Occupied Eastern Territories.
Records of the Reichsführer SS and Chief of the German Police.

Other Records Deposited in the National Archives

Records of the Berlin Document Center, including incomplete records of the RMfVP, the Reich Culture Chamber, the Bormann Collection, and the NSDAP personnel files.

United States Government, Records of the Foreign Broadcast Intelligence Service, 1941–1945, Federal Communication Commission.

———, Records of the Office of War Information, 1942–1945, Federal Communication Commission.

Records Deposited in the Hoover Library on War and Peace, Stanford, California

"Vertrauliche Informationen für die Hauptschriftleitung," "Tagesparolen des Reichspressechef," RMfVP.

Himmler Files.

Nationalsozialistische Deutsche Arbeiter Partei, Hauptarchiv, German Microfilm Collection.

"Politischer Dienst; Arbeitsmaterial für Presse und Publizistik," RMfVP, Abteilung Deutsche Presse.

Die Lage, Zentralinformationsdienst der Reichspropagandaleitung der NSDAP und des Reichsministeriums für Volksaufklärung und Propaganda.

Aufklärungs-und Redner Informationsmaterial der Reichspropagandaleitung der NSDAP und des Reichspropaganda-Amtes der Deutschen Arkeitsfront.

"Tätigkeitsberichte," RMfVP.

Records Deposited in the Yivo Institute for Jewish Research, New York City

Scattered documents, RMfVP.

Records Deposited at the Bundesarchiv, Koblenz, Germany

Complete collection of the "Nachrichtenblatt" of the RMfVP.

Incomplete records of the Propaganda Section of the RMfVP.

Collection "zur Presse Politik des Dritten Reiches": Brammer Collection—Notes taken at secret press conferences of the Reich government by the Berlin representative of the Pressebüro Dienstag and editor of the *Korrespondenz Brammer*. Oberheitmann Collection—"Tagesparolen des Reichspressechef," "Vertrauliche Informationen," "Sonderinformationen," daily distributed to the editors of German newspapers by the RMfVP. This particular collection was made by the editor in chief of the *Weilburger Tageblatt*, Theodor Oberheitmann. Nadler Collection.

Complete collection, Reports of SD, Reichssicherheitshauptamt.
Hasso von Wedel, *Die Wehrmachtpropaganda 1939–1945*; Dokumentation in Maschinenschrift, vol. I: *Die Abteilung für Wehrmachtpropaganda im Oberkommando der Wehrmacht (OKW/WPr)*, 1957; vol. II: *Die Propagandatruppe*, 1958.

Records Deposited in the Institut für Zeitgeschichte, Munich

The Goebbels Diaries.
Protocol Collection, the Nuremberg Trials.
"Persönliche Dokumente Gen: Ob. v. Fritzsch."
Zeugenschriftum.

Other Documentary Sources

Newspapers, periodicals, Nazi internal organization propaganda

Die Aktion (Kampfblatt für das Neue Europa), Berlin.
Das Archiv, Berlin.
Berliner Börsenzeitung.
Berliner Illustrierte.
Berliner Morgenpost.
Deutsche Allgemeine Zeitung.
Deutsche Post aus dem Osten, Berlin.
Deutschland im Kampf, Berlin, ed. Ministerialdirigent Alfred-Ingemar Berndt (RMfVP) and Generalmajor Hasso von Wedel (OKW/WPr). Berlin: Otto Stollberg, 1939–1944.
Frankfurter Zeitung.
Schulungsdienst der Hitler Jugend, BDM-Werk Glaube und Schönheit.
Die Innere Front, Pressedienst der NSDAP, RMfVP.
Mitteilungen für die Truppe, OKW/WPr.
Münchner Neueste Nachrichten.
Nationalsozialistische Monatshefte, Berlin.
Panzerbär (Kampfblatt für die Verteidiger Gross-Berlins, 1945).
Das Reich, ed. Joseph Goebbels.
Das Schwarze Korps, organ of the SS.
Unser Heer, Oberkommando des Heeres.
Völkischer Beobachter.
Die Wehrmacht, Oberkommando der Wehrmacht.

Tapes and Recordings of Radio Broadcasts, 1939–1945

Library of Congress.
RIAS Berlin.
Hessische Rundfunk, Frankfurt.

Collections of Films, Library of Congress, Bundesarchiv, and Bavaria-Film, Munich

Complete collection of Deutsche Wochenschauen, 1939–1945.
Morgenrot, 1933.
Der ewige Jude, 1940.
Jud Süss, 1940.
Der Feldzug in Polen, 1939.
Sieg im Westen, 1940.

Bismarck, 1940.
Wunschkonzert, 1940.
Feuertaufe, 1940.
Stukas, 1941.
Ich klage an, 1941.
Der grosse König, 1942.
Europa bekämpft dem Bolschewismus, 1942.
Im Walde von Katyn, 1943.
Der Führer schenkt den Juden eine Stadt, 1944.
Kolberg, 1945.

Printed Documentary Sources

Aldag, Peter. *Juden beherrschen England.* Berlin: Nordland, 1939.
Andreas-Friedrich, Ruth. *Berlin Underground, 1939–1945.* Trans. Barrows Mussey. London: Latimer House, 1948.
Baur, Flugkapitän Hans. *Ich flog Mächtige der Erde.* Kempten: Albert Pröpster, 1962.
Berndt, Alfred-Ingemar and Hasso von Wedel, eds. *Deutschland im Kampf.* 58 vols. Berlin: Otto Stollberg, 1939–1944.
Bezymenskii, Lev Aleksandrovich. *The Death of Adolf Hitler: Unknown Documents from Soviet Archives.* New York: Harcourt, Brace, World, 1968.
Boberach, Heinz, ed. *Meldungen aus dem Reich: Auswahl aus den geheimen Lageberichten des Sicherheitsdienstes der SS 1939–1944.* Neuwied and Berlin: Luchterhand, 1965.
Bormann, Martin. *The Bormann Letters.* Ed. H. R. Trevor-Roper. London: Weidenfeld and Nicholson, 1954.
Churchill, Winston. *Their Finest Hour.* Boston: Houghton Mifflin, 1949.
———. *The Gathering Storm.* Boston: Houghton Mifflin, 1948.
Ciano, Count Galeazzo. *The Ciano Diaries 1939–1943.* New York: Doubleday, 1946.
Delmer, Sefton. *Black Boomerang.* New York: Viking Press, 1962.
Dibelius, Martin. *Britisches Christentum und britische Weltmacht.* Berlin: Junker and Dünnhaupt, 1940.
Dietrich, Otto. *12 Jahre mit Hitler.* Munich: Isar Verlag, 1955.
———. *Auf den Strassen des Sieges.* Munich: Franz Eher, 1940.
Diewerge, Wolfgang. *Deutsche Soldaten sehen die Sowjetunion.* Berlin: W. Limpert, 1941.
Dohms, Gerhard. "Was ich im Osten sah," *Die Aktion*, October 1941, pp. 531–32.
Dwinger, Edwin Erich. *Wiedersehen mit Sowjetrussland.* Jena: E. Diederichs, 1943.
Eckart, Dietrich. *Der Bolschewismus von Moses bis Lenin: Zwiegespräch zwischen Adolf Hitler und mir.* Munich: Hoheneichen-Verlag, 1924.
Elser, Johann Georg. *Autobiographie eines Attentäters: Aussage zum Sprengstoffanschlag im Bürgerbräukeller, München am 8. November 1939.* Ed. Lothar Gruchmann. Stuttgart: Deutsche Verlags-Anstalt, 1970.
Europas Soldaten berichten über die Sowjetunion. Berlin: Erasmusdrück, 1942.
Frank, Hans. *Im Angesicht des Galgens.* Munich: Beck Verlag, 1953.
Fraser, Lindley M. *Propaganda.* London: Oxford University Press, 1957.
Fredborg, Arvid. *The Steel Wall: A Swedish Journalist in Berlin 1941–1943.* New York: Viking Press, 1944.
Friedrichs, Axel. *Deutschlands Weg zur Freiheit 1935.* Vol. III of *Dokumente der deutschen Politik*, Deutsche Hochschule für Politik/Berlin. Ed. Reg. Rat Paul Meier-Benneckenstein. Berlin: Junker and Dünnhaupt, 1937.
Fritzsche, Hans. *Hier spricht Hans Fritzsche.* Zurich: Interverlag, 1948.
———. Affadavit submitted to the Nuremberg Tribunal, Document Nr. 3469-PS, in *Nazi Conspiracy and Aggression*, VI, 184–90.
———, and Moritz Augustus von Schirmeister. Testimony delivered at Nuremberg,

in *International Military Tribunal*, XVII, 153–54, 158–64, 172–75, 186, 242, 250–53.

Germany. Auswärtiges Amt. *Amtliches Material zum Massenmord von Katyn.* Berlin: Franz Eher, 1943.

————. *Bolschewistische Verbrechen gegen Kriegsrecht und Menschlichkeit.* 2 vols. Berlin: Deutscher Verlag, 1941–42.

————. *Dokumente zur Vorgeschichte des Krieges.* Berlin: Reichsdruckerei, 1939.

————. *Zusammenstellung der Standardthesen und Richtlinien für die deutsche Auslandspropaganda* (Nur für den Dienstgebrauch). n.p., 1943.

Gilbert, Felix. *Hitler Directs His War.* New York: Oxford University Press, 1950.

Gödecke, Heinz, and Wilhelm Krug. *Wir beginnen das Wunschkonzert für die Wehrmacht.* Berlin and Leipzig: Niebelungen Verlag, 1940.

Goebbels, Dr. Paul Joseph. *Der Angriff: Aufsätze aus der Kampfzeit.* Munich: Franz Eher, 1935.

————. *Das Eherne Herz: Reden und Aufsätze aus den Jahren 1941/42.* Munich: Franz Eher, 1943.

————. *The Goebbels Diaries 1942–1943.* Ed. Louis Lochner. New York: Doubleday, 1948 (incomplete).

————. "Goebbels vor Offizieren im Juli 1943." Ed. Hildegard von Kotze. *Vierteljahrshefte für Zeitgeschichte*, XIX (January 1971), 83–112.

————. *Goebbels Reden.* Ed. Helmut Heiber. 2 vols. Vol. I: *1932–1939.* Vol II: *1939–1945.* Düsseldorf: Droste Verlag, 1971–1972.

————. *Kriegspropaganda 1939–1941: Geheime Ministerkonferenzen im Reichspropagandaministerium.* Ed. Willi A. Boelcke. Stuttgart: Deutsche Verlags-Anstalt, 1966.

————. *Rede vor der Generalität: Der Krieg als Weltanschauungskampf, Posen, January 25, 1944.* Berlin: NS-Führungsstab des Oberkommandos der Wehrmacht, 1944.

————. *Rede des Reichsministers Dr. Goebbels auf der Reichs-und Gauleiter Tagung in München, February 23, 1944.* Munich: Franz Eher, 1944.

————. *Der Steile Aufstieg: Reden und Aufsätze aus den Jahren 1942/43.* Munich: Franz Eher, 1944.

————. *Das Tagebuch von Joseph Goebbels 1925/26.* Ed. Helmut Heiber. Schriftenreihe der *Vierteljahrshefte für Zeitgeschichte*, no. 1. Stuttgart: Deutsche Verlags-Anstalt, 1961.

————. "*Wollt Ihr den totalen Krieg?" Die geheimen Goebbels-Konferenzen 1939–1943.* Ed. Willi A. Boelcke. Stuttgart: Deutsche Verlags-Anstalt, 1967.

————. *Die Zeit ohne Beispiel: Reden und Aufsätze aus den Jahren 1939/40/41.* Munich: Franz Eher, 1941.

Gral, Ferdinand. *Englands Kriege: Die Geschichte der britischen Kriege in 5 Erdteilen.* Berlin: Verlag der deutschen Arbeitsfront, 1940.

Grossdeutschland im Weltgeschehen: Tagesbildberichte 1941. Ed. Ernst Braeckow, RMfVP. Berlin: Verlag Joh. Kasper, 1942.

Hadamovsky, Eugene. *Propaganda und Nationale Macht.* Oldenburg: Gerhard Stalling, 1933.

Halder, Franz. *Kriegstagebuch: Tägliche Aufzeichnungen des Chefs des Generalstabes des Heeres 1939–1942.* Ed. Arbeitskreis für Wehrforschung. 2 vols. Stuttgart: W. Kohlhammer, 1962–1963.

Härtle, Heinrich. "Bolschewismus als Wissenschaft," *Nationalsozialistische Monatshefte*, XII (August 1941), 650–55.

Harlan, Veit. *Im Schatten meiner Filme.* Gütersloh: Sigberg Mohn Verlag, 1966.

Hassell, Ulrich von. *The von Hassell Diaries 1938–1944.* Garden City, N.Y.: Doubleday, 1947.

Hedin, Sven. *Ohne Auftrag in Berlin.* Trans. from Swedish by Jürgen Schröder. Buenos Aires: Dürer, 1949.

Heiber, Helmut, ed. "Der Generalplan Ost," *Vierteljahrshefte für Zeitgeschichte*, V (July 1958), 281–325.

————. *Reichsführer! Briefe an und von Himmler*. Stuttgart: Deutsche Verlags-Anstalt, 1968.

Hesse, Kurt. *Der Feldherr Psychologos*. Berlin: E. S. Mittler, 1922.

Hitler, Adolf. *Hitler: Reden und Proklamationen 1932–1945*. Ed. Max Domarus. 4 vols. Munich: Süddeutscher Verlag, 1965.

————. *Hitler's Lagebesprechungen: Die Protokollfragmente seiner militärischen Konferenzen 1942–1945*. Stuttgart: Deutsche Verlags-Anstalt, 1962.

————. *Hitler's Secret Book*. Ed. Gerhard Weinberg. New York: Grove Press, 1961.

————. *Hitler's Secret Conversations 1941–1944*. Trans. Norman Cameron and R. H. Stevens. New York: Farrar, Strauss, and Young, 1953.

————. *Hitler's Weisungen für die Kriegsführung 1939–1945*. Ed. Walther Hubatsch. Frankfurt-am-Main: Bernard & Graefe, 1962.

————. *Mein Kampf*. Munich: Franz Eher, 1943.

————. "Rede Hitlers vor der deutschen Presse, November 10, 1939." Ed. Wilhelm Treue. *Vierteljahrshefte für Zeitgeschichte*, VI (April 1958), 175–91.

————. *The Speeches of Adolf Hitler, April 1922–August 1939*. Ed. Norman H. Baynes. 2 vols. London: Oxford University Press, 1942.

————. *The Testament of Adolf Hitler: The Hitler-Bormann Documents, February–April, 1945*. London: Cassell, 1961.

Hofer, Walther. *Der Nationalsozialismus: Dokumente 1933–1945*. Frankfurt-am-Main: Fischer, 1957.

Ike, Nobutaka, ed. *Japan's Decision for War: Records of the 1941 Policy Conferences*. Stanford, Calif.: Stanford University Press, 1967.

International Military Tribunal. *Nazi Conspiracy and Aggression, Opinion and Judgment*. Office of United States Chief of Counsel for Prosecution of Axis Criminality. 8 vols. and supplements A and B (Red Series). Washington, D.C.: Government Printing Office, 1947.

————. *Trial of the Major War Criminals before the International Military Tribunal, 14 November 1945–1 October 1946*. 42 vols. (Blue Series). Nuremberg, 1947–1949.

————. *Trials of War Criminals before the Nuremberg Military under Control Council Law No. 10, October 1946–April 1949*. Vols. I–XV (Green Series). Washington, D.C.: Government Printing Office, 1949–1954.

Jenkner, Hans. *Bayreuth*. Berlin: Kintzel Verlag, 1944.

Kardorff, Ursula von. *Berliner Aufzeichnungen*. Munich: Biederstein Verlag, 1962.

Keesing's Archiv der Gegenwart, vols. IX–XV (1939–1945).

Kissel, Hans. *Der Deutsche Volkssturm 1944/45: Eine territoriale Miliz im Rahmen der Landesverteidigung*. Beiheft 16/17 der *Wehrwissenschaftlicher Rundschau*, Arbeitskreis für Wehrforschung. Frankfurt-am-Main: E. S. Mittler, 1962.

Kleist, Peter. *Zwischen Hitler und Stalin*. Bonn: Athenäum, 1950.

Klöss, Erhard, ed. *Der Luftkrieg über Deutschland*. Nördlingen: Deutscher Taschenbuch Verlag, 1963.

Koerber, Walther, Hermann Wanderscheck, and Hans Zugschwert. *Mord! Spionage! Attentat! Die Blutspur des englischen Geheimdienstes und der Münchner Bomben-Anschlag*. Berlin: Verlag Wehrfront Alfred Becker, 1940.

Kuby, Erich. *Das Ende des Schreckens: Dokumente des Untergangs, Januar bis Mai 1945*. Sonderdruck der Süddeutschen Zeitung. Munich: Süddeutscher Verlag, 1955.

Last Letters from Stalingrad. Trans. Franz Schneider and Charles Gullans. New York: William Morrow, 1962.

Lehndorff, Hans Graf von. *Ein Bericht aus Ost-und West-preussen 1945–1947*. Bundesministerium für Vertriebene, Flüchtlinge und Kriegsgeschädigte. Ed. Werner Conze et al. Düsseldorf: Oskar-Leiner-Druck KG, 1960.

Lüdde-Neurath, Walter. *Regierung Dönitz: Die letzten Tage des Dritten Reiches*. Göttingen University, Institut für Völkerrecht. *Göttinger Beiträge für Gegenwartsfragen*, vol.

II. Göttingen: Musterschmidt Wissenschaftlicher Verlag, 1950.

Ludendorff, Erich. *Meine Kriegserinnerungen 1914–1918.* Berlin: E. S. Mittler, 1919.

Mosse, George. *Nazi Culture.* New York: Grosset and Dunlap, 1966.

Müller, Georg Wilhelm. *Das Reichsministerium für Volksaufklärung und Propaganda.* Schriften zum Staatsaufbau, Hochschule für Politik, vol. 43. Berlin: Junker und Dünnhaupt, 1940.

Münzenberg, Willi. *Propaganda als Waffe.* Paris: Éditions du Carrefour, 1937.

Murawski, Erich. *Der deutsche Wehrmachtbericht.* Boppard: Harold Boldt Verlag, 1961.

————. *Der Durchbruch im Westen: Chronik der holländischen, belgischen, und französischen Zusammenbruchs.* Oldenburg: Gerhard Stalling, 1940.

Nationalsozialistische Deutsche Arbeiter Partei. *Judentum und Bolschewismus.* Munich: Franz Eher, 1943.

Nationalsozialistische Deutsche Arbeiter Partei. Hauptkulturamt in der Reichspropagandaleitung. *Unsere Feier: Richtlinien zur Fest-und Feiergestaltung, Muttertag, 1944.* Munich: Franz Eher, 1944.

Nationalsozialistische Deutsche Arbeiter Partei. Reichsorganisationsleiter der NSDAP. *Material zur Gestaltung von Mittwinterfeiern im kleinen Kreis der Ortsgruppen.* Munich, no date.

Nationalsozialistische Deutsche Arbeiter Partei, Partei-Kanzlei. *Verfügungen/Anordnungen/Bekanntgaben.* 5 vols. Munich: Franz Eher, 1941–1943.

Nationalsozialistische Deutsche Arbeiter Partei. Der Reichsführer SS, SS Hauptamt. *Bolschewismus—Jüdisches Untermenschentum.* Berlin: Nordland, 1941.

————. *Dieser Krieg ist ein weltanschaulicher Krieg.* Berlin, no date.

————. *Der Untermensch.* Berlin: Nordland, 1942.

————. *Vorschläge für die Abhaltung einer Totenfeier.* Berlin, no date.

Nationalsozialistische Deutsche Arbeiter Partei. SS Hauptamt-Schulungsamt. *Grenzkampf Ost.* Berlin: Nordland, no date.

Nobécourt, R. G. *Les secrets de la propagande en France occupée.* Paris: Librairie Artheme Fayard, 1962.

Oberkommando des Heeres. *Die Soldatische Tat: Der Kampf im Osten.* Ed. Erhard Wittek. 2 vols. Vol. I: *1941/1942.* Vol. II: *1942/1943.* Berlin: Im Deutschen Verlag, 1943.

Oberkommando der Wehrmacht. *Die Berichte des Oberkommandos der Wehrmacht.* 3 vols. (1941–1943). Berlin, 1942–1944.

————. Wehrmachtführungsstab. *Kriegstagebuch des Oberkommandos der Wehrmacht 1940–1945.* 4 vols. Ed. Percy Ernst Schramm and Helmuth Greiner. Hans-Adolf Jacobsen, vol. I, 1940–1941. Andreas Hillgruber, vol. II, 1942. Walther Hubatsch, vol. III, 1943. Percy Ernst Schramm, vol. IV, 1944–1945. Frankfurt-am-Main: Bernard & Graefe, 1961.

————. *Die Wehrmacht: Der Freiheitskampf des grossdeutschen Volkes.* Berlin: Verlag die Wehrmacht, 1940.

————. *Die Wehrmacht: Um die Freiheit Europas.* Berlin: Verlag die Wehrmacht, 1941.

Oven, Wilfred von. *Mit Goebbels bis zum Ende.* 2 vols. Buenos Aires: Dürer Verlag, 1949, 1950.

Pechel, Rudolf. *Zwischen den Zeilen: Aufsätze 1932–1942.* Wiesentheid: Droemersher Verlag, 1948.

Peter, Karl Heinrich. *Spiegelbild einer Verschwörung: Die Kaltenbrunner Berichte an Bormann und Hitler über das Attentat vom 20. Juli 1944.* Geheime Dokumente aus dem ehemaligen Reichssicherheitshauptamt, Archiv Peter für historische und zeitgeschichtliche Dokumentation. Stuttgart: Seewald Verlag, 1961.

Poliakov, Leon, and Joseph Wulf. *Das Dritte Reich und seine Diener.* Berlin: Arani, 1959.

Prien, Günter. *Mein Weg nach Scapa Flow.* Berlin: Deutscher Verlag, 1940.

Rosenberg, Alfred. *Der Bolschewismus als Aktion einer fremden Rasse: Rede gehalten auf dem Reichsparteitags-Kongress am 12. September 1935 zu Nürnberg*. Munich: Franz Eher, 1935.

———. *Europa und sein Todfeind. Vier Reden über das Bolschewistische Problem*. Bolschewismus Schriftenreihe, Nr. 6. Munich: Franz Eher, 1938.

———. *Memoirs of Alfred Rosenberg*. Ed. Serge Lang and Ernst von Schenck. Chicago: Ziff-Davis, 1949.

———. *Der Mythos des 20. Jahrhunderts*. Munich: Hoheneichen-Verlag, 1934.

Rotbuch der Anti-Komintern. Warum Krieg mit Stalin? Berlin and Leipzig, 1941.

Rüdiger, Karlheinz. "Die Freiheit Europas wird im Osten erkämpft," *Nationalsozialistische Monatshefte*, XII (August 1941), 643–49.

———. "Front gegen den Osten," XII (July 1941), 618–20.

Schaumburg-Lippe, Friedrich Christian, Prinz zu. *Dr. G.* Wiesbaden: Limes Verlag, 1963.

Schellenberg, Walter. *The Labyrinth*. New York: Harper & Row, 1956.

Schirach, Baldur von. "Die Fahne ist mehr als der Tod," *Schulungsdienst der Hitler Jugend*, no. 6, March 1941.

———. *Ich glaubte an Hitler*. Hamburg: Mosaik, 1967.

Schmidt, Adolf. *Jugend im Reich*. Berlin: Junge Generation, 1942.

Schmidt, Paul. *Statist auf diplomatischer Bühne 1923–1945*. Erlebnisse des Chefdolmetschers im Auswärtigen Amt mit den Staatsmännern Europas. Bonn: Athenäum, 1953.

Schultz, Joachim. *Die Letzten 30 Tage: Aus dem Kriegstagebuch des Oberkommando der Wehrmacht*. Ed. Jürgen Thorwald. Stuttgart: Steingruben, 1951.

Semmler, Rudolf. *Goebbels—The Man Next to Hitler*. London: Westhouse, 1947.

Sieg im Westen: Der Kriegsfilmbericht des Heeres. Ed. OKW/WPr. Berlin: 1941.

Sommerfeldt, Martin. *Das Oberkommando der Wehrmacht gibt bekannt: Ein Augenzeugenbericht des Auslandssprechers Oberkommando der Wehrmacht*. Frankfurt-am-Main: Westdeutsche Verlag, 1952.

Sontag, Raymond. *Nazi-Soviet Relations 1939–1941*. Documents from the Archives of the German Foreign Office, Department of State, Washington, D.C. New York: Didier, 1943.

Speer, Albert. *Erinnerungen*. Berlin: Propyläen Verlag, 1969.

Sündermann, Helmut. *Die Entscheidungen reifen: Berichte und Bekenntnisse aus grosser Zeit*. Munich: Franz Eher, 1943.

Taubert, Dr. Eberhard. *Der antisowjetische Apparat des deutschen Propagandaministeriums*. By the author, undated.

United States Strategic Bombing Survey. *The Effects of Strategic Bombing on German Morale*. 2 vols. Washington, D.C.: Government Printing Office, 1947.

Volz, Hans. *Der Kampf gegen den Osten 1941*. Vol. 9 of Dokumente der deutschen Politik, Reihe: Das Reich Adolf Hitlers. Berlin: Junker and Dünnhaupt, 1943.

Weiss, Wilhelm. *Der Krieg im Westen: Dargestellt nach den Berichten des "Völkischen Beobachters."* Munich: Franz Eher, 1940.

Wirsing, Giselher. *100 Familien regieren England*. Berlin: Deutsche Informationsstelle, 1940.

Wulf, Joseph. *Theater und Film im Dritten Reich*. Gütersloh: Sigbert Mohn Verlag, 1964.

Zeitschriftendienst/Deutscher Wochendienst. Weekly bulletin to editors of German periodicals containing directives from the RMfVP. Berlin.

Ziegler, W. *Ein Dokumentenwerk über die englische Humanität*. Im Auftrag des Reichsministeriums für Volksaufklärung und Propaganda. Berlin: Deutscher Verlag, 1940.

German Military Literature

Assmann, Kurt. *Deutsche Schicksalsjahre.* Wiesbaden: Eberhard Brockhaus, 1950.

Bor, Peter. *Gespräche mit Halder.* Wiesbaden: Limes Verlag, 1950.

Doerr, Hans. *Der Feldzug nach Stalingrad.* Darmstadt: E. S. Mittler, 1955.

Dönitz, Karl. *Zehn Jahre und zwanzig Tage.* Frankfurt-am-Main: Athenäum, 1960.

Freidin, Seymour, and William Richardson, eds. *The Fatal Decisions.* New York: William Sloane Associates, 1956.

Görlitz, Walther. *Paulus: "Ich stehe hier auf Befehl."* Frankfurt-am-Main: Bernard & Graefe, 1960.

Guderian, Heinz. *Panzer Leader.* Trans. Constantine Fitzgibbon. London: Michael Joseph, 1952.

———. "Erfahrungen im zweiten Weltkrieg," *Bilanz des zweiten Weltkrieges.* Oldenburg: Gerhard Stalling, 1953.

Halder, Franz. *Hitler as War Lord.* Trans. Paul Findlay. London: Putnam, 1950.

Heusinger, Adolf. *Befehl im Widerstreit—Schicksalstunden der Deutschen Armee 1923-1945.* Stuttgart: R. Wunderlich, 1950.

Liddell-Hart, B. H. *The German Generals Talk.* New York: William Morrow, 1948.

Lossberg, Bernhard von. *Im Wehrmachtführungsstab: Bericht eines Generalstabsoffiziers.* Hamburg: H. H. Nolke, 1949.

Manstein, Erich von. *Lost Victories.* Ed. and trans. Anthony G. Powell. Chicago: Henry Regnery, 1958.

Middeldorf, Eike. *Taktik im Russlandfeldzug.* Darmstadt: E. S. Mittler, 1956.

Philippi, Alfred, and Ferdinand Heim. *Der Feldzug gegen Sowjetrussland 1941 bis 1945.* Stuttgart: W. Kohlhammer, 1962.

Schröter, Heinz. *Stalingrad.* Trans. Constantine Fitzgibbon. New York: Dutton, 1958.

Tippelskirch, Kurt von. *Geschichte des zweiten Weltkrieges.* Bonn: Athenäum, 1951.

Warlimont, Walter. *Im Hauptquartier der deutschen Wehrmacht 1939-1945.* Frankfurt-am-Main: Bernard & Graefe, 1962.

Weltkrieg 1939-1945, Ehrenbuch der Deutschen Wehrmacht. Stuttgart: H. Riegler, 1954.

Secondary Sources

Albrecht, Gerd. *Nationalsozialistische Filmpolitik: Eine soziologische Untersuchung über die Spielfilme des Dritten Reiches.* Stuttgart: Enke Verlag, 1969.

Ansel, Walter. *Hitler Confronts England.* Durham, N.C.: Duke University Press, 1960.

Arendt, Hannah. *Eichmann in Jerusalem.* New York: Viking, 1963.

———. *The Origins of Totalitarianism.* New York: Meridian, 1958.

Armstrong, Anne. *Unconditional Surrender.* New Brunswick, N.J.: Rutgers University Press, 1961.

Axelrad, Sidney. "The German Front Reports in the Russian Campaign." Ph.D. thesis, New School for Social Research, New York, 1950.

Barghoorn, Frederick C. *Soviet Foreign Propaganda.* Princeton, N.J.: Princeton University Press, 1964.

Bilanz des Zweiten Weltkrieges: Erkenntnisse und Verpflichtungen für die Zukunft. Oldenburg: Gerhard Stalling, 1953.

Bon, Gustave Le. *The Crowd.* 5th ed. London: T. Fischer Unwin, 1908.

Bracher, Karl Dietrich. *Die Auflösung der Weimarer Republik.* Vol. 4 of Schriften des Instituts für politische Wissenschaft. Berlin, Villingen: Ring Verlag, 1960.

———. *Die deutsche Diktatur.* Cologne-Berlin: Kiepenheuer & Witsch, 1969.

Bramsted, Ernest K. *Goebbels and National Socialist Propaganda 1925-1945.* East Lansing: Michigan State University Press, 1965.

Brassey's Naval Annual 1948. Ed. H. G. Thursfield. London: Clowes & Sons, 1948.

Brausch, Gerd. "Der Tod des Generalobersten Werner Freiherr von Fritsch," *Militär-geschichtliche Mitteilungen,* VII (January 1970), 95–112.

Briggs, Asa. *The History of Broadcasting in the United Kingdom.* 3 vols. Vol. III: *The War of Words.* London: Oxford University Press, 1970.

Broszat, Martin. *Der Nationalsozialismus.* Stuttgart: Deutsche Verlags-Anstalt, 1960.

———. *Nationalsozialistische Polenpolitik 1939–1945.* Stuttgart: Deutsche Verlags-Anstalt, 1961.

Buchheim, Hans. *Das Dritte Reich.* Munich: Kösel-Verlag, 1958.

———. *Totalitäre Herrschaft.* Munich: Kösel-Verlag, 1962.

———, et. al. *Der Führer ins Nichts.* Rastatt and Baden: Grote, 1960.

Buchheit, Gert. *Hitler der Feldherr.* Rastatt: G. Grotesche Verlag, 1958.

Bullock, Alan. *Hitler, a Study in Tyranny.* Completely revised edition. New York: Harper & Row, 1962.

Carsten, F. L. *The Rise of Fascism.* Berkeley: University of California Press, 1964.

Chakotin, Serge. *The Rape of the Masses.* New York: Alliance, 1940.

Collier, Basil. *The Defense of the United Kingdom.* London: Her Majesty's Stationery Office, 1957.

Dallin, Alexander. *German Rule in Russia, 1941–1945: A Study of Occupation Policies.* London: MacMillan, 1957.

Deakin, F. W. *The Brutal Friendship: Mussolini, Hitler, and the Fall of Italian Fascism.* New York: Harper & Row, 1962.

Douglas-Hamilton, James. *Motive for a Mission: The Story behind Hess's Flight to Britain.* London: St. Martin's, 1971.

Dulles, Allen Welsh. *Germany's Underground.* New York: Macmillan, 1947.

Ebermayer, E., and H. Roos. *Gefährtin des Teufels: Leben und Tod der Magda Goebbels.* Hamburg: Hoffmann und Campe, 1952.

Ehrenstein, Walther. *Dämon Masse.* Frankfurt-am-Main: Verlag Dr. Waldemar Kramer, 1952.

Entscheidungsschlachten des zweiten Weltkriegs. Ed. H. A. Jacobsen and J. Rohwer. Frankfurt-am-Main: Bernard & Graefe, 1960.

Fabry, Philipp. *Der Hitler—Stalin Pakt 1939–1941.* Darmstadt: Fundus Verlag, 1962.

Feis, Herbert. *Churchill-Roosevelt-Stalin.* Princeton, N.J.: Princeton University Press, 1957.

Fitzgibbon, Constantine. *20 July.* New York: W. W. Norton, 1956.

Friedländer, Saul. *Prelude to Downfall: Hitler and the United States.* Trans. A. Werth. New York: Knopf, 1967.

Friedrich, Carl J., and Z. K. Brzezinski. *Totalitarian Dictatorship and Autocracy.* Cambridge, Mass.: Harvard University Press, 1956.

Fuller, J. F. C. *The Second World War 1939–1945.* New York: Duell, Sloan, & Pearce, 1949.

George, Alexander. *Propaganda Analysis: A Study of Inferences Made from Nazi Propaganda in World War II.* White Plains: Roe Peterson, 1959.

Gisevius, Hans Bernd. *Adolf Hitler.* Munich: Rütten & Loenig Verlag, 1963.

Görlitz, Walther. *Der zweite Weltkrieg 1939–1945.* 2 vols. Stuttgart: Steingrüben Verlag, 1951–1952.

Gruchmann, Lothar. *Nationalsozialistische Grossraumordnung: Die Konstruktion einer "Deutschen Monroe-Doktrin."* Vol. 4 of Schriftenreihe der *Vierteljahrshefte für Zeitgeschichte.* Stuttgart: Deutsche Verlags-Anstalt, 1962.

———. *Der zweite Weltkrieg.* Munich: Deutscher Taschenbuch Verlag, 1967.

Hagemann, Walter. *Publizistik im Dritten Reich: Ein Beitrag zur Methodik der Massenführung.* Hamburg: Hansischer Gilden Verlag, 1948.

Hale, Oron J. *The Captive Press in the Third Reich.* Princeton, N.J.: Princeton University Press, 1964.

———. "Hitler as Feldherr," *Virginia Quarterly Review,* XXIV (Spring 1948), 198–213.

Heiber, Helmut. *Joseph Goebbels*. Berlin: Colloquium Verlag, 1962.

Hillgruber, Andreas. *Hitler's Strategie: Politik und Kriegführung 1940–1941*. Frankfurt-am-Main: Bernard & Graefe, 1965.

Hoch, Anton. "Das Attentat auf Hitler im Bürgerbräukeller," *Vierteljahrshefte für Zeitgeschichte*, XVII (October 1969), 383–413.

———. "Der Luftangriff auf Freiburg am 10. Mai 1940," *Vierteljahrshefte für Zeitgeschichte*, IV (October 1956), 115–44.

Hoffmann, Peter. *Widerstand, Staatsstreich, Attentat*. Munich: Piper Verlag, 1969.

Höhne, Heinz. *The Order of the Death's Head*. Trans. R. Barry. New York: Coward-McCann, 1970.

Holt, Robert T., and Robert W. van de Velde. *Strategic Psychological Operations and American Foreign Policy*. Chicago: University of Chicago Press, 1960.

Hubatsch, Walther. *Weserübung*. Göttingen: Musterschmidt Verlag, 1960.

Huizenga, John. "Yosuke Matsuoka and the Japanese-German Alliance," *The Diplomats: 1919–1939*. Ed. Gordon A. Craig and Felix Gilbert. Princeton, N.J.: Princeton University Press, 1953. Pp. 641–45.

Hull, David Stewart. *Film in the Third Reich*. Berkeley: University of California Press, 1969.

International Council for Philosophy and Humanistic Studies with the assistance of UNESCO. *The Third Reich*. London: Weidenfeld & Nicholson, 1955.

Jacobsen, Hans-Adolf. *Fall Gelb: Der Kampf um den deutschen Operationsplan zur Westoffensive*. Wiesbaden: Franz Steiner, 1957.

Janssen, Gregor. *Das Ministerium Speer*. Berlin and Frankfurt-am-Main: Verlag Ullstein, 1968.

Kimche, Jon. *The Unfought Battle*. London: Weidenfeld & Nicholson, 1968.

Kirkpatrick, Ivone. *Mussolini: A Study in Power*. New York: Hawthorn Books, 1964.

Kitterman, David H. "National Diary of German Civilian Life during 1940: The SD Reports." PH.D. dissertation, University of Washington, 1972.

Kluke, Paul. "Nationalsozialistische Europaideologie," *Vierteljahrshefte für Zeitgeschichte*, III (July 1955), 240–75.

Kogon, Eugen. *Der SS-Staat*. Stockholm: Bermann-Fischer Verlag, 1947.

Kracauer, Siegfried. *From Caligari to Hitler: A Psychological History of the German Film*. Princeton, N.J.: Princeton University Press, 1947.

Kreuzberger, Hans. "Die deutsche Wochenschrift 'Das Reich.' " Dissertation. Vienna, 1950, microfilm collection, LOC.

Kris, Ernst, and Hans Speier. *Rerman Radio Propaganda: Report on Home Broadcasts during the War*. London: Oxford University Press, 1944.

Laqueur, Walter. "Hitler and Russia 1919–1923," *Survey*, VIII (October 1962), 89–113.

———. *Russia and Germany*. Boston: Little, Brown, 1965.

Lasswell, Harold D. "The Strategy of Soviet Propaganda," *The Process and Effects of Mass Communication*. Ed. Wilbur Schramm. Urbana: University of Illinois Press, 1954.

Lewy, Guenter. *The Catholic Church and Nazi Germany*. New York: McGraw-Hill, 1964.

Linebarger, Paul. "Warfare Psychologically Waged," *Propaganda in War and Crisis*. Ed. Daniel Lerner. New York: George Stewart, 1951.

McNeill, William H. *America, Britain, and Russia: Their Cooperation and Conflict 1941–1946*. Ed. Arnold Toynbee. *Survey of International Affairs*. London: Oxford University Press, 1953.

Maxon, Yale C. *Control of Japanese Foreign Policy: A Study of Civil Military Rivalry 1930–1945*. Berkeley: University of California Press, 1957.

Meskill, Johanna M. *Hitler and Japan: The Hollow Alliance*. New York! Atherton, 1966.

Moltmann, Günter. "Goebbels Rede zum totalen Krieg," *Vierteljahrshefte für Zeitgeschichte*, XII (January 1964., 13–43.

Mosse, George L. *The Crisis of German Ideology: The Intellectual Origins of the Third Reich.* New York: Grosset & Dunlap, 1964.

Neumann, Franz. *Behemoth, the Structure and Practice of National Socialism.* New York! Oxford University Press, 1942.

Nolte, Ernst. *Der Faschismus in seiner Epoche.* Munich: R. Piper & Co., 1963.

Presse im Fesseln: Eine Schilderung des N.S. Pressetrusts. Berlin: Archiv und Kartei, 1947.

Qualter, Terence H. *Propaganda and Psychological Warfare.* New York: Random House, 1962.

Reitlinger, Gerald. *The Final Solution.* London: Vallentine, Mitchell, 1953.

———. *The House Built on Sand: The Conflicts of German Policy in Russia, 1939–1945.* New York: Viking Press, 1960.

———. *The SS: Alibi of a Nation.* London: Heinemann, 1956.

Richards, Denis. *Royal Air Force 1939–1945.* London: Her Majesty's Stationery Office, 1953.

Roskill, S. W. *The War at Sea 1939–1945.* London: Her Majesty's Stationery Office, 1954.

Rothfels, Hans. *Die deutsche Opposition gegen Hitler.* Frankfurt-am-Main: Fischer Bücherei, 1958.

Rozek, Edward J. *Allied Wartime Diplomacy.* New York: John Wiley, 1958.

Ruge, Friedrich. *Der Seekrieg.* Stuttgart: Koehler Verlag, 1954.

Scheurig, Bodo. *Freies Deutschland.* Munich: Nymphenburger, 1960.

Schmeer, Karlheinz. *Die Regie des öffentlichen Leben im Dritten Reich.* Munich: Verlag Pohl, 1958.

Schroeder, Paul W. *The Axis Alliance and Japanese-American Relations: 1941.* Ithaca, N.Y.: Cornell University Press, 1958.

Shirer, William. *Berlin Diary.* New York: Knopf, 1942.

———. *The Rise and Fall of the Third Reich.* New York: Simon and Schuster, 1960.

Sington, Derrick, and Arthur Weidenfeld. *The Goebbels Experiment: A Study of the Nazi Propaganda Machine.* New Haven: Yale University Press, 1943.

Smith, Howard K. *Last Train from Berlin.* New York: Knopf, 1942.

Steinert, Marlis G. *Hitlers Krieg und die Deutschen: Stimmung und Haltung der deutschen Bevölkerung im Zweiten Weltkrieg.* Düsseldorf: Econ, 1970.

Stern, Fritz. *The Politics of Cultural Despair: A Study in the Rise of the Germanic Ideology.* Berkeley: University of California Press, 1961.

Trevor-Roper, H. R. *The Last Days of Hitler.* New York: Macmillan, 1947.

Weber, Eugen. *Varieties of Fascism.* New York: Van Nostrand, 1964.

Weinberg, Gerhard. *Germany and the Soviet Union 1939–1941.* Leiden: E. J. Brill, 1954.

Werth, Alexander. *The Year of Stalingrad.* New York: Knopf, 1947.

Wheeler-Bennett, John W. *The Nemesis of Power.* London: Macmillan, 1964.

Winkler, Hans-Joachim. *Legenden um Hitler.* Berlin: Colloquium Verlag, 1961.

Wuorinen, John. *Finland and World War II 1939–1944.* New York: Ronald Press, 1948.

Zawodny, J. K. *Death in the Forest.* Notre Dame, Ind.: University of Notre Dame Press, 1962.

Zeller, Eberhard. *Geist der Freiheit: Der Zwanzigste Juli.* 4th ed. Munich: G. Muller, 1963.

Zeman, Z. A. B. *Nazi Propaganda.* London: Oxford University Press, 1964.

INDEX

Index